Multimodal Literacy Studies in the Age of AI

Jason D. DeHart
https://orcid.org/0009-0005-5210-4738
The University of Tennessee, USA

IGI Global
Scientific Publishing
Publishing Tomorrow's Research Today

Published in the United States of America by
IGI Global Scientific Publishing
701 East Chocolate Avenue
Hershey, PA, 17033, USA
Tel: 717-533-8845 | Fax: 717-533-7115
Website: https://www.igi-global.com E-mail: cust@igi-global.com

Library of Congress Cataloging-in-Publication Data

Names: DeHart, Jason D., 1982- editor
Title: Multimodal literacy studies in the age of AI / edited by Jason D. Dehart.
Description: Hershey, PA : IGI Global Scientific Publishing, 2026. | Includes bibliographical references and index. | Summary: "This book aims to continue advancing conversation concerning multimodal thinking and practice as AI tools and other technologies emerge and evolve"-- Provided by publisher.
Identifiers: LCCN 2025042357 (print) | LCCN 2025042358 (ebook) | ISBN 9798337369860 hardcover | ISBN 9798337369877 paperback | ISBN 9798337369884 ebook
Subjects: LCSH: Computers and literacy--Case studies | Artificial intelligence--Educational applications--Case studies
Classification: LCC LC149.5 .M85 2026 (print) | LCC LC149.5 (ebook)
LC record available at https://lccn.loc.gov/2025042357
LC ebook record available at https://lccn.loc.gov/2025042358

British Cataloguing in Publication Data
A Cataloguing in Publication record for this book is available from the British Library.

Table of Contents

Detailed Table of Contents

closely connected to cognitive, cultural and socio-technical processes with the help of the available literature within the field of literacy, learning sciences, and AI ethics. Lastly, the chapter proposes the future-oriented agenda to multimodal literacy research during the AI age that necessitates the critical digital pedagogy, culturally sustaining pedagogues, ethical literacy systems, and cross-disciplinary research alliances.

This chapter explores the multiversal work of comics in light of the rises in technology in recent years. The chapter features a textual case study of a comics work alongside more general reflection on "What If" and "Elseworlds" storytelling modes, suggesting the malleability of narrative. The links between these changes and fandom are explored, as are implications for both identity and literacy instruction. From reading theory to philosophy, this work speculatively engages with continued questions of what text means.

This chapter conceptualizes gaming literacy as a critical multimodal pedagogy that positions digital games as texts embedded with systems, values, and ideological structures. Drawing on game studies, critical literacy, and educational research, the chapter argues that gaming literacy extends beyond gameplay to include meaning-making practices, relational ecosystems, and ethical forms of agency enacted both in and out of game worlds. Through examples drawn from commercial digital games, the chapter illustrates how player agency emerges through identity negotiation, emotional engagement, and embodied decision-making. The discussion is further expanded to contemporary debates on artificial intelligence in education, challenging assumptions of technological neutrality and optimization. Finally, the chapter highlights the relevance of gaming literacy for understanding learning, curriculum, and assessment in increasingly automated educational contexts.

practices while safeguarding democratic agency, cultural-linguistic diversity, and ethical accountability.

Sovannaroth Chheang, Department of Education, Sovanna Elton Foreign Language School (SELS), Phnom Penh, Cambodia
Sovanna Loch, Department of English, Nava Nalanda Mahavihara (Deemed to be University), Bihar, India
Phearun Tep, Department of English, University of Delhi, India
Sovanna Huot, Department of Education, National Institute of Education (NIE), Phnom Penh, Cambodia

This chapter demonstrates the powerful influence of artificial intelligence in changing multimodal literacies in various educational settings. It suggests that AI is a catalyst for providing learners with the ability to create, communicate, and critically interact with knowledge, while prompting consideration of ethical, equitable, and culturally responsive challenges. This regards AI, based on theories, historical context, and analysis from various parts of the world as a creative partner and a communicative facilitator. These studies demonstrate the capability of AI in aiding the facilizes of storytelling, collaboration, translation, and visualization of data and highlight the challenges of bias, misinformation, and dependency. The author proposes pedagogical models such as inquiry-based, project-based, and critical digital literacy as frameworks for responsible integration. The recommendations include educators, curriculum developers, and policymakers, as well as teachers and educational researchers, focusing on the duration of the impact, cultural integration, and justice.

This chapter examines the role of meta-analysis in synthesizing research evidence within multimodal literacy studies, particularly as artificial intelligence transforms educational landscapes. Meta-analytic approaches provide systematic methods for aggregating findings across diverse studies examining AI integration in multimodal learning environments. The chapter analyzes key meta-analyses investigating AI literacy development, generative AI impacts on learning outcomes, multimodal learning analytics, and digital literacy frameworks. Through critical examination of methodological approaches, effect sizes, and moderating variables, this synthesis reveals consistent positive effects of AI-enhanced multimodal interventions on student achievement, alongside challenges including over-reliance risks and implementation variability.

This chapter examines multivoice work as a foundational construct for understanding multimodal literacy practices in AI-enhanced educational contexts. Drawing on dialogic pedagogy and sociocultural theories, it explores how generative artificial intelligence transforms traditional notions of authorship, voice, and meaning-making in academic writing and digital composition. The chapter presents a comprehensive framework integrating multiple voices—human learners, educators, AI systems, and cultural-historical resources—within multimodal literacy practices. Through analysis of contemporary research and pedagogical applications, it demonstrates how AI-mediated environments create new possibilities for polyphonic learning while raising critical questions about agency, authenticity, and literacy competencies.

This chapter introduces the concept of Semiotics 5.0 to describe meaning-making in the algorithmic age, where human communication is increasingly co-shaped by multimodal signs and machine-driven processes. Unlike earlier semiotic models focused primarily on language and visual codes, Semiotics 5.0 highlights how textual, visual, auditory, and interactive forms now intersect with algorithmic mediation, personalization, and generative technologies.Multimodal literacy in this context extends beyond decoding symbolic content; it requires the ability to critically interpret algorithmic infrastructures, recommendation systems, and data-driven filters that influence visibility, meaning, and cultural participation. The chapter examines how hashtags, metadata, emojis, and AI-generated outputs operate as hybrid sign systems, blurring the boundaries between human and machinic authorship.

This chapter reviews the role of AI and multimodal literacies in Cambodia's education systems as a means of promoting more sustainable and inclusive development. It reviews technologies; AI writing apps for translation and digital storytelling, reshape learning in schools, higher education, and the community education sector. The chapter focuses on Cambodia's attempts to integrate multimodal literacy into educational frameworks and reform initiatives, as well as the efforts toward combining education with creative and culturally sensitive and equitable frameworks.

Preface

READING, WRITING, AND COMPOSING IN TANDEM WITH A CHANGING WORLD

This volume stems from the transformations that have occurred in recent years relative to technology and concepts of literacy. Indeed, the word transformation occurs often throughout the chapters contained here. As Book 1, the focus of these chapters is placed on *Multimodal Literacy Studies in the Age of AI.* The conversation continues in Book 2: *AI, Literacy, and Human Agency in Education* in which chapters probe further questions of the implications of AI and literacy development.

From a definitional stance, multimodality is a set of theoretical concepts that reaches across disciplines to encompass a study of the ways that meaning can be made across multiple modes of transmission. Jewitt et al. (2025) have explored multimodality as both a means of conversation analysis and a way of exploring social semiotics.

In recent years, Artificial Intelligence (A.I.) has developed at a rapid pace and has become a focal point of interest and controversy in education, arts, and media. The role of the individual/community regarding human voice and creativity has been at center in this conversation (Tkach et al., 2025).

Chapters in this volume reflect the wide corpus of work that is actively compiled relative to these concepts and this context. Linking the literacy focus with technological questions, authors speak to creative possibilities and limitations across contexts with a focus on implications in educational environments. What does multimodal literacy mean when the landscape of digital possibilities is changing?

Particularly, in this collection of scholarly voices, contributors consider the implications of AI for multimodal work in educational spaces focused on language and literacy. As such, authors consider both pedagogical theory and practice throughout these chapters in a variety of contexts.

VOLUME CONTENTS

Contributors Khajoboeva Nodira, Ravikumar Natarajan, Aarthi Selvakumar, Dilmurod Turaev, and Turdiev Abdullo Sagdullaevich lead this collection of voices in Chapter 1, "Reading Beyond Words: Multimodal Meaning-Making in AI-Mediated Literacy Classrooms." These authors consider the implications of AI for student meaning-making and understanding across modes of communication, beginning the conversation in what it means to be a reader in the age of AI. The authors place specific emphasis on the potential for Generative Artificial Intelligence (GEAI) in assistance and design of composition, as well as ethical/critical concerns that surround this type of production. The notion of reading beyond the words, as these authors explore in this chapter, is an essential initial avenue of discussion for this volume.

Following this discussion of reading, Amit Kumar Jain contributes Chapter 2, "Multimodal Literacy in the Age of Artificial Intelligence," deriving direction from the title of this collection and thoughtfully exploring the varied factors in this volume's consideration. This author explores the context that has sparked the current researched conversation, and seeks to define what literacy means in light of AI, including the juxtaposition of multimodality and AI in their respective developments over time. In thematic terms, this chapter broadens the conversation from reading quite intentionally and considers the concept of literacy. The chapter includes focus on pattern, practice, and ontology, including a call for reconstruction of literacy from a definitional stance to account for advances in technology and learning sciences. This culminates in a future-focused pedagogical vision.

In Chapter 3, the editor contributes "Multiversal and Multimodal Autoethnographic Interpretations: Comics Narratives in the Age of AI." This chapter unites ideas of technological integration with the multiversal movements in storytelling that authors and creators have designed in the past forty years, including Marvel's "What If" title and DC's "Elseworlds" imprint. While these two stands of analysis might not be immediately obvious, the juxtaposition of a speculative approach to literacy alongside the malleability of narrative is presented through both philosophical and theoretical foundations in reading. I place emphasis on both pedagogy and the implications of fandom for multimodal and technologically-afforded (re) presentations. This material focus acts as an example to cap the first two chapters.

Fabielle Rocha Cruz contributes Chapter 4, "Gaming Literacy as Critical Multimodal Pedagogy," including a necessary and helpful focus on gaming literacy and the relationship of this multimodal corpus to critical pedagogy. In this author's view, digital games are positioned as texts that contain a number of layers and fascinating structures for storytelling and meaning-making. Cruz explores the complexities of player agency and embodiment within a foundation of game studies, along with theoretical strands of critical literacy. Through this chapter, the author probes notions of neutrality, explores possibilities of multimodal engagement and world building, and establishes the relevant role of gaming literacy for contemporary (and future) educational spaces. Where previous chapters begin broadly from a defining point and then move to specific spaces for consideration, this author provides a unique multimodal and textual space for additional thinking.

Authors Kishin Khajiboyev, Aarthi Selvakumar, Ravikumar Natarajan, Dilmurod Turaev, and Turdiev Abdullo Sagdullaevich then consider creativity, authorship, and ethics relative to the focus of this volume in Chapter 5, "From Page to Platform-Ethical and Creative Literacies in Human-AI Multimodal Practices." These authors offer a salient look at moving from page-based literacy to a multimodal set of practices in human-AI dynamics, drawing on multimodal literacy theory, concepts of digital ethics, and platform studies. They give focus to example case studies relative to the concepts that are central to the chapter, with analysis of interactions serving as a corpus of data. The authors channel this conversation into recommendations for a considerate pedagogical framework that incorporates a range of literacy practices as steps for meaning-making and technology continue to change. The role of the human being as creative/maker and the human voice is a salient element of this conversation.

Ashraf Alam shares Chapter 6, "Designing AI-Mediated Multimodal Literacy Pedagogy and Translanguaging in K-12 and Higher Education: Frameworks, Classroom Models, and Policy Pathways" in which the author interrogates the multiple strata of multimodal literacy across instructional levels in the context of AI. The authors synthesize paradigms including New Literacy Studies and translanguaging to enable a reconsideration of the ontological nature of text with actionable steps for educators and policymakers to consider and implement. This chapter neatly combines notions of policy and pedagogy across linguistic barriers in light of multimodality and AI.

In Chapter 7, "AI-Augmented Multimodal Literacies: Rethinking Creativity, Communication, and Critical Engagement in Education" Sovannaroth Chheang, Sovanna Loch, Phearun Tep, and Sovanna Huot probe AI's influence on multimodal literacies, noting the role of AI for creativity, criticality, and communication methods. The authors envision institutions of learning in partnership and facilitation, including pedagogical models for engaging with AI in this way. This work includes recommendations for further research and practice. The crucial factor of criticality is at play in this chapter.

In Chapter 8, "Meta-Analysis in Multimodal Literacy Studies: Synthesizing Evidence in the Age of Artificial Intelligence," Brijendra Parasnath Gupta, Negmatov Bobir, Kunduz Irisbaeva, Diloram Ergasheva, Bakhtiyor Qayumov, Shoira Abdullaeva, Karimov Hikmat, and Qalandarova Bonu probe meta-analytic approaches in light of AI integration into multimodal learning environments, offering themes and threads from extant literature. These threads include but are not limited to AI literacy development, the impact of generative AI on educational outcomes, and frameworks for digital literacy. For empirical clarity, the authors' data analysis focuses on effect sizes and considerations of methodology, as well as variables within studies, and the authors conclude that results are generally positive relative to student achievement. Along with this positive tendency alongside potential drawbacks, such as over-reliance on AI support.

In Chapter 9, "Multivoice Work: Dialogic Approaches to Multimodal Literacy in the Age of Artificial Intelligence," authors Deepak Gupta, Surayyo Eshboyeva, Safarova Svetlana, Inoyatova Saodatxon Joxongir Qizi, Narzulloeva Salomatbonu, Juraqobilova Xamida, and Kamolova Ozodakhon employ multivoice work to engage in the questions that are essential to this volume. The authors utilize dialogic pedagogy as well as sociocultural theories to trace the transformational impact of generative AI on notions including authorship in academic/digital composition. From this process, the authors share a framework that focuses on integration of voices, both digital and human as well as current and historical, to consider multimodal literacy practices. Thematic implications include ideas about agency and authenticity, adding to the previous chapters' focus on development with specific domains in mind.

Syed Ibad Ali offers Chapter 10, "Semiotics 5.0: Multimodal Literacy in the Algorithmic Age." The linking of machine and humanity is a central thread in this conversation, and Ali notes how semiotic models have developed over time to incorporate a wider range of modes for meaning-making with interwoven questions of authorship. The author further considers the capacity for students to engage in practices of critical interpretation and digital filtering in the context of generative AI. Particular digital features in this consideration include hashtags, metadata, and more, offering an examination of how particular features shape meaning and might be juxtaposed with concepts of humanity.

Returning to geographic considerations and continuing the conversation about innovation and positive impacts, Chapter 11 is entitled, "AI and Multimodal Literacies in Cambodia: Pathways of Positive Developmental Progress in Education and Society," and is authored by Sovanna Huot, Sovanna Loch, and Chheangkhy Hok. The geographical/educational focus for the chapter is Cambodia, with findings that include implications for sustainable and inclusive developments across contexts. The authors include a helpful focus on AI writing apps, notably exploring how these tools enable translation features and narrative work. The authors consider the ways that multimodal literacy influences structures and standards in this context with emphasis on cultural awareness and equity, as well innovation.

The editor concludes this first part of these collected voices with Chapter 12, "Toward an Effectual Stance of Reading." As a final exploration of the theoretical implications of literacy in the current context and as a means of peering into the next possible transformations to occur, I draw attention to the ethical and justice-oriented affordances of multimodal literacy. Extending Rosenblatt's theory of the efferent and aesthetic, I posit a third space for reading interaction that surrounds reauthoring and a social justice lens. Tentatively called the effectual stance, given the change and influence-focus of this interaction, I intend to continue a researched conversation about the roles of readers and how these roles change over time in response to/in preparation for social and cultural transformations. In the final analysis, multimodal literacy in the age of AI is less about competencies and more about a philosophical set of principles which can be taken up and expanded on.

IMPLICATIONS AND FURTHER CONSIDERATIONS

Literacy is a concept that extends beyond a limited framework of traditional materials to encompass the embodiment and meaning-making that occurs, including critical steps and reflection, across forms of communication. Work has been underway to consider transformational and meaningful frameworks for literacy (Jeon et al., 2026). I intend for this volume to be a space where scholars and teachers can locate information on these topics and further the conversation as trends emerge and further transformations occur. I also intend a balanced conversation around the positive implications of technological innovation alongside the real and present issues that arise and have already been noted.

What is certain from having collected a number of contributions for this volume is that both concerns and possibilities abound. While the structure and nature of essential literacy practices and processes might be debated in terms of transformations, technology is continuing to develop in ways that suggest an unpredictable element of the future. By means of a conclusion to this preface, I offer some questions for reflection as you read.

1. What is the role of community members and educators in fostering critical literacy practices in a world shaped by AI?
2. What is the essential role of human creativity in literacy education and where does AI sit within/outside of that role (if at all)?
3. In what ways can educators and policymakers explore literacy practices in light of digital evolution?
4. How does literacy act with flexibility with transformations in meaning-making tools/methods?
5. What is the role of the community and institutional system to respond to and support navigation of changes in meaning-making and communication?

Jason D. DeHart
The University of Tennessee, USA

REFERENCES

Jeon, J., Coronel-Molina, S. M., & Lee, S. (2026). The AI turn in literacy practices: Toward an inclusive educational framework. *Literacy*, *60*(1), e70018. DOI: 10.1111/lit.70018

Jewitt, C., Bezemer, J., & O'Halloran, K. (2025). *Introducing multimodality*. Routledge. DOI: 10.4324/9781003513698

Tkach, M., Kozyr, A., Mymryk, M., Holubytska, N., & Khomych, I. (2025). Effectiveness of multimodal communicative practices in higher artistic education: An analysis of contemporary approaches. [JETDE]. *Journal of Educational Technology Development and Exchange*, *18*(1), 240–260. DOI: 10.18785/jetde.1801.13

Chapter 1
Reading Beyond Words: Multimodal Meaning-Making in AI-Mediated Literacy Classrooms

Khajoboeva Nodira
Mamun University, Khiva, Uzbekistan

Ravikumar Natarajan
http://orcid.org/0009-0009-3705-1681
Marwadi University, Rajkot, India

Aarthi Selvakumar
http://orcid.org/0009-0006-9064-2091
Marwadi University, Rajkot, India

Dilmurod Turaev
Termez University of Economics and Service, Termez, Uzbekistan

Turdiev Abdullo Sagdullaevich
Alfraganus University, Tashkent, Uzbekistan

ABSTRACT

The introduction of Artificial Intelligence (AI) is transforming the concept of literacy education by broadening meaning-making to encompass other practices of meaning-making except through texts. In this chapter, the author focuses on AI-mediated multimodal literacy, which focuses on how students comprehend and create meaning through text, image, sound, data, and interaction in digitally-enriched classrooms. Special focus is made on how Generative Artificial Intelligence (GEAI) can assist in multimodal composition, iterative design as well as creative exploration, but also provoke critical concerns about agency, authorship and fair use. Basing on the theoretical insights and the current educational trends, the chapter advocates the

DOI: 10.4018/979-8-3373-6986-0.ch001

significance of teacher mediation towards the maintenance of critical interpretation and learner autonomy. It focuses on AI as a socio-technical actor in the changing ecologies of literacy and the necessity of human-centered, ethical, and reflective practices of literacy education in AI-enhanced ecologies.

INTRODUCTION

The introduction of Artificial Intelligence to the classroom has brought the educational environment into an enormous overhaul of the literacy processes, breaking the current dogma about the way the reading, writing, and meaning-making process takes place. In modern classrooms, literacy is becoming transcendent of the alphabetic text to encompass the process of making and producing meaning in terms of images, sound, movement, data and interactive electronic objects. The active mediation of Artificial Intelligence (AI) systems in the form of generative language models, multimodal content generators, adaptive learning systems, and analytics-based platforms is able to influence the way learners experience, process, and build knowledge (Chen et al., 2020). These changes necessitate a rethinking of literacy in terms of dynamic, socially situated, and multimodal practice and not as a linguistic ability. With AI systems being involved in the production, editing, and manipulation of texts, they affect cognitive knowledge, reading approaches, and authority dynamics concerning learning environments. The introduction prefigures the necessity of critically analysing the ways in which AI transforms the literacy classrooms not only as the technological addition to their work, but as the socio-technical force that operates within the cultural, ethical, and pedagogical frames (Shiri, 2024). Placing literacy in ecologies mediated by AI, this chapter forms the basis of the comprehension of reading beyond words as a necessary ability to learners operating in more and more complicated and hybrid spaces of meaning-making.

Transformation of Literacy in AI-Mediated Educational Contexts

The process of literacy in the educational setting has also experienced significant change with the introduction of Artificial Intelligence in the everyday teaching and learning activities. Linear reading and writing based traditional models of literacy are being increasingly complemented or replaced by processes of engaging with smart systems that create, adjust and assess content. The AI-mediated environment allows the learner to interact with dynamically, personalised, and multimodal texts, involving language, visual, auditory, and data-driven components (Black et al., 2024a). These changes change the process of accessing and negotiating meaning as learners have to decipher not only content but also the logic and influence of algorithmic systems beneath it. Literacy, in turn, cannot be separated in connection to the comprehension of how AI influences the process of representation, focus, and meaning. The classroom becomes a place in which the meaning is co-created between learners, teachers, and intelligent tools, which demand new manifestations of critical awareness and reflexivity. This change prompts the idea that the definition of literacy competencies will have to be reimagined, with an emphasis on the interpretative flexibility, design consciousness, and the ability to be critically involved in the processes of AI-mediated reading or writing in a variety of educational environments (Black et al., 2024b).

From Word-Centric Reading to Multimodal Meaning-Making

The transition towards the multimodal interpretation of meaning rather than the focus on words demonstrates the wider transformation of the organisation of communication and knowledge in the digital and Artificial Intelligence based setting. The meaning is also increasingly being presented via the multi-modal interplay of various modes, among them being pictures, sounds, gesture, spatial design and interactive components, as well as the written word. The use of AI technologies increases this change through facilitating the smooth integration and creation of multimodal content, which commonly blurs the line between the author, the reader and the system (Crawford Camiciottoli & Campoy-Cubillo, 2018). Reading in its turn is moving through complex semiotic landscapes where the meaning making is anchored to the coordination of various representational resources. Students should learn to pay attention to visual displays, tonal details, data visualizations, and interactive affordances as well as critically assess the aspects of information prioritization or framing in AI systems. This reading practice requires new forms of analysis not based on reading a text but analyzing connections between modes (Hull & Nelson, 2005). For this reason, multimodal meaning-making takes centre stage in modern literacy pedagogy, making it essential to take design, interpretation and critical cross-modal engagement as central aspects in pedagogical work.

Purpose, Scope, and Structure of the Chapter

This chapter aims to explore the ways of Artificial Intelligence transforming multimodal meaning-making processes in modern literacy classrooms and clarify the pedagogical, ethical, and equity-related consequences of the developments. The chapter concentrates on both the K-12 and the higher education where AI mediated tools are gaining more importance in reading, writing, and interpretive practices. Its areas of coverage include theoretically oriented views of multimodal, sociocultural, and critical literacy traditions and didactic classroom activities that depict how students interact with multimodal texts that are supported by AI. The chapter is arranged in such a way that at the beginning of the chapter conceptual and theoretical background has been set, and the review of literature relying on the objectives of the research is given. The recent case studies are then discussed to show the practical use and have identified the rising challenges. The discussion summarizes the research findings to emphasize the changing literacy practices and instructional roles whereas the following section discusses future research and implications to the managerial level. This systematic methodology aids in the comprehensive reading of beyond word reading in an AI mediated literacy setting.

BACKGROUND TO THE STUDY

The context of the current study is based on the intersections of digital media, multimodal communication, and Artificial Intelligence in educational contexts. The research on literacy, in turn, has seen in the past decades that the meaning-making process should not be confined to print-based texts, but rather to a broad assortment of semiotic resources that are culturally, socially, and technologically conditioned. The accelerated progress of AI accelerates this change, as it brings the systems with the ability to produce, modify and analyze multimodal content in large quantities (Domínguez Figaredo & Stoyanovich, 2023). These advancements pose significant concerns in defining, teaching and testing of literacy in classrooms where smart technologies are involved in the process of learning. To conceptualize this background, it would be necessary to place AI-mediated literacy in the context of larger historical changes in digital learning and within the more established theoretical frameworks that explain power, culture, and representation. The research relies on sociocultural and semiotic traditions to analyze the negotiation of meaning between the learners, tools, and contexts (Ng et al., 2021). This section provides the conceptual background through which the modern practices of literacy and their impact on the creation of equitable and ethical learning conditions can be analyzed by researching the evolution of multimodal literacy and the emergence of AI in education.

Evolution of Multimodal Literacy in Digital Learning Environments

Multi-modal literacy was created to address the increased consciousness that communications in a digital space are based on more than written language co-ordination. With the emergence of educational technologies, the interaction between learners in visual and audio texts as well as animation and interactive texts changed the conventional way of reading and writing. The online learning space has also increased the scope of the representational resources which may be used in making senses and it has accorded precedence to the designing, navigation and decoding of the modes (Apata et al., 2025). This transformation altered the traditional literacy pedagogies that focused on print literacy to cast doubt and researchers transformed the concept of literacy to be a multimedia and socially constructed practice. Multimodality became increasingly significant as well as a result of networked and participatory media in which learners are currently capable of creating and publishing advanced digital objects. Knowing in this prospect was not the only meaning of literacy, nor to have the capacity to design and read multimodal texts critically (Hafner, 2014). These trends established the background of the thinking concerning the continuation of the multidimensional literacy by the automatization, personalization, and transformation of meaning-making process in the modern classrooms. Table 1 The major modalities of primary meaning-making (text, image, sound, data, interaction) are presented and the use of these modalities in AI-mediated literacy.

Table 1. Key Modes and Semiotic Resources in Multimodal Literacy

Mode	Description	Role in Meaning-Making	Literacy Skill Developed
Text	Written or symbolic language	Conveys explicit ideas, arguments, and explanations	Reading comprehension, critical analysis
Image	Visual representations such as photos, icons, diagrams	Supports interpretation, symbolism, and visualization	Visual literacy, inferencing
Audio	Sound, speech, music, and narration	Adds emotional tone and emphasis	Listening comprehension, affective literacy
Data	Charts, graphs, numerical representations	Enables evidence-based reasoning	Data literacy, analytical thinking
Interaction	Clicks, simulations, navigation, feedback loops	Encourages active engagement and exploration	Digital literacy, problem-solving

Emergence of Artificial Intelligence in Literacy Classrooms

There has been an increased use of Artificial Intelligence in literacy classrooms with the aid of content generating tools, personalization, assessment, and feedback. Adaptive reading, automated writing assistants, generative text and image systems and multimodal analytics are now affecting text-and text-based interaction with learners and teacher-based instructional design. These technologies not only change the nature of affordances, e.g. real-time feedback and personalized learning courses, but they also transform the nature of authority and authorship to literacy practices. AI systems do not passively provide material but actively mediate its interpretation by pointing out patterns, proposing corrections or coming up with alternative displays.

This mediation brings up the issues of learner agency, critical engagement, and a transparency of the algorithmic processes (Bacon, 2017). With the introduction of AI into the daily practices of literacy, classrooms can be seen as a space of hybrid existence as human and machine input overlap. Coming to terms with the existence of AI in the field of literacy education would involve considering the potential of the technology and its drawbacks, especially in the aspects of bias, over-procession, and the danger of devaluing the concept of running more critical readers should it be engaged without skepticism (Ravikumar & Aarthi, 2025). Table 2 varies popular AI-powered tools with functions of facilitating reading, interpretation, and multimodal composition.

Table 2. AI Tools and Their Roles in Multimodal Literacy Classrooms

AI Tool Category	Example Functions	Supported Literacy Practice	Pedagogical Value
Generative Text Systems	Drafting, summarizing, paraphrasing	Reading and writing enhancement	Idea development, language scaffolding
Image Generation Tools	Visual creation, illustration	Visual-text integration	Multimodal composition
Adaptive Learning Platforms	Personalized content sequencing	Differentiated reading support	Individualized learning pathways
Multimodal Analytics	Pattern recognition, feedback	Reflective interpretation	Metacognitive awareness
Intelligent Feedback Systems	Automated suggestions and revisions	Writing and revision practices	Timely formative feedback

Sociocultural and Semiotic Foundations of Multimodal Meaning

The theories of sociocultural and semiotic ensure necessary premises in the interpretation of multimodal meaning-making in the context of AI-mediated literacy. In sociocultural terms, literacy is considered a socially located practice that is entailed in cultural norms, power relations and institutional contexts. Meaning is constructed in the connection between individuals, tools and communities, and does not exist in texts only. Semiotic frameworks also underscore the idea that meaning is built up with the signs in different modes, which have various affordances and constraints (Kustini, 2023). These conceptual views are very significant in AI-mediated settings where intelligent systems serve as mediational resources to manipulate representation, interpretation, and participation. The AIs created in the form of texts and images are not neutral objects; they are designed by data, design decisions, and assumptions that are implemented into algorithms (van Leeuwen, 2015). The critical analysis of AI reworking meaning-making processes and procedures through the sociocultural and semiotic lens can be conducted, as to what voices are voiced or are not voiced, and how to establish agency in technologically mediated literacy activities through bargaining. These are some of the pillars that are significant when studying equity, ethics and critical literacy in the contemporary classroom.

RESEARCH OBJECTIVES

Very specific research goals inform the chapter and strive to examine how Artificial Intelligence and multimodal literacy education are transforming their connection in a systematic manner. As AI-mediated tools become increasingly influential on the way of reading, processing, and creating meaning in any of the modes, there is need to articulate certain objectives that encompass the pedagogical, ethical, and equity-related facets. The objectives are aligned with the theoretical basis and practice orientation of the chapter and enable a systematic study of the effects of AI on the status of literacy practices nowadays.

- To examine the role of Artificial Intelligence in shaping multimodal literacy practices, including the interpretation and production of meaning across text, image, sound, data, and interactive media.
- To analyze how AI-mediated tools transform traditional reading practices into multimodal meaning-making processes within educational settings.
- To investigate pedagogical shifts in literacy instruction, with particular attention to changes in teacher roles, instructional design, and learner agency in AI-supported classrooms.
- To identify ethical challenges associated with AI-mediated literacy, including issues of authorship, originality, algorithmic bias, and transparency.
- To examine equity-related implications of AI-enabled multimodal literacy practices, focusing on access, representation, cultural voice, and inclusion across diverse learner populations.

CONCEPTUAL MODEL

The multimodal literacy theoretical framework in this chapter transforms Artificial Intelligence into an ecosystem in which it is the active mediator rather than an instructional facilitator. The model hypothesizes the processes of learning literacy as being dynamic and influenced by relationships between the learners, the different semiotic modalities, the intelligent systems and the pedagogical orientations. The interpretation and composition of text, image, sound, data and interaction that is meaning-making that occurs in this ecosystem is determined by the synchronised interpretation and creation process and is influenced by the processes of personalisation, generation and analytics that are algorithmic. The sociocultural and semiotic are integrated in the model to emphasize the fact that the practices of literacy are social and affected by power, representation and access (L. Zhao et al., 2022). It is also anticipatory of the teachers in mediating the use of the AI in order to sustain the critical engagement and agency of the learners. The model highlights the proliferation of meaning-making between human and non-human actors through making AI an element of an extended literacy ecology. This theoretical framework provides a systematic approach to classroom practice, pedagogical change and moral issues associated with AI-mediated multimodal literacy. Table 3 shows the main aspects of the conceptual model and such elements as learners, modalities, AI systems, and teacher mediation.

Table 3. AI-Mediated Multimodal Literacy Conceptual Model Components

Component	Description	Function within the Model
Learners	Active interpreters and designers of meaning	Construct and negotiate multimodal meanings
Semiotic Modalities	Text, image, sound, data, interaction	Provide diverse representational resources
AI Systems	Generative, adaptive, and analytical tools	Mediate and transform meaning-making
Teacher Mediation	Instructional guidance and scaffolding	Sustain critical engagement and agency
Sociocultural Context	Cultural, institutional, and ethical factors	Shape access, interpretation, and values

AI-Mediated Multimodal Literacy Ecosystem

The AI-mediated multimodal literacy ecosystem signifies the interdependent environment where learners are able to interact with different forms of meaning using intelligent technologies. Generative Artificial Intelligence (GEAI) models, adaptive platforms, and multimodal analytics are some of the AI systems in this ecosystem that work alongside traditional and digital texts, and influence information presentation, interpretation, and transformation. The unique role of GEAI is that it produces both text and images and multimodal artifacts, which allows the learner to interact with the alternative representations, experiment with meaning-making, and repeat design processes. Literacy in this ecosystem is seen as the result of the interaction between learners, cultures, and technological systems as opposed to being an individual skill (Yi & Siquan, 2025). The ecosystem approach to AI applications highlights that they do not just affect the delivery of content, but also the choice, order, and focus of semiotic assets. Such influences are related to the manner in which learners build meaning, rank information, and strategies of interpretation. The model recognizes the interdependence of a technological affordance, institutional practices, and sociocultural factors by putting AI and especially GEAI in context in an ecosystem. This framing facilitates comprehensive conceptualization of multimodal literacy which takes into consideration the complexity, variability and sensitivity of contexts in educational settings where AI is enhanced (Biagini, 2024). Fig1 is a multi-domain trusted architecture which integrates and combines multimodal biometric authentication, AI proctoring, explainable assessment scoring, and blockchain-supported compliance to create secure, transparent, and institutionally controlled digital examinations.

Figure 1. Secure GEAI-Enabled Multimodal Assessment and Proctoring Framework

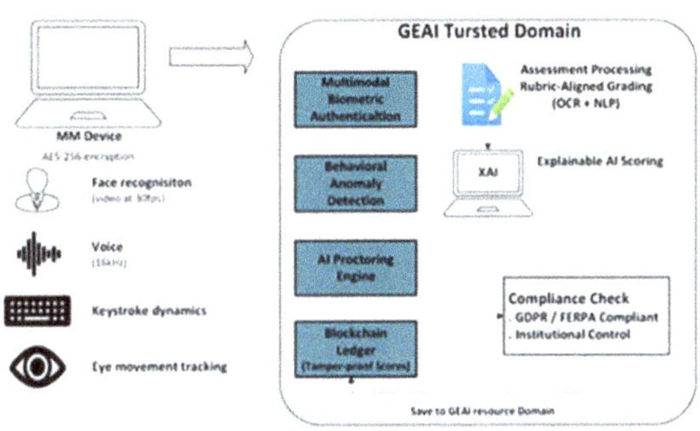

Interactions among Learners, Modalities, and Intelligent Systems

The interactions between the learners, multi-modal representations, and intelligent systems that mediate the meaning-making processes are the centre of conceptual model. Students interact with texts that are a combination of linguistic, visual, auditory, and interactive and are often created or edited by AI-driven software. Such systems shape the combination, focus or conversion of modes, which affect interpretive pathways of learners. Meaning-making is a process that is repeated where the learners engage with the prompts, visualizations, or feedback that are generated by AI and at the same time add their own meanings and designs (Asad et al., 2024). The interactional focus points out the fact that learning literacy is not a straight forward process of decoding but a dialogical process of negotiation between the human cognition and the semiotic resources as well as an algorithmic mediation. This interactive process demands that learners learn to manage the coordination of modes, assess AI inputs and critically consider the way of how intelligent systems constitute meaning. The model therefore highlights interaction as one of the primary processes by which multimodal literacy is formed in AI-mediated situations.

Teacher Mediation and Learner Agency within the Model

The conceptual model is based on teacher mediation and learner agency, which provide that AI-mediated literacy practices are not deprived of pedagogical meaning and ethical foundations. The role of teachers is in the capacity to act as critical mediators who help the learners to interpret multimodal texts, challenge AI-created texts, and make sense of how the algorithms affect meaning-making. The model does not set AI as an independent authority but focuses on the instructional practice that prefigures the human judgment, reflection, and situational knowledge. Teacher mediation assists learners in building metacognitive awareness about the way that meanings are produced as well as design decisions influencing the way that meanings are interpreted (Lomelí, 2023). Meanwhile, learner agency is highlighted with the opportunities of choice, creativity, and criticality of multimodal resources. Students are placed as active negotiators and decoders of meaning, and not mere consumers of the products of AI. The model helps to create responsible and reflectionary AI use, as well as agency in multimodal literacy education by balancing teacher protection and learner autonomy. Figure 2 below is a theoretical model that shows how AI can be used as a tool and platform in mediation of relationships between instructors and students, students and students, and students and self during instruction, collaboration, and learning processes.

Figure 2. AI-Mediated Pedagogical Relationship Model

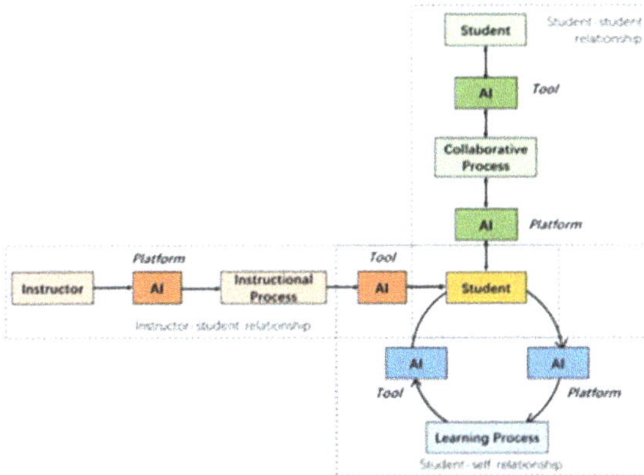

RESEARCH METHODOLOGY

The methodology of the research used in this chapter is aimed at studying AI-mediated multimodal literacy practices in the modern educational settings in a systematically organized manner. The methodological approach is supported by a qualitative and interpretive orientation that allows oversight into the process of meaning-making where there are interactions among learners, teachers and intelligent systems. The sociocultural and semiotic perspectives, which focus on context, interaction and representation in literacy practices are consistent with the methodology (Hendricks-Sturrup et al., 2023). The methodology promotes a comprehensive view of the pedagogical process instead of broad-scale assessment because it combines theoretical analysis and case-specific evidence. The analytic coherence, transparency, and ethical rigor are the methodological frameworks that focus on the maintenance of the interpretations that are based on previously stipulated literacy theories and recorded classroom practices. The complexity of multimodal participation and mediation of AI technologies is considered without simplifying these phenomena to separate variables (Miller, 2013). In this section, the research design, data sources, and ethical issues that will guide the study will be outlined, which will give the researchers an understanding of how insights will be generated, although the constraints inherent to an exploratory research, especially in fast changing AI-mediated learning settings.

Research Design and Analytical Approach

The research design used by the study is qualitative and exploratory based on interpretive and constructivist paradigm. The design suits the investigation of new practices related to literacy which are influenced by Artificial Intelligence in which meanings are negotiated in social interaction and multimodal representation. The method of analysis is based on the multimodal discourse analysis and the thematic analysis in order to study the role of text, image, sound, and interaction in learning activities mediated by AI (Christ-Brendemühl, 2025). Conceptual synthesis is used to synthesize the theoretical literature and make an observation on the basis of the observed practices recorded in the classroom and case studies. The method does not need to establish hypotheses but tries to discover patterns, relations, and educational consequences of AI-mediated multimodal meaning-making. Systematic coding, repeated cross-source comparison, and correspondence to the known literature models of literacy are used to make sure that the analysis is rigorous. This approach can enable an intricate and contextual understanding of how AI changes literacy practices, and it can be designed so as to be sensitive to the variability of practices in education and learner experience.

Data Sources and Contextual Settings

To receive a comprehensive view of the mediated AI-mediated multimodal literacy practices, the discussion will be grounded in different qualitative data materials. The main sources will be documented classroom activities, published case studies, and empirical research findings about the situation of K-12 or higher education where AI-assisted tools are used in literacy teaching. The other materials are the policy statements, curriculum policy and examples of AI created multimodal objects such as digital stories, visualization and interactive texts. The sources are in various learning environments to show disparities in technology availability, learning and student profiles. (Bahroun et al., 2023). It is possible to analyze the impact of institutional, cultural, and technological contexts on the adoption and use of AI in literacy classrooms using the contextual focus. The study utilizes diverse sources thus capturing instructional desires and experiences of learners thereby encouraging meaningful analysis of multimodal meaning-making in relation to various learning contexts and levels. Table 4 describes the research design, method of analysis, data collection sources and settings of the research study.

Table 4. Summary of Methodological Design and Data Sources

Aspect	Description
Research Design	Qualitative and interpretive
Analytical Approach	Multimodal discourse analysis and thematic synthesis
Data Sources	Published case studies, classroom reports, AI-generated artifacts
Educational Contexts	K–12 and higher education settings
Theoretical Alignment	Sociocultural, semiotic, and critical literacy frameworks
Ethical Considerations	Bias, authorship, transparency, and data privacy

Ethical Considerations and Methodological Limitations

The research methodology entails aspects of ethics especially considering the role of Artificial Intelligence in literacy practices. The discussion focuses on ethical portrayal of both learners and educators without being overgeneralized or blindly approving AI tools. The focus is placed on such problems as the data privacy, authorship, and algorithmic bias as it is applied to the reviewed literature and classroom activities. Acknowledgement is given to methodological shortcomings such as the use of secondary data and case study examples instead of empirical research on a large-scale basis (Akgun & Greenhow, 2022). The temporal stability of evidence is also constrained by the high dynamism of AI technologies since tools and practices can evolve within a short period of time. Also, the insights have limited transferability due to contextual variability in educational contexts. The methodology offers some useful exploratory insights on AI-mediated multimodal literacy despite these constraints. The study is transparent and endorses accountable interpretation of results in the context of current literacy research by clearly stating ethical issues and the methodological constraints.

LITERATURE REVIEW

Literacy education literature is becoming more aware of the fact that meaning-making is not confined to alphabetic text, but it also involves a variety of semiotic modalities that are informed by social, cultural and technological conditions. In this literature, the concept of multimodal literacy has become a problematic point of reference in the interpretation and construction of meaning by learners through the combined communication activities of language, pictures, sounds, gesture, and digital communication (Liu et al., 2025). Later, the concept of introducing Artificial Intelligence into the educational setting has escalated the academic interest in the mediation of intelligent systems in literacy practices. Available literature has both emphasized the pedagogical promise of AI to enable individualized and creative learning and given the challenges of AI to agency, critical interpretation and ethical responsibility of learners (S. Zhang et al., 2025). The theoretical and empirical views are synthesised in this review and are consistent with the purpose of the chapter, which offers the basis of the analysis of AI-mediated multimodal meaning-making in modern classrooms.

Theoretical Perspectives on Multimodal and Critical Literacy

Theoretical approaches to multimodal literacy stress that there is an interaction of representational modes to make meaning and not just language. In semiotic approaches, modes are conceptualized as socially constructed resources and each of them has its own affordance to communication and interpretation. The sociocultural theories also contextualize the literacy practice in the practices of cultural norms, institutional practices, as well as in power relations. In this sense, the role of literacy learning is to be able to engage in meaning-making through the mediation of tools and social interaction (Lin et al., 2025). Critical literacy theories carry these arguments a step further by pre-empting problems of power, representation and ideology, and inviting their learners to wonder how the texts are placing the reader, and favouring some voices over others. When applied to the AI-mediated environments, these theories emphasize the necessity of investigating the impact of intelligent systems on meaning in terms of design options, the selection of data, and prioritization of algorithms (Yan et al., 2025). Multimodal and critical literacy theories combined will give a powerful perspective to explain literacy as a socially situated dynamic practice that has to be critically scrutinized in technologically mediated contexts.

Empirical Studies on AI-Supported Literacy Practices

Empirical research on AI-based literacy practices states that there is an increasing use of intelligent tools to improve reading, writing, and multimodal composition. The uptake of adaptive reading platforms, automatic writing feedback, and generative tools, which help in generating text image combination, digital stories, and interactive art objects, are documented in research. The results are that these tools could be used to enhance the engagement, give prompt feedback, and offer differentiated learning trajectories (Qiu, 2025). Research also shows that AI-facilitated multimodal spaces stimulate collective sensemaking and exploration of a variety of different ways of expressing meaning. Nevertheless, there is empirical evidence showing ambivalent results concerning critical engagement, and some learners simply extensively use AI-generated outputs without paying enough attention to them. It is observed in research that there is fluctuation in teacher readiness and organizational assistance, and it determines the extent that AI tools integrate into literacy teaching (Quan, 2025). Altogether, the empirical studies reveal both possibilities and obstacles that require the use of pedagogical mediation to make sure that AI promotes, but does not limit the development of multimodal literacy.

Gaps in Existing Research and Positioning of the Chapter

Regardless of increased attention, current literature indicates that there are a number of gaps in the knowledge of AI-mediated multimodal literacy. A significant part of the literature is devoted to tool effectiveness or learner performance and little has been done regarding the underlying meaning-making processes and interpretive agency. Multimodal, sociocultural, and critical literacy perspectives have not been integrated well in AI-supported classroom studies. Issues that are ethical and equity based, such as bias, representation and access are usually considered but not analyzed in a systematic manner (Wang, 2025). Also, there is a lack of studies that provide comprehensive conceptual frameworks that consider relations between learners, teachers, modalities, and intelligent systems. This chapter fits in these gaps by establishing theories and providing examples to anoint the future of meaning-making, agency, and ethics. The chapter is a critical and integrative addition to the current literacy studies by putting AI into the frame of an active member of literacy ecologies.

CASE STUDIES

This part provides current and exemplary case studies that support how Artificial Intelligence has been introduced in multimodal literacy practices in various learning settings. The case studies shedding light on the role of AI-based tools and pedagogical practices in the meaning-making of learners in various modes, i.e. text, image, audio and interaction, by comparing the particular implementation in K12 and higher education environments. The cases also illuminate the process of mediation by educators and active use of technologies, critical interaction of learners with AI-generated materials, and practice-based challenges (Li & Wu, 2025). The chosen examples are based on the existing research and the reported practical applications of the last two years, which indicate the dynamism and quick development of AI-mediated literacy teaching. This section presents the evidence of the way AI tools are contextualized in terms of classroom activity, how they influence learner cognition and collaboration, and how systemic and contextual influences impact implementation. Inter-case comparisons also highlight similarities and differences in context, as far as AI-enabled multimodal learning of literacy is concerned.

Case Study I: AI-Supported Multimodal Literacy in K–12 Education

A recent K-12 education case study that examined how multimodal Machine Learning tools can be utilized to support AI literacy and multimodal meaning-making in an elementary classroom had been discussed (Ravikumar, Aarthi, et al., 2025). In this experiment, learners were engaged in activities, based on which they worked on AI-enhanced systems that combined textual stimulation, pictorial representations, and interactive analytics to artificially recreate the socially constructed knowledge (Casal-Otero et al., 2023). The AI tools enabled the integration of many forms of representation that enabled the learners to participate in the process of interpreting and producing highly detailed digital objects that were an amalgamation of text, images, and data visualizations. The guided tasks assisted the students in exploring topics along with the tools, developing multimodal narratives, and commenting on the meaning-making processes. (Yue et al., 2022). Teachers have reported that learners were more engaged and engaged in more in-depth interpretations of complex semiotic environments that developed due to AI. Educators were very instrumental in mediating the interaction of learners with the technology, which led to the consideration of how the AI system produced suggestions and how the meaning might vary among modes (Ravikumar, Aarthi, Ruzimova, et al., 2025). Although the advantages were apparent, the case raised such challenges like the level of different digital competence in students and professional development as reasons to facilitate successful multimodal instruction. The paper highlights the possibilities of AI tools to enhance multimodal literacy, and it focuses on instructional mediation. Figure 3 model that puts students and teachers at the core of using AI, under human supervision, fairness, transparency, privacy, and explainability in the education systems.

Figure 3. Human-Centered Responsible AI in Education Model

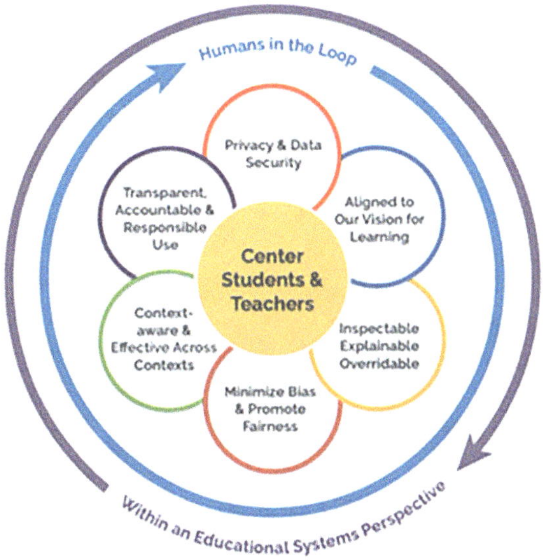

Case Study II: Multimodal Meaning-Making in Higher Education Contexts

Research studies on AI application to multimodal composition and meaning-making in university-level literacy and education courses have been conducted in higher education. Among these studies was the study that examined the utilization of generative AI systems by preservice teachers, who would produce multimodal compositions (text, images, interactivity) as an aspect of coursework. Students were in iterative design and reflective processes, relying on the suggestions of AI to expand ideas and consider other possible representations. The researchers discovered that multimodal composing activities enhanced through AI assisted students in enhancing their interaction with difficult texts and by exploring different means of expression. Students said that AI-based tools made it easier to prototype multimodal artifacts in a short time and increased their knowledge of design options in communication. Nevertheless, there were difficulties in the balancing of AI support and critical thinking because some of the students were willing to take AI generated content without undergoing adequate analysis (Nouri, 2019). To react to the challenge, instructors incorporated metacognitive prompts and peer-review tasks to make learners evaluate the outputs provided by AI critically and explain their choice of a multimodal design. As a case, one can note the dual role of AI as an instrument of creativity and critical reflection in the practices of higher education literacy. Figure 4 model that involves AI literacy as a product of computer science, data science, design thinking, media literacy, digital literacy, and ethics.

Figure 4. Integrated AI Literacy Competency Framework

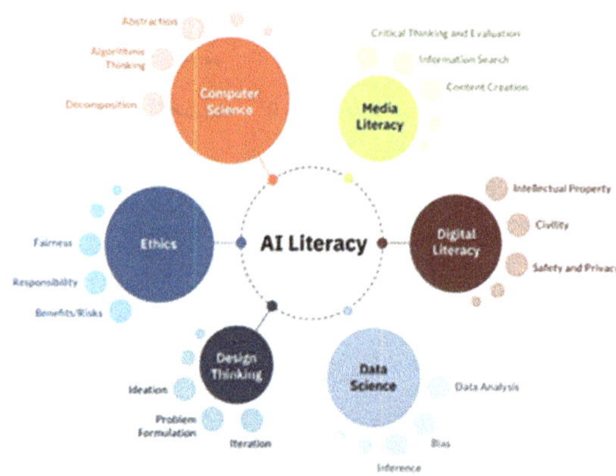

Cross-Case Observations and Comparative Insights

In the two cases, it is possible to outline a number of shared themes. To begin with, AI devices with multimodal features can be used to increase the engagement of learners and open up possibilities of creative meaning-making, especially when a text, images, and interaction should be synthesized. Learners in both K-12 and higher education environments were able to utilize the visual and interactive capabilities of AI systems, which implied that multimodal integration facilitates more in-depth thinking and interpretation. Second, teacher mediation played an essential role in directing learners on how to critically engage with AI-generated content, without teacher scaffolding the learners were likely to follow AI recommendations without adequate analytical consideration (Tadimalla & Maher, 2025). Lastly, issues of digital competence and equal access occurred in both environments, as they put the importance of professional growth and inclusive design approaches in focus. Although the level of education and the context varies, these lessons highlight the fact that multimodal literacy teaching based on AI requires a harmonious mixture of technological devices and their applications, pedagogical support, and reflective practices. Table 5 Comparisons between the K-12 and higher education case studies are based on the context, AI tools, literacy practice, and the main outcomes.

Table 5. Comparative Overview of Recent Case Studies

Dimension	Case Study I (K–12)	Case Study II (Higher Education)
Educational Level	Elementary and secondary	University and teacher education
AI Tools Used	Multimodal ML platforms, adaptive systems	Generative AI and design tools
Literacy Focus	Multimodal reading and storytelling	Multimodal composition and critique
Learner Engagement	High engagement through interaction	High engagement through design and reflection
Key Challenges	Digital skill variability	Over-reliance on AI outputs
Role of Teacher	Strong scaffolding and guidance	Critical facilitation and reflection

RESULTS AND DISCUSSION

The case studies and the literature analysis suggest that there are drastic changes in the practice of literacy as the process of Artificial Intelligence integration into the multimodal learning setting becomes internalized. It is found that AI-mediated tools transform the processes of interaction between learners and texts, taking reading beyond the linear decoding to dynamic interaction processes of texts, designs, and multiple mode interactions. The process of meaning construction is becoming more and more dependent on the combination of the linguistic, visual, auditory, and data-driven content which can be mediated by intelligent systems that affect the representation and focus (Fountoulakis, 2024). These transformations do not only influence the way learners read and create texts but also the way they conceptualize authorship, credibility and interpretation. The discussion notes the fact that the integration of AI increases the chances of interaction and innovation, at the same time, presenting new cognitive and ethical issues. The impact of pedagogical practices on the results is a determining factor because it is the methodical instructions that make an AI tool beneficial to critical literacy or lead to unthinking usage of the generated electronic content. In general, the results indicate that the integration of AI reduces the literacy classrooms to hybrid meaning-making environments in which the intersectional process of human judgment, technological mediation, and sociocultural context exists, and intentional instructional and ethical processes are necessary.

Changes in Reading Practices and Meaning Construction

The findings reveal that there is a definite shift in the reading, as learners showed more and more interest in multimodal and non-linear ways of meaning formation.

Instead of paying attention to written text only, learners decode information by integrating pictures, visual patterns, interactive elements, and AI-based proposals. Reading is transformed into a process of navigating and synthesising various semiotic resources which in many cases involves interaction with intelligent systems through repetitive interactions (Danielsson & Selander, 2016). The way information is framed through the application of AI tools emphasizes patterns, produces summaries or an alternative representation, which also influences interpretive routes. The fact that learners have to decide on relevance, coherence and credibility across forms broadens the thinking needs of reading. Such a shift promotes more active consumption of content and, at the same time, requires critical consideration of the mediating role of AI systems (Damayanti & Febrianti, 2020). The results indicate that multimodal reading practices contribute to interpretive flexibility and design awareness, although the learners have to be helped in critically assessing the content as well as the algorithmic forces that mediate the learners reading experiences.

Learner Engagement, Cognition, and Interpretive Agency

The involvement of learners improved significantly in AI-mediated multimodal literacy conditions due to the curiosity and continued focus of interactive and visually rich texts. The active exploration and experimenting of the tools supported by AI encouraged the learners to test ideas, revise interpretations, and construct the meaning together. Cognitive engagement was spread to a point that is far greater than comprehension to analysis, synthesis and reflection of the way meanings are generated across modes (Hutchison & Woodward, 2014). Nevertheless, tensions of interpretive agency are also observed. Although the scaffolding and creative prompts were offered by the AI tools, there was a danger of learners relying on algorithmic responses to make a judgment. The interpretive agency was the most effective in cases where learners had an incentive to doubt AI recommendations, present design decisions, and explain interpretations (Tan & Guo, 2009). These results show that AI is able to boost the cognitive activity provided that learners are active participants, not passive receivers. The instructional strategies that should be used in supporting the agency include metacognitive reflection and learner responsibility in processes related to making meaning.

Pedagogical and Ethical Implications of AI Integration

There are significant pedagogical and ethical implications of the introduction of AI into the learning of literacy. Pedagogically, the results indicate the need to have instructional designs that specifically focus on multimodal interpretation, critical appraisal, and reflective application of AI tools. The role of teachers in mediating the use of technology is crucial because teachers should present AI as a means of enquiry as opposed to a source of meaning. Ethical issues affecting the authorship, originality, and bias became the main problem (Ciampa et al., 2023). Students should be instructed to learn what lies within the scope of the human input and what falls under the machine-created material and the possibility of the AI systems reproducing the prevalent opinion or misinformation. The equity aspect also plays a major role since the access to the AI tools differently and the level of digital literacy may affect learning. The discussion highlights the fact that in the integration of AI in literacy education, constant consideration of ethics, transparency, and inclusivity practices that are human centred in judgement and critical literacy is the best.

FUTURE RESEARCH DIRECTIONS

Further studies of multimodal literacy in Artificial Intelligence era should go beyond the description of the adoption of tools, to more theoretically based studies that are longitudinal. Because AI systems are coming to mediate the manner in which learners read, interpret, and design meaning in across modes, there is a necessity to continue to inquire over the long run the manner in which the practices transform the development of literacy. Studies need to also investigate the effects of AI on cognitive, social, and cultural aspects of meaning-making in particular as learners engage with more autonomous and generative systems (H. Zhang et al., 2022). The mixed and longitudinal studies would be beneficial to the future studies as a method to capture the changing learner competencies, instructional practices, and institutional responses. Diversity in educational settings also needs to be given attention and it is imperative that AI mediated literacy practices are conditioned by cultural norms, language practices, and technology access (Topalidou Laskaridou et al., 2022). Future research will educate more just, reflective, and pedagogically rational literacy education methods in AI-rich learning classrooms by enriching theory and existing knowledge.

Advancing Multimodal Literacy Theory in AI-Rich Contexts

The future development of multimodal literacy theory in AI-intensive situations demands reconsideration of the key premises of agency, authorship, and mediation. Conventional multimodal models need to be expanded in order to take into consideration intelligent systems that actively constitute, modify and prioritize meaning across modes (Aarthi et al., 2025). Conceptualization of AI as a tool rather than a semiotic actor that influences the possibilities of representation and interpretive directions should be the future of theoretical work. This growth paradigm demands the incorporation of learning sciences, human-computer interaction, and critical algorithm studies insights into the literacy theory (Sabatini et al., 2023). More effort should be put on the negotiations of meaning by the learners when working with the AI-generated texts and the way in which power and ideology are incorporated into the algorithm design. Through theoretical models that are further developed to incorporate a human-AI dynamic in constructing meaning, then scholarship can be used to describe emerging literacy practices and to justify instructional strategies which maintain critical awareness and agency among learners in technologically mediated contexts.

Longitudinal and Cross-Cultural Research Opportunities

Multimodal literacy development in AI conditions can be studied more thoroughly with the help of longitudinal and cross-cultural studies. Prolonged research could prove the impact of long-term exposure to AI-enhanced learning conditions on literacy abilities, interpretive, and critical awareness in the long-term. This research will be necessary as it may outline developmental patterns and possible long-term advantages or dangers of AI inclusion. The cross-cultural studies may enlighten the multimodal literacy practices in different linguistic, cultural and educational settings and the significance of local values and norms in the formation of AI usage. Comparative research has also the ability to reveal inequalities in access, infrastructure and pedagogical provision affecting learning outcomes (Cappello et al., 2019). Through various contexts, researchers will be able to keep their assumptions more universal and help to create fewer universal theories of literacy that are more inclusive and context-sensitive. These strategies facilitate evidence-based guidelines that are sensitive to the global learning diversity as well as technological inequality.

Emerging Technologies and Evolving Literacy Ecologies

The potential to replace literacy ecologies with emerging technologies like immersive environments, adaptive multimodal analytics and intelligent agents are likely to see more change in the years ahead. Through research, it should be expected that these technologies will coexist with AI to form more sophisticated meaning-making worlds that incorporate physical, digital, and virtual worlds. Future research investigations should focus on the navigation of learners in multimodal texts in an augmented or immersive environment and how AI may aid or limit real-time interpretation (Srinivasan et al., 2024). Moreover, the changing literacy ecologies pose concern to the attention, embodiment, and social interaction beyond the conventional classroom setting. To study the developments, interdisciplinary methods have to be used that involve education, media studies and research on technology.

The future research can shape proactive pedagogical patterns by investigating new technologies in the shifting literacy ecologies that focus on ethical design, critical thinking, and humanistic learning in fast evolving educational contexts.

MANAGERIAL IMPLICATIONS

Implications of learning Multimodal literacy education with Artificial Intelligence have significant managerial implications on educational leaders, institutions, and policy stakeholders. These can only be effectively implemented through strategic decision making and alignment between the technological adoption and the pedagogical objectives, ethical standards and equity considerations. Educational leadership has a pivotal role in institutional vision, resources allocation as well as the creation of governance frameworks to sustain responsible AI application in the teaching of literacy (Alm, 2025). Managers and administrators will have to strike the right balance between innovation and responsibility and make sure that AI tools support learning without compromising critical literacy or human judgment. The planning of institutions needs to deal with the alignment of the curriculum, the infrastructure preparedness, and the long-term sustainability of the AI-enabled programs. Also, the leadership should acknowledge that the implementation of AI requires the capacity of the teacher and continued professional guidance. Managers can achieve this by having a systems-level approach to design environments where multimodal literacy flourishes by considering multimodality, having inclusive policies, and reflective practice (Rod & Jamie, 2021). In this section, the main managerial issues that can be identified in terms of leadership, institutional strategy, and professional growth are described in the frame of AI-mediated multimodal literacy education. Table 6 Summarizes instructional, ethical, and leadership inferences emerging out of AI incorporation in literacy education.

Table 6. Pedagogical, Ethical, and Managerial Implications of AI-Mediated Multimodal Literacy

Dimension	Key Implications
Pedagogical	Emphasis on multimodal interpretation and critical literacy
Ethical	Address authorship, bias, and transparency
Equity	Ensure access and inclusive representation
Leadership	Align AI use with curriculum and values
Institutional Policy	Establish governance for responsible AI adoption
Professional Development	Train educators in AI-mediated multimodal instruction

Implications for Educational Leadership and Curriculum Design

It requires educational leadership to facilitate the use of AI in the curriculum of literacy based on logical decisions and coherent vision. The design of the curriculum needs to go beyond the isolated use of technology to incorporate multimodal literacy competencies in learning outcomes, assessment practices, and instructional activities. The role of leaders is to make sure that the curricula focus on the importance of critical interpretation, ethical awareness, and learner agency in addition to technical proficiency (Kayumova & Sadykova, 2019). Curriculum alignment Strategic curriculum alignment is useful in avoiding piecemeal implementation and in assuring consistent learning experiences across grade levels and across disciplines. Inclusivity also requires the leadership to ensure that various needs of learners, their language backgrounds, and accessibility are put into consideration so that they can select and design AI-supported resources (Pernaa et al., 2024). Educational leaders can encourage consistent and sustainable multimodal literacy programs by encouraging curriculum designers, teachers, and technology experts to work together. Such activities contribute to a moderate stance where AI can supplement pedagogical practice and strengthen the topic of educational values and the aim of critical literacy.

Institutional Strategies for Responsible AI Adoption

Literacy education institutions are supposed to develop tangible actions that will inform responsible and ethical AI application. This includes establishing governance frameworks that are concerned with privacy of data, transparency and accountability in the application of smart systems. The institutions should be clear in their policies in terms of selection of AI, its implementation and its evaluation to ensure that it aligns with the educational goals and ethical standards. It is also advisable that in the strategic planning, the infrastructure preparedness which includes quality technology availability, support services, etc should be taken into consideration (Lérias et al., 2024). Another major issue is the problem of equity because the unequal access to AI tools can only exacerbate the existing inequity among learners and institutions. The introduction of inclusive practices should be introduced to learning institutions that will result in equal access and cultural sensitivity in the use of AI-mediated resources. The systems of continuous assessment have to track the impacts of AI in education and learning and alter practices as the technologies evolve. In collaboration with thoughtful institutional strategies, AI can be integrated in such a way that it will allow expanding the innovation and safeguarding the educational integrity.

Professional Development for Multimodal Literacy Instruction

The significance of the professional development is rather significant in assisting the educators to make proper use of AI in multimodal literacy teaching. Teachers must have an opportunity to acquaint themselves with technical information about AI devices and pedagogical strategies to facilitate learning in the techniques of how the learners may develop critical and creative meaning-making practices in the modes. Professional learning programs must be dominated by the reflection practice, which will help educators to analyze how AI influences the interpretation, authorship, and learner agency. Knowledge sharing and experimentation with multimodal instructional designs can be encouraged with the help of collaborative models of professional development including communities of practice (Z. Zhao et al., 2025). Ethical considerations such as bias, transparency and responsible usage of the AI-generated material should also be mentioned in training. Institutions can invest in long and context-specific professional growth to enable the teachers to become informed mediators and not technological passive followers. This will help enhance the quality of instruction as well as make sure that AI-based practices of multimodal literacy can be learner-centered, fair, and pedagogically grounded.Top of Form

CONCLUSION

The chapter has investigated the way in which the nature of literacy education is being transformed by the combination of Artificial Intelligence and the increased popularity of multimodal meaning-making, suggesting the need to reconceptualize reading outside of word-focused cultures. In modern classrooms, literacy is becoming a process of meaning-making, whether via text, image, sound, data, and interaction, which is mediated by intelligent systems that actively affect the process of representation and interpretation. The conceptualization of literacy as a multimodal and AI-mediated practice shows the necessity to focus on AI not as a supportive tool only but as a socio-technical agent placed in the context of larger cultural, pedagogical, and ethical frameworks. The discussion displays that, although AI has the potential to increase the chances of engagement, creativity, and personal learning, there are risks of agency, bias, authorship, and mindless dependence on the outputs of algorithms. The maintenance of human judgment and critical interpretation thus comes out as a key requirement in AI-dominated literacy education. The mediation of AI use is a critical role of a teacher, who will instruct the learner to question, evaluate, and reflect on the construction of meanings and whose views are presented. The development of learner agency is also a crucial factor to consider because it is necessary to make sure that students are active creators and decoders of AI-generated content instead of passive consumers. This chapter will be part of the current discussions on literacy studies through synthesis of theoretical views, empirical evidence, and illuminating examples to predict ethical awareness, equity and critical engagement as fundamental elements of multimodal literacy. Finally, it will be necessary to practice reading beyond words in the era of AI by balancing the technological innovativeness with the human values, cultural sensitivity, and reflective learning so that learners can develop the skills to read and discern the complex multimodal texts in the increasingly AI-mediated classrooms with responsibility and discretion.

REFERENCES

Aarthi, S., Ravikumar, R. N., Khudayberganov, S., Ismailov, A., & Khujaniyozova, O. (2025). Using Intelligent Tutoring Systems to enhance student engagement. In *Advances in Computational Intelligence and Robotics* (pp. 155–188). IGI Global. DOI: 10.4018/979-8-3373-1827-1.ch008

Akgun, S., & Greenhow, C. (2022). Artificial intelligence in education: Addressing ethical challenges in. *AI and Ethics*, *2*(3), 431–440. DOI: 10.1007/s43681-021-00096-7 PMID: 34790956

Alm, A. (2025). Reconceptualising literacy as co-literacy in language education with AI. In *Insights into AI and Language Teaching and Learning* (pp. 53–76). Castledown., DOI: 10.29140/9781763711600-04

Apata, S. B., Owojori, O. M., Shogbesan, Y. O., & Ugom, M. K. (2025). Artificial intelligence and multiliteracies: Preparing learners for a technologically evolving world. *International Journal of Nursing Education*, *15*(15). Advance online publication. DOI: 10.24310/ijne.15.2025.21332

Asad, M. M., Shahzad, S., Shah, S. H. A., Sherwani, F., & Almusharraf, N. M. (2024). ChatGPT as artificial intelligence-based generative multimedia for English writing pedagogy: Challenges and opportunities from an educator's perspective. *International Journal of Information and Learning Technology*, *41*(5), 490–506. DOI: 10.1108/IJILT-02-2024-0021

Bacon, C. K. (2017). Multilanguage, multipurpose: A literature review, synthesis, and framework for critical literacies in English language teaching. *Journal of Literacy Research*, *49*(3), 424–453. DOI: 10.1177/1086296X17718324

Bahroun, Z., Anane, C., Ahmed, V., & Zacca, A. (2023). Transforming education: A comprehensive review of generative artificial intelligence in educational settings through bibliometric and content analysis. *Sustainability (Basel)*, *15*(17), 12983. DOI: 10.3390/su151712983

Biagini, G. (2024). Assessing the assessments: Toward a multidimensional approach to AI literacy. *Medical Education*, *15*(1), 91–101. DOI: 10.36253/me-15831 PMID: 38279173

Black, N. B., George, S., Eguchi, A., Dempsey, J. C., Langran, E., Fraga, L., Brunvand, S., & Howard, N. (2024a). A framework for approaching AI education in Educator Preparation Programs. *Proceedings of the AAAI Conference on Artificial Intelligence*, *38*(21), 23069–23077. DOI: 10.1609/aaai.v38i21.30351

Black, N. B., George, S., Eguchi, A., Dempsey, J. C., Langran, E., Fraga, L., Brunvand, S., & Howard, N. (2024b). A framework for approaching AI education in Educator Preparation Programs. *Proceedings of the AAAI Conference on Artificial Intelligence, 38*(21), 23069–23077. DOI: 10.1609/aaai.v38i21.30351

Cappello, M., Wiseman, A. M., & Turner, J. D. (2019). Framing equitable classroom practices: Potentials of critical multimodal literacy research. *Literacy Research: Theory, Method, and Practice, 68*(1), 205–225. DOI: 10.1177/2381336919870274

Casal-Otero, L., Catala, A., Fernández-Morante, C., Taboada, M., Cebreiro, B., & Barro, S. (2023). AI literacy in K-12: A systematic literature review. *International Journal of STEM Education, 10*(1), 29. Advance online publication. DOI: 10.1186/s40594-023-00418-7

Chen, L., Chen, P., & Lin, Z. (2020). Artificial intelligence in education: A review. *IEEE Access : Practical Innovations, Open Solutions, 8*, 75264–75278. DOI: 10.1109/ACCESS.2020.2988510

Christ-Brendemühl, S. (2025). Leveraging generative AI in higher education: An analysis of opportunities and challenges addressed in university guidelines. *European Journal of Education, 60*(1), e12891. Advance online publication. DOI: 10.1111/ejed.12891

Ciampa, K., Wolfe, Z. M., & Bronstein, B. (2023). ChatGPT in education: Transforming digital literacy practices. *Journal of Adolescent & Adult Literacy: A Journal From the International Reading Association, 67*(3), 186–195. DOI: 10.1002/jaal.1310

Crawford Camiciottoli, B., & Campoy-Cubillo, M. C. (2018). Introduction: The nexus of multimodality, multimodal literacy, and English language teaching in research and practice in higher education settings. *System, 77*, 1–9. DOI: 10.1016/j.system.2018.03.005

Damayanti, I. L., & Febrianti, Y. (2020). Multimodal literacy: Unfolding reading path in children's picture book and its potential for EFL classrooms. *Indonesian Journal of Applied Linguistics, 9*(3), 616–627. DOI: 10.17509/ijal.v9i3.23212

Danielsson, K., & Selander, S. (2016). Reading multimodal texts for learning – a model for cultivating multimodal literacy. *Designs for Learning, 8*(1), 25–36. DOI: 10.16993/dfl.72

Domínguez Figaredo, D., & Stoyanovich, J. (2023). Responsible AI literacy: A stakeholder-first approach. *Big Data & Society, 10*(2), 20539517231219958. Advance online publication. DOI: 10.1177/20539517231219958

Fountoulakis, M. S. (2024). Evaluating the impact of AI tools on language proficiency and intercultural communication in second language education. *International Journal of Second and Foreign Language Education*, *3*(1), 12–26. DOI: 10.33422/ijsfle.v3i1.768

Hafner, C. A. (2014). Embedding digital literacies in English language teaching: Students' digital video projects as multimodal ensembles. *TESOL Quarterly*, *48*(4), 655–685. DOI: 10.1002/tesq.138

Hendricks-Sturrup, R., Simmons, M., Anders, S., Aneni, K., Wright Clayton, E., Coco, J., Collins, B., Heitman, E., Hussain, S., Joshi, K., Lemieux, J., Lovett Novak, L., Rubin, D. J., Shanker, A., Washington, T., Waters, G., Webb Harris, J., Yin, R., Wagner, T., & Malin, B. (2023). Developing ethics and equity principles, terms, and engagement tools to Advance Health Equity and Researcher Diversity in AI and machine learning: Modified Delphi approach. *JMIR AI*, *2*, e52888. DOI: 10.2196/52888 PMID: 38875540

Hull, G. A., & Nelson, M. E. (2005). Locating the semiotic power of multimodality. *Written Communication*, *22*(2), 224–261. DOI: 10.1177/0741088304274170

Hutchison, A., & Woodward, L. (2014). A planning cycle for integrating digital technology into literacy instruction. *The Reading Teacher*, *67*(6), 455–464. DOI: 10.1002/trtr.1225

Kayumova, A., & Sadykova, G. (2019). Implementing a multimodal online program for very young learners of Russian: Educators' perspective. *Indonesian Journal of Applied Linguistics*, *9*(1). Advance online publication. DOI: 10.17509/ijal.v9i1.13323

Kustini, S. (2023). A project-based multiliteracies instruction to improve students' multimodal literacy. In *Advances in Social Science, Education and Humanities Research* (pp. 632–647). Atlantis Press SARL. DOI: 10.2991/978-2-38476-054-1_54

Lérias, E., Guerra, C., & Ferreira, P. (2024). Literacy in artificial intelligence as a challenge for teaching in higher education: A case study at Portalegre Polytechnic University. *Information (Basel)*, *15*(4), 205. DOI: 10.3390/info15040205

Li, N., & Wu, D. (2025). The auxiliary function and realization mechanism of artificial intelligence in cross-cultural traditional music education. *Journal of Cases on Information Technology*, *27*(1), 1–18. DOI: 10.4018/JCIT.388947

Lin, Z., Dai, Y., & Ng, O.-L. (2025). Constructionism in K-12 AI literacy education: A systematic review of pedagogical designs, student outcomes, and learning mechanisms. *Journal of Educational Computing Research*, *63*(7–8), 1748–1781. DOI: 10.1177/07356331251360442

Liu, X., Wang, J., & Luo, Y. (2025). Acceptance and use of technology on digital learning resource utilization and digital literacy among Chinese engineering students: A longitudinal study based on the UTAUT2 model. *Behavioral Sciences (Basel, Switzerland)*, *15*(6), 728. DOI: 10.3390/bs15060728 PMID: 40564510

Lomelí, K. (2023). The work of growing young people con Cariño: A reconstructive lens on one white teacher's anti-racist approach to teaching immigrant-origin Latinx students. *English Teaching*, *22*(1), 45–60. DOI: 10.1108/ETPC-03-2022-0040

Miller, S. M. (2013). A research metasynthesis on digital video composing in classrooms. *Journal of Literacy Research*, *45*(4), 386–430. DOI: 10.1177/1086296X13504867

Ng, D. T. K., Leung, J. K. L., Chu, K. W. S., & Qiao, M. S. (2021). AI literacy: Definition, teaching, evaluation and ethical issues. *Proceedings of the Association for Information Science and Technology*, *58*(1), 504–509. DOI: 10.1002/pra2.487

Nouri, J. (2019). Students multimodal literacy and design of learning during self-studies in higher education. *Technology Knowledge and Learning*, *24*(4), 683–698. DOI: 10.1007/s10758-018-9360-5

Pernaa, J., Ikävalko, T., Takala, A., Vuorio, E., Pesonen, R., & Haatainen, O. (2024). Artificial intelligence chatbots in chemical information seeking: Narrative educational insights via a SWOT analysis. *Informatics (MDPI)*, *11*(2), 20. DOI: 10.3390/informatics11020020

Qiu, G. (2025). On the relationship between students' perceived support, students' self-efficacy, and affect-emotions in AI -enhanced learning environments. *European Journal of Education*, *60*(3), e70180. Advance online publication. DOI: 10.1111/ejed.70180

Quan, Y. (2025). The influence of teachers' clarity and credibility on Chinese EFL students' willingness to attend AI -powered classrooms: A qualitative inquiry. *European Journal of Education*, *60*(4), e70295. Advance online publication. DOI: 10.1111/ejed.70295

Ravikumar, R. N., & Aarthi, S. (2025). Federated Learning and privacy-preserving search. In *Role of Library Resources for Higher Education in the Digital Era* (pp. 71–108). IGI Global Scientific Publishing., DOI: 10.4018/979-8-3373-3005-1.ch004

Ravikumar, R. N., Aarthi, S., Ruzimova, F., & Mamadiyarov, Z. (2025). Training and development in AI-driven education scaling solutions. In *Advances in Computational Intelligence and Robotics* (pp. 267–298). IGI Global Scientific Publishing. DOI: 10.4018/979-8-3373-2185-1.ch010

Ravikumar, R. N., Aarthi, S., Sapaeva, B., Jumaniyozov, Y., Manoj Praveen, V., & Siddheswaran, V. (2025). Revolutionizing education with NLP and ML. In *Advances in Computational Intelligence and Robotics* (pp. 293–324). IGI Global Scientific Publishing. DOI: 10.4018/979-8-3373-6791-0.ch011

Rod, P., & Jamie, M. (2021). Critical literacy and semiotic juxtaposition: The possibilities of multimodal pedagogy in Korea. *STEM Journal*, *22*(2), 73–92. DOI: 10.16875/stem.2021.22.2.73

Sabatini, J., Graesser, A. C., Hollander, J., & O'Reilly, T. (2023). A framework of literacy development and how AI can transform theory and practice. *British Journal of Educational Technology*, *54*(5), 1174–1203. DOI: 10.1111/bjet.13342

Shiri, A. (2024). Artificial intelligence literacy: A proposed faceted taxonomy. *Digital Library Perspectives*, *40*(4), 681–699. Advance online publication. DOI: 10.1108/DLP-04-2024-0067

Srinivasan, M., Venugopal, A., Venkatesan, L., & Kumar, R. (2024). Navigating the pedagogical landscape: Exploring the implications of AI and chatbots in nursing education. *JMIR Nursing*, *7*, e52105. DOI: 10.2196/52105 PMID: 38870516

Tadimalla, S. Y., & Maher, M. (2025). AI literacy as a core component of AI education. *AI Magazine*, *46*(2), e70007. Advance online publication. DOI: 10.1002/aaai.70007

Tan, L., & Guo, L. (2009). From print to critical multimedia literacy: One teacher's foray into new literacies practices. *Journal of Adolescent & Adult Literacy: A Journal From the International Reading Association, 53*(4), 315–324. DOI: 10.1598/JAAL.53.4.5

Topalidou Laskaridou, A., Papadopoulos, N., & Koutsogiannis, D. (2022). Contemplating post-digital narrativity: Co-active, multimodal meaning-making on Instagram and its implications on learning. *Punctum International Journal of Semiotics*, *08*(02), 119–142. DOI: 10.18680/hss.2022.0019

van Leeuwen, T. (2015). Multimodality in education: Some directions and some questions. *TESOL Quarterly*, *49*(3), 582–589. DOI: 10.1002/tesq.242

Wang, C. (2025). Exploring students' generative AI-assisted writing processes: Perceptions and experiences from native and nonnative English speakers. *Technology Knowledge and Learning*, *30*(3), 1825–1846. DOI: 10.1007/s10758-024-09744-3

Yan, Y., Liu, H., & Chau, T. (2025). A systematic review of AI ethics in education. *Journal of Global Information Management*, *33*(1), 1–50. DOI: 10.4018/JGIM.386381

Yi, Z., & Siquan, X. (2025). The impact of pre-service language teachers' basic psychological needs on behavioural intentions to utilise artificial intelligence (AI) in teaching: AI literacy and self-efficacy as mediators. *European Journal of Education, 60*(3), e70160. Advance online publication. DOI: 10.1111/ejed.70160

Yue, M., Jong, M. S.-Y., & Dai, Y. (2022). Pedagogical design of K-12 artificial intelligence education: A systematic review. *Sustainability (Basel), 14*(23), 15620. DOI: 10.3390/su142315620

Zhang, H., Lee, I., Ali, S., DiPaola, D., Cheng, Y., & Breazeal, C. (2022). Integrating ethics and career futures with technical learning to promote AI literacy for middle school students: An exploratory study. *International Journal of Artificial Intelligence in Education, 33*(2), 1–35. DOI: 10.1007/s40593-022-00293-3 PMID: 35573722

Zhang, S., Ganapathy Prasad, P., & Schroeder, N. L. (2025). Learning about AI: A systematic review of reviews on AI literacy. *Journal of Educational Computing Research, 63*(5), 1292–1322. DOI: 10.1177/07356331251342081

Zhao, L., Wu, X., & Luo, H. (2022). Developing AI literacy for primary and middle school teachers in China: Based on a structural equation modeling analysis. *Sustainability (Basel), 14*(21), 14549. DOI: 10.3390/su142114549

Zhao, Z., An, Q., & Liu, J. (2025). Exploring AI tool adoption in higher education: Evidence from a PLS-SEM model integrating multimodal literacy, self-efficacy, and university support. *Frontiers in Psychology, 16*(1619391), 1619391. DOI: 10.3389/fpsyg.2025.1619391 PMID: 40989284

KEY TERMS AND DEFINITIONS

AI-Mediated Literacy: Literacy practices in which Artificial Intelligence tools actively influence how texts are produced, interpreted, and evaluated.

Algorithmic Influence: The ways in which AI systems shape content, interpretation, and visibility through data-driven rules and processes.

Artificial Intelligence (AI): Computer-based systems that simulate human intelligence to generate, analyze, or adapt content and support learning processes.

Critical Literacy: An approach to literacy that emphasizes questioning power, representation, bias, and ideology within texts and media.

Ethical AI Use: Responsible application of AI that considers fairness, transparency, privacy, authorship, and inclusivity in educational contexts.

Learner Agency: The capacity of learners to make informed choices, exercise judgment, and actively participate in their own meaning-making processes.

Meaning-Making: The process through which learners construct understanding by interpreting and integrating information across different modes and contexts.

Multimodal Literacy: The ability to interpret and create meaning using multiple modes such as text, images, sound, gestures, data, and digital interaction.

Multimodal Meaning-Making: The coordinated use of multiple semiotic resources to construct and communicate meaning beyond written language alone.

Teacher Mediation: The instructional role of educators in guiding, scaffolding, and critically framing learners' interactions with texts and technologies.

Chapter 2
Multimodal Literacy in the Age of Artificial Intelligence

Amit Kumar Jain
http://orcid.org/0009-0008-6942-9987
Poornima University, India

ABSTRACT

With the rapid integration of the artificial intelligence (AI) into education and communication practices, the definition of literacy has been completely changed to be far beyond the traditional print-based perception of literacy. This chapter has explained how multimodal literacy has evolved in the presence of AI through historical patterns of literacy research, such as classical patterns of reading and writing to digital and multimodal patterns. The chapter substantiates the idea that literacy ought to be reconstructed as an AI mediated multimodal practice that are closely connected to cognitive, cultural and socio-technical processes with the help of the available literature within the field of literacy, learning sciences, and AI ethics. Lastly, the chapter proposes the future-oriented agenda to multimodal literacy research during the AI age that necessitates the critical digital pedagogy, culturally sustaining pedagogues, ethical literacy systems, and cross-disciplinary research alliances.

INTRODUCTION: WHY MULTIMODAL LITERACY IS IMPORTANT NOW

The social, technological and communicative environments of the first decades of the twenty-first century have experienced changes that are disruptive to conventional

DOI: 10.4018/979-8-3373-6986-0.ch002

conceptions of literacy. The multimedia of the multiformity, the omnipresence of digital interfaces, and the emergence of artificial intelligence (AI) as a meaning-making force together necessitate the broadening of the conceptual and pedagogical perspective of literacy studies. Here, I would contend that (i) multimodal literacy is no longer an option but a foundation (ii) AI, in particular, generative and multimodal AI, both exposes and demands more of multimodal literacies (iii) as a reaction, the literacy theory and pedagogy should also change accordingly to respond to these changing conditions.

THE MONOMODAL/MULTIMODAL PARADIGM SHIFT: MULTILITERACIES IN HISTORY

The New London Group issued A Pedagogy of Multiliteracies: Designing Social Futures (1996) with the argument that changes in communication technologies and the growing cultural and linguistic diversity required a wider understanding of literacy than that offered by print-centric methodologies. The authors argue that not only linguistic modes, but a combination of several semiotic modes, visual, audio, spatial, gestural, and interaction among them, should be struggled by the learners (New London Group, 1996). Such an approach to multiliteracies views literacy as social, multi-modal, and design based: learners participate in meaning-making by composing multimodally, which entails being involved in discourse of power, culture and design.

Later social semiotics scholarship (e.g. Kress, van Leeuwen) heightened the focus on the grammar or affordance of non-linguistic modes and the multimodal coordination of meaning. The concept of the reading path of visual arrangement, pictures, text and space organization leading to interpretation reflects how multimodal texts require specific semiotic work on the part of the reader (Kress, 2003). The channels of attention in digital media are non-linear, hyperlinked or can be rearranged dynamically, which only worsens the semiotic pressures on readers.

Multiliteracy pedagogy usually projects four practices: situated practice, explicit teaching of metalanguages, critical framing, and transformed practice (Cope & Kalantzis, 2009). Situated practice means that the learners work with texts based on their lifeworld's; explicit instruction provides them with meta-vocabulary and practices to discuss mode, design, and medium; critical framing allows them to question power, ideology and design decisions; as well as transformed practice allows learners to be seen as designers who can adapt and reassemble modes in new settings. This pedagogical model was applied to visual narratives, interactive media, game designs, data visualisation and other multimodal spaces, as digital and multimodal artifacts became increasingly ubiquitous.

But, not long ago, a substantial amount of that work has been confined to human writing and to human affordance. The entry of AI and its models that create images, audio, and multimodal artifacts based on hybrid objects trigger a transformation in the functioning of composition, reception, and semiotic design.

Table 1. Evolution of Literacy

Literacy Stage	Timeframe	Definition / Focus	Key Characteristics
Traditional Literacy	Pre-20th century	Reading & writing	Print-based, alphabetic, text-focused
Digital Literacy	Late 20th century	Use of digital tools	Multimedia, online communication, basic ICT skills
Multimodal Literacy	Early 21st century	Integration of multiple modes	Text, visuals, audio, interaction
AI-Mediated Literacy	2020s onward	AI-enhanced learning & creation	Generative AI, immersive environments, adaptive learning

The Rationale behind Multimodal Literacy Now with the Age of AI

Multimodal literacy is increasing the stakes of multimodal AI in several ways:

- **AI as Semiotic Producer and Co-designer:** Semiotic agents Generative AI models (text-to-image, text-to-video, vision + language, etc.) are becoming increasingly productive: they create, recombine, and manipulate multimodal artifacts. The user does not have to be the sole designer anymore; immediate design, model decision, and output curation is part of the compositional process. Effectively, teachers and learners need to interact with model literacies, which are the learning environment and influence on output, through model architecture, training data, biases, and prompt heuristics. As AI is a co-designer, multimodal literacy will have to extend beyond human-led design; it will have to include human-AI cross-design practices.
- **Greater Volume, Speed and Interactivity:** The AI can be used to speed up ideation, provide multimodal drafts which can be rapidly prototyped, and explore between modes through iterative exploration. One prompt could produce many visual sketches, where a student picks one, develops and alters them. This velocity and multiplicity distort the time of composition, increasing the number of cycles of variation and curation possible, and consequently

increasing the demands of evaluative literacies the process to choose which version rhetorically, ethically, or representationally best.

- **Cross-Modal Translation and Mediation:** AI can change modalities: images can be captioned or described, audio can be transcribed and remixed, video frames can be summarised, and textual prompts can create visual or audio artifacts. These affordances expand the capabilities of multimodal work and make it more accessible (e.g., alt-text, audio descriptions). But such reconfigurations are mediated through model constraints and biases; critical multimodal literacy needs to entail critique of the way in which these cross-modal conversions can lure meaning or advantage some forms of representation.
- **The problems of Opacity, Bias, and Authorship:** The training data, representational biases and internal heuristics are often black box: users cannot see them. Outputs can encode stereotypes, falsely represent marginalized groups, or can make uncanny or hybrid artifacts that cannot be easily read by humans. Researchers have started to research the ways in which large multimodal foundation models in education introduce novel interpretability, fairness, and trustworthiness concerns (Claman & Sezgin, 2024). Moreover, there are more questions of authorship and originality: when an AI system adds a lot of value to an image or composition, who is the author? How is it that plagiarism occurs with hybrid human-AI multimodal texts? These problems dictate that the literacy framework should be now equipped with ethical and critical AI literacies.
- **Equity-Risks and uneven Access:** The ability to use state-of-the-art multimodal AI tools is not evenly distributed: licensure, cost, hardware issues (e.g., GPUs), network infrastructure also differ depending on socio-economic and geographic contexts. In this regard, access disparities can further enhance existing educational disparities in multimodal literacy access. Therefore, a justice-based multimodal literacy agenda must be mindful of inequality of access, infrastructural limitations and literacies that are culturally situated.
- **Generative AI as Re-invention of Meaning and Multiplicity:** AI can create several different interpretations of a prompt; it is able to reformulate meaning, combine cultural objects, or create hybrids of genres. Multiplicity affordance implies that one prompt can result in more than one semiotic path, thus, encouraging learners to compare and contrast and choose. Such a multiplicity dislodges the concept of a finished text and shifts literate practice to the practices of selection, negotiation and curation of multimodal variants. It requires the learners not only to write, but also to discriminate between model-generated choices.

To a Multimodal Literacy Framework

As a continuation of the multiliteracies background and the disruptive changes of AI, a new multimodal literacy framework, needs to incorporate the following principles:

1. Design-weep hybridity: Have the learners become hybrid human-AI designers and make prompt making and model steering compositional decisions.
2. Awareness of meta-model: Integrate into the curriculum a metalanguage to reason about constraints of models, datasets, bias and interpretability.
3. Iterative ethical curation: Promote the idea that AI outputs should be viewed as drafts and be open to interrogation, editing, and re-design.
4. Multimodal reflexivity: As well as asking learners to reflect on the interplay between modes (such as how image and text go together), ask them to reflect on how AI is mediating the interactions.
5. Access and equity orientation: Proactively scaffold access to learners with limited access (e.g. lightweight AI tools, offline modes) and power disparities in model access.
6. Provenance, attribution, authorship literacy: Develop literacies of traceability (prompt logs, versioning, model metadata) and ethical attribution of AI contributions.

HOW AI CHANGES MULTIMODAL COMPOSITION AND RECEPTION

New Affordances

The multimodal literacies affordances brought by AI have not only increased the range of what can be accomplished but have also changed the conventional compositional phases and augmented the resources that can be used by the learners.

- **Improved Invention and Idea Generation:** Inspiration In generative AI applications (e.g., text-to-image, text prompts, image editing), rapid idea generation, visual or audio inspiration, and ideation scaffolding are offered. Jiang et al. discovered that during multimodal composition projects, tools such as Adobe Firefly and DALL·E were helpful during the invention stage because they proposed visual metaphors and aesthetics and enabled students to rethink problems they otherwise would have never imagined (Jiang, 2024).

- **Revision, Design Variation, Iteration:** The ability of AI to produce variants enables students to experiment and test with designs, adjust visual/audio/textual combinations, trim unwanted features, and improve their multimodal artifacts. Jiang et al. (the same study) report that the students additionally used the AI output as a draft of their compositions and then critically revised them. It was also found that preservice teachers were writing under the influence of iterative prompting, trying out unforeseen results, humour, surprise, and playful discovery when they used AI tools. These affective creative dynamics belong to AI affordances (Smith et al., 2024).
- **Multicultural/Linguistic Support:** Multimodal AI works with multiple languages, visual aids, and translation, and they can be used to access and scaffold curriculum, particularly culturally and linguistically diverse ones. Hong Kong high school studies provided proof that AI assistance is beneficial in digital multimodal compositions, indicated that students who took advantage of generative AI in studies of vocabulary, grammar, and structure, and AI assistance proved to be particularly beneficial when dealing with multilingual texts (Lin et al., 2024).
- **Feedback, Scaffolding, and Collaboration:** The AI tools can provide either immediate feedback or suggestions (textual, visual), act as a brainstorming/design collaborator, act as a critic/editor of multimodal texts. Such affordances make design fewer delays and more reflectively revised. As an example, AI proposals can be used by some students to narrow or even delete undesired information in graphics or design materials.
- **New Modes & Cross-Modal Translation:** AI makes it possible to make cross-modal transformations: text to image, speech to text, image to description, and so on. Such cross-media translations assist in accessibility (e.g., alt text), in intermedia translation between student ideas, as well as in understandings of media interrelations. Also, on the literature, there are activities in which students demonstrate scientific epistemic reading in multiple modalities, involving both organizational and representational meaning in visual terms (Cheung et al., 2024).

Risks, Limitations, and Tensions

On the one hand, AI opens new opportunities, but, on the other hand, there are considerable restrictions, uncertainties, and tensions. They have pedagogical design implications, ethics implications and literacy interpretation implications.

- **Opacity, Bias and Represented Fairness:** Generative models are usually black-box: training data, innuendos within, and the logic is not completely transparent to the users. Prejudice in created material can support stereotypes, inaccurately represent culture or identity, or disenfranchise the voices. New research in generative bias has found examples of underrepresentation or biased image generation by AI regardless of whether biased training data is explicitly used (Huang and Huang, 2025). The cognitive perception of algorithmic bias of the text-to-image models by children also shows the perception of unfair or stereotyping results by the learners, which leads to the necessity of critical literacy (Vartiainen et al., 2024).

- **Authorship, Originality and Intellectual Property Concerns:** In cases of AI tools, the question is who an owner is or credited in a composition, or part thereof. In multimodal composition, (Kostopolus, 2024) argues that intellectual property and academic honesty is complicated because the students use AI-generated images or audio, which could be based on training data that the creators have little to no control over.
- **Quality, Coherence and Compositional Understanding:** The outputs of AI are not always coherent, particularly in multimodal complex scenes with numerous objects or relationships. Models can also not understand compositional scenes well; recent comparisons have indicated that even high-end text-to-image and vision-language models are significantly worse than humans when given the task of generating scenes that involve multiple objects and associations (Fu et al., 2025). Also, cross-mode consistency (e.g. between text and image) can also break down: images can be inconsistent with the intended story or theme, or text can misunderstand images. Learners will have to negotiate and rectify disjunctions.
- **Overdependence, Flattening of Creative Process, and Attribution Problems:** Moreover, the rights and attributions of sources that AI models are based upon are also invisible at times. Teachers need to scaffold the knowledge of provenance in students and teach them to critically review AI-generated text and modify it instead of taking it at face value.

Reception Alteration: The AI Impact on Reception, Interpretation, and Audience

The effect of AI is not just felt in the writing of the texts, but in their reception, interpretations, propagation, and evaluation. In this context, the researcher emphasizes the importance of critical writing by being able to read AI-mediated texts, examine media, and develop skills in pertinent and meaningful writing.

- **Critical Reading of AI-Mediated Texts:** In this regard, the researcher highlights the significance of critical writing in being able to read AI-mediated texts, analyze the media, and learn to write, in a relevant and meaningful way. The users of multimodal texts produced (or in part produced) through AI will be forced to acquire literacies to be sceptical of authorship, bias, data provenance, model limitations, and ethical considerations. As an example, a learner should consider whether the visualized image was created with biased data, whether the approximate or the hallucinated material can be deceptive, or whether the style replicates the unacknowledged work.

- **The interpretation of Multiplicity and Variation:** Due to the ability of the AI tools to generate various variant outputs of the same prompt, the readers or audiences can be exposed to different instantiations of the same concept. Such multiplicity requires interpretive abilities: making comparisons between versions, finding which one is most suited to a rhetorical purpose or an ethically desirable presentation. Having variant drafts implies that it is more negotiable what will be considered final.
- **Change in Audience Expectation, Authenticity, and Trust:** AI generated images or sound can alter viewer conventions regarding what is considered as high production value, reality, or fidelity. On one hand, audiences might believe that a picture is real, whereas in reality, it is an AI product, or they might assume that any multimodal artifact is refined, even when it was created by a student because of seeing professional AI products. This may put strain on the student designers and sometimes mistrust or doubt in some situations.
- **Effect on Voice, Identity, and Designer Presence:** In multimodal compositions, mode, aesthetic, style and semiotic choice are used by the learners to convey identity, voice and perspective. At the hands of skilled users, AI tools can be used to enhance voice; however, they also may be used without a critical mindset, and in such cases, homogenize voice or replace it with model defaults. One recent qualitative paper (Purposeful Remixing with Generative AI: Constructing Designer Voice in Multimodal Composing) investigates the ways in which students tried to assert their uniqueness by their AI-remixed images, however, with limitations since their prompts were not enough to create their authorial impact (Tan et al., 2024).

Pedagogical Implications Curriculum, Instruction and Teacher Preparedness

Here I discuss how the dynamic needs on AI-mediated multimodal literacies must transform the curriculum design, instructional strategies, and teacher professional development (PD).

Table 2. Pedagogical Approaches in AI-Mediated Multimodal Literacy

Approach	Definition	AI Integration	Expected Outcomes
Constructivist	Learning by doing	AI scaffolding and content generation	Deeper conceptual understanding
Sociocultural	Collaborative learning	AI-mediated collaborative platforms	Enhanced peer interaction & cultural literacy
Personalized Learning	Adaptive & individualized	AI recommendation systems	Increased learner engagement & motivation

Multimodal Literacy Curriculum Design Principles of AI-Inflected Multimodal Literacy

The implementation of generative and multimodal AI in literacy education means the redefinition of learning outcomes, scaffolds, and progression. These are some of the most important concepts that should be considered when redesigning literacy curricula.

- **Explicit Multimodal + AI Literacies:** Not only mode literacies (visual, audio, gestural, spatial) but also AI literacies (prompt design, model interpretation, validation, and ethical awareness) should be clearly expressed in curriculum. These literacies must not be regarded as peripheral ones and they should be incorporated into the learning outcomes of multimodal composition. As an example, as part of their literate competence, learners may be asked to explain how timely changes can change visual affordances or criticize bias in AI-generated images.
- **Scaffolded development of Low-Stakes to High-stakes Tasks:** Since AI tools are both potent and unreliable, curriculum must proceed through guided, low-stakes exploration (e.g., prompt manipulation of small images) toward more open, high-stakes projects (e.g., projects facing external audiences). During the initial stages, educators may offer initial prompts, defined scaffolds to refine them, or filtered AI results to interpret design choices.
- **Reflection and Metacognition as Fundamental Elements:** Since many AI models are black-box, based on their relevance to the curriculum, repeated metacognitive reflection has to be embedded in the curriculum, and students need to record histories of prompts, decision-making rationale, and revisions. Design logs or reflection journals serve as intermediaries between the black box AI processes and human cognition. The learners develop model-conscious literacies through such reflective practices.

- **Framing Ethical and Socio-Cultural:** Multimodal AI composition does not happen in a dispassionate vacuum. The design of the curriculum should actively incorporate critical framing, which entails asking the students to consider who is presented and who is marginalized, how stereotypes can be perpetuated and which power structures are embedded in the training data. This is in harmony with the critical framing focus of multiliteracies theory (New London Group, 1996). One way such framing can be operationalised is via case study, ethical audit of prompt ethics, and discussion of dataset provenance.
- **Accommodation:** Since not everyone has access to state-of-the-art AI tools, curricula must contain options (e.g. lower weight local models, low-tech multimodal activities) and must allow students with different levels of access to equitably engage. AI-infused assignments should also be designed keeping bandwidth, hardware, and software in consideration. Moreover, AI can be used in curriculums to scaffold learner disparities such as adaptive multimodal scaffolds, auto-generated visuals, or proposed alternative prompts provided that the design is clear and can be controlled by the learners.
- **Interdisciplinary and Intergenic Integration:** The multimodal AI literacy cannot be isolated in English or media classes. Instead, it must trickle down the disciplines (science, social studies, arts, language) and genres (explainers, narratives, argument, data visualizations). As an example, a science course may require students to create visualizations of a natural phenomenon and then create a multimodal description, which they are expected to revise based on the variants suggested by AI. Recent science education research suggests that it is possible to incorporate multimodal large language models (MLLM) into the inquiry of discipline-specific inquiry without disrupting pedagogical balance and human control (Bewersdorff et al., 2025).

Instructional Strategies and Classroom Practices

The process of translating principles of the curriculum into classroom practice includes developing tasks, scaffold, interactions and assessments that utilize AI affordances and develop student agency and criticality.

- **Prompt Labs & Prompt Workshops:** One of the underlying classroom methods is the prompt lab: a classroom in which students are tasked with creating prompts to generate text, images or audio, comparing versions and commenting on how small modifications to a prompt influence generation. Educators have the option to model prompt moves (e.g. changing style cues, constraints or compositional terms) and invite students to collaboratively remix prompts. With time students learn prompt-design heuristics as multimodal writing repertoire. Scaffolding of prompts to progressive constraints can be done with template prompts and then gradually, open-ended prompts. Students can be taught to debug on the fly, to analyse errors (e.g. Why did the tree not appear?), and to check output (check meaning, check representation, check style).

- **Think-Aloud Design Sessions:** Think-aloud design sessions can be performed by teachers or more advanced students, as they describe their choices on-the-fly, the logic of model choice, the logic of evaluation of output and the logic of revision. This makes their compositional argument (in multimodal/ AI situations) more external and assists beginner learners to visualize the way the design moves are mediated by the AI. This scaffolding resembles pedagogical actions of composition theory except that now it applies to AI-mediated design.
- **Human AI Pairing:** In classroom projects students can be divided into human-AI design teams, where students write prompts, examine the AI output, and make collaborative corrections. The human has to be the ultimate design; the AI is a co-designer or assistant. By doing so students will be taught to negotiate with the affordances, introduce an intervention where AI outputs are concerned, and to avoid blind acceptance.
- **Remix, Attribution and Transparency Exercises:** An interesting pedagogical genre is the remix attribution exercise: students are given or create multimodal AI artifacts, which they then need to remap, remix, re-author, or recontextualize, while following the histories of prompts, model versions, and editorial decisions. Students will need to add a provenance fold (a mini-report) about timely logs, model used and their changes. This creates transparency and makes them regard AI outputs as rough materials, rather than final products.
- **Scaffolded Multimodal Portfolios:** Teachers can scaffold students to create iterative multimodal portfolios over a semester or a course instead of having single assignments. With every artifact, there are design rationales, prompt histories, variants in comparison, and reflective commentary. Portfolios make it possible to provide formative feedback, track student development, and conduct meta-analysis regarding the temporal dynamics of prompt/AI interaction.
- **Hybrid Technologies that are Low-Tech:** All students will not have equal access to AI. The low-tech backup activities that teachers should plan (i.e., drawing, collage, oral narration) should be arranged in such a way that learning goals are modality, design and reflection-based instead of being based on the novelty of the tool. The use of hybrid classes can be alternated between

AI-enhanced and analog multimodal design tasks, which makes them equally fair and more conceptually sound in regard to the modes exclusively generated by AI.

Teacher Education, Professional Development and Institutional Support

Teacher preparation and institutional structures need to develop together in order to have AI-inflected multimodal literacy be successful.

- **Developing AI + Multimodal Theory-Practice Bridges:** Multimodal semiotics needs to be incorporated in teacher education programs along with fluency of AI tools. Multimodal design tasks that involve the use of generative AI should be performed by pre-service teachers, as well as the consideration of model affordances, prompt heuristics, and ethical concerns. Making AI iterations embedded into methods courses is consistent with the idea that pedagogical theory and the fluency of tools should be co-created.

According to the scoping review by Sperling et al. the existing body of literature conceives AI literacy through the conceptual framework of teacher knowledge (content, pedagogy, ethics) but seldom creates a sustained disciplinary AI-infused design capacity (Kajiwara and Kawabata, 2024). The teacher growth should not be limited to a simple how-to-use-the-tool training but should be grounded more deeply in concepts and be more iterative.

- **Sustained Professional Learning Communities (PLCs):** Transformative change cannot be done in short workshops. Schools and districts must also facilitate long-lasting PLCs whereby teachers work together to co-create AI-enhanced multimodal units, exchange immediate heuristics, debug outputs, and carry out mini action research. The teacher knowledge concerning AI-mediated multimodal literacy in these communities develops in enactment and reflection cycles.
- **Teacher Reflective Tools based on analytics:** The upcoming research suggests multimodal analytics tools that might assist teacher reflection on hybrid human-AI classrooms (e.g., movement, student-AI interactions) (Adiguzel et al., 2023). These tools may assist teachers to track the interaction of students with AI, in which failures promptly take place, and how to scaffold more effectively. One example of this might be a tool that visualises how often many revisions are made, how many hours students spend reviewing AI output, or how many times students switch modes.

- **Equity, Access and Infrastructure:** The institutional support is essential: the license, hardware, network capacity and equitable access to AI tools should be insured. Schools should have tool access policies (e.g. licensing, offline), and osmotic across classroom mechanisms. In the absence of this infrastructure, AI multimodal pedagogy will be prone to perpetuate inequities.

EVALUATION AND ASSESSMENT MULTIMODAL LITERACY IN THE AGE OF AI

Recent advances of generative and multimodal AI demand the re-conceptualization of teacher-conceptualization, design, and practice of evaluation in the field of literacy education. Conventional models of assessment, an assumption of linearity as the primary evaluative approach and text-based writings, along with human-produced products, as the key evaluation tools are getting increasingly out of scope with the complexity, hybridity, and cyclicality of AI-mediated multimodal compositions. This section will examine how the assessment practices should change, with regard to new standards, sources of evidence, and instruments of assessment that will be useful in the AI age in order to support the multimodal literacy skills.

The Multimodal Era of Assessment the Multimodal Era of Assessment

Conventional literacy testing has long been concerned with such discrete skills as grammar, coherence, vocabulary, and structure of argument. However, multimodal texts (such as visual, gestural, spatial, and even linguistic ones) demand more measures of evaluation that are multidimensional. Multimodality, according to Jewitt and Kress, brings about orchestration of semiotics where meaning is created through the interaction between modes and not necessarily through linguistic text. This problem is escalated by the fact that AI is incorporated, introducing additional levels of co-authorship, prompts design, and algorithmic mediation.

The evaluation should be now based not just on what students create (the final artifacts) but also how they plan, provoke, recycle, and critically interact with AI mechanisms. Composition process, rationale of choices of modal, prompting and refinement strategies and the fact that an ethical consideration has been incorporated into the work itself become as important as the product (Cope & Kalantzis, 2009).

Multimodal Assessment Principles Amid AI

- **Process-Oriented Evaluation:** The AI-mediated multimodal literacy is iterative and tends to be non-linear in compositional process. Students create numerous artifacts, test prompts, curate products, and improve on them. Evaluation should thus not be confined to summative product evaluation, but it should be accompanied by documentation and reflection on the process. Timely logs, history of iterations, design diaries can be critical sources of information about student learning and decision making (Crompton & Burke, 2020).
- **Focus on Human Agency and Criticality:** Since AI has the capability to automate composition, assessment should be able to distinguish between the use of tools passively and proactively and critically. The evaluators are to seek agency indicators among the students such as the questioning of model outputs, the purposeful choice of design, and bias or representation critique. Activities that make students explain their design decisions or compare and critique AI results can help identify how well students have the skills of critical literacy.
- **Multimodal Coherence:** The important criterion of assessment is the level at which the various modes collaborate to attain communicative objectives. Rubrics should focus on coherence, rhetorical consistency, and awareness of the audience. This means more than merely the quality of visual, textual, auditory and spatial elements; it is a matter of their integration. It has been argued that the complexity of multimodal work is better reflected by the evaluation of modal orchestration, as opposed to being evaluated in single modal.
- **Socio-Technical and Ethical Awareness:** The awareness of the ethical considerations of the students such as representation, data provenance, bias, copyright and authorship should be included in the assessment framework. Such criteria could be whether students recorded model sources, had cogitated about possible biases, or considered the ethical consequences of their design choices. With the spread of AI-generated content, multimodal competence can no longer be considered outside of ethical literacy (Floridi & Chiriatti, 2020).

Model and Frameworks of Assessment

To apply this set of principles, a series of models of assessment that were established to deal with AI-mediated multimodal literacy could be applied in education systems and by teachers.

- **Layered Portfolio Assessment:** Initial drafts, AI-generated work, revisions, logs at prompt, reflective essays may all be included in portfolios. Evaluation is also concerned with the end product, but also with the learning paths and the complexity of the decision-making process among students. Indicatively, in a course in media design, students could have a series of created images, a note on how the prompts were adjusted to get them to be more appropriate, and a final product. This gives the evaluators an overview of student learning and agency.
- **Collaborative Assessment and Peer Review:** Peer assessment is an important component in multimodal literacy education. Formal peer review procedures may encourage students to share their design decisions, be subject to a wide range of feedback and be able to critically assess multimodal compositions of others. Peer review with AI-sensitive rubrics also aids students to acquire meta-linguistic and meta-design vocabularies to enhance assistive literacy.

Table 3. Challenges and Barriers in AI-Mediated Multimodal Literacy

Category	Description	Example	Potential Mitigation
Technological	Limited access to AI tools	Low-resource schools	Cloud-based AI, open-source platforms
Pedagogical	Teacher readiness & skill gap	Lack of AI training	Professional development & workshops
Ethical / Social	Bias, privacy concerns	AI-generated misinformation	Transparent, explainable AI systems
Cultural	Multilingual & cross-cultural adaptation	Non-English learners	Multilingual AI models & inclusive content

Future Directions and Challenges of Assessment

Despite the innovations discussed above, there are some issues regarding the measurement of multimodal literacy in the era of AI:

- **Authorship and Attribution:** There is still controversy about the definition of human and machine authorship. Evaluation systems have to deal with the issues of originality and academic integrity.
- **Bias and Opacity on Results:** The AIs can encode bias or error on the output and this may be hard to detect. The educators should come up with ways of

determining the degree of consciousness and mitigation of these concerns among the students.

Workload Process-oriented and portfolio testing is time consuming and demands the professional expertise of the instructor. Institutions have to invest in training, tools, and workload change to maintain such assessments.

- **Changing Tools and Standards:** With the progress of AI, the evaluation standards will have to be constantly altered, so that they are always timely and effective.

The automatic assessment tools which should be included in the human assessment, the analytics dashboards to reveal the pattern of interaction between the student and the AI, and the cross-institutional frameworks to certify the AI-mediated multimodal competencies will be studied in the future.

RESEARCH AND PRACTICE METHODOLOGICAL PATHWAYS

With the maturation of the study of literacy to the age of multimodal texts mediated by AI, our methodological toolbox will have to alter. The complexity of the co-composition between human and AI as well as multimodal semiotic orchestration and the changing literate practices cannot be adequately represented through conventional means of qualitative or quantitative research. This sub-section suggests and critically discusses methodological paths in which the research on multimodal literacy in the AI usage can be conducted. Notable approaches include design-based research, multi-modal discourse analysis, Multi-modal learning analytics (MMLA) and AI-enabled analytics, longitudinal mixed methods, participatory and critical methods and meta-analyses. In both I talk of affordances, design issues and design heuristics.

AI-Mediated Multimodal Literacy Design-Based Research (DBR).

Design-based research (DBR) remains a key method of educational innovation especially when interventions (e.g. AI-assisted multimodal composing) are intimately connected with sequential improvement and theory. DBR can assist with the co-cutting tool, scaffold, rubrics, and curriculum sequence process in the context of AI, and research how learners engage with generative models in the real-world situation.

Affordances

DBR lets the intervention cycles adjust to students behaving in emergent ways, and to model affordances or constraints not originally anticipated.

It facilitates the incorporation of design justification and scientific evidence, which results into usable knowledge by practitioners.

Intervention infrastructure can be incorporated with logging, prompt tracking and versioning, which provide rich data capture.

Challenges and Heuristics

Needs Replications Since AI models change (e.g., new models, model updates), replications need to consider changing baselines.

Models, prompt libraries and scaffold artifacts should be planned to be version controlled, with each cycle recorded as to which version of model was used.

Mixed assessment (qualitative observation + process logging + analysis of artifacts) is a necessity.

When implementing AI tools in students, ethical supervision is necessary on a continuous basis.

AI- multimodal literacy DBR is well-positioned to help integrate curriculum design and research question, though should take specific care of the changing baseline of AI tools over time.

Multimodal Discourse Analysis/Semiotic Tracing.

The Multimodal discourse analysis (MDA) continues to be an influential qualitative approach to unpack the relationship between the modes (text, image, audio, spatial layout) in artifacts. In the case of AI, MDA should be extended to have prompt histories, variants generated by the model, and explanation of decisions.

KEY METHODOLOGICAL MOVES

Quick-Artifact Alignment: The outputs of variant prompts are assigned to specific versions of prompts, with particular focus on the degree to which subtle prompt alterations can result in a semiotic change.

Modal Interdependence Mapping: Visualize the evolution of image, text, audio, gesture and layout, lineage of coherence, tension and variation of affordances.

Revision Trajectories: These are the interventions of the learners to intervene (edit, re-prompt, remix) recursively across the modes, and comment on this intervention.

Model Transparency Layer: Record where possible what known model biases or tendencies may have influenced a particular artifact (e.g. default style, preference towards prototypical visual).

When paired with MDA and timely logs and design rationale, semiotic tracing provides the opportunity to closely read human-AI design conversations. Not only the content of multimodal texts is prefigured by this technique, but also their existence.

Multimodal Learning Analytics (MMLA) and AI-Enhanced Analytics

Multimodal Learning Analytics MMLA has emerged as a rapidly becoming field of study, with methodological promise to capture and interpret multimodal student activity in deep, time-prolonged settings, in an automated or semi-automated way. One recent systematic review of AI + MMLA demonstrates that numerous studies currently combine AI techniques of learning features, fusion, and prediction in multimodal pipelines.

Basic procedure pipeline of AI-enhanced MMLA

Data capture and synchronization: Minimize multimodal sensors or logs (video, audio, keystroke logs, eye tracking, gesture data, physiological sensors).

Pre-processing and feature extraction Clean, segment, and extract features (e.g. visual features, speech prosody, gesture dynamics). Guerrero-Sosa et al. conduct a thorough overview of the data modalities and pipelines in learning institutions (Guerrero-Sosa et al., 2025).

Fusion & modeling: Fuse with methods such as early/late/hybrid fusion, deep learning models, attention models, ensemble methods.

Interpretation & intervention: Predictive models can be used to generate predictive signals in scaffold requirements or create visualizations that can be interpreted by researchers/teachers.

Affordances

MMLA can extract fine-grained patterns of modality transitions, prompts-response cycles and design contingencies that would be difficult to extract manually.

Example: Design Process Scaffolding and adaptive feedback can be provided by real-time or near-real-time analytics.

Issues & Design Principles

Multimodal stream synchronization and alignment is computationally and error intensive.

Critical Model interpretability: black-box deep models do not necessarily provide information about teacher actions.

Trade-offs between scalability and ecological validity: Lots of MMLA systems are lab systems and not field-deployable systems.

Ethical, fairness, privacy: questions of surveillance, consent and access to data will have to be pre-empted. Prinsloo and Slade address privacy issues in MMLA situations (Prinsloo et al., 2023).

Lens of FATE (Fairness, Accountability, Transparency, Ethics): Jin et al. believe that the student perceptions of fairness and transparency should also be examined in the real-life context (Jin et al., 2024).

New work extends latent class analysis to MMLA to reduce multimodal patterns to interpretable classes (e.g., collaborative vs solitary modes) in high-fidelity simulations (Yan et al., 2024).

Altogether, AI techniques integration into MMLA has strong avenues to relate information of micro-interactions with multimodal literacy design, but requires critical methodological, interpretative, and ethical designing.

Mixed Methods and Learning Trajectory Analysis Longitudinal

A longitudinal examination of the process of multimodal literacy development is invaluable in learning how the timely literacies, design fluency, and critical sensibility of the learners develop over a period. Longitudinal mixed methods designs are combination:

- QT analysis (trend analysis of timely logs, revision logs, change of modal over time)
- The qualitative case studies can be conducted in the form of interviews, reflective journals, and stories of artifacts.
- Growth modeling (e.g., hierarchical linear modelling, latent growth curve models) to find links between process measures and learning outcomes or change in disposition.

Participatory, Critical, Culturally Responsive Methods

- Design with students and communities: Work with students to design prompt scaffolds, genres of artifacts and criteria of evaluation. This ensures that the methods are reflective of semiotic repertoires and culture sensibilities of the students.

- Critical reflexivity procedures: The researchers are required to keep reflexive records concerning power relations, assumptions, and model prejudices.
- Ethnographic / micro ethnographic research: The invisible work of literate design can be revealed by observing how students practice in contexts that involve the use of AI (classrooms, community labs).
- Cultural probes and narrative inquiry: Prompt learners to recount their experience using AI-generated multimodal design, their experience of voice, and how they associate model affordances to their situations.
- These approaches assist in bringing to the fore the side-lined views, local sense making activities, and challenges to AI affordances.

Meta-Analyses, Scoping Reviews and Comparative Studies

To integrate knowledge and find gaps, meta-analytical, scoping, and comparative cross-contextual approaches should be embraced by the field:

- Scoping reviews visualize the terrain of AI + multimodal literacies (e.g. how many studies in classrooms, what domains, what populations). Mohammadi et al. have already performed a systematic review of AI in MMLA with gaps in scale, interpretability and cross context deployment.
- Meta-analyses can quantify the effects of AI interventions (e.g., the effect of prompt scaffolding on the quality of multimodal composition) across studies.
- Comparative cross-contextual studies (e.g. resource-rich vs resource-constrained, L1 vs multilingual settings) can be used to test the effect of context on AI-mediated literacy practices.
- Combined they might assist in establishing evidence-based heuristics and theory-building in a variety of contexts.

Methodological Integration & Pragmatic Triangulation

- No single method suffices. Triangulation of numerous approaches will be the most fruitful research designs:
- E.g. Pair DBR interventions with MMLA instrumentation and semiotic tracing to record both macro and micro dynamics.
- Growth can be tracked longitudinally using longitudinal mixed methods, supported by participatory design to root in the context.
- Bury meta-analytic syntheses to intersect emergent patterns between studies.

An imaginary example protocol could be as follows:

- By engaging and collaborating with teachers and students, co-design a multimodal-AI composition project.
- Integrate immediate logging, version management and sensor capture.
- In enactment, use real-time analytics scaffolding mid-course changes.
- Perform semiotic tracking of objects and trigger change.
- Track students over time on several activities.

Ethical, Validity and Practical Concurrencies

To achieve methodological rigor in AI-infused environments, it is important to pay close attention to:

- Informed consent, privacy and data management: especially sensor, video or physiological data within classrooms (Prinsloo et al., 2023).
- Validity and reliability of analytics models: ensure that the models are validated, transparent and not overfit, there should be human interpretability in the model, and it should be always verified.
- Altering tool ecosystems: AI models are always being modified, requiring researchers to keep track of versions, tool licenses, prompt libraries and migration plans.
- Scalability vs field validity: trade-offs between sophistication in the laboratory and the potential of implementation to the classroom.
- Reflexivity of researcher positionality: the researchers must be aware of how model design conventions and affordances, and resource constraints affect the definition of good multimodal literacy.

UNDERSTANDING AI-MEDIATED MULTIMODAL LITERACY: EQUITY, ETHICS AND SOCIO-CULTURAL CONSIDERATIONS

Equity of Access and Opportunity

These differences will potentially widen the literacy gap unless purposeful design and policy intervention is implemented. Digital Access and Resource Distribution (DA): The Department of Information Technology will oversee the provision of digital services and resources to every citizen.

Digital Access and Resource Distribution

Equity will start by making sure that hardware, software, and network infrastructure will be provided in a variety of learning settings. When possible, schools and universities should place a premium on device-delivery, cloud-based platform delivery, and offline options. The studies have shown that inequality in access to digital tools is highly associated with the inequality in engagement and the results of learning. To illustrate, students who do not have regular access to AI platforms have a reduced ability to take part in the iterative multimodal design procedures or undertake a portfolio-based assessment.

Pedagogical Differentiating and Inclusive Design

The various levels of AI literacy and modality proficiency should be accommodated in the instructional and curriculum design. This entails scaffolding assignments to provide multiple points of entry to the learners who might possess different technological, cognitive and linguistic differences. UDL frameworks may be applied to the practices of AI-mediated instructions to ensure that assignments are choice-based, flexible, and mode-representative.

Linguistic and Cultural Inclusivity

In AI, the models employed are generally trained on skewed data sets that favor more powerful languages and cultural norms, which are not sensitive to students whose native language or cultural background is over- or under-represented in the data set. Different repertoires of semiotic legitimize the pedagogical effectiveness and support multilingual and culturally based multimodality. Generative AI models can be employed to facilitate translation, generate local content, culturally responsive prompts, etc. using creative applications, although such applications will require intentional attention and adjustment.

Ethics in AI-mediated Literacy

AI-mediated multimodal composition also requires more than technical competency; it includes critical reflection on the socio-technical consequences of using AI. The primary issues are bias, copyright, privacy, transparency and authorship.

- **Bias and Algorithmic Fairness:** With only a few exceptions, generative AI systems recreate the biases found in their training data, generating stereotypical or exclusionary results. In order to prevent the harmful impacts of

AI, students need to be directed to critically assess AI outputs as biased and make conscious decisions. Some of the pedagogical practices are bias audits, immediate change-exercises, and AI-generated content reflectively (Bender et al., 2021). Ethical literacy requires insight into the underlying ethics of the algorithm, rather than the superficiality of bias in its results.

- **Copyright and Authorship:** The artificial content produced by AI makes conventional concepts of authorship, intellectual property, and scholarly integrity difficult. Teachers and schools need to design evident standards in attribution such as recording immediate histories, AI involvement, and student interventions. Future policy discourse proposes to incorporate co-authorship and provenance tracking throughout the design of assignments in a way that is transparent but academic responsibility is upheld.
- **Privacy and Data Governance:** Multimodal composition mediated by AI authorship frequently demands students to provide personal information, photographs or videos. Ethical models need to be privacy, informed consent, and secure storage-based with particular focus to sensitive demographic/biometric information which is personal and sensitive. The policies of the institutions must be congruent with the standards like GDPR or COPPA, and the students must be enabled to learn about the risks and implications of the data sharing (Ng'ambi et al., 2016).
- **Transparency and Explainability:** Ethical literacy is largely dependent on transparency in AI. Students ought to be taught to read model outputs, evaluate reliability, and make valid justification of immediate decisions. Transparent and accountable practice can be facilitated with the help of instructional scaffolds like annotated prompt logs, step-by-step output documentation, comparative model analyzes, etc. (Floridi et al., 2018). The postponement of over a month is due to the risk incurred when renting a building in the city where the event will be held.

Socio-Cultural Responsiveness

This is because renting a building in the city where the event will take place poses a risk of a delay of more than a month. Multimodal literacy is by its nature placed in social, cultural, and linguistic context. The practices of AI should not impose normative and homogenizing structures but reflect and enhance the various cultural identities of people.

- **Contextualized Pedagogy:** The curricular designers are encouraged to inculcate culturally significant contents and activities, which enable students to access the knowledge and vernacular literacies of their communities, as well as the local multimodal repertoires. This practice is consistent with the concepts of culturally sustaining pedagogy, which insists on continuity between the real lives of students and the classroom literacies.

- **Critical Cultural Literacy:** It is recommended that students should challenge AI-generated representations critically in terms of cultural assumptions, stereotypes or misrepresentation. The pedagogical practices can be based on the analysis of how AI presents the historically marginalized groups and on the development of the multimodal stories challenging the mainstream discourses. Such critical reading develops media literacy, morality and socio-political consciences.
- **Community-Based and Collaborative Practices:** In multimodal projects of AI, the socio-cultural responsiveness is enhanced in collaboration and community-bearing practices. To provide an example, the students can collectively create multimodal campaigns of the local social issue, such as the perspectives of the community, or translate the stories to another language. Staying ethically accountable and maintaining AI-mediated literacy in a social context does not only require participation design but also makes it possible to engage.

Intersectionality and Auditing Inclusion

- Analysis The most evident point of collision in equity and ethics is assessment. The multimodal AI literacy tests should be receptive, allowing and responsive to the background and skills of students.
- Differentiated rubrics can consider the varying degrees of access, modality knowledge and language proficiency.
- Process-oriented evaluation is also interested in critical thinking, iteration and reflection, and not in the quality of raw output.
- Reduction of grading bias will ensure that AI-mediated artifacts do not discriminate students, in terms of language, culture and socio-economic background.

Policy and Institutional Implications

- Institutional policy is not the only aspect of fairness and morals that can be practiced in the classroom:
- Institutions are to come up with AI guidelines in assignments, privacy and IP.
- Professional development- AI ethical training, bias awareness, culturally responsive pedagogy.

- Policy makers therefore need to give equal access to AI platforms in the under-resourced schools or communities.

CHALLENGES, LIMITATIONS, AND FUTURE RESEARCH OPPORTUNITIES

These are technological, pedagogical, ethical, socio-cultural and institutional issues. Here, I have enumerated the most crucial obstacles to successful implementation, highlighted some of the methodological and conceptual limitations, and outlined the future research directions that can guide the future creation of AI-integrated multimodal literacy research.

- **Quickly Slipping AI Tools:** To illustrate, a generative AI device could provide inconsistent outcomes because of its iterative nature in updating, and this aspect could affect the effect on reproducibility in the classroom intervention and research study.
- **Multi-platform Integration:** Of most AI-mediated multimodal literacy situations, there is a need to integrate text, audio, visual and interactive media. The compatibility of the data, the interoperability of the tools and the synchronization of multimodal outputs are the challenges of integration. Weak integration may leave the learners to fragmented working processes that do not encourage engagement and comprehension.
- **Model Bias and Limitations:** The AI models tend to be built on the bias of the training data, resulting in stereotypical or culturally blind or inaccurate results. These biases must be challenged by teachers and students in order to avoid making inequalities stronger. The analysis of bias reduction methods including prompt engineering and dataset diversification is a young field that needs to be developed (Bender et al., 2021).
- **Preparedness and Professional Development of Teachers:** The process should be digital and AI literate enough on the part of the teaching personnel and should have been designed, be multimodal, and be ethically responsible in time. The prospect of AI-mediated literacy programs might be limited with the absence of the relevant training and professional development programmes.
- **Complexities of assessment and evaluation:** The traditional assessment and evaluation methods may fail to reflect the iterative, multimodal, and AI mediated learning processes. The development of evaluation structures which will not only assess process and product but also the moral and critical engagement is difficult.

- **Student Overdependence on AI:** The overdependence potential on the result of AI may block the critical thinking, creativity and problem-solving process. There must be the pedagogical strategies that promote the active human agency of the multimodal composition and use AI as the facilitation tool.
- **Equity and Access:** Technological access, internet access, and device access can help to exacerbate educational inequities. Learners in less-resource-rich settings may not be as able to learn AI-mediated multimodal learning.
- **Privacy and Data Security:** Multimodal literacy tools have high chances to hold sensitive data, which include video, audio and biometrics. The prevention of ethical misconduct requires the data to be stored in secured storage, consent should be informed, and all privacy regulations should be followed (Ngambi et al., 2016).
- **Culture and language inclusion:** The AI models that have been trained to be most helpful in the most popular cultures or languages can discriminate against learners of underrepresented populations.
- **Limitations of a Longitudinal Study:** Longitudinal tracking can be challenging due to the change in AI tools over time; also, the longitudinal tracking can affect the comparability of data. The researchers can apply the findings to the parent population as the sample is accurately representative of the parent population.
- **Externalizability to Parent Population:** The sample is representative of parent population, and therefore the results can be extrapolated. Most research conducted is conducted in controlled or well-resourced classroom environments and cannot be generalized to various classroom environments or other international sources. The access variance in terms of access differences, cultural setting and technological infrastructure should be considered in the research designs.

CONCLUSION AND IMPLICATIONS

The inquiry of AI-mediated multimodal literacy proves the disjointed potentials of bringing the concept of artificial intelligence into the literacy study field, and the convergence of technological innovation, pedagogy, and socio-cultural responsibility. This chapter has followed the development, theoretical basis, practices in education, evaluation systems, ethical aspects, and the future tendencies of multimodal literacy in the AI age. The results indicate that there are opportunities and challenges of learning, teaching and institutions that may want to maneuver through this complicated terrain.

Shifting the Definition of Literacy

The paradigm of traditional literacy, which is mainly based on reading and writing, is becoming progressively inadequate in the multimodal and interactive communication processes and through the mediating effects of AI. Literacy now encompasses:

- Digital and AI literacy, such as the faculty to critically consume AI-generated content.
- Multimodal competence- The combination of text, images, audio, and interaction modalities in ways that make sense.
- Ethical and cultural literacy, which allows learners to work within the socio-cultural diverse communicative background in a responsible manner.

Pedagogical Implications

Multimodal literacy mediated by AI changes the process of teaching and learning, by supporting:

- Customized, personalized, and co-creative learning experiences by using AI to scaffold learners.
- Interconnected and shared learning, which enables international interaction and cross-cultural competency.
- Reflective and metacognitive practices, which allow the development of ethics and critical thinking in the production of multimodal content.

Assessment and Evaluation

The practices of assessment should be changed to reflect the process and products of AI-mediated multimodal learning:

- Portfolio-based, performance-based and formative strategies are offering a holistic assessment.
- Multimodal learning analytics (MMLA) and AI-assisted feedback systems can be used to improve real-time assessment and self-regulation by the learner.
- Assessment frameworks that are ethically, inclusive, and culturally responsive are effective in the provision of equitable assessment in different settings.

Ethical, Social and cultural dimensions.

Introducing AI into the multimodal literacy of raises serious concerns about:

- Accountability, transparency and algorithmic bias.
- Fairness and equity, so that everyone gains out of AI-mediated opportunities.

Currently, there is an emphasis on: cultural representation, facilitating multilingual, multicultural, and contextually based literacy practices.

For Lifelong Learning

- Providing learners with the ability to critically evaluate AI-generated information.
- Promoting lifelong, self-directed and networked learning.

For Research and Policy

- Creation of moral, open, and culturally responsive AI applications in education.
- Longitudinal research on multimodal literacy development and learning performance.
- Educational policies encouraging fair access, inclusivity and accountable AI control.

REFERENCES

Adiguzel, T., Kaya, M. H., & Cansu, F. K. (2023). Revolutionizing education with AI: Exploring the transformative potential of ChatGPT. *Contemporary Educational Technology, 15*(3), ep429. DOI: 10.30935/cedtech/13152

Bender, E. M., Gebru, T., McMillan-Major, A., & Shmitchell, S. (2021). On the Dangers of Stochastic Parrots. *Proceedings of FAccT*, 610–623. DOI: 10.1145/3442188.3445922

Bewersdorff, A., Hartmann, C., Hornberger, M., Seßler, K., Bannert, M., Kasneci, E., Kasneci, G., Zhai, X., & Nerdel, C. (2025). Taking the next step with generative artificial intelligence: The transformative role of multimodal large language models in science education. *Learning and Individual Differences, 118*, 102601. DOI: 10.1016/j.lindif.2024.102601

Cheung, K. K. C., Pun, J., Kenneth-Li, W., & Mai, J. (2024). Exploring students' multimodal representations of ideas about epistemic reading of scientific texts in generative AI tools. *Journal of Science Education and Technology*. Advance online publication. DOI: 10.1007/s10956-024-10182-0

Claman, D., & Sezgin, E. (2024). Artificial intelligence in Dental Education: Opportunities and Challenges of large language models and Multimodal foundation Models (Preprint). *JMIR Medical Education, 10*, e52346. DOI: 10.2196/52346 PMID: 39331527

Cope, B., & Kalantzis, M. (2009). "Multiliteracies": New literacies, new learning. *Pedagogies, 4*(3), 164–195. DOI: 10.1080/15544800903076044

Crompton, H., & Burke, D. (2020). Mobile learning and pedagogical opportunities: A configurative systematic review of PreK-12 research using the SAMR framework. *Computers & Education, 156*, 103945. DOI: 10.1016/j.compedu.2020.103945

Floridi, L., & Chiriatti, M. (2020). GPT-3: Its nature, scope, limits, and consequences. *Minds and Machines, 30*(4), 681–694. DOI: 10.1007/s11023-020-09548-1

Floridi, L., Cowls, J., Beltrametti, M., Chatila, R., Chazerand, P., Dignum, V., Luetge, C., Madelin, R., Pagallo, U., Rossi, F., Schafer, B., Valcke, P., & Vayena, E. (2018). AI4People—An Ethical Framework for a Good AI Society: Opportunities, risks, principles, and recommendations. *Minds and Machines, 28*(4), 689–707. DOI: 10.1007/s11023-018-9482-5 PMID: 30930541

Fu, S., Lee, A. J., Wang, A., Momennejad, I., Bihl, T., Lu, H., & Webb, T. W. (2025, March 29). *Evaluating compositional scene understanding in multimodal generative models*. arXiv.org. https://arxiv.org/abs/2503.23125?utm_source=chatgpt.com

Group, N. N. L.The New London Group. (1996). A Pedagogy of Multiliteracies: Designing Social Futures. *Harvard Educational Review*, *66*(1), 60–93. DOI: 10.17763/haer.66.1.17370n67v22j160u

Guerrero-Sosa, J. D. T., Romero, F. P., Menéndez-Domínguez, V. H., Serrano-Guerrero, J., Montoro-Montarroso, A., & Olivas, J. A. (2025). A Comprehensive review of multimodal analysis in Education. *Applied Sciences (Basel, Switzerland)*, *15*(11), 5896. DOI: 10.3390/app15115896

Huang, L. T., & Huang, T. (2025). Generative bias: Widespread, unexpected, and uninterpretable biases in generative models and their implications. *AI & Society*. Advance online publication. DOI: 10.1007/s00146-025-02533-1

Jiang, J. (2024). When generative artificial intelligence meets multimodal composition: Rethinking the composition process through an AI-assisted design project. *Computers & Composition*. *Computers and Composition*, *74*, 102883. DOI: 10.1016/j.compcom.2024.102883

Jin, Y., Echeverria, V., Yan, L., Zhao, L., Alfredo, R., Tsai, Y., Gašević, D., & Martinez-Maldonado, R. (2024). FATE in MMLA: A Student-Centred Exploration of Fairness, Accountability, Transparency, and Ethics in Multimodal Learning Analytics. *arXiv (Cornell University)*. https://doi.org//arxiv.2402.19071DOI: 10.48550

Kajiwara, Y., & Kawabata, K. (2024). AI literacy for ethical use of chatbot: Will students accept AI ethics? *Computers and Education Artificial Intelligence*, *6*, 100251. DOI: 10.1016/j.caeai.2024.100251

Kostopolus, E. (2024). Student use of generative AI as a composing process supplement: Concerns for intellectual property and academic honesty. *Computers & Composition*. *Computers and Composition*, *75*, 102894. DOI: 10.1016/j.compcom.2024.102894

Kress, G. R. (2003). *Literacy in the new media age*. http://eprints.ioe.ac.uk/14914/

Lin, C., Zhou, K., Li, L., & Sun, L. (2024). Integrating generative AI into digital multimodal composition: A study of multicultural second-language classrooms. *Computers & Composition*. *Computers and Composition*, *75*, 102895. DOI: 10.1016/j.compcom.2024.102895

Ng'ambi, D., Brown, C., Bozalek, V., Gachago, D., & Wood, D. (2016). Technology enhanced teaching and learning in South African higher education – A rearview of a 20 year journey. *British Journal of Educational Technology*, *47*(5), 843–858. DOI: 10.1111/bjet.12485

Prinsloo, P., Slade, S., & Khalil, M. (2023). Multimodal learning analytics—In-between student privacy and encroachment: A systematic review. *British Journal of Educational Technology*, *54*(6), 1566–1586. DOI: 10.1111/bjet.13373

Smith, B. E., Shimizu, A. Y., Burriss, S. K., Hundley, M., & Pendergrass, E. (2024). Multimodal composing with generative AI: Examining preservice teachers' processes and perspectives. *Computers & Composition. Computers and Composition*, *75*, 102896. DOI: 10.1016/j.compcom.2024.102896

Tan, X., Xu, W., & Wang, C. (2024, March 28). *Purposeful remixing with generative AI: Constructing designer voice in multimodal composing*. arXiv.org. https://arxiv.org/abs/2403.19095?utm_source=chatgpt.com

Vartiainen, H., Kahila, J., Tedre, M., López-Pernas, S., & Pope, N. (2024). Enhancing children's understanding of algorithmic biases in and with text-to-image generative AI. *New Media & Society*. Advance online publication. DOI: 10.1177/14614448241252820

Yan, L., Gašević, D., Zhao, L., Echeverria, V., Jin, Y., & Martinez-Maldonado, R. (2024). From complexity to parsimony: Integrating latent class analysis to uncover multimodal learning patterns in collaborative learning. *arXiv (Cornell University)*. https://doi.org//arxiv.2411.15590DOI: 10.48550

Chapter 3 Multiversal and Multimodal Autoethnographic Interpretations: Comics Narratives in the Age of AI

Jason D. DeHart
http://orcid.org/0009-0005-5210-4738
The University of Tennessee, USA

ABSTRACT

This chapter explores the multiversal work of comics in light of the rises in technology in recent years. The chapter features a textual case study of a comics work alongside more general reflection on "What If" and "Elseworlds" storytelling modes, suggesting the malleability of narrative. The links between these changes and fandom are explored, as are implications for both identity and literacy instruction. From reading theory to philosophy, this work speculatively engages with continued questions of what text means.

INTRODUCTION

Through iterations of self, the author reflects on their experiences as a scholar, educator, and reader on the cusp of the Generation X and Millennial boundaries. Kumar et al. (2024) noted the leaps in development that comics generation with artificial intelligence (AI) has made in the 2020s. This chapter seeks to explore the ways in which fluid cultural thinking and definitions have emerged from comics

DOI: 10.4018/979-8-3373-6986-0.ch003

narratives over time, and seeks to comment theoretically on what multimodality and creativity mean – with a particular view to comics – in the current time.

In terms of methodology and organization, this chapter is intended as a review of relevant comics literature, particularly with links to fandom and (trans)formation of identity. The author begins with a review of comics literature, followed by a linking of progressive technology and multimodality with comics conceptualizations of the multiverse. Prior to exploring a number of practical and theoretical implications, the author showcases the textual and identity linking of a multimodal text in what might be termed a textual case study.

Because of the literary nature of this chapter, professional literature and comics examples will be explored in categories throughout the discussion rather than as a separate section.

COMICS OF TOMORROW

What is AI if not a reconceiving of worlds through existing elements in a mosaic formulation afforded by technology? It is a blending, not exactly generation, but more like regeneration in nature. The trend in comics stories to share "What If" and "Elseworld" stories, as well as "Multiverses" in general, points to something akin to reconceiving of existing elements. Unlike the case with AI, these elements are woven from preexisting materials; the comic still likely offers something new in terms of authorship. Jenkins (2012) has noted the malleability of characters and concepts through multiple threads of cultural representation, as well as the ways in which individuals take up elements of media as they consider expression, identity, and self. This notion of linked networking and multiversal work is not separated from theoretical explorations of AI, or of literacy/literacies. Indeed, Forte (2025) has explored the relationship of AI and multiverse thinking, with attention to aesthetics.

The "What If" narratology is divergent beginning and ending a new thread of inquiry, and instead poses a remixing and repairing, with some elements usually offered that are unique. The concept of a multiverse includes a move on the part of writer and reader to unite diverse elements to weave in all strands into what can be conceived as the larger story in its entirety. Thus, authors/artists capture popular characters in (re)render them. Like many comics materials and nostalgic stories, they are passed on as visual and verbal storytelling, linking with memory and identity. The purpose of this authorial move is, again, relatively commercial in some cases, particularly in terms of bringing together disparate elements of a disjointed storyline, but also holds implications for what it means to take up elements of character and worldbuilding in reading practice.

While the capitalistic interest of exploring multiple iterations of characters is briefly addressed again here and acts as the material foreground, there are additional considerations embedded in these fields of inquiry. Readers make decisions about the existence and placement of credulity, and also encounter moments where they either reframe or discard previous understandings in our development of identity and thought. This is part of developing as a cognitive being, regardless of belief. I draw on Voltaire's *Candide* for a textual example of the extreme application of the absence of this kind of critical thought. Voltaire posited elements of experience which must be acknowledged by communities of ritualized thinking, rather than discredited as drawbacks to a more blissful view of the world.

How much compromise of reality's evidential working is held up as we weave together an understanding of representation and ritual? Ultimately, the focus on the connecting thread of legitimacy, the linking of thinking and action, and the notions of ownership/authorship arrive at play. AI opens up not only a wide range of possibilities, but also a number of questions to explore.

TIES TO IDENTITY IN MULTIMODAL SPACES

Just as with popular characters, there are constants and creative touchpoints when thinking about literacy practices in virtual and fandom spaces. There have also certainly been moments of difficulty. In terms of literacy instruction, as hooks (2014) noted, teaching is a very public and open act. There is a sense of physical manifestation and display that occurs in traditional pedagogical models – an embodiment. Often, the classroom is formulated as a gathering of young people, sitting in desks that are arranged in rows, while an adult facilitates/presents/disseminates informative and activity at the front of the room. Popular media depictions of pedagogy vary from the compassionate educator, the life-changer who enters a troubled classroom climate, or the strict disciplinarian who attempts to establish rule even as the youthful protagonist questions and searches for boundaries to push.

In this consideration of the reflection of multivariate storytelling propagation, I am again reminded of the Elseworlds comic book imprint for additional textual support in exploring the ways that characters are transmuted across multiple narratives and yet retain an essential sense of their ontology. There is more than simply another permutation here, as readers work to constrain or define what constitutes a world, in view of contradictory elements. In the same way, the ontology of a classroom can be transported to a new space, even a new planet, in comics work, but the manifest elements that are consistent provide anchor points of connection across boundaries of experience and imagination.

What happens when the story folds in on itself, or when a universe needs to be reshaped? In a recent example across media, director James Gunn retconned a scene from the streaming series *Peacemaker*, replacing characters that were previously included with characters from his own rebooted universe. Only character remained constant. From all ostensible purposes, Gunn did not make this creative decision or "rewriting" as an insult or move of aggression – he and the previous creative team/director appear to have an amiable relationship. This was multiversal fun and a play with continuity, from my analysis, for telling a continued story while creating a nod to the past.

The marker of a such a move is the decision point for following or resisting from fandom. It is perhaps for the innovative work of a storyteller that we next hope, or we turn away from the story, or we start an entirely new narrative on our own. We cast and recast, even ourselves, seeking what is true and what is essential as we engage in identity work and, mosaic-like, form and reform our philosophies.

In narrative form, we can remove a character like Wonder Woman from her typical narrative location, either in terms of time or space, and we can even transform her into an animal character, as was done in the work, *JLA: Island of Dr. Moreau* (Thomas et al., 2002). Indeed, the stuff of the world can be reshaped with reflecting points in science fiction and fantasy, the genre in which we might place superhero narratives. The DC Comics universe take on *Moreau* acts as another example from the range of titles that were published as part of Elseworlds, and additional narrative reworkings occurred in futuristic settings, the old American west, the French Revolution, and a wide range of other spaces and within other encounters.

The ways in which we sum up a character, or share a sense of personhood, revolve around a set or package of preconceived or previously-shared features. In the case of a DC Comics character, these features might include the origin of the character, some sense of their motivation, and certainly a sense of their appearance. When this essence is compromised, we encounter new steps forward or abandonment of the ideal.

That moment or central feature from which all of aspects of a character issue is of some sense of flexibility, but is always retained in some sense. In the book *Catwoman: Guardian of Gotham* (Moench, 1999), for example, the character of Batman is depicted as an adversary. This is a mingling and movement of character elements and anchor points from previous narratives, reworked for fun, in the same that one can re-envision one's self through AI methods. This is perhaps the greatest stretch of the character's essential nature in the Elseworlds universe – yet, that sense of who the character is has not disappeared from the narrative. What is essential and nonessential to a character proves to part of this discussion, and were a character to change too greatly, they would be considered an homage instead of a reworking.

Batman may be depicted as a mad person and villain in the story, but his positive characteristics are transposed to the titular character, Catwoman. In this way, the typical dynamic between the two figures is playfully disrupted. Gavaler and Goldberg (2019) explored a view of multiverses as a kind of retconning and rebooting practice among creators, and pointed the metaphysical changes in reality for the characters. These authors define a multiverse as "a linear restart of a story world where the history of the story world is mostly forgotten but not categorically nullified" (p. 125). As an audience, we take up these threads and travel with the changes posed in the universe we encounter, for responses both good and ill.

Perhaps an absolute nullification of the previous universe would feel like a cheat to the reader, or perhaps this is sometimes a creative move to continue to pull material from the preexisting universe to inform the new one. This is more than a fragment of a previous narrative that is separated and treated as a stand-alone, one-time venture. It is a unity with the other worlds, suggesting not only an alternative view but an entirely new consideration of what ontology means in universal terms. If the world is always allowing for possibilities and permutations, this is more than an individual authorial move – it is an essential characteristic of the world itself, suggesting an all-encompassing malleability.

ENTER THE MULTIVERSE

The streams of popular culture thought that are embraced and interwoven in multimedia responses to characters and storylines embrace a sense of tension and duality in the same way that a variety of approaches are made to the practicing of religious ritual. The individual's aesthetic response and particular perspective is embraced by a variety of interpretations of what enacting spiritually-informed experience looks like. To limit the boundaries of how identity is taken up and to place fences around the individual as contributor and thinker in such spaces is work of barrier-making, and is fundamentally problematic.

This possibility for multiple threads is contained with the comics continuum as creators play with the ways that storylines work, and I note the presence of multiple interpretations not simply in the storylines themselves but in the individual artist's representation of characters and mythologies. The work of Alex Ross, for example, punctuated the *Kingdom Come* storyline, offering (for lack of a better term) Rossian renditions of popular characters.

My affection for the Elseworlds storyline is part and parcel of my own textual experience, and I further recall through pictorial images the creation of multiple renditions of characters through paint and craftwork applied to action figures I collected as a child. *Heroes Illustrated* proved to be one inspiration for these "textual" moves with toys, and I would then arrange characters I (re)created alongside characters that already existed as a means of stationary storytelling with pictures I could take with my camera.

These static images worked for me in displaying scenes, as depicted in the comic books and films I enjoyed as a child, but also now lend an architecture of textual work to remind me of the ways I constructed stories with action figures. Sometimes these toys combined in a shared universe experience, from Marvel to DC and beyond, and often popular films informed my storytelling choices.

For example, if I saw a particular frame in a film, I would use my eye as the camera and frame the scene that way in my childhood play. If specific music was used in a film, I would play that part of the movie's soundtrack on cassette during my plan. In this way, I attempted to recreate multimodal ensembles in live action play based on the ways in which stories were told in film and in books. The story had to be continued, and my approximations in play recreated the media experience in as many ways as possible.

It was a quick and natural jump from these moments of play to composing my own texts in notebooks, which are now sadly lost to time. Most strikingly in terms of spiritually-oriented play, I recall employing *Clash of the Titans* and other mythological action figures in combination with my comics universe toys to no creative dissonance in my mind. There was no dissonance in this work on my part; in fact, I already had a Thor action figure. Positioning popular characters alongside action figure representations from other stories I knew was simply uniting storytelling work for the purposes of play.

In effect, I was enlarging the cast of characters who could then be featured in the stories I was telling through enactment, bringing universes together seamlessly. The terms Marvel and DC did not hold particular story boundaries as my characters could meet each other just as naturally as they stood side-by-side on my bedroom shelf, or jumbled together in a storage bin.

To me, the superpowers of Zeus exemplified in film and other media aligned with much of the characterization I saw in characters like Superman and, not too surprisingly, Thor. Hephaestus was akin to a misshapen Hulk. These characters mingled in my mind, and held a common place alongside *Star Wars* and *Masters of the Universe* heroes and villains, as well. When I encountered characters I did not know, I incorporated them into mythology in the way that made most sense to me, as was the case the first time I discovered the now-popular character of Harley Quinn in a Batman playset. I dubbed the character "Katrina," after a girl I knew from school, and assigned attributes to this character before realizing that she was an altogether different identity in the animated series in which she was introduced. I did not allow this hindrance in knowledge to stop me from incorporating a character of my own transactional molding.

In these ways, I not only embraced the multiversity that allowed for multiple actors to play the same characters, creating a sense of impermanence about the characters I loved, but I also constructed my own universe of play, inviting and reshaping characters to fit the stories that I wanted to tell. When I did not know a character immediately upon their arrival in the story, I named them and reframed them myself. The work I was doing also hints at strands of reality, and the ways I hoped superhero narratives joined the living world. Somewhere inside of me, I hoped that Batman was a real character, while also noting the tension between the Adam West and Michael Keaton incarnations, not to mention the multitudes of Catwomen that populated the multiverse of media I encountered.

I negotiated all of this with a sense of embracing that allowed for humorous and dark incarnations, while seeing a thread of consistent characterization in these representations. It did not matter that they were vastly different; I subsumed them and loved them in my roles as viewer, collector, reader, and enactor. In the multiverse of my own making, Batman could encounter Satan as easily as Dracula, and individual comic book universes could be subsumed for the purpose of nothing else save play and fandom. In fact, this very storyline was sketched out in one of my childhood notebooks, drawing on the work of artists Kelley Jones and Mike Mignola. Proctor (2017) noted the ways that both Marvel and DC have adopted these narrative stances, allowing for multiple story-threads. According to this researcher, within DC Comics-related stories there is a narrative proper, or city limits of the page, with other stories operating outside of that scope. This unites with a sense of the canonical, as well as the apocryphal.

The presence of infinite earths runs parallel with this notion, allowing multiple stories to exist in multiple universes. On the other hand, Marvel has presented stories in a long line of narrative framing, uniting these story threads with what Proctor (2017) referred to a kind of universal canonization of storytelling in all threads and across all platforms, including television, film, and the printed or digital page. Such positioning of multiple worlds as a prelude to spiritual formulation is hardly relegated to the comic book medium, as Purdy (1999) contended that the presence of a multiverse in the James Joyce novel *Finnegan's Wake* might be an implication of a religious narrative contained within the text.

For my work as a young reader, the intentions of the publisher were of little to no concern, and I barely paid attention to the names of the creators at the beginning masthead until much later in my early adolescence when I began to note the appreciation I held for some artists and authors. Early on, Batman was Batman was Batman, and I would reframe the narrative as I saw fit in order to juxtapose all of the elements I wished to include. These formulations became endemic to my formation.

What we encounter in life is sometimes much more difficult to contend with, and that is embracing a sense of multiversity in world views. To say we exist in the same world but see this space differently, or see our identity on our own terms, is a move that calls for a compassionate response rooted in learning and exploration. If justice does not sit at the heart of both our theology and our pedagogy, then we have much to reconsider. We must always be ready to listen, learn, and reframe when needed.

EXPLORING AND EXTENDING BOUNDARIES: A COMICS CASE

One of the joys of being an educator has been discovering the value inherent in the voices that authors share in their stories. Gathering stories from a range of experiences and voices makes for a rich classroom experience. Moreover, one of the charges of being a thoughtful and compassionate teacher is to build positive regard for all students (and stories), including nonbinary narratives. Educators are now challenged to think about the ways we view gender identity and gender expression, and to reconsider our assumptions about identity. Meanwhile, authors and artists like Mollie Knox Ostertag translate some of these concepts into visual narratives that teachers can draw on to explore concepts of identity and acceptance in the classroom – and beyond.

My love of the visual medium is not simply subsumed in the sign-making that occurs, but in the possibilities for thinking and rethinking about the world. Graphic novels provide one literary space for a variety of stories to be told, through the combination of words and images. In my middle school classroom, graphic novels were reliable sources of interest and were often checked out by students. There is something vivid and engaging about the combination of artistic images, bright colors, and text.

The Witch Boy has the potential for critical reading and dialogue with students, and can serve as one textual space where nonbinary students can see representations of their experiences that are honored as part of classroom reading material. In this next section, I will explore this book's use of supernatural narrative and concepts of heroism within the context of critiquing bias and forming identity.

From the reality of the issue, Forbes reported that 331 trans people were] "murdered, hanged, or lynched" in 2019. The author of this piece, Jamie Wareham noted that even more trans people were killed in the previous year – 369, to be exact. Transphobia is not a tragic element of our global community that is going to go away quickly, and certainly not without the thoughtful work of advocates who are willing to step into talk around concepts of acceptance and troubling our assumptions about what it means to be a man, woman, or even a human. There is a real and earth-bound hatred in the world, and Darkseid need not be blamed. We have forces to contend with in our daily lives that call to mind the action of heroes who seek to shape the world into more compassioned reality, and the image of God that is sacred and foremost in religious communities cries out against loss of any life. My development spiritually also includes a sense of advocacy.

These realities in our culture, and in the wider world, speak to the importance of emphasizing the humanity that binds us all, in spite of creed or identification. Inviting texts can be a powerful vehicle for this kind of work, particularly in the hands of an expert reading teacher. Superheroes see the humanity in the world around them and take up arms to fight injustice, even if they encounter differences. This is human work, even if the agent is superhuman. In *The Witch Boy*, Mollie Knox Ostertag affords us the opportunity to discuss gender norms within the boundary of a fictional universe – but the realities we can uncover in this text extend to both here and now.

In the first book in this series, *The Witch Boy*, Ostertag introduces us to Aster, a young male whose expected societal role is that of warlock. What happens instead is that Aster feels himself drawn to the witchcraft orientation that is acceptable among females in his society. This is a feeling that is not met openly by his teachers and wider community. When Aster is caught practicing witchcraft, he is chastised and sent out of the day's lesson. It is this sense of otherness and being othered that is again striking in this story.

Speaking with his mother, Aster shares that this treatment is not fair. She tells him, "Aster, that Magic isn't for you" (Panel 1, p. 8). Aster will not back down in his desire to learn a practice that is female-oriented in his society. To this, his mother responds: "Women and men have different types of magic, and witches pass down their knowledge from mother to daughter. That's how it is and how it's always been, my son" (Panel 3, p. 8). A bit later she affirms in the same panel, "You'll be one of the men." Aster still resists this notion, and his mother tells him the story of another character who was poisoned by their play outside of gender boundaries.

In this case, Ostertag's use of supernatural gifts acts as a clever conceit for considering what happens to young people when they operate in ways that are not honored and embraced by the culture in which they live. Ostertag explores the initial rejection Aster feels, his struggles with his identity, and the dangers presented by a malevolent being who has undergone a similar rejection. It is in the mirror of this antagonist that we, as the audience, glimpse the potentially fatal and tragic outcome of Aster's journey. It is ultimately choice to embrace his role in society, even in the face of adversity, or to wither away and ultimately reject himself. In this book, this self-rejection transmogrifies a character, Mikasi, into a dragon. Here again is the mirrored self or cautionary tale rendered as nemesis.

While Aster begins to come to terms with identity in *The Witch Boy*, some of his struggles continue in *The Hidden Witch*, the book's sequel. The questions presented in this second book resonated with me as a teacher in that Aster meets rejection yet again – again, at the hands of a female instructor in the early pages of the book. It is a scene that demonstrates how even a simple word or gesture in pedagogical practice can create a barrier between student and teacher. These personal hurts add strength to Aster's decision to seek another mentor.

Ostertag uses both *The Witch Boy* and *The Hidden Witch* to consider challenges youth face, including the experience of identifying with a nonbinary gender identity. More of her artwork can be seen, along with scripting by Brennan Lee Mulligan, in the webcomic *Strong Female Protagonist.* The identity of the superhero is taken to new places in Ostertag's work, and the result is a range of representation that is not readily encountered in all storylines. Are these superhero narratives? I do believe that it takes heroic and courageous qualities to be fully ourselves and to explore our identity and intersections of identity in a world that does not always welcome, and in fact often violently resists, these stances of exploration. May the faith communities of the world never subscribe, or cancel their subscriptions, to hatred as an aspect of creed in all its realized forms. These are real problems with which we must contend and lovingly confront.

Comic book work is certainly affinity work for me, but reading this medium has lately shown me the wide number of possibilities for sharing stories that have gone beyond my expectations and assumptions. I still position myself as learner when it comes to seeing life from another person's perspective. Some of these stories not only have the promise of capturing students' interest, but moving beyond engagement to critical awareness of relevant issues, including the reality of transphobia and questions of what it means to trouble gender norms. A superhero who reifies boundaries and hatred is no hero at all, and a religion that seeks to pull others down is to be critiqued, reframed, and questioned.

I am a cisgender reader and as a graphic novel fan, certainly, but also as a teacher whose desire is for students to see themselves reflected in text, with a commitment for students to consider what it means to be a compassion human being if they encounter someone whose identity or expression challenges their assumptions. My desire is that students can find voices, including their own, in the pages of texts so that our pedagogy can begin to offer possibilities for conversation and threads of cultural counternarrative. Graphic novels present this sense of narrative in multimodal fashion and, I suspect, contain and convey their own sense of invitation for readers to render their stories along a range of meaning-making practices.

There is still a mountain of work to do in building a kind world that views people as valuable, regardless of gender, race, ethnicity, ableness, age, sexuality, political orientation, and a host of other facets of identity that are so often used to form barriers. Graphic novels like *The Witch Boy* are one literary space where teachers can begin to work with students to accomplish the work of shaping classrooms of love and support, with the hope that one day these conversations will transform the world that is reflected in that classroom. It is this quest for identity which is often met with creed-oriented disregard, and which ultimately speaks to the need for compassion and equity in educational communities.

IMPLICATIONS FOR FANDOM (AND BEYOND)

In whatever case exists, the choice is ours to continue reading and engaging, or to find a new character and story-thread to pick up on, or to reject fandom entirely if we become beleaguered with the endless prospects or if our belief in the logic of the universe wanes. What informs that choice is a matter of some potential discussion, including (a) devotion to the character based on a personal history with the creative world; (b) particular relationship in terms of personal or lived experience connection to the settings, characters, and general world-building that are established; (c) a persistent hope among readers that the story will generate more curiosity and perhaps even return to its former structure; (d) a continued appreciation of the ways that the new structure of the story add to, reshape, and redefine the previous story-thread. I am most likely to continually engage with stories that resonate mostly deeply with my earliest reading experiences, or with characters which hold a certain sense of complexity or allure. In a recent example in reading and viewing life, I attempted to pick up on season two of a popular superhero television show.

While I engaged readily and hungrily with the first season, there was too much strain on the narrative, too many fragments to be explored in this second season to maintain my interest. I did not have the background knowledge nor the prior experience necessary to maintain my engagement, and so I stopped at episode three. Such is the prerogative of the fan, and no doubt other viewers who are more tethered to the storyline as a continuing narrative in their lives and who possess more awareness of the characters and developments, have a more affection response for this new season.

The authentic expression of voice is salient in words and images; the integration of multiple/mosaic previous representations is a mere simulacrum. Sufficing to take up space, the AI generated multimodal product is a novelty. The individual infusion of identity work for more global and interactive applications is a thriving heart of literacy (in this metaphor, a creature with many hearts and chambers of being and logic).

Yet, there must be an unchanging element that remains part of a dominant thread, including the presence of an ethic or code to inform the interactions that surround the character and the choices they make. In this case, the concept of boundless love and care unites the role of mother and father. Or else, we simply maintain obedience to the character as a fan, even when understanding of the character is temporarily unresolved. It is the unknowing, yet hoping, that sometimes most defines fidelity to the story as we anticipate another turn.

IMPLICATIONS FOR FURTHER IDENTITY WORK

These questions of ontology are hardly relegated only to text or to a theoretical framing of spiritual practice or awareness. They are questions inherent in our thinking about our own being, our decisions about how and to what degree to invite and include others, and our practice of shaping community together. To think on such matters is to return to what we consider human and purposeful.

For example, being an educator at any level, from my worldview, involves the idea of including and valuing all voices. This sense of value creates particular challenges when working in schools where the vast majority of students come from a dominant cultural group, or when divisions are clear among members of the community. This was the case for me as an English teacher in rural schools. I looked for authentic ways to interact with students who often found themselves working at the margins, and I sought to balance my advocacy and alliance without stepping into "White savior" mode. Here, my desire to help is complicated by the very real truth that I am not the person who is equipped to help everyone. However, I can speak to the need for linking together in our common humanity, and I can confront racism, sexism, and other injustices when I see them. Being necessarily issues into doing, even when I forget the original foundation of being because I become so lost in to-do lists and routines. I need sometimes to be reminded of my theoretical and philosophical foundations, the "why" that informs the other questions of when, where, what, and how.

Very often, I served a small population of students who brought perspectives outside of a dominant culture. Afterall, I too am white and much of my identity and experiences lines up with the dominant ethnic group from which I speak, but I take these notions into account as I consider the ways stories are told and which practices are honored in terms of acknowledging and combating my own privilege. A new dimension of my love for graphic novels is taking shape as I appreciate the voices of other racial, ethnic, gender, and social identities through visual storytelling, including Jason Reynolds, Jerry Craft, and Molly Knox Ostertag, to name a few. These folx have not only helped me expand my notions of what is possible in comics, but also helped me expand my views about lived experience. I feel my call is to first and foremost love people.

The narrative flexibility I find in the multiverse demonstrates a notable trajectory in comics work, one that is autobiographically centered, and one that extends the idea of what a superhero/hero/heroine can be. This focus on experiences outside of my own is rooted in what I consider to my most honest enactment of spiritual development in the world around me, but also finds its impetus in my interest in the ways that stories contain possibilities for representing all people and all experiences. In alignment with thinking about multiverse, I acknowledge multiple realities, multiple experiences, and the very real and authentic intersections of identity that exist within the human spectrum. I also value these differences and note the possibilities for a richer understanding of life and being by practicing a willingness to listen and learn from a range of voices.

No one should be left out of the comics page, or the dialogic space, and these creators point to that reality. So much of the genre has been rooted in superhero narrative, but what happens when the work of the graphic novel page is brought to earth in clearer terms? The capacity for capturing the individual and unique voice in literacy expression should provide pause when thinking about the inherent narrative entropy of AI generation.

IMPLICATIONS FROM TEXTUALITY

There is something of the outsider pressing in, searching for belonging, that is present in both the superhero narrative and in the work of Ostertag.

The possibility of the multiverse as a narrative or ritualistic move decentralizes a primary narrative, and moves the story into a kind of prismatic view, where a variety of approaches to characters and settings are not simply seen as narrative one-offs, but as an endemic feature or a larger structure. It is the kind of juxtaposition of pluralistic perspectives that is so often craved and yearned for in academic discourse – and so often difficult to attain and balance in these same environments. This is a kaleidoscope, not a telescope.

It is perhaps this sense of fandom in multiplicity which ties in closely with a hewing to a commonly-held set of beliefs. We allow the tensions of our expectations and understandings to sit with our lack of knowledge and the incomprehensibility of ontology in simultaneous moments. This terminology is hardly divorced from Platonic ideal versus conceptual reality and speaks to the concept of transformation. We are both what we are and what we hope to be, shaping each moment. The idealized thought of how the story works informs the action of storytelling.

What is the uniting thread between my affection for the characters I encountered, allowing me to experience their tensions and divides simultaneously, and this conception of being? Within this nexus of love and creativity, there is a sense of ludic wonderment. This is one of the primary aspects of literacy which links to multimodality and can be inspired, not replaced, by AI work.

Voltaire's *Candide* acts as example of a moment in literary history when alliance with systems transcends reason and circumstance, and the portrait is not flattering. This a treatment of faith that refuses to see, listen, and acknowledge, instead favoring a reconceptualization of the world that remains static, even when new voices attempt to be known. It would be the equivalent of throwing away or ignoring a new character or storyline completely, and pretending that the only narrative that exists is the one, original story.

Yet, perhaps that is too much to ask that a reasonable sense of hope may be prevalent and continue engaging readers in superhero narratives. The thought that someone would dedicate their lives to helping others, even in some small way, is radical redemptive work that extends beyond the self and promises (threatens?) to reshape the universe in which such a person finds themselves. Paolo Freire would no less remind us that this is the transformational work of access to literacy, and Louise Rosenblatt might add that it is through text that we are transformed together, reader, student, teacher, and author together in an assembly of meaning-making.

In Voltaire's *Candide* we discover the dark side of belief; an ignorant and reality-denying sense of faith that refuses to take into account the true challenges of the world. It is a cloistered idea that refuses to be changed, even in light of other engaging perspectives. In this way, the resetting or rebooting that is often so essential in the sense of a multiverse is ignored. Rather than rebooting, the story continues.

The result is troubling and Frankensteinian, as the lead speaker in the story continues to act as though events have not occurred. It is the metaphorical image of singing on the sinking ship, not as an act of bravery but of denial. The original thread persists, even as the ghastly elements of story changes exist at the corners of the storying space. When the story is held in a frozen sense, even in the face of injustices and even in the face of mourning, and when the old answers continue to be brought forward in retread, the complicated work of faith encountering reality and speaking to the existence of valid questions (not to mention the presence of a range of perspectives and ideas), the narrative seems jarring. No reader likely wants to be Candide, continuing a charade of simple responses in the face of great evil, just as readers do not value a character who encounters wrongdoing and pretends victory in spite of the very credible and visible presence of defeat.

In this moment, reframing, rethinking, and multiverse storytelling is refused and bound up in an ongoing Campbellian refusal of the call to move forward, a closing off of the narrative self and the potential for possibility so that a preferred or dominant narrative can be retained instead. The story then hides in shelter, waiting for the questions for challenges to pass by, rather than to challenge and reframe based on new responses. It is hardly satisfying to those who see the storm.

CONCLUSIONS AND IMPLICATIONS FOR INSTRUCTION

I now fuse these elements together in a way of thinking about their applications for the community we build we students in the classroom. Once more, my positioning from the reading field helps me in my resolution of these threads, particularly in the relationship of theory and practice.

Storytelling is complicated work across all forms and with all audiences. To this end, who gets to be part of this multiverse? In previous research work, I have expanded my work with comic books by including students as characters in the comics. For example, I will create an illustration of the tutee in superhero form, with a name like "Super-Jim" (pseudonym). I will then incorporate elements of the lesson into the story, fashioning five or six panels as we go through the content.

Depending on the age and language level of the student, the text we create can be more or less complex. We issue into creation both as a way of achieving higher levels of learning, but also by means of practice of being. We are both relational and creative. Some students have engaged in multiple lessons, and their stories continue for a number of pages. Many of the lessons include animals, ideas about adaptations, or hobbies. These are relatively simple to incorporate into a simple storyline as the "super" version of my student encounters creatures that are represented in the lesson and ultimately wins the day based on whatever conflict seems relevant to the lesson. In at-home literacy practice, students often draw on the materials they have at hand. What are the possibilities for continued instruction through maker kits and how can both original creations and AI tools be part of maker kits for learners?

It is a bit of a rush to put sketches together in a short lesson, but the teacher can take artistic and pedagogical freedom in providing brief illustrations that touch on key points. Both images and words convey a sense of voice and story, working together in multimodal texts. Teachers who are not illustrators and comic book lovers at heart can also consider using simple drawings, AI representations, or even cutouts to assemble from existing books.

The payoff is that we work we do with reading and writing invites the learner into the text, not just as passive receptor, but as creator and even character within the story. AI, in this perspective, is a tool and a space for critique more so than a replacement for authentic and original thinking. These are questions of reader identity and agency – but they are also questions of invitation, belonging, identity, and community. To what degree do we raise barriers in the ways that we frame questions of theory and practice? Where do we draw the lines of community when it comes to literacy and fandom? Who gets to be part of the narrative, and how do we conceive of and construct the larger vision of a narratological multiverse?

REFERENCES

Forte, M. (2025). Exploring multiverses: Generative AI and neuroaesthetic perspectives. *Heritage*, *8*(3), 102. DOI: 10.3390/heritage8030102

Gavaler, C., & Goldberg, N. (2019). *Superhero thought experiments: Comic book philosophy*. University of Iowa Press. DOI: 10.2307/j.ctvn5twvb

hooks, b. (2014). *Teaching to transgress*. Routledge.

Jenkins, H. (2012). *Textual poachers: Television fans and participatory culture*. Routledge. DOI: 10.4324/9780203114339

Kumar, J. T., Babu, H., & Srinivasan, N. (2024, February). Comic Generation Using AI–A Review. In *International Conference on Computational Intelligence in Data Science* (pp. 156-166). Cham: Springer Nature Switzerland.

Ostertag, M. K. (2017). *The witch boy*. Graphix.

Proctor, W. (2017). Schrödinger's cape: The quantum seriality of the Marvel multiverse. Retrieved from http://eprints.bournemouth.ac.uk/29352/7/Quantum_Seriality.pdf

Purdy, S. B. (1999). Is there a multiverse in "Finnegan's wake", and does that make it a religious book? *James Joyce Quarterly*, *36*(3), 586–602.

Thomas, R., Pugh, S., & Mulvihill, P. (2002). *The island of Dr. Moreau (JLA)*. DC Comics.

Wareham, J. (2019). "Murdered, hanged and lynched: 331 trans people killed this year." Retrieved from https://www.forbes.com/sites/jamiewareham/2019/11/18/murdered-hanged-and-lynched-331-trans-people-killed-this-year/#4ca3092a2d48

KEY WORDS AND DEFINITIONS

Comic: A text which uses both words and images, juxtaposed, to create meaning. The form also includes elements like panels, word bubbles, and grids.

Elseworlds: The DC Comics imprint that begin in the 1990s in which popular characters were recast across time and in a variety of contexts.

Graphic Novel: A lengthy comics work that often stands on its own or is anthologized.

Identity: An individualized means of expression that represents a way of being and understanding, with possibilities for linking with wider networks of experience.

Multimodality: The communication of ideas through multiple modes, or spaces of meaning-making.

Multiverse: The narrative structure employed by popular comics publishers wherein multiple versions of the same character can exist simultaneously, albeit in different but connected realities.

Transmedia: The phenomenon of stories and characters being represented across forms of media (e.g., television and comics; toys and film).

Chapter 4

Gaming Literacy as Critical Multimodal Pedagogy

Fabielle Rocha Cruz
http://orcid.org/0000-0001-6364-8603
University of Calgary, Canada

ABSTRACT

This chapter conceptualizes gaming literacy as a critical multimodal pedagogy that positions digital games as texts embedded with systems, values, and ideological structures. Drawing on game studies, critical literacy, and educational research, the chapter argues that gaming literacy extends beyond gameplay to include meaning-making practices, relational ecosystems, and ethical forms of agency enacted both in and out of game worlds. Through examples drawn from commercial digital games, the chapter illustrates how player agency emerges through identity negotiation, emotional engagement, and embodied decision-making. The discussion is further expanded to contemporary debates on artificial intelligence in education, challenging assumptions of technological neutrality and optimization. Finally, the chapter highlights the relevance of gaming literacy for understanding learning, curriculum, and assessment in increasingly automated educational contexts.

WHY GAMING LITERACY NOW?

When literacy is discussed, traditional notions about reading and writing still dominate educational discourse. Literacies are still about reading and writing, but they are no longer limited to these practices. What has changed is how these two verbs are understood: literacy is not restricted to reading printed text and producing written

DOI: 10.4018/979-8-3373-6986-0.ch004

language. It encompasses the recognition that meaning-making extends far beyond print literacy. More importantly, it acknowledges that, in a world where people can read and write across spaces, even digitally, information is shaped by perspectives, biases, and ideologies, often in ways that are not neutral nor well-intentioned.

This issue becomes pressing when we consider that much of schooling prioritizes performance over citizenship through critical engagement. Educational institutions frequently equate literacy with technical proficiency, overlooking the fact that the contemporary world is hyperconnected and that meaning emerges in modes other than verbal. We live in a society saturated with artificial intelligence (AI), images, sounds, and other semiotic resources that circulate through multimodal channels. Understanding content in this context requires more than knowing what a word means, exceeding the boundaries of linguistic fluency.

As a result, the challenge is no longer mere access to information, but interpretations and uncertainty in light of credibility. When schools view reading and writing from the perspective of print literacies, they risk creating a bubble in which students succeed because they know how to write well-structured texts while lacking the necessary discernment to distinguish what is reliable or what is misleading, what is human-made or AI-generated, or what constitutes intentional misinformation. In this light, it is worth questioning whether school performance, through grades and positive feedback, reflects the level of critical competence that a student demonstrates to act in both real and digital worlds, which they already inhabit through smartphones, computers, social media, or digital games.

It also reveals a crucial point that deserves our attention: if these multimodal devices and resources are already embedded in students' households and lives all over the world, why does school insist on privileging literacy based on written, verbal text? Moreover, how might these resources be mobilized to teach students to construct meaning and interpret multimodal texts with the confidence of individuals equipped to question the intent, validity, and implications of the texts they come across?

As an example, digital games can be a compelling entry point into this discussion. Games, in general, have been part of people's lives for over 2500 years (Cruz, 2022; McGonigal, 2011). Historically, games were used to distract people from a famine that plagued the kingdom of Lydia and to bring good omens to a deceased pharaoh, and today they continue to define and represent cultures, positions, and ideologies. As they are now just a click away, digital games reshape and reconfigure what it means to read and write, situating literacy into a hyper-multimodal space that requires more than identifying and knowing the isolated meaning of words. In such environments, for instance, the W, A, S, and D keys are not used to spell a word, but commonly function as embodied commands that move a character in computer games.

Schools may already incorporate digital games into the classroom. Yet, it is important to break with the constant idea that digital games are restricted to fun and playfulness, as this framing deprives commercial games of their pedagogical potential and devalues them as complex semiotic systems. Furthermore, it raises the question of whether people would have to constantly discuss issues such as addiction, isolation, and negative impacts if educational contexts helped students engage with them as texts, providing tools to play and reflect critically. The field still lacks sufficient research that treats digital games as rich semiotic resources, approaching different ways of reading the world (Freire, 1985, 1987), with practices that formal education tends to underemphasize.

Against this backdrop, the guiding question of this chapter is: *In what ways can gaming literacy function as a critical multimodal pedagogy capable of challenging traditional notions of literacy while responding to the ethical and epistemological demands of education in the age of AI?* In response, this chapter discusses the dominant traditions in schools and prevailing views of digital games, arguing that an expanded understanding of the term "literacy" is needed to critically engage with what is produced and circulated in the digital realm (including AI-generated content, digital games, and social media posts). In this framework, digital games are positioned as epistemological practices speaking directly to the contemporary student, who lives in a hyperconnected world.

Ultimately, this chapter invites readers to consider three interconnected shifts. The first is *ontological*, regarding the understanding that digital games should not be limited to mere entertainment. The second is *epistemological*, recognizing that *gaming literacy* is not about gamer identity but about an attitude towards games and the critical stances enacted in play. The third one is *axiological*, valuing critical thinking beyond narrowly defined academic content. Together, these three axes position digital games as spaces for meaning-making and prompt a reconsideration of teaching, learning, and the formation of individuals in an era marked by artificial intelligence and multimodality.

FROM MULTIMODALITY TO GAMING LITERACY

To understand how gaming literacy emerges as a critical pedagogical practice, we should examine how digital games evolved as multimodal systems. In the early 1970s, computers were becoming increasingly accessible on a personal level, as they no longer required an entire room. Amid the exponential growth in the acquisition of personal computers, Atari, Inc. was created in 1972 and soon released *Pong* (Atari, 1972), one of the first digital games to achieve widespread commercial success. What was special about *Pong* was the simulation of a tennis or a ping-pong match, represented by two parallel bars that moved up and down, pushing a ball from one side of the screen to the other. Whilst it may not sound as amazing today, it was one of the first games to translate an activity that was rooted in the sports field and replicate it in a virtual environment, relying on players' cultural understandings of a paddle, a ball, and motion to generate meaning on screen.

In the nearly sixty years since the release of *Pong*, the digital games industry has expanded dramatically, evolving along with technological advancements and the development of graphics. As a result, games like *Pong* are categorized as "classic" or "vintage". By contrast, the contemporary game industry is shaped by beautiful or well-designed games with more content, driven by a multimodal generation that understands the construction of meaning in many dimensions. For example, games like *World of Warcraft* (WoW; Blizzard Entertainment, 2004), a landmark Massive Multiplayer Online Role-Playing Game (MMORPG), far exceeded just two bars and a ball, despite being released 21 years ago. Their narrative, quest systems, and complexities demand interaction beyond player-computer relations, encompassing interactions, communities, paratexts, and ongoing dialogue with developers.

What this snippet into the history of video games reveals is the transition from a simple meaning-making system, based on the player's ability to interpret a ball and two bars as a tennis or ping-pong simulation, to a complex semiotic ecosystem. In said environments, a myriad of semiotic means are used to make meaning, giving rise to a relational ecosystem that depends on sound, image, movement, gestures, text, and more. Although not as innovative when compared to what the television or film industries have done over the decades, there is a crucial difference: in gaming, multimodality depends on the player's participation for meaning-making.

This transition invites a closer reflection on what is the meaning of *multimodality*. Emerging from the field of social semiotics and multiliteracies research in the late 1990s, multimodality is often associated with Gunther Kress (2010) and Theo van Leeuwen (2004). Kress (2010) defines multimodality as a framework that helps identify which semiotic modes are being used to construct the meaning intended by the author of a text, such as color, style, design, and movement. Although multimodality is not exclusive to video games, it is fundamental to the player's ability to interpret, act, and participate within the gameworld. As Kress (2010, p. 5) emphasizes, the significance of multimodality is anchored in the fact that "the world of communication has changed and is changing still; and the rules for that lie in the vast web of intertwined social, economic, cultural, and technological changes."

Building on the studies of Kress and van Leeuwen (2001), Hawreliak (2019, p. 3) reiterates that communication is never "ahistorical or immaterial, but happens in particular contexts—social, cultural, economic, technological, etc.—through a particular medium that is indelibly linked to its usage by actual humans and begins in time and space." When applied to digital games, Hawreliak points out that the semiotic modes that make up a game do not necessarily maintain their meaning when combined, which highlights the importance of the meaning-making process to understand how color + sound + text construct a new concept. This indicates that the combination of two or more semiotic modes will always have a greater meaning than each part individually (Hawreliak, 2019; Jewitt, 2009; Kress, 2010; Kress & van Leeuwen, 2001; van Leeuwen, 2004).

Therefore, if multimodality allows us to identify which semiotic modes compose a text, a central question that emerges is: what is necessary to interpret digital games as multimodal, participatory, and ideological texts? How is meaning negotiated, resisted, and performed within these relational ecosystems?

The answer lies in *gaming literacy*. While many researchers and scholars in the field discuss the correct terminology between the terms "game," "games," and "gaming," this chapter focuses on studies proposed by Steinkuehler (2010), Salen (2007), and Zimmerman (2008), who employ the gerund to emphasize that literacy as a practice emerges from the act of playing. Thus, the use of the term is consistent with the understanding of digital games as multimodal texts whose meanings are produced and dependent upon player participation.

Gaming Literacy

Building on the discussion of multimodality, gaming literacy is understood as a way of "reading" the multimodal text, in the broad and interpretive sense. Like other forms of literacy, it develops over time and requires more than just exposure. This implies that, just as individuals who appreciate art are not necessarily artists or understand deep artistic nuances, those who play digital games are not "automatically equipped to critically, culturally and creatively respond to these texts" (Partington, 2010, p. 84). This also reinforces the idea that gamers may demonstrate uneven patterns of knowledge: sometimes, they may display extensive procedural or technical understanding, while at other times, they may lack a critical perspective on digital games as texts.

Through the lens of Lemke (2006) and Salen (2007, p. 63), gaming literacy emerges from "gaming attitudes," which are stances of creativity, improvisation, and subversion enacted during gameplay. Echoing Steinkuehler (2010) and Zimmerman (2008) in adopting the gerund "gaming", Salen (2007, p. 63) emphasizes that this literacy concerns how digital games "support a performative and often transgressive learning stance based in play, which in turn, owes much of its specific character to the status of games as dynamic, rule-based systems." Returning to the example of *World of Warcraft*, gaming literacy does not operate exclusively in-game; rather, as is common in many MMOs, it extends to out-of-game resources, including FAQs, walkthroughs, forums, and other paratextual contexts.

At the same time, positioning it as a form of literacy centered on gaming also raises a persistent tension with the field of education, particularly the perceived divergences between games and classrooms. Digital games contain discourses, themes, and ideologies that are deemed inadequate or that reflect narrow, distorted views of society. These shortcomings frequently serve as justification to resist digital games in educational contexts (Steinkuehler, 2008, 2010), even when it hinders the opportunities for the development of gaming literacy. If gaming literacy offers an interpretative and performative lens to examine the semiotic modes that compose the digital game as a multimodal text, it simultaneously serves to criticize, rethink, and debate (Partington, 2010; Salen, 2007; Steinkuehler, 2006, 2010). Gaming is a narrative co-constructed with the player, through which other literacies, such as digital literacies, are articulated via game design and gameplay.

Within game studies, several models have been proposed to help structure gaming literacy practices in the field of education. One influential framework is Zimmerman's (2008) triad *systems-play-design*. In this model, *systems* refer to the attitudes that allow us to understand, navigate, and rethink how people live, relate, and work, for example. In gaming literacy, systems manifest as the rules and mechanics that govern a digital game. They only work because they are embedded in a context, in a structure that shapes and is shaped by the player, which Zimmerman (2008) calls *play*.

Play also includes the relational ecosystems that cause the personal experience to be validated or questioned. Thus, both the rules and mechanics, as well as the structure of the game experience, need *design* for gaming literacy to make sense, since design is understood as "the process by which a designer creates a context, to be encountered by a participant, from which meaning emerges" (Salen & Zimmerman, 2004, p. 41). Without design to give meaning to systems and play, gaming literacy would not account for the meaning-making process.

However, while the *systems–play–design* triad provides a foundational framework for understanding gaming literacy, it proves insufficient to fully address the multimodal, relational, and ethical demands that characterize contemporary digital games. This limitation raises a central question for the present discussion: how can gaming literacy be expanded to engage more meaningfully with critical pedagogy?

GAMING LITERACY AS CRITICAL PEDAGOGY

Considered one of the most influential role-playing games of the twenty-first century, *Persona 5* (Atlus, 2016) is the fifth entry in a Japanese game series centered on Jungian psychology and coming-of-age narratives, following a classic hero's journey structure. The game follows Joker, a high school protagonist who was unjustly accused of a crime involving a prominent politician and subsequently has to move to Tokyo. With the support of friends and powers that come from accepting the darker aspects of the self (an interpretation of Jungian concepts of "shadow" and "persona"), Joker confronts challenges that permeate contemporary societies, such as corruption, abuse of power, violence, and media manipulation.

Although lengthy, *Persona 5* presents an engaging narrative that requires the player's involvement and the activation of prior knowledge to make sense of its gameworld. When interpreted through Zimmerman's (2008) perspective, *systems* encompass the rules of the game, its linear calendar-based progression, and the organization of the character's multiple "selves". *Play* is reflected in social bonds, which emerge through player-game interaction, and the turn-based combat that allows for strategic decision-making. *Design* manifests through visual style, color scheme, the incorporation of mythological and religious figures as personas, and the overarching narrative that serves as the guiding thread for shaping the game's events.

However, it is precisely the narrative depth of *Persona 5* that reveals a need to expand Zimmerman's (2008) model for gaming literacy to account for the player's *funds of knowledge* (González, Moll & Amanti, 2005; Vélez-Ibáñez & Greenberg, 1992) and how they are mobilized and transformed in gameplay. The expansion of this framework does not dismiss Zimmerman's (2008) original framework; rather, it proposes a breakdown of the triad into new components to foreground a multimodal and multiliterate vision that is already implicit in the model.

Funds of Knowledge and Agency

To address this limitation, a central element in this expanded framework is the concept of *funds of knowledge* (FoK), which recognizes that students (referred to here as players) bring a vast knowledge of different areas, cultures, experiences, and practices. Thus, in any literacy practice, FoK shape what players already know and how they engage with information. As discussed in the previous section, when Steinkuehler (2010) argues that games are narratives co-created with the player and Partington (2010) states that learners often demonstrate uneven experience across domains, FoK are what determine the extent and how it works.

When extended beyond their original educational context, FoK can be applied to digital games as multimodal texts. In *Pong*, discussed in the previous section, recognizing the two bars and the ball as an analogy to tennis or ping-pong activates FoK related to symbolism in sports culture. In *World of Warcraft*, FoK is no longer just visual and mechanical, as players with prior knowledge of how RPGs work, for example, better understand conventions, narrative expectations, and strategic decision-making. At the same time, a game like *WoW* also requires engagement with lore, in-game history, community practices, and paratexts that are created within and around the game. In this case, FoK enhances both performance and engagement with the game as a complex semiotic system.

Persona 5 takes it even further by inviting the player to activate or seek FoK related to contemporary Japanese society, power relations, media discourse, authority structures, and Jungian psychology. Importantly, FoK are not a prerequisite for participation. As Moll et al. (2009) argue, FoK are a resource to be valued regardless of depth, and the game as a multimodal text encourages the player to learn by playing. There is an incentive to walkthroughs, FAQs, and knowledge created, organized, and disseminated by the community, just as important and valuable as what the player already knows. In *Persona 5*, if the player does not know the Japanese high school system, the game will not punish them. On the contrary, it scaffolds through the experience of the game itself. This example illustrates how gaming literacy not only draws on prior knowledge but also actively expands through gameplay.

This dynamic foregrounds a key principle discussed in multiliteracies theory (Cope & Kalantzis, 2000, 2015; Gee, 2007; Luke, 2012; New London Group, 1996): agency. In games, player agency is both ontological and epistemological; that is, it lies in the player's participation in meaning-making and their ability to question, interpret, and act upon the gameworld. FoK constitutes the first step towards agency, whether it is what the player already knows or through knowledge they actively seek in and out-of-game to understand the gameworld. Agency emerges when the player is able to recognize and question what they know, identify what they do not know, and decide to engage with both through learning. In this sense, gaming literacy sees FoK as a mobilizable framework rather than a requirement, and rewards players with the expansion, demonstrating that playing is not passive (Gee, 2007; Lemke, 2006), but is also about learning how to learn about the game.

Critical Literacies & Pedagogies

When player agency is understood as both ontological and epistemological, critical engagement become central to gaming literacy. As presented in the previous section, many researchers identify and recognize violence and controversial themes as potential downsides of digital games in education (Partington, 2010; Salen, 2007; Steinkuehler, 2006, 2010), and the player's interaction with these themes is part of player agency.

Although it may appear counterintuitive, gaming literacy extends beyond playing and/or technical proficiency, and it is not about liking, consuming, or defending games. Its core is centered on reading, interpreting, questioning, and even rejecting a game when necessary, positioning it as a multimodal text to be selected like a book, a film, or a song. This understanding, aligned with reading a text through critical lenses (Freire, 1987; Luke, 2012), validates the ontological position of the player in relation to the game, as well as the epistemological boundaries of what a player accepts as meaningful or legitimate. Consequently, saying "no," as in rejecting a gameworld or a narrative, constitutes an enactment of agency in and of itself within gaming literacy.

Luke (2012), alongside Jordão and Fogaça (2007), points out that critical literacy is grounded on the critical pedagogy proposed by Freire (1985, 1987), who argued that reading the world precedes reading the word. In other words, critical literacy is based on recognizing the world and all discourses, ideologies, and power relations that shape social realities, and taking a stance on acting against or in favor of it. This premise holds in digital games as well: gaming literacy embraces criticality as a way to promote the player's agency and their freedom to challenge the game, the narrative, the mechanics, and the intentions behind its development and underlying its design.

First-person shooters (FPS) and action games have long been criticized for allegedly promoting violence, although studies have shown that they have the same impact as watching a football game or other sporting competition (Prensky, 2007). Game series such as *Fallout* (Bethesda Game Studios, 1997–2018) and *Borderlands* (Gearbox Software, 2009–2025) exemplify action games with complex narratives, how violence operates in them, and how gaming literacy presents different avenues for employing agency to challenge, criticize, and certainly reject them. Critical skills here operate in conjunction with what the player holds as values or morals, rather than inviting them in unreflective consumption.

The *Fallout* series, for example, combines action game with role-playing game elements that move beyond a simple shooting game with pointless, gratuitous violence. Although it has elements of violence, the atompunk narrative (which follows a retrofuturistic aesthetic) raises pertinent questions about the future of the world in the face of a post-apocalypse caused by atomic bombs. One of the most striking characteristics, which expands in-game agency, is the karma system, which changes according to how the player behaves in dialogues and in the gameworld. There are narrative consequences stemming from reputation and moral alignment, culminating in irreversible choices, forcing the player to often externalize what they consider justifiable or what they would like to experience. Ontologically, the mechanics in *Fallout* propose a world in which the player uses their agency to refine, evaluate, question, test, and visualize who they are in and out-of-game.

In contrast, *Borderlands* depicts violence as satire and exaggeration, an interpretation that stems from distancing itself from the "good versus evil" moral dichotomy. Ontologically, it implies the question "*Who are you if you need to survive?*" While it follows a classic narrative of a game about finding an artifact and saving the world, it never explicitly demands that the player position themselves as someone morally righteous within a world that is about to end. The game's main design is the use of humor through caricatured representations, exaggeration, and sarcasm to explain the deliberate absence of moral realism, rendering violence absurd rather than normalized. Critical skills and agency, in this game, occur in accepting or refusing the conditions and making or reframing meaning from the interpretation of humor. Importantly, this does not mean that *Borderlands* does not have deep and reflective scenes, but that they also depend on FoK to make sense and engage with the player.

These two examples illustrate how gaming literacy operates as a form of critical pedagogy, functioning as an expansion or, perhaps, a situated enactment of agency. The act of playing transcends the boundaries of interpretation and becomes pedagogical when it enables reflection, ethical choice, positioning, and the activation of prior knowledge, especially when the game is treated as a multimodal text and gameplay as a situated pedagogical practice. It is, once again, a foreground to the ontological and epistemological positioning that gaming literacy requires to be developed, welcoming those who lack specific FoK, acknowledging those who refuse to play, and profoundly stimulating the constant process of meaning-making in a multimodal environment.

Expanding on the Framework

When gaming literacy is seen as a natural developmental movement, much like earlier expansions of other literacies, such as digital literacy, it becomes possible to revisit what Zimmerman (2008) proposed in terms of gaming literacy and extend it as a response to contemporary research in game studies and education. The *systems-play-design* triad remains a foundational framework and contributed significantly to naming it "gaming literacy" before it became widespread. However, advances in critical pedagogy, multimodality, game studies, and increasingly AI-mediated environments require that gaming literacy be repositioned to account for emergent practices and theoretical developments from research and application.

Building from the original triad, a logical next step is to observe what emerges from the intersections between its elements, since it is evident that there is room to expand what Zimmerman (2008) originally outlined based on critical literacy and pedagogy. As Figure 1 illustrates, gaming literacy operates at a central level through the original triad, and at a secondary level through the intersection of design and play, play and systems, and systems and design. This expanded framework can be extended to other interactive and algorithmic systems, such as AI-mediated settings, where meaning algo emerges through interaction.

Figure 1. Diagram illustrating the expansion of Zimmerman's (2008) gaming literacy framework, highlighting the unfolding of meaning at the intersections of its core elements.

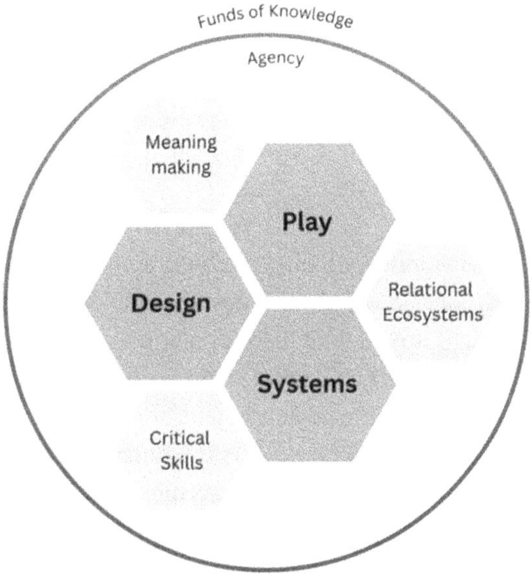

Design encompasses the developers' intentionality, including the color palette, aesthetics, typography, and the organization of the game in terms of framing, soundtrack, and dialogue, for example. As such, it becomes the core that shapes the gameplay understanding. However, it is for this very reason that design cannot be meaningfully separated from play, which is the player's own performance within the game, including issues of embodiment, time, rhythm, and reaction. Although design and play elements present themselves differently according to each genre and even each game, the space between them is populated by *meaning-making*. The intersection of *design + play* is what gives digital games the characteristics of multimodal text, positioning them as an artifact that, alone, has no meaning. Meaning emerges from playing and from the player, expanding notions of social semiotics (van Leeuwen, 2004), multimodal literacy (Kress, 2010; Serafini, 2015), and embodied meaning-making (Hulston, 2019; Mills et al., 2022).

In this same sense, we have play intersecting with systems. In other words, we have the rules and structures that make the game work, plus the actions that players take within those rules. *Systems + play* give rise to *relational ecosystems*, both in and out-of-game. As observed in community literacies (Higgins et al., 2006), players organize themselves into affinity spaces (Gee, 2007) that emerge within a broader participatory culture (Jenkins et al., 2006). Players organize themselves into interest groups that play together and create content such as FAQs, walkthrough videos, fan fiction, and streaming as support for the community. In this relational ecosystem, paratexts function as negotiation, dissemination, discussion, and (meta)reflection, transforming platforms like *Discord*, *Reddit*, and *Twitch*, for example, into spaces where players interact and reframe the meaning-making process collectively.

As it is an extension of digital and critical literacies (Bacalja, 2018; Steinkuehler, 2010), this framework cannot be discussed without considering critical skills, which stem from the connection between *design + systems*. At this intersection, critical skills are not only developed within the game environment but are required for the development of gaming literacy itself, as the player becomes more familiar with identifying and evaluating values, ideology, ethics, and positioning, not only of the players but also of the game creators and developers. While Zimmerman (2008) already implicitly included this idea in his proposition, it is worth naming it to emphasize that gaming literacy as ethical positioning and ideological reading. It is about choosing a game, rejecting a theme or genre, and producing paratexts that help the community in challenges. This intersection is the foundation of gaming literacy as a critical pedagogical practice, grounding it in critical literacy (Freire, 1987; Luke, 2012), equally necessary in AI contexts, where systems are wrongly perceived as neutral despite being shaped by bias and underlying ideologies (Holmes et al., 2019).

Across the triad and its intersection, agency becomes an emergent condition of gaming literacy. Agency emerges when FoK are mobilized within design, systems, and play, reinforcing the assumption of game studies and multiliteracies that digital games, as multimodal texts, are about "reading." Agency is not an attribute; it underpins critical skills (to what extent do I want to interact with this text and how did I choose to read it?), the relational ecosystems (how can I contribute or seek help from the community?), and meaning-making (what do I know that helps me or distances me from this game?). Importantly, agency in gaming literacy goes beyond the creation of a character or avatar in gaming literacy, at a surface-level. In life simulation games, such as *The Sims 4* (Maxis, 2014), character creation anchors the experience without defining the gameplay, as what the player chooses to do with the character determines the agency, including career choices, housing, relationships, preferences, and more.

Finally, situated beyond the game while still intrinsic to the experience are the Funds of Knowledge. As discussed earlier, FoK are crucial for meaning-making, critical skills, and participation in relational ecosystems without being a prerequisite imposed by the game. FoK supports the activation of prior knowledge while also encouraging the learning of new information to make the game more approachable or interesting. However, it operates as a mobilizable, accessible, and expandable repertoire, not limited to a set of skills or compartmentalized into what a player needs to know before playing. Like agency, it permeates and conditions the entire gaming experience, repositioning gaming literacy as a critical, multimodal, pedagogical practice. This perspective also reinforces the relevance of gaming literacy as a bridge between education and emerging literacies, especially AI literacy (Long & Magerko, 2020), where meaning-making remains central in critical engagement.

EMBODIMENT, IDENTITY & POSITIONALITY

Gaming literacy does not depend on a specific type of game, but on the situated relationship between body, choice, rhythm, and meaning. From this perspective, what matters is not the genre but the digital game as text and the relationship established with it through play. For example, while role-playing games are often particularly efficient for exploring several aspects of the framework discussed earlier, they are neither the only genre capable of instigating critical literacies practices nor a prerequisite for engaging with emotions, positionality, and identities. Not all games need to be choice-heavy to provoke reflection, discomfort, or epistemological engagement.

Winner of the *Best Narrative* award at the 2017 Game Awards and frequently cited as one of the games that best represent video games as an art form (Bogost, 2011; Tavinor, 2009), *What Remains of Edith Finch* (Giant Sparrow, 2017) is an excellent example of an adventure and exploration game that guides the player through storytelling with easy mechanics and simple action. With fewer than three hours of gameplay, its value lies in activating emotions and mobilizing the player's FoK to narrate the story of a family from the perspective of 17-year-old Edith and through objects, memories, and fragmented narratives related to each of her relatives. Multimodality is central for ambiguity in the game (Hawreliak, 2019; Kress, 2010; Serafini, 2015), as genre, style, mechanics, sounds, framing, and intention shift according to each family member. Through said shifts, the story subverts the life-death dichotomy, presenting death as inevitable, while life is the most fragile and the greatest surprise.

What *Edith Finch* performs is an epistemological turn that foregrounds emotion as an integral component of knowledge construction. Although the game affords limited agency in terms of choices within the narrative (since it guides the player in a journey through the family's history), the emotional weight of the game produces consequences for the player, establishing agency in the sense of recognizing when to stop or even give up on the game. Because it is centered on the theme of loss, memory, grief, and mortality, the game demonstrates that knowledge does not solely come from meaning-making, but from the emotional and physical reactions embodied by the player as they engage with each family member and their metaphors.

In digital games, emotion frequently moves from the virtual to the physical space, especially because of the different identities enacted during gameplay as a response to the game's demands, narratives, and representations. This movement emerges from the question "*who does the game assume I am and why do I feel this way?*", highlighting that it is about what the player feels, and more specifically, to the point of what the player feels when embodying another person (a game character or an avatar, for example) within the gameplay. In alignment with the expanded framework discussed in the previous section, this process constitutes an enactment of identities within a relational ecosystem, which is not limited to players alone, but also includes the representation and positioning of the player in virtual space.

Identities Collide

The concept of "identity," when taken in isolation, is inherently risky to define, as its meaning is based on the area of study, theoretical traditions, and the positionality of researchers. Therefore, for gaming literacy, the choice is to conceptualize it within games and literacies studies, after all, it is a recurring term in both areas, with affinities that bridges perspectives from education, communication, and media studies.

In game studies, the study of identity in relation to the game is commonly associated with the enactment of who the player is within the gameworld. It is not restricted only to the avatar or playable character, but extends to how this representation reflects, refracts, or challenges who the player is out-of-game and how this is transposed in-game. Research on meaning-making in gameplay (Chess, 2017; Isbister, 2017; Kankainen, 2024) frequently draws on the study of selfhood to emphasize the ontological dimension of identity in games, reinforcing that play is situated and embodied, thus, the same happens to identities.

Bridging a gap between game studies and literacies, Gee (2007) offers a widely adopted framework that addresses the issue of identity in his seminal work, "*What video games have to teach us about learning and literacy*?" For the author, playing is not limited to a single identity; it depends on what happens when three identities are enacted at the same time. The first identity, called "*virtual identity*," is represented by the avatar or playable character, with its characteristics, strengths, weaknesses, and strategies. In a game like *What Remains of Edith Finch*, this means playing as Edith and all the other characters, relatives of the protagonist, that the player momentarily embodies. In a game like *Fallout*, it is the avatar created by the player, developed from what he can and cannot do in the game world based on player choice and systemic constraints.

The virtual identity is designed by the game developers and directly supports narrative progression or gameplay mechanics. Even when the game allows for avatar customization, the game imposes limitations (at the intersection of systems, play, and design) that regulate agency, according to expectations and end goals. Often, the limitations can result in misrepresentation, prompting players to question, resists or abandon the game altogether, an act of informed agency decision. This is only possible with the second identity, called "*real-world identity*." For Gee (2007, p. 50), this is (per)formed by real identities (e.g., gender, race, profession, nationality) and "become relevant only as they affect and are filtered through my identity as a video game player." In other words, these identities activate the FoK and, consequently, enable the player to have agency in the game even with the limitations imposed by the systems.

The third identity, then, arises at the intersection of real-world and virtual identities as they collide inside and outside the game. According to Gee (2007), a "*projective identity*" is "the hardest identity to describe but the most important one for understanding the power of games," as it encompasses who the player is and who the game invites or allows the player to be. This identity exists in a space where morals, personalities, and ambitions are questioned. Projective identity is what makes gaming literacy critical, insofar as the player is aware that what happens in the game is a representation or a space for experimentation with new ways of seeing the world, even when these reflections remain distant from lived reality.

Earlier, when relational ecosystems were positioned as a component of gaming literacy, paratexts and community practices were highlighted as extensions of gameplay. These practices are made possible precisely through the three identities. In-game experience motivates or prompts the player to seek out the community, whether to share strategies, such as the drop rate of a rare item, or to create a walkthrough for a difficult puzzle. The relational ecosystem exists because the game is not confined to the gameworld. It expands and unfolds in sharing experience, strategic dialogues, and participatory culture, even if the games are single-player. These literacy practices, grounded in care, community, collaboration, and text creation, intersect with other literacies, reinforcing gaming literacy as situated, relational, and embodied.

Emotion & Embodiment

Perhaps this is the moment to question why players get irritated, distressed, or emotionally affected when they play, after all, it's "just a game." The most immediate answer is, once again, that a digital game is a multimodal text, much like a movie, novels or a comic book. However, challenging the standard understanding of the game as passive, the complex answer to this question concerns identity conflict, a breakdown in ethical alignment, and a clash of positionality. Positionality emerges precisely when the player is placed in a situation that challenges them (whether in terms of skill, morality, affect, or comfort, for example) and must decide how to react or respond. Games tease players to react to different moments in-game, and the result evokes feelings such as sadness, irritation, and giving up, but these elements are not synonymous with failure or weakness. Notably, when the audience has an emotional reaction to a movie or a book, it seems to be widely accepted, while they are often dismissed or trivialized when elicited by games.

A compelling example that reflects this positioning is *Papers, Please* (Galactic Cafe, 2013), a popular single-player empathy game in which the player assumes the role of an immigration agent responsible for approving or denying entry into the fictional country of Arstotzka. Recently emerging from a violent political conflict with its neighboring nation, Kolechia, Arstotzka operates under strict bureaucratic and ideological control as the countries diverge in terms of political systems. In gameplay, the player must follow the guidelines of the Ministry of Admissions and listen carefully to the stories told by the immigrants, and then make an "informed" decision, weighing in on veracity, inconsistencies, and moral implications. However, the ethical tension in *Papers, Please* goes beyond the immigration booth: if the player lets an unauthorized individual enter the country, the impact falls on the agent's own family (Cruz, 2024). In this sense, the game proposes a dual agency, within and beyond the gameworld, where emotion comes from the ethical conflicts that the player goes through, with embodied reactions and the sustained engagement with a broader relational ecosystem, particularly for those players who want to achieve the best among the game's twenty possible endings.

What happens in *Papers, Please* is a meaning-making process based on FoK and simulates the player's own embodied experiences of power, responsibility, and moral compromise (Gee, 2008). As Gass (2022, p. 1) claims, "to play a videogame is to experiment and play with embodied difference," in which the three identities (real-world, virtual, and projective) operate simultaneously to shape the experience. In gameplay, this experience provokes emotions that become embodied responses and, often, work to question, reframe, and validate the game. In turn, gameplay becomes embodiment, which gives meaning to the game through FoK. Gee (2007, 2008) emphasizes that embodiment thinking is central in many games, though not all, as this embodiment comes from inhabiting the real and the virtual worlds, from "attempting, within that framework, simultaneously to realize goals and values that are part of the 'core self' (built from our own personal history) we bring to any social identity we enact" (Gee, 2008, p. 261).

Gee's argument expands the notion of FoK beyond disciplinary or factual knowledge. Emotional repertoires and individual reactions to affective experience are constitute FoK, enacted through identities. If, in digital games, "we play with life as if life were a toy" (Gee, 2008, p. 261), positionality within the multimodal text becomes the condition through which meaning-making occurs, agency is enacted, and experience becomes critical. While this perspective is not far from Zimmerman's (2008) understanding, it further articulates the overlapping parts of the framework to situate the content of gaming literacy within this critical view of emotion and embodiment.

Papers, Please exemplifies embodiment by transposing the real and the imagined realities of transnational movements (Cruz, 2024) by and when activating the FoK of history education and contemporary news discourse. Yet, embodiment in gaming literacy is not limited to overtly political or emotionally intense scenarios. Even when it seems like nothing is really happening, as is the case with *The Stanley Parable* (Pope, 2013), moving can pose a hard decision-making setting. In this game, players navigate the office life with the help of a narrator who describes each of Stanley's actions, sometimes with contentment, sometimes with sarcasm, as the player explores the mystery surrounding his missing co-workers while "contradiction follows contradiction, the rules of how games should work are broken, then broken again" ("The Stanley Parable," n.d.). Agency, in this case, resides not in a traditional choice structure. It is about the player's embodiment of discomfort, curiosity, and investment in storytelling while willing to engage with uncertainty and epistemological disruption.

Together, these two games illustrate how positionality, emotion, and embodiment extend gaming beyond the game itself, placing the player in ethically questionable positions, which provoke and encourage the development of FoK and agency. It's not about choosing good games or those that fit within the framework, but about understanding that gaming literacy can and should be expanded to other contexts, as gameplay becomes a site of learning, positioning, and meaning-making that can and should inform broader discussions of literacy, education, and critical pedagogy.

GAMING LITERACY IN THE AGE OF AI: IMPLICATIONS FOR EDUCATION

When we position gaming literacy as a critical pedagogy practice, we accept the implication that digital games are not neutral artifacts. This stance represents one of the most significant contributions to the field of education, particularly in how gaming literacy informs the use of other technologies and resources, such as artificial intelligence. As with digital games, there is a pervasive false sense of neutrality in the use of AI. However, a more sensible approach is to recognize that agency is not equivalent to algorithmic functioning. Algorithms are shaped by bias, ideologies, and power, much like the design choices made by game producers and developers.

By expanding gaming literacy to the field of AI literacy, AI-generated content is positioned as texts that require critical world readings (Long & Magerko, 2020). In this sense, interacting with AI also mobilizes FoK, which shapes the outputs and the interpretations. This is because the products of human-AI interaction carry values, decisions, and priorities that are often constrained by the data and assumptions embedded in Large Language Models (LLM). At the same time, there is a significantly growing body of research in game studies to investigate the use of AI in digital games, focusing on meaning-making and the player-game relationship at an epistemological level, which reiterates the overlapping area between the two literacies. One of the key points highlighted is precisely the fact that AI is not an autonomous agent, but acts according to certain pre-established structures and rules. This is a reminder that AI models may seem real, but they are based on experience, not ontology (Rana et al., 2018), which raises the question: how does gaming literacy help researchers and educators conceptualize the role of AI in educational contexts?

From Play to Optimization: What AI Promises Education

This section does not seek to either defend or demonize the use of AI in education. Instead, the aim is to understand how AI literacy mobilizes mechanisms similar to those found in digital games and how to use in-game or out-of-game examples to inform its application in the educational context (Long & Magerko, 2020). In fact, discussions about the use of AI, especially in the sense of chatbots, have existed since the mid-twentieth century, when the chatbot ELIZA was developed as a simulation of psychotherapy (Norvig, 1992). What the literature of the last six decades presents is the focus that matters for this discussion, to establish the importance of criticality and the conscious use of these artifacts. Early interactions with chatbots such as ELIZA already exposed the tension between perceived intelligence and enacted agency in a way that some games, such as *The Stanley Parable*, do. In both cases, the illusion of autonomy dissolves when users become aware of the underlying structures guiding responses and outcomes.

What is notably missing from much of the contemporary discourse surrounding AI, particularly educational AI, is a sustained critical examination of the dominant discourse. Frequently, AI is framed as a promise of efficiency and instantaneous feedback, often without taking into account the particularities of the educational system, classroom dynamics, and learner diversity. Moreover, AI is increasingly positioned as an immediate solution, rhetorically aligned with consolidated educational theories such as sociocultural and constructivist (Shah, 2023), in a search for optimization. When viewed through lenses borrowed from gaming literacy, however, it becomes evident that chatbots and virtual agents also operate within a system-design-play dynamic (where "play" can be understood as interaction). From this perspective, what education asks for is a pedagogical approach that uses AI as a co-creator or as support, but not as a miraculous resource.

Recently, Xu et al. (2024) combined game-based learning and AI in a study that investigates higher-order thinking skills and academic performance. Their findings suggest improved performance among students who engaged with gamified chatbots, offering a compelling snapshot of where gaming and AI literacies converge. Even so, there are two conclusions drawn by the authors that resonate directly with the arguments advanced in this chapter. First, education must remain fundamentally student-centered, accounting for the evident differences in cognitive and behavioral terms among learners. Second, there is a clear gap in research that critically examines the use of AI across educational contexts, particularly given that the focus of this research was on a higher education information technology course.

One argument proposed by the authors is that "embedding an AI chatbot into digital games does not diminish students' learning motivation; instead, it creates more challenges, making learning more enjoyable" (Xu et al., 2024, p. 14), which reiterates the point that gaming and AI literacies serve the purpose of changing the student's perspective on the object of study. Although the authors mention enjoyment as an important dimension, other factors contribute to these results, such as the active use of these tools through critical literacy practices, scaffolded support that respects learners' pacing, and opportunities for gradual engagement with complex tests and systems. These elements reinforce the assumption that optimization is not equivalent to learning when, in fact, AI chatbots serve as pedagogical support within relational and multimodal ecosystems, rather than as a locus of agency.

AI, Games & Agency

In digital games, agency manifests in different ways, depending on the genre, mechanics, and design, as already discussed in this chapter. Games structured around choice, for instance, tend to require the player to engage with their FoK more actively, thereby enabling greater agency by comparison. When this understanding is transposed to AI literacy, it becomes possible to assume that different AI-based resources also demand or afford agency in distinct ways, especially because AI systems do not assume values or take responsibility for the discourse they generate (Holmes et al., 2019). In this sense, agency necessarily includes moments of discomfort or friction, which involve deciding *how*, *when*, and to *what extent* to engage with algorithmic systems.

Gee (2007, 2008) reminds us that agency emerges when action is meaningful and has perceived consequences. Because AI does not deliberate in a critical or ethical sense of the word, agency must be enacted by the user. This reflection, drawn from gaming literacy, reiterates that agency emerges from relationships and interactions in the field of artificial intelligence and not from the algorithm (Holmes et al., 2019). Thus, the interaction between player-game or player-AI is different from the machine's autonomy. Gaming literacy and AI literacy alike depend on their users: whether players or students, agency constitutes an ethical stance grounded in positionality, responsibility, and critical awareness.

Furthermore, this understanding is central to demystifying AI as a miraculous solution to all educational challenges (Holmes et al., 2019; Williamson & Eynon, 2020). By foregrounding agency, gaming literacy brings back discussions of critical literacy to the center of the conversation once again. This distinction is essential to avoid reducing education to optimization, automated feedback loops, or performance metrics.

What This Means for Education

Before concluding the chapter, it is worth taking one final, more in-depth look at gaming literacy in educational contexts. If digital games are an integral part of the contemporary world and have been gaining more and more space with mobile games, their impact directly relates to the classroom. It isn't a call for teachers to compete with digital games, nor a return to the topic of screen time, which remains essential but insufficient. Actually, it is an invitation to consider what is part of gaming literacy that can be meaningfully extended to other domains, including AI literacy (Holmes et al., 2019).

One of the primary areas gaming literacy challenges and supports is the curriculum itself. For some time, educational games have been implemented in formal and informal contexts, guided by instructional objectives. However, gaming literacy turns any commercial game into a multimodal text that can be read, discussed, evaluated, and created in the classroom. For the curriculum and, consequently, for assessment, gaming literacy contributes to less predictability, emphasizing that mistakes are welcome and that school, for example, should be the place to learn from them. Here, digital games and AI are introduced as resources, not as criteria, emphasizing that choice is still a priority.

Articulating these resources within the curriculum may seem a challenge. However, just as teachers have been testing new activities and tools for years, opening the doors to digital games represents an alignment with students' lived realities. As Freire (1985, p. 15) reminds us, "our tendency as teachers is to start from the point at which we are and not from the point at which the students are. The teacher has to be free to say to students 'You convinced me.' Dialogue is [...] a natural part of the process of knowing."

This alignment between gaming literacy and the curriculum is part of critical pedagogy as discussed earlier. For the curriculum to be ethically and pedagogically articulated with digital games and other resources (such as AI), teachers need to be ethical mediators, critical of the tools they have brought to their classrooms. This reiterates the importance of teacher agency, recognizing the affordances and limitations in each resource, and fostering an epistemological positioning. For example, the axiological movement of questioning "*why this tool and not another one*?" or "*what does this resource allow/limit me from doing*?" opens space for dialogue and, consequently, cultivates student agency. As in gaming literacy, where a player gives up or chooses to interrupt gameplay, whatever resource the teacher brings should be used with the awareness that "dislike" is a legitimate form of agency, just as "using it perfectly."

Assessment in gaming literacy cannot be reduced to performance or metrics that measure how "correctly" a game is played. Instead, it must consider how students critically engage with multimodal texts through their FoK, demonstrating agency in their interpretations and choices. Assessing may be formative, through reflective practices, multimodal productions, or dialogic activities that express questioning, reasoning, and interpreting. This can be used for both games and AI-generated content, positioning assessment as an evidence-based process of meaning-making (Williamson & Eynon, 2020).

Finally, gaming literacy reinforces the centrality of multimodal resources in the classroom, especially those that question ideology, power, and positioning. AI, digital games, and any resources are built with a purpose and, therefore, carry the bias of whoever created them. Thus, questioning a chatbot or a particular game title or genre is an enactment of critical literacy and critical pedagogy. Such engagement represents a confrontational yet generative stance, by both the teacher and the student, towards available resources, drawing from funds of knowledge, and cultivating the critical skills acquired through critical reading of multimodal texts.

GAMING LITERACY IS AN ETHICAL PROJECT

As this chapter has demonstrated, gaming literacy constitutes an expansion of media and digital literacies grounded in critical pedagogies, which do not approach digital games through neutral or merely playful lenses. In fact, the core of gaming literacy lies in critical engagement and the conceptualization of digital games as multimodal texts, composed of different semiotic resources that, when combined, generate new meanings. This premise is what sustains the claim central to the chapter: when systems, play, and design are articulated, gaming literacy is about agency and the articulation of funds of knowledge in three major intertwined domains: meaning-making, relational ecosystems, and critical skills.

The purpose of this chapter was not to exhaust the discussion, but to provide a broader and more in-depth view of the topic. At the beginning of the twenty-first century, when digital games were already part of people's lives, although not yet studied in such depth, authors such as Gee (2007) and Zimmerman (2008) began to give more space to this transitional movement between game studies and education, which consolidated the term "gaming literacy." Despite ongoing disagreement among scholars on the use of “game,” “games,” and “gaming,” one point is certain: literacy emerges from engagement with digital games as text, and its practice resides in gameplay, in the gameworld, and in the paratexts produced in and out-of-game.

It is also important to note that the examples included here are a very small sample of everything that has been published and continues to be developed by the digital game industry. This limitation underscores the expansive potential of digital games as objects of inquiry, with room for discussion within the topic, especially since the area still lacks research more focused on educational aspects. Nevertheless, the examples included were intended to illustrate and apply the concepts discussed, and should not be seen as limitations in terms of genre, narrative, or mechanics. On the contrary, gaming literacy can and should be applied to all games, with the awareness that refusal or discomfort with a particular game is a legitimate practice of agency. This is what allows us to look at a simple game, with basic mechanics like match 3 games, and still see the potential to be approached as sites for questioning, rethinking, and generating new meanings. How many people play games like these, and where is the appeal in moving colored pieces across a smartphone screen? Gaming literacy offers a framework through which such questions can be critically examined.

Gaming literacy is a framework, as well as a set of critical pedagogy practices, that enables these questions. In contemporary education, its contributions lie in looking at agency as choice and decision, including refusing to play, testing and experimenting with scenarios, putting different identities to the test, and, in a way, finding a space for self-reflection. As such, it is subject to expansion, questioning, and research, especially to adapt more and more to what current education needs are.

Within formal education settings, gaming literacy highlights how the classroom is an inherently multimodal and political space. However, technology is also shaped by material conditions, such as digital infrastructure and broader socioeconomic factors. Hence, ethical engagement in gaming literacy requires attention to equity, including issues of accessibility, students’ diversity needs related to disabilities and language skills, and broader considerations of inclusion.

Technologies are never neutral, especially when it comes to a system increasingly mediated by algorithms and the promise of automated learning. Unlike models that focus solely on predictability and content optimization, which have been constantly done with artificial intelligence, gaming literacy encourages ambiguity, error, and ethical positioning. Thus, gaming literacy is a stance of pedagogy that resists and challenges the neutralization of thought, reaffirming the relevance of human agency even in moments mediated by technology.

Finally, returning to the question from the introduction, *In what ways can gaming literacy function as a critical multimodal pedagogy capable of challenging traditional notions of literacy while responding to the ethical and epistemological demands of education in the age of AI*, this chapter responds to contemporary epistemological demands without positioning gaming literacy as a methodological prescription or as a blind celebration of digital games. Conversely, by adopting this stance as a pedagogical response to contemporary educational challenges and the context of use by the students themselves, gaming literacy is presented as an ethical project that values choice, critical thinking, and responsibility in an increasingly automated environment.

REFERENCES

Atari. (1972). *Pong* [Video game]. Atari.

Atlus. (2016). *Persona 5* [Video game]. Atlus.

Bacalja, A. (2018). What critical literacy has to offer the study of video games. *Australian Journal of Language and Literacy*, *41*(2), 111–122. DOI: 10.1007/BF03652016

Bethesda Game Studios. (1997–2018). *Fallout series* [Video game series]. Bethesda Softworks.

Blizzard Entertainment. (2004). *World of Warcraft* [Video game]. Blizzard Entertainment.

Bogost, I. (2011). *How to do things with videogames*. University of Minnesota Press. DOI: 10.5749/minnesota/9780816676460.001.0001

Chess, S. (2017). Playing with Identity. In Ready Player Two: Women Gamers and Designed Identity (pp. 31–58). University of Minnesota Press. DOI: 10.5749/j.ctt1pwt7z7.5

Cope, B., & Kalantzis, M. (Eds.). (2000). *Multiliteracies: Literacy learning and the design of social futures*. Routledge.

Cope, B., & Kalantzis, M. (2015). *A pedagogy of multiliteracies: Learning by design*. Palgrave. DOI: 10.1057/9781137539724

Cruz, F. R. (2022). *Jogando palavras: Tecnologia e gamificação no ensino de língua portuguesa*. InterSaberes.

Cruz, F. R. (2024). "Papers, Please": transposições entre o real e o imaginário de comunidades de refugiados. *RE@D - Revista de Educação a Distância e E-learning, 7*(2), e202416. DOI: 10.34627/redvol7iss2e202416

Freire, P. (1985). Reading the world and reading the word: An interview with Paulo Freire. *Language Arts*, *62*(1), 15–21. DOI: 10.58680/la198525786

Freire, P. (1987). *Reading the word and the world*. Bergin & Garvey.

Galactic Cafe. (2013). *The Stanley Parable* [Video game]. Galactic Cafe.

Gass, A. B. (2022). *The body in play: Embodiment in and through videogames* (Doctoral dissertation). University of Chicago.

Gearbox Software. (2009–2025). *Borderlands series* [Video game series]. 2K Games.

Gee, J. P. (2007). *What video games have to teach us about learning and literacy* (2nd ed.). Palgrave Macmillan.

Gee, J. P. (2008). Video games and embodiment. *Games and Culture, 3*(3-4), 253–263. DOI: 10.1177/1555412008317309

Giant Sparrow. (2017). *What remains of Edith Finch* [Video game]. Annapurna Interactive.

González, N., Moll, L. C., & Amanti, C. (Eds.). (2005). *Funds of knowledge: Theorizing practices in households, communities, and classrooms*. Lawrence Erlbaum Associates.

Hawreliak, J. (2019). *Multimodal semiotics and rhetoric in videogames*. Routledge.

Higgins, L., Long, E., & Flower, L. (2006). Community literacy: A rhetorical model for personal and public inquiry. *Community Literacy Journal, 1*(1), 9–43. DOI: 10.25148/CLJ.1.1.009529

Holmes, W., Bialik, M., & Fadel, C. (2019). *Artificial intelligence in education: Promises and implications for teaching and learning*. Center for Curriculum Redesign.

Hulston, S. J. (2019). Embodied meaning making: A case study investigating the use of gesture in the responses of year 1 children to a wordless picturebook. *Cambridge Open-Review Educational Research e-Journal, 6*, 13–33.

Isbister, K. (2017). *How games move us: emotion by design*. The MIT Press.

Jenkins, H., Clinton, K., Purushotma, R., Robison, A. J., & Weigel, M. (2006). *Confronting the challenges of participatory culture: Media education for the 21st century*. The John D. and Catherine T. MacArthur Foundation.

Jewitt, C. (Ed.). (2009). *The Routledge handbook of multimodal analysis*. Routledge.

Jordão, C., & Fogaça, F. (2007). Ensino de inglês, letramento crítico e cidadania: um triângulo amoroso bem-sucedido [English teaching, critical literacy and citizenship: A harmonious intersection. *Línguas & Letras, 8*(14), 79–105. DOI: 10.5935/rl&l.v8i14.906

Kankainen, V. (2024). Curating the Self-Identity: Tabletop Game Hobbyist Online Practices as an Extended Leisure Experience. *Leisure Sciences*, •••, 1–20. DOI: 10.1080/01490400.2024.2305666

Kress, G. (2010). *Multimodality: A social semiotic approach to contemporary communication*. Routledge.

Kress, G., & van Leeuwen, T. (2001). *Multimodal discourse: The modes and media of contemporary communication*. Arnold.

Lemke, J. (2006). *Everywhere now: Three dialogues on kids, games and learning*.

Long, D., & Magerko, B. (2020). What is AI literacy? Competencies and design considerations. *Proceedings of the 2020 CHI Conference on Human Factors in Computing Systems*, 1–16. DOI: 10.1145/3313831.3376727

Luke, A. (2012). Critical literacy: Foundational notes. *Theory into Practice*, *51*(1), 4–11. DOI: 10.1080/00405841.2012.636324

Maxis. (2014). *The Sims 4* [Video game]. Electronic Arts.

McGonigal, J. (2011). *Reality is broken: Why games make us better and how they can change the world*. Penguin Books.

Mills, K. A., Scholes, L., & Brown, A. (2022). Virtual Reality and Embodiment in Multimodal Meaning Making. *Written Communication*, *39*(3), 335–369. DOI: 10.1177/07410883221083517

Moll, L. C., Amanti, C., Neff, D., & González, N. (1992). Funds of knowledge for teaching: Using a qualitative approach to connect homes and classrooms. *Theory into Practice*, *31*(2), 132–141. DOI: 10.1080/00405849209543534

New London Group. (1996). A pedagogy of multiliteracies: Designing social futures. *Harvard Educational Review*, *66*(1), 60–92. DOI: 10.17763/haer.66.1.17370n67v-22j160u

Norvig, P. (1992). *ELIZA: Paradigms of artificial intelligence programming*. Morgan Kaufmann Publishers.

Online dialog posted to http://community.macfound.org/openforum

Partington, A. (2010). Game literacy, gaming cultures and media education. *English Teaching*, *9*(1), 73–86.

Pope, L. (2013). [Video game]. *Papers, Please*, *3909*, LLC.

Prensky, M. (2007). *Digital Game-Based Learning*. Paragon House.

Rana, P., Bhardwaj, P., & Singh, J. (2018). Artificial Intelligence (AI) in Video Games. *International Journal of Computer Applications*, *181*(19), 1–3. DOI: 10.5120/ijca2018917818

Salen, K. (2007). Gaming literacies: A game design study in action. *Journal of Educational Multimedia and Hypermedia*, *16*(3), 301–322.

Salen, K., & Zimmerman, E. (2004). *Rules of play: Game design fundamentals*. MIT Press.

Serafini, F. (2015). Multimodal Literacy: From Theories to Practices. *Language Arts, 92*(6), 412–423. https://www.jstor.org/stable/24577533. DOI: 10.58680/la201527389

Shah, P. (2023). *AI and the future of education: Teaching in the age of artificial intelligence*. Jossey-Bass.

Steinkuehler, C. (2006). Massively multiplayer online video gaming as participation in a discourse. *Mind, Culture, and Activity, 13*(1), 38–52. DOI: 10.1207/s15327884mca1301_4

Steinkuehler, C. (2008). Cognition and literacy in massively multiplayer online games. In Coiro, J., Knobel, M., Lankshear, C., & Leu, D. J. (Eds.), *Handbook of research on new literacies* (pp. 611–634). Erlbaum.

Steinkuehler, C. (2010). Video games and digital literacies. *Journal of Adolescent & Adult Literacy, 54*(1), 61–63. DOI: 10.1598/JAAL.54.1.7

Tavinor, G. (2009). *The art of videogames*. Wiley-Blackwell. DOI: 10.1002/9781444310177

The Stanley Parable. (n.d.). https://www.stanleyparable.com/

van Leeuwen, T. (2004). *Introducing social semiotics*. Routledge. DOI: 10.4324/9780203647028

Vélez-Ibáñez, C. G., & Greenberg, J. B.Carlos G. Vélez-Ibáñez ProfessorJames B. Greenberg Associate Research Professor. (1992). Formation and transformation of funds of knowledge among U.S. Mexican households. *Anthropology & Education Quarterly, 23*(4), 313–335. DOI: 10.1525/aeq.1992.23.4.05x1582v

Williamson, B., & Eynon, R. (2020). Historical threads, missing links, and future directions in AI in education. *Learning, Media and Technology, 45*(3), 223–235. DOI: 10.1080/17439884.2020.1798995

Xu, Y., Zhu, J., Wang, M., Qian, F., Yang, Y., & Zhang, J. (2024). The impact of a digital game-based ai chatbot on students' academic performance, higher-order thinking, and behavioral patterns in an information technology curriculum. *Applied Sciences (Basel, Switzerland), 14*(15), 6418. DOI: 10.3390/app14156418

Zimmerman, E. (2008). Gaming literacy: Game design as a model for literacy in the twenty-first century. In Perron, B., & Wolf, M. J. P. (Eds.), *The video game theory reader 2* (pp. 23–31). Routledge.

ADDITIONAL READING

Consalvo, M. (2007). *Cheating: Gaining advantage in videogames*. MIT Press. DOI: 10.7551/mitpress/1802.001.0001

Deterding, S., & Dixon, D. (2011). From game design elements to gamefulness. In *Proceedings of the 15th International Academic MindTrek Conference* (pp. 9–15).

Flanagan, M. (2009). *Critical play: Radical game design*. MIT Press. DOI: 10.7551/mitpress/7678.001.0001

Galloway, A. R. (2006). *Gaming: Essays on algorithmic culture*. University of Minnesota Press.

Jenkins, H. (2006). *Convergence culture: Where old and new media collide*. NYU Press.

Murray, J. H. (1997). *Hamlet on the holodeck: The future of narrative in cyberspace*. MIT Press.

KEY TERMS AND DEFINITIONS

Agency: Agency refers to the capacity to act consciously and meaningfully within a system, making choices that have implications or consequences. In gaming literacy, agency does not reside in the game. It emerges through interactions between the player, systems, design, and contexts.

AI Literacy: AI literacy is the ability to critically evaluate, engage, and interpret artificial intelligence systems and their artifacts as non-neutral technologies. AI literacy emphasizes human responsibility and ethics when interacting with AI-generated content.

Critical Pedagogy: Critical pedagogy is an educational approach centered on acknowledging that education is inherently political and ideological. Its practices prioritize dialogue, reflexivity, and questioning of structures and systems, focusing on student-centered activities.

Funds of Knowledge: Funds of knowledge refer to the historically accumulated knowledge, experience, skills, and cultural practices particular to each individual. They can be accessed or activated through different practices as a way to support meaning-making, agency, and critical engagement with texts.

Gaming Literacy: Gaming literacy is a critical, multimodal literacy that emerges through the act of playing games. It expands beyond reading, including interpreting, questioning, and making meaning from games as complex semiotic systems.

Meaning-Making: Meaning-making is the process of interpreting semiotic resources in relation to context and prior knowledge to construct understanding. Meaning-making is participatory and embodied, drawing on funds of knowledge.

Multimodal Text: A multimodal text is a communicative artifact in which two or more different semiotic modes come together. It does not necessarily refer to written text, but image, gesture, movement, space, and sound.

Positionality: Positionality refers to the stance an individual occupies in relation to a text, a situation, or a system. Positionality can be epistemological, ontological, cultural, emotional, and even ethical. It is a reflection of enacted identities.

Relational Ecosystems: Relational ecosystems are networks of social, cultural, and participatory practices around a group, an object, or a setting. In gaming literacy, it refers to the communities, paratexts, and collaborative spaces where meaning-making is fostered, debated, and challenged.

Chapter 5
From Page to Platform:
Ethical and Creative Literacies in Human-AI Multimodal Practices

Kishin Khajiboyev
Mamun University, Khiva, Uzbekistan

Aarthi Selvakumar
http://orcid.org/0009-0006-9064-2091
Marwadi University, Rajkot, India

Ravikumar Natarajan
http://orcid.org/0009-0009-3705-1681
Marwadi University, Rajkot, India

Dilmurod Turaev
Termez University of Economics and Service, Termez, Uzbekistan

Turdiev Abdullo Sagdullaevich
Alfraganus University, Tashkent, Uzbekistan

ABSTRACT

The growing nature of the integration of Artificial Intelligence in the education platform is transforming literacy as a multimodal, platform-mediated, and ethically challenging practice. This chapter explores transitioning to page-based literacy to the human-AI multimodal meaning-making such that the ethical and creative aspects of literacy within AI-enabled spaces are highlighted. The chapter is based on the multimodal literacy theory, digital ethics, and platform studies to analyze the interaction between learners and AI as a co-creative agent (text, image, sound, and interactive media). The discussion is based on recent example case studies in K-12 and higher education and shows the way AI platforms can affect creativity,

DOI: 10.4018/979-8-3373-6986-0.ch005

authorship, and ethical awareness. The chapter states that, to build successful literacy education in the age of AI, educational theories must combine ethical reasoning with creative agency to maintain human judgment in automated literacy ecosystems.

INTRODUCTION

The modern learning and teaching settings are experiencing a radical shift in literacy due to the fast adoption of Artificial Intelligence in daily learning, communication, and creative activities. Conventional theories of literacy, based on page reading and writing in a linear manner, are becoming less and less powerful to explain how meaning is created, moved and decoded in digitally mediated contexts. The AI-enhanced systems bring agency of algorithms to the literacy practices to redefine the manner in which texts are produced, selected, assessed, and distributed in multimodal spaces. Such developments require re-defining of literacy as an active process socially situated and involving interaction between humans, technologies and institutional structures. Within the educational field, learners are currently interacting with text, image, sound, data and interactive media using adaptive, recommendation, and real-time generating platforms (Samo & Highhouse, 2025). The transformations present a great challenge of authorship, creativity, ethical responsibility and power in the construction of knowledge. Ethical rationale and utmost judgment, which are created by the application of AI systems as co-producers and meaning makers, demand that literacy education should never be limited to technical capacity alone (Ibrahim, 2024).

The introduction helps to put the chapter in this dynamic space, where literacy is regarded as a multimodal, ethical, and creative practice that is reshaped in human-AI alliances within ecosystems founded on platforms. In this context, conventional literacy theories mean print and early digital literacy models that have a focus on linear text, fixed authorship and meaning-making as controlled by humans. The chapter concentrates on AI-mediated literacy in secondary and higher education, mostly on platform-based learning, which involves English, in which algorithms actively mediate reading, writing, and multimodal writing. The concept of algorithmic agency in this chapter describes AI functionality where educators adopt a new technology that involves generative models, suggestion tools, automatic feedback, and adaptable assessment as part of their literacy practices. These systems affect the text production, selection, assessment and distribution by prompting, ranking, feedback and interface designs due to their positioning algorithms as active participants in meaning-making as well as the human judgment.

TRANSFORMATION OF LITERACY IN AI-MEDIATED EDUCATIONAL CONTEXTS

The artificial intelligence-mediated situations in education are also altering the very meaning of literacy by attempting to introduce the intelligent systems into the process of reading, writing and meaning-making. Literacy is no longer restrictive to reading fixed texts but to an interface where it is adaptive, or to using generative tools or to being responded to by an algorithmic curation. The AI-based platforms customize the learning journeys, automate the feedback mechanisms, and produce multimodal results, which affects the way learners process the information and communicate their knowledge (Vartiainen & Tedre, 2024). These systems are prolific in influencing cognitive and creative processes by prefiguring some manifestations, styles, and viewpoints through the models driven by data. Consequently, literacy practices are spread within the judgment of humans and computer-generated suggestions. This change brings pedagogical assumptions of acquiring, understanding, and evaluating skills into question. It is necessary that learners be able to critically assess AI-generated pieces, learn its limitations, and be aware of the sociotechnical circumstances in which it is created. AI-mediated literacies therefore demand an augmented skill, one that combines technical engagement with critical awareness and ethical sensitivity as well as creative judgment in the numerous modes of representation.

From Page-Based to Platform-Based Multimodal Practices

The fact that page based to platform-based literacy practices are on the rise is indicative of a wider change in the organization and experience of knowledge within digital contexts. Although page-based literacy has traditionally focused on stability, linearity, and author-driven meaning, these attributes are not unique to print per se, and flexibility and interactivity to digital ones. Instead of providing a firm dichotomy, page-based literacies and platform-based literacies are presented in this chapter as intersecting practices, and the uses of AI-mediated platforms enhance a set of practices of adaptability, personalization, and algorithmic mediation limited or tacit before. Education platforms combine text and images, audio, video, data visualizations with interactives that allow students to compose and make sense of messages using multiple semiotic modes (Tan et al., 2025). The algorithms that are inherent to these platforms also shape the engagement with levels of prioritizing content, proposing creative paths, and modifying the interface according to the behavior of the user. It therefore follows that meaning-making is a dynamic process; it will depend on the intention of man as well as the rationality of the computation. This change necessitates new literacy types that include navigation skills and multimodal composition and critical platform awareness (Hryciw et al., 2023). The learners should be able to not only generate content but also learn how platforms organize visibility, participation and interpretation. Multimodal practices are thus repositioned through platforms, which make literacy a situated practice within the technological, cultural and institutional settings.

Ethical and Creative Imperatives in Human–AI Literacy Engagements

Human-AI literacies involve human engagements that present ethical and creative demands that go beyond the simple functional utilization of technology. With the introduction of AI systems into the idea generation process, text construction, or the appearance of visual artifacts, the issues of originality, authorship, and responsibility become the focal point of the process of literacy education. Artificial intelligence-based creative practices have the potential to increase the range of expressiveness, but may also lead to homogenization, the amplification of bias, and dependence on automated results (Jobin et al., 2019). Ethical literacy is required thus to make certain that creative agency stays focused on human values including fairness, transparency, and cultural sensitivity. The learners should be coached to think about the way AI systems are conditioned, the opinions of whom are encoded in the results and the impact of the algorithmic decisions with representation and voice. In AI, creative literacy is a process of making informed decisions regarding taking, modifying, or opposing machine-based recommendations (Yan et al., 2025). Creative imperatives and ethical imperatives can therefore not be separated and literacy education should be used to cultivate reflective judgment in collaboration with experimentation and innovations in human-AI interactions.

BACKGROUND TO THE STUDY

The context behind this work lies in the intersection of the multimodal literacy theory, digital learning and the increasing role of AI-based platforms in the educational setting. The study of literacy has increasingly over the last twenty years outgrown models that are driven by print to address the significance of visual, auditory and interactive forms of communication. At the same time, educational technologies have shifted the position of the inert digital materials to the smart systems that can produce content, customize teaching, and manipulate student behavior (Akgun & Greenhow, 2022). This convergence has exacerbated ethical issues surrounding the use of data, algorithmic bias and sharing of creative power between humans and machines. Although the current literature covers the concept of multimodality and digital literacy, not many frameworks have been able to combine ethical reasoning with creative practices in AI-mediated settings.

This background section provides the theoretical underpinnings that must be used to explore literacy as a technologically mediated practice that is socially embedded (Holmes et al., 2022). It identifies the necessity to comprehend how the historic development in bimodal literacy intertwine with the modern AI developments to form new opportunities and challenges that teachers, students, and institutions will face when functioning within the educational ecosystem of platforms. Still, although the literature in multimodal literacy and digital creativity is massive, the issue of ethics is often considered as a policy-level issue, but not a part of creative practice. Research in AI-ethics revolves around governance and bias, but their counterparts in creativity research are expression and engagement. Very little has been done to analyze ethical thinking in AI-assisted creative work, and in this chapter, the author fills this gap by connecting the ethical literacy with creative agency. Table 1 summarizes a shift in print literacy to platform based, multimodal and AI mediated literacy practices.

Table 1. Evolution of Literacy from Page-Based to AI-Mediated Platforms

Aspect	Page-Based Literacy	AI-Mediated Platform Literacy
Mode of communication	Primarily text	Text, image, audio, video, data
Structure	Linear and fixed	Interactive and adaptive
Role of technology	Supportive	Active mediator
Meaning-making	Human-centered	Human–AI collaborative

Evolution of Multimodal Literacy Studies

Multimodal literacy has been developed in reaction to the shortcomings of the print-based approaches to meaning-making, and it focuses on the idea that communication is multimodal: it involves language, image, gesture, sound, and spatial design. One of the earliest frameworks was the emphasis of interaction of various modes to create meaning and learning especially in media and digital-rich settings. As time passed, the research became broader to encompass social, cultural, and critical aspects, since it became appreciated that multimodal practices are embedded within power relationships and institutional contexts. Multimodal literacy in education has been associated with engagement, inclusivity, and creative expression, particularly in diverse linguistic and cultural groups of learners. Nonetheless, the literature on the matter largely precedes the proliferation of generative Artificial Intelligence and adaptive websites (Apata et al., 2025). Consequently, the conventional multimodal theorists tend to believe that there are human-directed design processes, and representational decisions that are constant. The development of multimodal literacy studies can give a critical ground to the ways in which AI undermines the prevailing assumptions by introducing algorithmic agency into the formation and analysis of multimodal compositions. Figure 1 Shows how literacy research has evolved over time through print-based methods to digitally mediated, inclusive, and AI-driven multimodal approaches to literacy.

Figure 1. Evolution of Multimodal Literacy Studies

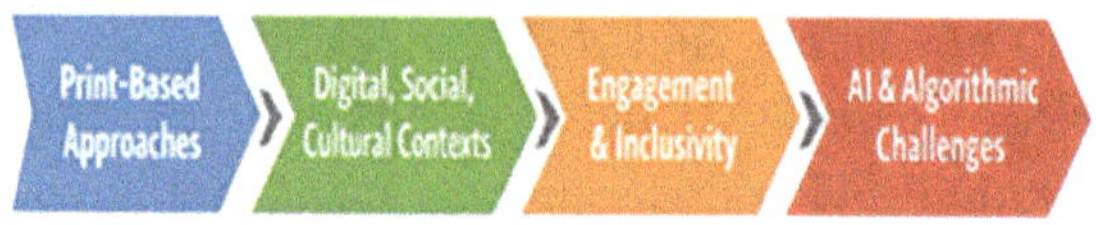

Emergence of Generative AI and Algorithmic Platforms in Education

In education, some applications of AI mediation can be found in systems that combine generative writing applications, automatic feedback, recommendation systems, and adaptive interfaces. Multimodal composition is implemented using learning management systems, which have AI-assisted grading tools and generative design tools, and resource visibility is determined by recommendation-driven platforms. There is empirical evidence of the impact of these systems on learner choices, pacing, and representational practices in addition to technological presence in education. Generative AI and algorithm platforms have brought major changes to learning environments by introducing intelligent automation to the most fundamental literacy practices.

Learning management systems, creative applications and assessment environments now contain tools that are able to produce text, images, audio and multimodal artifacts (Aarthi et al., 2025). Such platforms are based on high-volume data and machine learning models to predict, recommend and generate content, and frequently mediate the experience of learning invisibly. The personalization, efficiency, and increased creativity have beckoned them to be adopted (Ibrahim & Lianingsih, 2025). Nevertheless, the use of algorithmic platforms creates some opacities in the decision-making process that cast doubt on the issue of transparency, accountability, and pedagogical control. Generative AI poses a challenge to traditional divisions between author and tool, learner and system. The need to comprehend how these technologies appear is urgent enough to make it contextualized or rather make it understandable on how literacy practices are being redefined not only by digital media but also by intelligent systems that become active participants of meaning making processes.

Ethical Challenges and Creative Opportunities in AI-Supported Literacy

The idea of AI-aided literacy is a complex blend of moral issues and aesthetic opportunities. On the one hand, AI-driven tools are able to popularize multimodal composition, provide various demands to learners, and promote experimentation with the modes and with the genres. On the other hand, they also create ethical issues of discrimination, surveillance, possession of data and erosion of the human authorship. These systems of algorithms have the potential to normalise the prevailing standards of linguistics, reinforce cultural stereotypes, or integrate the effort of constructing training data (Guo & Zhang, 2025).

All of these challenges suggest that ethical literacy can be viewed as one of the building blocks of AI-assisted education. In the meantime, AI can be employed to open the doors to the creativity provided it is approached as a companion rather than a substitute to human judgement. Hospitable pedagogical frameworks can assist learners to become considerate users of AI products, recombine multimodal elements, and manifest personal opinions. Good literacy practices in AI-based educational settings are dependent on the need to remain ethically conscious and creative.

RESEARCH OBJECTIVES

The guiding force of this chapter is a variety of research objectives that guide the systematic research of the sub-field of multimodality, Artificial Intelligence and educational platforms. The goals are set to go beyond the descriptive accounts of the AI application and to challenge how the human-AI relations refract the role of the creative agency, moral judgment and pedagogical accountability of the modern instruction on the literacy teaching. These objectives allow the systematic assessment of the AI-based multimodal meaning-making in the framework of learning by balancing the theoretical inquiry and the educational practice. The following are the main research questions:

- To examine the nature and dynamics of human-AI co-creation in multimodal literacy practices across educational settings.
- To analyze how generative AI tools and algorithmic platforms influence processes of meaning-making, authorship, and creative expression.

- To investigate the ethical dimensions of platform-mediated literacy, including issues of bias, transparency, data governance, and accountability.
- To explore learners' and educators' roles in critically engaging with AI-generated multimodal content and automated recommendations.
- To identify pedagogical implications and design principles that support equitable, inclusive, and ethically grounded AI-enabled literacy education.

CONCEPTUAL MODEL

The theoretical framework of the chapter provides the concept of literacy as a distributed, multimodal practice that can be established on the basis of the protracted interaction between learners, educators, AI systems, and digital platforms. The model has not adopted Artificial Intelligence as a neutral instrument, considering that it regards AI as a mediator, which informs the design, interpretation and appraisal of meaning in learning activities. Literacy is understood as an ecology in which human judgment, creative will, moral reasoning and process algorithm are in a constant state of engagement. This model merges the multimodal literacy theory and ethical/pedagogical strategies to describe the complexity of the learning environment on platforms (Sutrisno et al., 2024). It repeats the argument that not just is the production of meaning no longer the outcome of the individual thought it has been co-produced by the organization of sociotechnical organization which includes data and interfaces, and also institutional conventions.

The model highlights the need to balance both responsibility and innovation due to the foregrounding of both ethical literacy and creative agency as two factors that are very vital. Teachers and spaces are put in the position of primary mediators that regulate the interaction of learners with the AI systems and can define the opportunity to critically reflect, be incorporated and be creative. This conceptual model, therefore, offers a consistent structure on human-AI multimodal literacy practices in the modern education. Table 2 provides a description of the important dimensions, including multimodality, ethical literacy, creative agency, and algorithmic mediation.

Table 2. Core Dimensions of Human–AI Multimodal Literacy

Aspect	Page-Based Literacy	AI-Mediated Platform Literacy
Mode of communication	Primarily text	Text, image, audio, video, data
Structure	Linear and fixed	Interactive and adaptive
Role of technology	Supportive	Active mediator
Meaning-making	Human-centered	Human–AI collaborative

Human–AI Multimodal Literacy Ecosystem

Human AI multimodal literacy ecosystems consist of related relations among learners, AI technologies, content modalities, and sociocultural contexts. Happening in this ecosystem, meaning-making occurs when there is a relationship between text, image, sound, data and interactive media through algorithmic systems. Besides offering interpretive judgment, combined understanding and ethics, AI tools offer more multimodal content generation, editing and adaptation. The literacy practices are therefore not concentrated in a human being but distributed among the human and machine actors (Harry & Sayudin, 2023).

The ecosystem lens is a platform of knowing frameworks that to coordinate the involvement by organizing accessibility, visibility, and engagement on the platform in terms of interface design and recommendation frameworks. It also shows the role of data infrastructures and training models in mediating the process of determining which forms of expression are given priority (Gideon, 2025). Defining literacy as a kind of ecosystem allows taking a rather wide view of how creative and ethical issues may appear under the condition of a stable interaction between a human and AI in the process of continuous learning. Figure 2 shows the interaction between learners, AI systems, multimodal content and sociocultural contexts interacting to form a meaning-making in AI-mediated literacy space.

Figure 2. Human–AI Multimodal Literacy Ecosystem

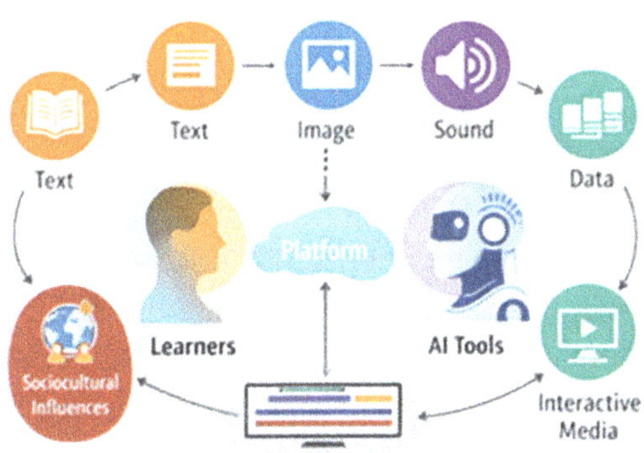

Integration of Ethical Literacy and Creative Agency

Ethical literacy and creative agency are the two core elements of the proposed conceptual model since these two aspects interact to determine responsible interaction with AI-mediated literacy practices. Creative agency is the ability of learners to undertake premeditated design decisions, experiment with multimodal, and express original attitudes. Ethical literacy is the complement to this as it allows critically evaluating the social, cultural, and political consequences of AI-generated content (Igbokwe, 2024). In the model, ethical reasoning is not considered as an external limitation to creativity but rather as a guiding model that informs creative decisions. The learners are urged to challenge the sources, prejudices, and constraints of AI products and proactively direct them to human values. This assimilation underpins a balanced approach whereby innovation is being correlated with accountability, fairness, and inclusiveness. The model fosters the growth of literacy within creative practice that will keep human judgment and responsibility alive in an increasingly automated setting by integrating ethical inquiry into creative practice.

Role of Educators and Platforms in Mediating Literacy Practices

The educators and digital platforms play the important mediating role that affects the way human-AI multimodal literacy practices are enacted. The role of the educators in this case is that of being ethical guardians and creating learning opportunities, organizing a meaningful and vital encounter, and training learners to read and evaluate the AI-generated information. Their pedagogical preferences will dictate how learners perceive AI, as authority, partner, or as a tool which requires assessment. On the other hand, platforms mediate literacy through the architecture of the interface (interfaces), algorithmic recommendations, and through personalization, which operates on the basis of data. These technological assemblies constitute the content that is undergone, the innovation that is encouraged and the participatory forms that are encouraged or restricted (Ranes, 2025).

The conceptual model pays attention to the educator and platform as a mutual accountability in the establishment of open, non-discriminative, and self-reflexive literacy conditions (Ravikumar, et al., 2025). It should also be mentioned that efficient mediation should be founded on a combination of pedagogical goal and platform development to ensure that the AI-mediated literacy practices sustain ethical thinking, creative agency and participatory fairness between diverse groups of learners.

RESEARCH METHODOLOGY

The research approach that has been used in this chapter is aimed at systematically analyzing human-AI multimodal literacy practices in a qualitative approach based on interpretive methods. Since both ethical and creative aspects of AI-mediated literacy are exploratory, the methodology is focused on contextual comprehension, but not quantification of the independent variables. The conceptual analytical framework is directed by the conceptualization of the study and is embedded in an analytical framework of multimodal literacy theory, ethical inquiry and platform studies to analyze the meaning-making process within the context of the AI-supported educational setting (Meylani, 2024). The case-based approach is used in order to record the practice that is situated in various learning environments where interactions between learners, teachers, and AI systems can be analyzed in-depth. This method upholds a subtle interpretation of how creative agency and ethical thinking is put into action. The methodological rigor is ensured by clear case selection, systematic analysis of data, and reflexive interpretation. Ethical considerations are inherent in the research process to be responsible in the data, participants and interpretation of AI-mediated practices (Alduais et al., 2025). The methodology offers a logical basis into studying literacy as a socially and technologically mediated process in the modern education.

Research Design and Analytical Framework

The study has a qualitative, multi-case study research design that is appropriate to explore contextualized literacy practices. This design allows studying human-AI interactions in their natural contexts of real-life learning, not in the controllable experimental conditions. The analytical framework combines the ideas of multimodal discourse analysis, critical digital literacy, and ethical analysis in order to inform the interpretation. The multimodal discourse analysis is applied to the analysis of the construction of meaning through textual, visual, and interactive components and critical digital literacy to determine how power relations are inscribed in the platform design and meditated by algorithms (Zawacki-Richter et al., 2019). Moral examination offers an approach that can be used to analyze matters like authorship, bias and accountability. All these views constitute a stratified system, which facilitates methodical but elastic analysis. Such a combination of design guarantees that the creative, ethical, and technological aspects are researched as a whole, and the process of research is correlated with the conceptual model presented in the chapter.

Data Sources and Case Selection Criteria

The study data are obtained using a variety of qualitative sources to describe the depth of AI-mediated multimodal literacy practices. Examples of such sources are classroom resources, student-created multimodal artworks, platform-based outputs, teaching materials, and teacher reflections. The purposive criteria applied in case selection are made to fit the objectives of the research. The chosen instances will present educational settings, where multimodal composition and learning with the help of generative AI tools and digital platforms are actively employed. Educational level, disciplinary focus, and learner demographics diversity is believed to facilitate the breadth of analytics (Dahlquist, 2023). The selection of cases is determined by their ability to provide different types of human-AI interaction, ethical bargaining, and creative practice. In this way, one can make a comparative analysis without losing depth in each instance. Open record keeping of the data sources, and the selection criteria will improve the validity and reusability of the results.

Analytical Procedures and Ethical Considerations

The manner of analytical procedures is iterative and reflexive comprising a combination of coding, thematic analysis, and interpretive synthesis. Information was structured and codified to establish trends associated with multimodality design options, AI inclusion, and moral logic. Themes have been subsequently formulated by comparison between cases, based on the manner in which creative agency and ethical literacy is practically enacted. In the course of the analysis, one is focused on how platforms and algorithms are used to form meaning-making processes. Analysis and reporting are inseparable aspects of ethics (Yim & Wegerif, 2024).

Information has been processed following the guidelines of informed consent, responsible representation, and confidentiality. The materials produced by AI are critically analyzed to prevent the attribution of agency and authorship mindlessly. The reason behind keeping reflexivity is to recognize the interpretive aspect of the researcher and the weakness of the data mediated by AI. These processes guarantee rigor in decisions and ethical uprightness during the research.

LITERATURE REVIEW

The discourse of literacy in digital and AI-facilitated space demonstrates a remarkable switch in the print-based concept to more comprehensive models that integrate multimodality, moral thinking, and human-technology interface. Educational research is gradually beginning to conceptualize literacy as a social practice, which is mediated by cultural, technological, and institutional forces. In this understanding, the meaning-making is not restricted to writing, but includes visual, auditory, and interaction to meaning-making, especially in platform-based learning situations. Simultaneously, the emergence of employing more algorithmic systems in education has raised new issues of authorship, biasness, and responsibility (Cohn et al., 2025).

The relevant literature reviewed in this chapter can be aligned with the objectives of the chapter because it looks at the convergence of multimodal literacy practices with ethical issues and creative agency in human-AI relationships. Instead of viewing AI as a neutral instructional tool, current research highlights the presence of AI in the creation of participation, representation, and the knowledge building process (Rafique et al., 2025). The field of investigation offers the basis to comprehend opportunities and threats of the AI-enabled literacy and emphasizes the necessity of integrated frameworks that can be used to address the connections between multimodal practice, ethical literacy, and pedagogical responsibility. Table 3 summarizes the key literature strands pertaining to multimodality, ethical literacy and human-AI collaboration.

Table 3. Summary of Literature Themes Aligned with Research Objectives

Theme	**Key Focus**
Multimodal literacy	Non-textual meaning-making
Digital literacy	Platform navigation
Ethical literacy	Algorithmic awareness
Human–AI collaboration	Creativity and authorship

Multimodality and Digital Literacy in Educational Research

The study on multimodality and digital literacy has increased the perception on how learners formulate meaning using various quasi-semantic systems. Research underscores that literacy entails the integration of language, images, symbols, sound, and spatial layout especially the digital environments. The educational research points to the potential of multimodal methodology to increase the level of participation, to facilitate various learning styles, and allow more inclusive expressivity (Peng et al., 2025). Digital literacy models also emphasize the necessity of navigation of platforms, judgment of information on the Internet, and awareness of the sociotechnical situations of communication. Along with the development of educational technologies, researchers are more prone to admit that interfaces, software affordances, and algorithmic structures dictate how literacy practices should be. Nevertheless, a significant proportion of the literature is dedicated to human-controlled digital tools, which provide little information on situations when AI systems both produce and filter content (S. Zhang et al., 2025). The gap highlights the importance of reconsidering multimodal theory of literacy in the context of AI-mediated platforms that are involved directly in the process of making meanings.

Ethical Literacy and Algorithmic Accountability

Ethical literacy is a recent dimension of education that has become a serious feature of contemporary education due to the increasing role of data-driven technologies. The sources underline the importance of learners learning about the functioning of algorithms, data collection and application, and the ability of automated systems to reproduce social biases. Accountability of the algorithm is a topic that is talked about as a collective effort between the designers, the institutions and the users (Wu et al., 2025). Research on education raises the issues of transparency, fairness, and the incomprehensibility of the AI decision-making process. In the literature on literacy, ethical literacy is currently being understood as the ability to ask critical questions of digital systems and their products. According to the scholars, in the absence of ethics, the learners might passively receive the content generated by algorithms as an objective or something that is authoritative (Lin, 2025). This is something also reflected in the literature on ethical issues where platform-based environments where power is entrenched in design decisions and data structures magnify ethical issues. Such deliberations confirm the significance of making ethical reasoning an ingredient of literacy education and not a peripheral issue.

Creativity, Authorship, and Human–AI Collaboration

The scholarship of creativity and authorship on AI-aided spaces displays the continued discussions on the essence of human-machine collaboration. Research indicates that the use of AI can improve creative practice by facilitating the ideation, experimentation, and composing in multiple modes. Meanwhile, there is also the worry of the human authorship becoming diluted and the standardization of creative output possible. Scholarly studies investigate the negotiate process of authorship in the context of AI involvement in the creation of content, which captures conflicts between originality and automation (Güneş & Kaban, 2025). There are studies that tend to view AI as a co-creative companion that supplements human potential whereas other researchers warn about excessive dependence on suggestions provided by the machine. In the literature, it is stressed that creative agency requires the ability of learners to critically define and contextualize AI outputs as opposed to appropriately accepting them. The literature affirms the importance to have pedagogical models that facilitate reflective, ethical, and creative human-AI work in literacy practices.

CASE STUDIES

In this section, I will provide two contemporary case studies, which demonstrate how human and AI interaction can influence multimodal literacy practices at different levels of learning. The cases are chosen so as to provide a difference in terms of the age of the learners, the context in which the institutions operate, and the pedagogical intent, although they have a constant focus on AI-assisted multimodal composition. Collectively, they offer empirical basis on which ethical reasoning, agency of creativity, and mediation of platforms can be explored practically. The former is K12 education where AI is implemented into the organized curricular setting to reinforce elementary literacy and creativity. The second scenario looks at the higher education scenarios where the learners interact with AI in a more autonomous way as creative co-authors of high-order multimedia work (Qi, 2023).

The two cases examine the level of engagement in learners, creative accomplishments and ethical understanding, utilizing the indicative values of percentages to depict the observed tendencies and the comparative knowledge. These findings are combined in the cross-case analysis to help point out similarities and differences in the context, which allows a better understanding of how AI-facilitated literacy practices develop in educational contexts. Table 4 illustrates case study comparison by level of engagement, ethics awareness, and creative agency (percentage indicators).

Table 4. Comparative Overview of Case Study Contexts and Outcomes

Aspect	K–12 Education	Higher Education
Engagement increase	~68%	~78%
Ethical awareness	38% → 62%	~69%
Creative modification	~70%	~78%
AI reliance	Moderate	Moderate–High

Case Study I: AI-Assisted Multimodal Composition in K–12 Education

The case study belongs to multimodal composition activities supported by AI that were introduced in a language arts curriculum in the middle-school. Students were provided with generative AI systems to aid in the creation of stories, visual representation, and audio narration through a teacher-led system. About 68% of students showed more engagement in multimodal narrative writing than with the traditional writing, where they had two texts alone. Almost 72% of learners had included visual and audio aspects which means that they operate across modes. In AI-assisted brainstorming, teachers said that students became less anxious about writing at the beginning of the task, especially students with poor literacy (Yim & Su, 2024). Ethical awareness was, however, still lopsided.

Although 55 out of 100 learners were able to recognize that images or text produced by AI were not wholly original, just 38 out of 100 learners were able to identify possible bias or mistakes in representation in generated content in the first place. The change in ethical recognition was measurable and the classroom discussions and reflective prompts, which were structured and guided, led to an increase of the ethical recognition to about 62% at the conclusion of the unit. An agency that was most creative happened when AI products were considered drafts and not final and 70% of students were willing to make amendments to the generated products (Van Brummelen et al., 2021). As the case demonstrates, guided pedagogical scaffolding is the key to striking the right balance when it comes to balancing the facets of creativity, ethical concerns, and learner agency in K-12 practices of AI-aided literacy. Figure 3 shows percentages of increase in learner engagement, ethical awareness, and creative agency caused by AI-based multimodal composition activities in K-12 classrooms.

Figure 3. AI-Assisted Multimodal Literacy Outcomes in K–12 Education

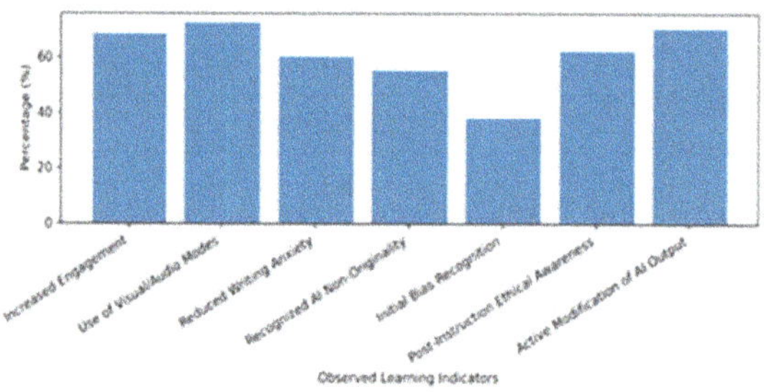

Case Study II: Human–AI Creative Practices in Higher Education

The second case study discusses creative practices between humans and AI in a media and communication undergraduate program. The undergraduate students were exposed to generative AI tools in creating multimodal projects that was a combination of the text, data visualization, images, and interactive elements. The analysis of the survey and artifacts revealed that 78% of learners viewed AI as the partner and not a threat to human imagination. More than three-quarters (74%) said that AI tools have increased the speed of ideation and experimentation, allowing multimodal designs of greater complexity and even short-term development. Of greater frequency in the ethical engagement context compared to the K-12 context (Oermann et al., 2025), almost 69% of students showed explicit authorship, attribution or bias in reflective statements. Nonetheless, as the dependence on default AI results was noted in approximately 31% of projects, this indicates that there are still continuing conflicts between efficiency and originality.

Peer critique and instructor feedback sessions also helped towards better critical engagement, and revised submissions demonstrated an increase of 22% in original multimodal restructuring. Creative agency was the most significant with those projects that involved a combination of AI-generated factors with personal data, lived-in experience, or contextual analysis (Leander & Burriss, 2020). This example underscores the fact that more ethical reflexivity is evident among the students of higher education, yet they still need pedagogical models to avoid the introduction of blind reliance on AI-generated materials. Figure 4 shows the percent-based measure of collaboration, ethical engagement, creative agency, and dependence on the AI tools by the students of higher education involved in AI-mediated multimodal composition.

Figure 4. Human–AI Creative Practices in Higher Education

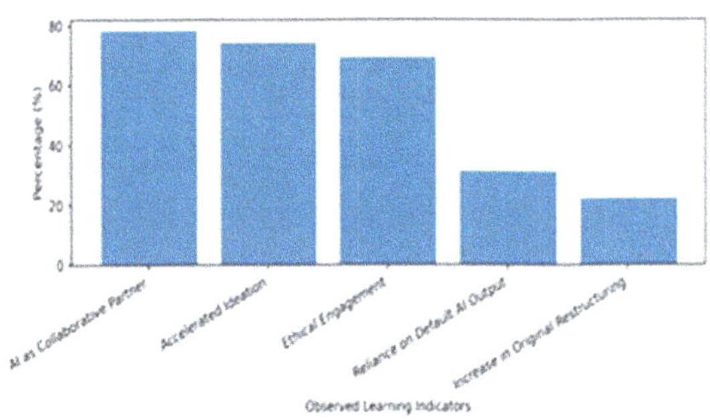

Cross-Case Insights on Ethics, Creativity, and Learner Agency

According to the cross-case analysis, there are certain paralleling patterns, as well as some variation of contexts of AI-enabled multimodal literacy practices. The involvement rates grew in both scenarios as were reported with the growth of the 65-78% that is suggestive of the motivational force of an AI-aided composition. The levels of awareness of the ethics increased faster as the level of education increased since the level of awareness at the first stage was about 69%, as opposed to 38% of the first K-12 conditions (Ojeda-Ramirez et al., 2024). Nevertheless, both instances showed that systematized pedagogical interventions raised ethical knowledge by 20-25%.

The best creative agency was found when the findings of AI were presented as temporary holders, and the active human regulation stipulated the 70% and 78% of the K-12 respondents and higher education respondents respectively. In general, in most cases, the use of absolute AI was associated with the decrease in originality in approximately 30% of work. These discoveries augment the importance of carrying out age-sensitive scaffolding and reflective activities in order to maintain ethical cognition and creative agency in human-AI multimodal literacy ecosystems (Lin, 2026). When comparing the results of percentages in the K-12 learning environment and the higher level of education, the figure 5 shows the spheres of engagement and awareness of ethical and creative agency, as well as reliance on AI in the multimodal literacy practices.

Figure 5. Cross-Case Insights on Ethics, Creativity, and Learner Agency

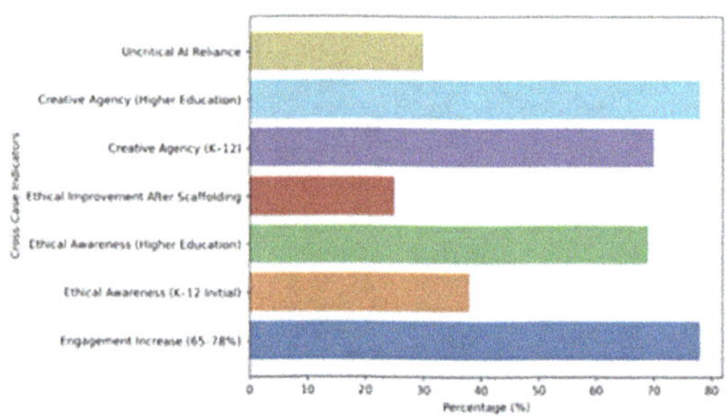

RESULTS AND DISCUSSION

The findings of the two case studies indicate that multimodal meaning is constructed, interpreted, and assessed in multimodal ways due to AI-enabled platforms. According to the findings, AI tools transform the literacy practice by facilitating composition faster, increasing access to multimodal resources, and mediating creative decisions by providing algorithmic recommendations. Simultaneously, the outcomes indicate that tensions between efficiency and originality, automation and moral accountability are still present. The engagement in both K12 and higher education environments also went up with gains of up to 65% to 78% perceiving the motivational affordances of AI-assisted platforms (Ng et al., 2021). Nevertheless, more interaction was not necessarily accompanied by critical or ethical literacy. Rather, the notions of ethical awareness and creative agency were closely intertwined with the concept of pedagogical scaffold and reflective intervention. These findings are contextualized in the discussion on platform-mediated literacy as AI systems are co-constructors of meaning and not tools. In general, the results indicate that AI platforms have the potential to make multimodal literacy richer in case of a carefully designed educational application, but may eradicate the diversity of creative practices and moral consciousness with unrefined use.

Influence of AI Platforms on Multimodal Meaning-Making

Multimodal meaning-making AI platforms have a quantifiable effect in influencing the process and the result of the literacy practice. In case of K-12, the percentage of learners using AI-generated visual or audio components in their compositions was around 72% points, which indicates the extended engagement of modalities. In post-secondary education, 74% of students said AI tools allowed them to ideate faster and integrate more extensively in multi-modal ways. These results imply that multimodal composition barriers are reduced through AI platforms and allow experimentation (Rowsell & Walsh, 2011). Nonetheless, algorithmic suggestions also oriented the creative directions, with traditional formats or style fads being prioritized. In the two scenarios, approximately 30% of outputs exhibited low variation, which indicates that one is inclined to approve default AI proposals. Meaning-making therefore became a hybridized process that is conditioned by human will and algorithm organization (Kustini, 2023). The findings underscore the fact that AI platforms do not passively facilitate multimodality, but they actively influence the representational options, something that should be enhanced by imperative platform consciousness in literacy education.

Ethical Awareness, Bias Recognition, and Responsibility

The awareness of ethics showed wide disparity in learning settings, and provided valuable insights into the manner in which students are aware of being influenced by algorithms and how they react to it. In the K-12 scenario, throughout the case study, bias or representational bias was only noted in the initial stages of learning by 38% of the learners, and went to about 62% after facilitated introspection. Higher education students had greater familiarity with the concept of ethical awareness as 69% of students who were asked to account reflectively included an answer on the issue of authorship or bias concerns (Kooli, 2023). With such gains, the blind consumption of AI-generated content continued in about one-third of outputs in both situations. Instructional design was strongly linked to ethical involvement and especially included discussion prompts, attribution rules, and peer critique. These results suggest that AI usage does not bring ethical literacy but needs a conscious pedagogical treatment. The findings support the perception that ethical responsibility in AI-mediated literacy is an acquired skill that should be developed along with technical and creative abilities.

Implications for Creative Agency and Knowledge Construction

The results indicate that creative agency and knowledge building in AI-mediated conditions are determined by the way learners locate themselves in the relations to the AI systems. Active human modification was present in 70% of K-12 projects and 78% of higher education projects when AI outputs were considered as provisional resources. Such cases were coupled with increased originality and conceptual consistency. On the other hand, those projects that mostly used unedited AI outputs (around 30% of the cases) were less deeply interpreted and poorly knowledge-built (Li & Huang, 2025). The findings indicate that creative agency can be maintained when the learners do not give up decision-making control and contextual judgment. Knowledge construction was developed as a process of collaboration, where AI aided the exploration, although it did not substitute human sense-making. These implicates the significance of pedagogical approaches that place more emphasis on reflection, revision, and critical engagement to make sure that AI can improve and not reduce creative and epistemic agency in multimodal literacy activities.

FUTURE RESEARCH DIRECTIONS

Future studies of the role of AI in mediating multimodal literacy should go beyond cross-sectional and temporary classroom-based studies and explore how ethical reasoning, creative agency, and literacy competencies change over time. With the current growth of AI technologies and their integration into the educational systems, the necessity to conduct long-term empirical research that would reflect the developmental trends over time is increasing. The current literature is mostly centered on short-term effects of interaction with AI platforms (engagement or productivity) and has little information on how repeated exposure to the AI platform influences the identity of learners, their judgment, and their meaning-making activities (Amiri et al., 2025).

Further studies should also focus on the growing diversity of learners and the situations of AI-assisted literacy training, such as informal learning settings and hybrid learning environments. Moreover, the high rate of technological change puts doubt on whether the existing ethical theories are sufficient to inform responsible literacy education. Future research can add to the theoretical foundation and practice through longitudinal, cross-cultural, and technology-oriented views, supporting the creation of the more robust theoretical frameworks and teaching methods. This research is critical to the assurance that the process of AI-mediated literacy development will be consistent with human values, educational equity, and the overall objectives of inclusive and responsible knowledge societies.

Longitudinal Studies on AI-Mediated Literacy Development

The longitudinal research is necessary to comprehend the impacts of the continued use of AI platforms on the development of literacy in the long run. Further research, including the development of the creative agency of learners, ethical awareness and critical judgment, should be analyzed at various levels of learning, starting with early school and further education. The long-term research may demonstrate whether the early-acquired positive results on engagement and multimodal competence are maintained or fade away with the normalization of AI tools. These studies can also investigate the influence of sustained exposure to algorithmic recommendation systems on cognitive habits, authorship practices and dependency on automated support (Zhang et al., 2022).

Longitudinal designs assist the researcher to establish the pattern of development, thresholds, and the possible risks involved in dependency or lack of originality. They also give some insight into the effects of pedagogical interventions as they pertain to long-term ethical literacy instead of temporary compliance. Future studies can also provide evidence-based recommendations on how to develop curricula that facilitate responsible and creative literacy acquisition in AI-mediated settings through the use of tracking learners on a long-term basis.

Cross-Cultural and Linguistic Perspectives on Multimodal AI Literacy

Multimodal literacy based on AI mediation, cross-cultural and linguistic perspective are essential in the further development of inclusive models. The future studies must examine the interplay between AI platform and the dissimilar cultural standards, language customs, and communicative customs. Numerous generative AI models are conditioned with overwhelming languages and culture, which may exclude minor voices and other forms of expression. The transregional and inter-language and inter-educational comparative analyses can highlight the way learners bargain meaning in the case when the AI results do not correspond to the cultural background (Nagapushpa et al., 2024).

This research can also address the way, in which multilingual learners can customize AI to make use of their multilingualism and translate linguistically sensitive multimodal composition. Cross-cultural investigation can shed light to power relations inherent in the world AI systems and its situational consequences to literacy education equity. The future studies will make it possible to predetermine the creation of AI systems and pedagogies that will facilitate pluralistic and contextualized literacy practices by foregrounding linguistic diversity and cultural specificity.

Emerging Technologies and Evolving Ethical Frameworks

The emergent technologies including immersive media, adaptive learning systems and intelligent agents will keep on transforming literacy practices. Future studies should focus on the interaction between these technologies and AI to form even more multimodal worlds. With the growth of technological capacity, moral codes should develop to meet the new authorship, use of data and algorithmic manipulation. Additional studies are required to understand how students and teachers understand ethical responsibility in situations when personalization occurs in real-time, data is biometric, or simulations are immersive (Ray & Ray, 2024). Research must also determine whether the current education policy and code of ethics is sufficient to deal with these changes.

The future scholarship can be valuable by exploring advancing technologies and the development of new ethical entities to defend proactive and not reactive methods in literacy education (Ravikumar et al., 2025). This research question is critical toward making sure that the innovation of AI-mediated literacy is informed by transparency, accountability, and humanistic values. Figure 6 The interactive process between new educational technologies and new ethical paradigms is dynamic, and it is necessary to bring transparency, accountability, and human-centered governance in the AI-mediated literacy spaces.

Figure 6. Emerging Technologies and Evolving Ethical Frameworks

MANAGERIAL IMPLICATIONS

The implications made by this chapter have grave managerial implications to educational leaders, administrators and policymakers that have to incorporate AI in the teaching and learning space. The practices of AI-literacy must be planned to ensure the utilization of technology does not oppose the ethical values, pedagogical goals and organizational values. The managers are supposed to realize that AI platforms do not merely influence the efficiency in operations, but also the construction of knowledge, expression of creativity, and agency of learners. Good leadership presupposes the transition to the coordination of technologies and the ethical rationale and creative development deployment in the institutional settings instead of an ad hoc use of technologies (Solanke Asia, 2024).

Based on the results, when there is no planned guidance, approximately 30% of AI-supported literary habits might become highly automated, and, therefore, less considered. In selecting and realizing AI systems, managerial decision-making should then be dominated by transparency, accountability and inclusiveness. The collaboration between teacher-technologist-ethics committees can enable institutions to make AI labor to enhance and not hamper literacy education. These management implications serve as an indication of the need to have structured actions that will lead to responsible innovation, equal accessibility, and continued human judgement in AI mediated learning processes. Table 5 Gives the Institutional, curricular and governance implications on findings.

Table 5. Managerial and Pedagogical Implications for Ethical AI-Enabled Literacy

Area	Key Implication
Institutional strategy	Ethical AI adoption
Curriculum design	Ethics-integrated creativity
Governance	Clear AI usage policies
Professional development	Educator capacity building

Institutional Strategies for Ethical AI Adoption in Education

The institutions will be at the center of influencing the way AI technologies are adopted and utilized in the educational environment. The principles of ethical use of AI should be determined through strategic planning, such as transparency of work of algorithms, data protection, and bias monitoring mechanisms. The uncritical use of AI tools can be minimized by institutional guidelines since it was found to be present in about 30% of learner outputs in the case studies (Alotaibi & Alshehri, 2023). The decision-makers are supposed to lean toward AI platforms that permit human control and personalization over complete automated generation of content. Informed decision-making can be facilitated using the help of cross-functional governance structures that include academic leadership, IT units, and ethics bodies. Also, the institutions must invest in the infrastructure that would provide just the access to the AI-enabled learning tools by eliminating the differences in the connectivity and digital literacy. Institutional strategies can enable responsible AI adoption by motivating responsible procurement, deployment, and evaluation procedures including embedding ethical considerations and contributing to multimodal literacy without compromising the trust and autonomy of the learners.

Curriculum Design for Ethical and Creative Multimodal Literacy

The design of the curriculum is a significant key to transferring the principles of ethical AI to the daily literacy activities. The results indicate that the ethical awareness was raised by 20-25% under the influence of the structured pedagogical interventions, which emphasizes the role of the conscious planning of the curriculum. AI-aided multimodal composition should be included in the curriculum alongside specific learning outcomes pertaining to the ability to think ethically, write, and be creative. Instead of ethics as an individual subject, the ethical question should be incorporated into creative assignments and evaluation guidelines (Brouwer et al., 2020).

Reflective activities, comparative work between human and AI-generated content, and revision-based workflows can be included in the curriculum design and facilitate critical interaction, the curriculum designers. Curriculum flexibility enables educators to make AI tools flexible to the needs of different learners without losing pedagogical integrity. The alignment of creative experimentation and ethical reflection by curriculum strategies can help to promote deeper learning and make sure that AI contributes to, but does not limit, multimodal literacy development.

Governance, Policy, and Professional Development Considerations

As a means to sustain ethical and creative AI-enabled literacy practices, it is important to have good governance and policy frameworks. The institutional policies are supposed to make clear expectations about the use of AI, attribution of authorship, rules of data management, and scholarly honesty. Policy direction assists in minimizing ambiguity and aids in the practice consistency among departments and levels of education. The professional growth is also paramount, with the educators to be constantly encouraged to learn how to operate within the changing AI technologies (Hesti et al., 2025). Having technical proficiency as the main theme of training program should be accompanied by ethical judgment, critical platform awareness and pedagogical integration. According to the case studies, educator-led scaffolding made a huge impact on enhancing ethical engagement, and the importance of focus on professional learning is emphasized. Professional development can be connected with governance structures that are able to enforce alignment between the vision of an institution and classroom practice. Governance, policy, and capacity-building can help institutions to proactively control the adoption of AI and maintain the quality of education, equity, and human-focused literacy outcomes.

CONCLUSION

The shift to platform-mediated AI-enabled literacy requires a new approach to the conceptualization of literacy education in modern learning settings. As it has been presented in this chapter, literacy is not restricted to individual processes of reading and writing anymore, but rather produces itself in the interactions between human beings, Artificial Intelligence systems, and multimodal platforms that inform the way meaning is created, distributed, and assessed. The increase in creative potential through the reduction of barriers to multimodal composition and the development of new modes of expression has been achieved by AI platforms, but has also raised issues of ethics including authorship, bias, transparency, and distribution of agency between humans and machines. The results show that ethical reasoning and expressiveness cannot be discussed as two different competencies in AI-mediated literacy practices. Rather, their combination is a key to the responsible development of literacy, which has to keep creative experimentation based on critical awareness and human values.

To maintain human judgment in the more automated literacy ecosystems, purposeful pedagogic format, institutional leadership, and self-reflection on the part of both learners and instructors is necessary. When AI is framed as a partner tool and not an autocratic source of knowledge, learners will have fewer reasons to replicate agency creatively and challenge algorithmic control, as well as build knowledge meaningfully. On the negative side, blindly following the output of automated tools may lead to the loss of creative diversity and deterioration of the ethical sense of responsibility. The chapter emphasizes the necessity to prepare learners not only to utilize AI instruments, but design the meaning in a responsible way, question the platform dynamics, and maintain a human judgment in the light of automation. The future of literacy learning in the era of AI platforms will be founded upon the development of ethically mindful and creatively empowered individuals who are able to negotiate and shape multimodal knowledge spaces in a manner that will promote equity, responsibility, and human well-being.

REFERENCES

Aarthi, S., Ravikumar, R. N., Khudayberganov, S., Ismailov, A., & Khujaniyozova, O. (2025). Using Intelligent Tutoring Systems to enhance student engagement. In *Advances in Computational Intelligence and Robotics* (pp. 155–188). IGI Global. DOI: 10.4018/979-8-3373-1827-1.ch008

Akgun, S., & Greenhow, C. (2022). Artificial intelligence in education: Addressing ethical challenges in K-12 settings. *AI and Ethics*, *2*(3), 431–440. DOI: 10.1007/s43681-021-00096-7 PMID: 34790956

Alduais, A., Qadhi, S., Chaaban, Y., & Khraisheh, M. (2025). The ETHICAL protocol for responsible use of generative AI for research purposes in higher education. *AI Magazine*, *46*(4), e70047. Advance online publication. DOI: 10.1002/aaai.70047

Alotaibi, N. S., & Alshehri, A. H. (2023). Prospers and obstacles in using artificial intelligence in Saudi Arabia Higher Education institutions—The potential of AI-based learning outcomes. *Sustainability (Basel)*, *15*(13), 10723. DOI: 10.3390/su151310723

Amiri, S. M. H., Islam, M. M., & Akter, N. (2025). Educating the future: AI's role in shaping next-generation pedagogies. *International Journal of Science and Research Archive*, *15*(1), 621–636. DOI: 10.30574/ijsra.2025.15.1.1036

Apata, S. B., Owojori, O. M., Shogbesan, Y. O., & Ugom, M. K. (2025). Artificial intelligence and multiliteracies: Preparing learners for a technologically evolving world. *International Journal of Nursing Education*, *15*(15). Advance online publication. DOI: 10.24310/ijne.15.2025.21332

Brouwer, C. L., Dinkla, A. M., Vandewinckele, L., Crijns, W., Claessens, M., Verellen, D., & van Elmpt, W. (2020). Machine learning applications in radiation oncology: Current use and needs to support clinical implementation. *Physics and Imaging in Radiation Oncology*, *16*, 144–148. DOI: 10.1016/j.phro.2020.11.002 PMID: 33458358

Cohn, C., Snyder, C., & Fonteles, J. H., Ashwin, Montenegro, J., & Biswas, G. (. (2025). A multimodal approach to support teacher, researcher and AI collaboration in STEM +C learning environments. *British Journal of Educational Technology: Journal of the Council for Educational Technology*, *56*(2), 595–620. DOI: 10.1111/bjet.13518

Dahlquist, M. (2023). Toward a framework for information creativity. *College & Research Libraries*, *84*(3). Advance online publication. DOI: 10.5860/crl.84.3.441

Gideon, L.A. (2025). The role of Ai in English education: Opportunities, challenges, and future directions. *International Journal of Law, Politics and Humanities Research*. DOI: 10.70382/caijlphr.v9i6.057

Güneş, A., & Kaban, A. L. (2025). A Delphi study on ethical challenges and ensuring academic integrity regarding AI research in higher education. *Higher Education Quarterly*, *79*(4), e70057. Advance online publication. DOI: 10.1111/hequ.70057

Guo, Y.-X., & Zhang, X. (2025). The impact mechanism of algorithmic transparency on user trust in intelligent recommendation systems of internet platforms. *Journal of Computers*, •••, 335–348. DOI: 10.63367/199115992025063603022

Harry, A., & Sayudin, S. (2023). Role of AI in education. [INJURITY]. *Interdiciplinary Journal and Hummanity*, *2*(3), 260–268. DOI: 10.58631/injurity.v2i3.52

Hesti, D. A., Ozora, G., Silalahi, V. M., Hanoselina, Y., & Helmi, R. F. (2025). Pemberdayaan Siswa dan Siswi dalam Pemanfaatan Kecerdasan Buatan (AI) Secara Etis dan Produktif di Lingkungan Sekolah. *Sosial Simbiosis : Jurnal Integrasi Ilmu Sosial Dan Politik*, *2*(2), 163–178. DOI: 10.62383/sosial.v2i2.1588

Holmes, W., Porayska-Pomsta, K., Holstein, K., Sutherland, E., Baker, T., Shum, S. B., Santos, O. C., Rodrigo, M. T., Cukurova, M., Bittencourt, I. I., & Koedinger, K. R. (2022). Ethics of AI in education: Towards a community-wide framework. *International Journal of Artificial Intelligence in Education*, *32*(3), 504–526. DOI: 10.1007/s40593-021-00239-1

Hryciw, B. N., Seely, A. J. E., & Kyeremanteng, K. (2023). Guiding principles and proposed classification system for the responsible adoption of artificial intelligence in scientific writing in medicine. *Frontiers in Artificial Intelligence*, *6*, 1283353. DOI: 10.3389/frai.2023.1283353 PMID: 38035200

Ibrahim, A. B. (2024). Assessing the knowledge and perception of artificial intelligence for teaching and research among lecturers in the faculties of arts in Nigeria. *Journal of Global Research in Education and Social Science*, *18*(2), 25–33. DOI: 10.56557/jogress/2024/v18i28671

Ibrahim, R. A., & Lianingsih, N. (2025). Digital rhetoric and algorithmic ethics: A literature review of digital communication. *International Journal of Linguistics. Communication & Broadcasting*, *3*(2), 45–49. DOI: 10.46336/ijlcb.v3i2.224

Igbokwe, I. C. (2024). Artificial intelligence in educational leadership: Risks and responsibilities. *European Journal of Arts. Humanities and Social Sciences*, *1*(6), 3–10. DOI: 10.59324/ejahss.2024.1(6).01

Jobin, A., Ienca, M., & Vayena, E. (2019). The global landscape of AI ethics guidelines. *Nature Machine Intelligence*, *1*(9), 389–399. DOI: 10.1038/s42256-019-0088-2

Kooli, C. (2023). Chatbots in education and research: A critical examination of ethical implications and solutions. *Sustainability (Basel)*, *15*(7), 5614. DOI: 10.3390/su15075614

Kustini, S. (2023). A project-based multiliteracies instruction to improve students' multimodal literacy. In *Advances in Social Science, Education and Humanities Research* (pp. 632–647). Atlantis Press SARL. DOI: 10.2991/978-2-38476-054-1_54

Leander, K. M., & Burriss, S. K. (2020). Critical literacy for a posthuman world: When people read, and become, with machines. *British Journal of Educational Technology*, *51*(4), 1262–1276. DOI: 10.1111/bjet.12924

Li, J., & Huang, Q. (2025). Navigating ethical dilemmas in AI-enhanced education. *International Journal of Knowledge Management*, *21*(1), 1–21. DOI: 10.4018/IJKM.382384

Lin, C.-S. (2026). Co-creating with AI: How communication students learn, think, and rely on intelligent systems. *Journal of Educational Computing Research*, *64*(1), 155–179. DOI: 10.1177/07356331251385944

Lin, H.-C. K. (2025). Writing is Coding. *International Journal of Online Pedagogy and Course Design*, *15*(1), 1–23. DOI: 10.4018/IJOPCD.385016

Meylani, R. (2024). Artificial Intelligence in the education of teachers: A qualitative synthesis of the cutting-edge research literature. *Journal of Computer and Education Research (ISSN 2148-2896)*, *12*(24), 600–637. DOI: 10.18009/jcer.1477709

Nagapushpa, Kanchana, & Monish. (2024). Revolutionizing art and design through AI: Balancing innovation, Ethics, and future preparedness. *INTERANTIONAL JOURNAL OF SCIENTIFIC RESEARCH IN ENGINEERING AND MANAGEMENT*, *08*(11), 1–7. DOI: 10.55041/IJSREM38443

Ng, D. T. K., Leung, J. K. L., Chu, K. W. S., & Qiao, M. S. (2021). AI literacy: Definition, teaching, evaluation and ethical issues. *Proceedings of the Association for Information Science and Technology*, *58*(1), 504–509. DOI: 10.1002/pra2.487

Oermann, M. H., Owens, J. K., Carter-Templeton, H., Peterson, G., & Bailey, H. E. (2025). Using artificial intelligence for scholarly writing. *The American Journal of Nursing*, *125*(11), 52–55. DOI: 10.1097/AJN.0000000000000179 PMID: 41128585

Ojeda-Ramirez, S., Ritchie, D., & Warschauer, M. (2024). AI literacy for multilingual learners: Storytelling, role-playing, and programming. *The CATESOL Journal, 35*(1). Advance online publication. DOI: 10.5070/B5.35861

Peng, P., Xu, L., Ng, D. T. K., Lee, C. S. Y., & Chu, S. K. W. (2025). Exploring the impact of AI -generated image, story and song creations on AI literacy and well-being among older adults: A mixed-methods study. *Proceedings of the Association for Information Science and Technology, 62*(1), 1045–1050. DOI: 10.1002/pra2.1337

Qi, W. (2023). Developing multimodal literacy in the Business English reading class: A case study of students' presentation PowerPoint slides. *Journal of Language Teaching and Research, 14*(3), 820–827. DOI: 10.17507/jltr.1403.30

Rafique, G. M., Mughari, S., & Khan, H. A. (2025). Unlocking potential: The role of AI literacy and creativity in medical librarians' task performance in Pakistan. *Information Development, 41*(3), 559–575. DOI: 10.1177/02666669251325444

Ranes, B. (2025). AI integration in facilitating learning: Its benefits, challenges and strategies for enhancement. *Divine Word International Journal of Management and Humanities (DWIJMH) (ISSN: 2980-4817), 4*(3), 2095–2109. DOI: 10.62025/dwijmh.v4i3.181

Ravikumar, R. N., Aarthi, S., Rai, P. K., & Mamadiyarov, Z. (2025). Intelligent code analysis and feedback generation. In *Advances in Computational Intelligence and Robotics* (pp. 137–170). IGI Global Scientific Publishing. DOI: 10.4018/979-8-3373-0598-1.ch006

Ravikumar, R. N., Aarthi, S., Ruzimova, F., & Mamadiyarov, Z. (2025). Training and development in AI-driven education scaling solutions. In *Advances in Computational Intelligence and Robotics* (pp. 267–298). IGI Global Scientific Publishing. DOI: 10.4018/979-8-3373-2185-1.ch010

Ray, S., & Ray, D. P. (2024). Artificial Intelligence in education: Navigating the nexus of innovation and ethics for future learning landscapes. *International Journal of Research -GRANTHAALAYAH, 11*(12). DOI: 10.29121/granthaalayah.v11.i12.2023.5464

Rowsell, J., & Walsh, M. (2011). Rethinking literacy education in new times: Multimodality, multiliteracies, & new literacies. *Brock Education Journal, 21*(1). Advance online publication. DOI: 10.26522/brocked.v21i1.236

Samo, A., & Highhouse, S. (2025). Artificial intelligence and art: Identifying the aesthetic judgment factors that distinguish human- and machine-generated artwork. *Psychology of Aesthetics, Creativity, and the Arts, 19*(5), 1084–1098. DOI: 10.1037/aca0000570

Solanke Shweta A, P., & Assistant Professor PR Pote Patil College of Engineering and Management Amravati Maharashtra India Southern Asia, C. S. E. D. (2024). The prospects of generative AI in higher education. *INTERANTIONAL JOURNAL OF SCIENTIFIC RESEARCH IN ENGINEERING AND MANAGEMENT, 08*(05), 1–5. DOI: 10.55041/IJSREM32533

Sutrisno, D., Abidin, N. A. Z., Pambudi, N., Aydawati, E., & Sallu, S. (2024). Exploring the benefits of multimodal literacy in English teaching: Engaging students through visual, auditory, and digital modes. *Global Synthesis in Education Journal, 1*(2), 1–14. DOI: 10.61667/xh184f41

Tan, T., Yan, Y., Yuan, X., & Gao, Z. (2025). Shaping Sustainable Futures on T ik T ok? Media Literacy, Youth Education and the SDG s. *European Journal of Education, 60*(4), e70270. Advance online publication. DOI: 10.1111/ejed.70270

Van Brummelen, J., Heng, T., & Tabunshchyk, V. (2021). Teaching tech to talk: K-12 conversational artificial intelligence literacy curriculum and development tools. *Proceedings of the AAAI Conference on Artificial Intelligence, 35*(17), 15655–15663. DOI: 10.1609/aaai.v35i17.17844

Vartiainen, H., & Tedre, M. (2024). How text-to-image generative AI is transforming mediated action. *IEEE Computer Graphics and Applications, 44*(2), 12–22. DOI: 10.1109/MCG.2024.3355808 PMID: 38285567

Wu, Q., Li, B. J., & Zhang, H. (2025). Observers, seekers, and professionals in AI adoption: An investigation of AI divide through social cognitive perspective. *Proceedings of the Association for Information Science and Technology, 62*(1), 1121–1125. DOI: 10.1002/pra2.1350

Yan, Y., Liu, H., & Chau, T. (2025). A systematic review of AI ethics in education. *Journal of Global Information Management, 33*(1), 1–50. DOI: 10.4018/JGIM.386381

Yim, I. H. Y., & Su, J. (2024). Artificial intelligence (AI) learning tools in K-12 education: A scoping review. *Journal of Computers in Education*. Advance online publication. DOI: 10.1007/s40692-023-00304-9

Yim, I. H. Y., & Wegerif, R. (2024). *Teachers' perceptions, attitudes, and acceptance of artificial intelligence (AI) educational learning tools: An exploratory study on AI literacy for young students*. Future in Educational Research., DOI: 10.1002/fer3.65

Zawacki-Richter, O., Marín, V. I., Bond, M., & Gouverneur, F. (2019). Systematic review of research on artificial intelligence applications in higher education – where are the educators? *International Journal of Educational Technology in Higher Education, 16*(1), 39. Advance online publication. DOI: 10.1186/s41239-019-0171-0

Zhang, H., Lee, I., Ali, S., DiPaola, D., Cheng, Y., & Breazeal, C. (2022). Integrating ethics and career futures with technical learning to promote AI literacy for middle school students: An exploratory study. *International Journal of Artificial Intelligence in Education, 33*(2), 1–35. DOI: 10.1007/s40593-022-00293-3 PMID: 35573722

Zhang, S., Ganapathy Prasad, P., & Schroeder, N. L. (2025). Learning about AI: A systematic review of reviews on AI literacy. *Journal of Educational Computing Research, 63*(5), 1292–1322. DOI: 10.1177/07356331251342081

KEY TERMS AND DEFINITIONS

Algorithmic Mediation: The influence of algorithms in shaping what content is generated, recommended, or prioritized within digital platforms

Artificial Intelligence (AI): Computer-based systems that perform tasks such as generating content, recognizing patterns, and making recommendations that typically require human intelligence.

Authorship: The recognition of human responsibility and ownership in content creation, even when AI tools contribute to the process.

Bias in AI: Systematic preferences or distortions in AI-generated outputs that result from training data, model design, or platform assumptions.

Creative Agency: The capacity of learners to make intentional choices, modify ideas, and produce original multimodal content rather than relying solely on automated outputs.

Ethical Literacy: The ability to critically understand and evaluate the ethical implications of AI use, including issues of bias, transparency, responsibility, and fairness.

Human–AI Collaboration: A mode of interaction in which humans and AI systems work together in creative or learning activities, with humans retaining decision-making authority.

Learner Agency: The extent to which learners actively control and shape their learning processes and outcomes in AI-mediated environments.

Multimodal Literacy: The ability to create, interpret, and communicate meaning using multiple modes such as text, images, audio, video, and interactive media.

Platform-Based Literacy: Literacy practices that occur within digital platforms where content is shaped by interfaces, algorithms, and user interaction.

Chapter 6

Designing AI-Mediated Multimodal Literacy Pedagogy and Translanguaging in K-12 and Higher Education:

Frameworks, Classroom Models, and Policy Pathways

Ashraf Alam
http://orcid.org/0000-0001-6178-1187
Department of Education, National Institute of Technology Calicut, India

ABSTRACT

This chapter interrogates AI-mediated multimodal literacy as a composite capability that entwines cognitive, affective, social, and infrastructural strata across K-12 and higher education. It synthesises New Literacy Studies, multimodality, multiliteracies, translanguaging, critical literacy, and posthuman-sociomaterial lenses to reconceptualise texts as algorithmically curated, synthetically generated semiotic ensembles. The chapter develops typologies of AI systems, an ecological framework, and comparative matrices of curriculum, pedagogy, assessment, and governance, situating AI as co-author, curator, assessor, and infrastructural condition. It foregrounds critical AI literacy, data justice, algorithmic fairness, and epistemic plurality to articulate normative architectures for just and sustainable design. The chapter advances actionable imaginaries for educators, policy makers,

DOI: 10.4018/979-8-3373-6986-0.ch006

and technologists who must orchestrate AI-infused translanguaging and multimodal practices while safeguarding democratic agency, cultural-linguistic diversity, and ethical accountability.

INTRODUCTION

Situating Multimodal Literacy in the Age of AI

Multimodal literacy is increasingly constituted within an expanded mediascape in which textual, visual, auditory, spatial, gestural, and computational codes interpenetrate through networked infrastructures and intelligent systems. The historical transition from print-centric regimes to screen-based ecologies has been intensified by the proliferation of generative and analytic artificial intelligence that composes, curates, and evaluates complex semiotic ensembles at unprecedented speed and scale (Carcamo, 2025; Lin et al., 2025; Maamuujav, 2025). In this conjuncture, learners in K-12 and higher education inhabit communicative environments where essays coexist with memes, podcasts, interactive simulations, dashboards, and synthetic images, all orchestrated through opaque recommendation engines and predictive models. AI does not simply augment existing literacies, it reconfigures the conditions under which texts are authored, circulated, and legitimated, while simultaneously reshaping what counts as rigour, originality, and criticality. Multimodal literacy in the age of AI therefore involves not only decoding and producing multi-channel artefacts, but also apprehending how intelligent infrastructures shape perception, attention, and epistemic authority.

Purpose, Scope, and Conceptual Orientation

This chapter develops a dense conceptual-theoretical cartography of *AI-mediated multimodal literacy* and *translanguaging* in K-12 and higher education that can orient curriculum design, classroom orchestration, and policy deliberation in diverse jurisdictions. Its scope spans formal institutions, para-institutional spaces such as makerspaces and writing centres, and informal ecologies such as social platforms, fan communities, and gaming environments that increasingly leak into classroom repertoires. The argument foregrounds literacy as *socio-technical practice* shaped by assemblages of hardware, software, data infrastructures, institutional norms, and human actors, rather than as discrete individual skills. The chapter mobilises constructs such as *multimodality*, *pluriliteracies*, *critical AI literacy*, *algorithmic culture*, and *epistemic justice* to articulate how AI systems become semiotic resources, cognitive partners, and governance mechanisms. The orientation is diagnostic and prospective at once, mapping existing conceptual terrains while also projecting plausible design pathways for future-ready, justice-oriented literacy education.

Guiding Questions and Core Problems

The analysis is structured around several interlocking problematics that underpin contemporary debates on AI and literacy. A first problematic concerns the meaning of being *multimodally literate* when large language models, image generators, and multimodal architectures participate in authoring and reauthoring texts, thereby destabilising inherited notions of authorship, creativity, and textual fixity. A second problematic addresses how constructs such as *New Literacy Studies*, *multimodality*, and *translanguaging* require reinterpretation once algorithmic curation, synthetic media, and predictive analytics saturate communicative ecologies. A third problematic interrogates the tensions between human judgement and automated optimisation, between open-ended critical inquiry and platform-driven engagement metrics, and between translanguaging repertoires and AI systems that normalise dominant languages and registers. A fourth problematic asks how pedagogical agency can be sustained when infrastructures, interfaces, and corporate standards preconfigure what teachers and learners can do with AI-mediated semiotic materials.

Audience and Positionality

The chapter addresses a heterogeneous readership that includes literacy scholars, applied linguists, curriculum experts, policy makers, school and university leaders, EdTech architects, and workforce-development professionals concerned with emerging competency frameworks. It assumes no singular disciplinary vantage point, but instead adopts a *transdisciplinary positionality* that treats education, linguistics, media studies, human-computer interaction, science and technology studies, and public policy as mutually informing lenses on the same socio-technical field. The contribution to the volume is threefold. Conceptually, it synthesises diverse constructs into an integrated account of AI-mediated multimodal literacy and translanguaging that is portable across sectors and systems. Architecturally, it proposes a multi-level framework that links classroom practices with institutional governance and macro-level policy imaginaries. Pragmatically, it offers typologies, matrices, and design logics that can be operationalised in curricular blueprints, professional learning programmes, and regulatory instruments without prescribing uniform templates.

Chapter Architecture and Method of Conceptual Synthesis

The chapter unfolds through a seven-part architecture that progressively thickens the conceptualisation of AI-mediated multimodal literacy. An initial foundational section reconstructs key theoretical lenses for understanding multimodal and translingual meaning-making in technologically saturated societies. A subsequent section interrogates AI, algorithmic culture, and platformisation as generative conditions for contemporary semiotic ecologies. A central section articulates an explicit multi-level framework that organises cognitive, affective, social, ethical, spatial, and infrastructural dimensions across learner, institutional, and systemic scales. This framework is then used to structure a conceptual treatment of curriculum, pedagogy, assessment, and teacher professionalism, followed by an exploration of ethics, governance, and policy imaginaries. Throughout, the chapter employs *narrative synthesis* and *conceptual mapping* as its primary methods, weaving constructs from multiple traditions into a coherent yet flexible schema. The concluding section crystallises cross-cutting insights and delineates normative commitments and future-oriented questions for an international community of practice.

THEORETICAL AND HISTORICAL FOUNDATIONS OF MULTIMODAL LITERACY

Moving from Autonomous Literacy Paradigms to Social Practice Perspectives

Theoretical accounts of literacy have shifted from autonomous skill taxonomies toward social practice perspectives that foreground contextual, relational, and power-saturated dimensions of meaning-making. Autonomous paradigms treat reading and writing as decontextualised cognitive routines that can be discretised into hierarchies of subskills and measured through standardised items, while social practice perspectives conceptualise literacy as patterned participation in *literacy events* and *literacy practices* that are organised by institutions, norms, and material infrastructures (Alam & Mohanty, 2024; Pool et al., 2023; Sari, 2025). Within this latter orientation, literacy is configured through *sponsorship*, gatekeeping, and recognition regimes that privilege certain genres, languages, and registers over others. When intelligent systems are layered onto these pre-existing hierarchies, AI-mediated text production and evaluation become additional mechanisms through which sponsorship operates (Lim, 2024; Serafini, 2023; Warriner, 2023). Learners in K-12 and higher education do not simply acquire neutral skills, they are inducted into socio-technical orders in which multimodal artefacts, assessment rubrics, and

AI-driven platforms collectively define what counts as legitimate literacy, authorship, and academic voice.

Multimodality, Social Semiotics, and Semiotic Repertoires

Within the *multimodality* and social semiotics tradition, meaning making is theorised as the orchestration of multiple modes, such as linguistic, visual, spatial, gestural, numeric, and auditory resources, each with distinct affordances, constraints, and histories of use. Texts are treated as *designed ensembles* in which sign-makers select, configure, and hybridise semiotic resources in response to audience expectations, genre conventions, and material conditions of production (Löfgren, 2025; López-Pérez & Bobadilla-Pérez, 2023; Mulcahy & Shaw, 2024). This view foregrounds *semiotic repertoires*, the heterogeneous arrays of scripts, symbols, emojis, diagrams, graphs, screenshots, animations, and interface conventions that learners mobilise to perform identities and construct knowledge. AI-mediated tools intensify this design space by generating synthetic images, adaptive layouts, and predictive prompts that pre-structure multimodal composition (Dewanthi et al., 2024; Kang & Kim, 2024; Saputra et al., 2024). In such ecologies, multimodal literacy involves meta-awareness of modal choice, cross-modal coherence, and the politics of default templates, as well as the capacity to improvise with, resist, or repurpose AI-generated configurations in ways that align with ethical, epistemic, and disciplinary commitments.

Multiliteracies, Translanguaging, and Pluriliteracies in AI-Saturated Ecologies

The construct of *multiliteracies* extends this semiotic orientation by emphasising global mobility, linguistic heterogeneity, and the proliferation of digital genres that require flexible navigation across languages, registers, and modes. It introduces pedagogical heuristics such as *situated practice*, *overt instruction*, *critical framing*, and *transformed practice* that support learners in moving between everyday repertoires and specialised discourses (Alam & Mohanty, 2023; Almeida et al., 2023; Rasul et al., 2023). *Translanguaging* and *pluriliteracies* further conceptualise learners as agents who fluidly mobilise multiple languages and disciplinary semiotics as a unified repertoire rather than as compartmentalised systems. Within AI-saturated ecologies, these constructs intersect with automated translation, speech recognition, and large language models that tend to normalise certain lingua francas, standard registers, and textual genres (Al Farabi & Rohmah, 2023; Henderson, 2023; Wong, 2025). The interaction between human translanguaging practices and machine translation pipelines generates complex dynamics of amplification, erasure, and reconfiguration that require careful theoretical articulation. These convergences are systematically contrasted with other lenses in Table 1, which synthesises how major theoretical traditions construe text, technology, and pedagogy under AI-mediated conditions.

Critical Literacy, Algorithmic Mediation, and Comparative Theoretical Synthesis

Critical literacy and *critical media literacy* position texts as sites of ideological struggle, where representational choices enact and naturalise particular social orders. Within this perspective, learners interrogate how narratives, images, and interfaces encode power relations, marginalise voices, and construct normative identities (Amer, 2025; Hashim et al., 2024; Pereira et al., 2023). Algorithmic mediation introduces new layers to this critique, since AI systems curate, personalise, and often generate the multimodal artefacts that circulate in classrooms and platforms. Recommendation engines, scoring algorithms, and generative models participate in shaping visibility, credibility, and affective resonance, which means that critical literacy must now extend to *critical AI literacy* that scrutinises data provenance, model assumptions, and platform governance (Guo & Wang, 2024; Hadjiconstantinou, 2023; Lim & Unsworth, 2023). To scaffold such analysis, Table 1 presents a comparative matrix of theoretical lenses, clarifying how each frames the nature of text, the role of technology, and the design of literacy pedagogy in AI-intensive environments.

Table 1. Comparative Theoretical Lenses for AI-Mediated Multimodal Literacy

Theoretical Lens	Core Conceptual Constructs	View of Text and Mode	Configuration of Technology and AI	Implications for Literacy Pedagogy
New Literacy Studies	Literacy as social practice, ideological model, sponsorship, situated participation	Text as socially embedded event, modes as culturally regulated resources	Technology and AI as institutional mediators that structure access, participation, and recognition	Pedagogy foregrounds communities, practices, and power, cultivates critical participation in socio-technical orders
Multimodality	Semiotic resources, modal affordances, design, orchestration, intersemiotic cohesion	Text as designed multimodal ensemble, modes as complementary and tension-filled channels	Technology and AI as expanded design palettes and layout engines that shape semiotic configuration	Pedagogy emphasises design thinking, cross-modal reasoning, and reflexive choice of semiotic resources
Multiliteracies and Translanguaging	Plurilingual repertoires, situated practice, critical framing, transformed practice, fluid language use	Text as hybrid configuration of languages and modes, oriented to diverse lifeworlds	Technology and AI as translators, mediators, and potential normalisers of dominant codes	Pedagogy valorises hybrid repertoires, designs tasks that integrate languages, modes, and AI tools in equitable ways
Critical and Media Literacy	Ideology, discourse, representation, hegemony, audience positioning, critical AI literacy	Text as ideological artefact, modes as vehicles of power and affect	Technology and AI as opaque infrastructures that shape visibility, bias, and affective economies	Pedagogy cultivates interrogation of algorithms, data flows, and platform architectures in relation to justice
Posthuman and Sociomaterial Perspectives	Assemblages, relational agency, material-discursive entanglement, actor-networks	Text as emergent from human-nonhuman couplings, modes as material-semiotic actants	Technology and AI as co-actors within assemblages that redistribute agency and responsibility	Pedagogy explores entanglements of bodies, tools, spaces, and codes, fosters ethical awareness of distributed agency

Table 1 functions as a conceptual hinge that links foundational theories of literacy with the specific challenges introduced by AI-mediated multimodality. By juxtaposing the lenses along dimensions such as view of text, configuration of technology, and pedagogical implications, the matrix highlights complementarities and tensions that might otherwise remain implicit. It invites educators, curriculum designers, and policy makers to consider which theoretical emphases they privilege when interpreting AI tools in classrooms, whether they foreground community participation, multimodal design, linguistic hybridity, ideological critique, or distributed agency.

This synthetic mapping also prepares the ground for the multi-level framework elaborated later in the chapter, where these lenses are re-situated within cognitive, social, ethical, and infrastructural strata of educational ecologies.

Postdigital, Posthuman, and Sociomaterial Approaches to AI-Mediated Multimodal Literacy

Postdigital, posthuman, and *sociomaterial* approaches argue that contemporary literacy cannot be understood through binary oppositions such as online and offline, human and machine, analog and digital. Instead, literacy practices are conceptualised as emergent phenomena within assemblages that couple bodies, devices, data streams, architectures, and regulatory regimes (Ledy, 2023; Parker, 2024; Sultan, 2023). The postdigital construct treats digitality as an ordinary, infrastructural condition rather than as an exceptional novelty, which aligns with classrooms where AI-driven tools are woven into routine tasks such as drafting, searching, captioning, and translating. Posthuman and sociomaterial perspectives extend this insight by attributing relational agency to nonhuman entities, including sensors, interfaces, algorithms, and datasets (Afifah et al., 2023; Indhra et al., 2025). When read alongside the lenses in Table 1, these approaches foreground questions of responsibility, accountability, and care in distributed networks where no single actor controls the semiotic outcomes. For AI-mediated multimodal literacy, they encourage educators to design pedagogies that sensitise learners to these entanglements, while still affirming human ethical obligations within complex assemblages.

AI, ALGORITHMIC CULTURE, AND SEMIOTIC ECOLOGIES

Mapping Contemporary AI for Multimodal Literacy

Artificial intelligence in contemporary education comprises a heterogeneous ensemble of computational architectures that reconfigure how texts are generated, classified, and circulated across multimodal channels. Large language models operationalise probabilistic language modelling and transformer-based attention to synthesise extended textual artefacts, while image and video generators instantiate diffusion, generative adversarial, and hybrid architectures to fabricate visual and audiovisual representations aligned with textual prompts (Komninos, 2023; Linder & Falk-Ross, 2024; Sofkova Hashemi, 2025). Speech recognition and synthesis pipelines convert between acoustic and orthographic codes, and machine translation systems perform cross-linguistic mapping that collapses spatial and temporal distance between discourse communities. Recommendation engines and predictive analytics orchestrate exposure to texts, videos, and interactive objects within learning platforms and social media, thereby curating the semiotic diet of learners (Alam & Mohanty, 2022; Harrington & Cox, 2024; Ryu & Kim, 2024). For K-12 and higher education, these AI strata act simultaneously as compositional resources, feedback mechanisms, and gatekeeping filters, which demands a fine-grained typology of their semiotic affordances and constraints, subsequently crystallised in the comparative schema of Table 2.

Algorithmic Culture, Platformization, and Data Infrastructures in Education

The construct of *algorithmic culture* captures how algorithmic procedures progressively mediate symbolic production, reception, and valuation within educational environments. Learning management systems, search engines, and social platforms implement ranking, recommendation, and filtering logics that operationalise engagement metrics, behavioural traces, and inferred preferences, resulting in highly stratified information ecologies (Hartmann, 2025; Tan et al., 2023; Tchetgen, 2025). Platformization in education embeds curricular resources, assessment artefacts, and communicative exchanges within corporate or institutionally controlled ecosystems that centralise authentication, data storage, and analytic dashboards. These ecosystems rely on extensive data infrastructures, including cloud architectures, content delivery networks, telemetry pipelines, and model hosting environments that collectively condition latency, availability, and scalability of AI services (Analido & Pratiwi, 2025; Duraisamy, 2025; Liu & Lo, 2025). For multimodal literacy, this means that textual and non-textual materials appear in patterned sequences that are co-produced by human design choices and machine-driven optimisation routines. The typological distinctions articulated in Table 2 help clarify how different AI subsystems participate in these algorithmic cultures, and how they differentially shape learner exposure to multimodal texts.

AI as Co-Author, Tutor, and Semiotic Resource in Literacy Ecologies

In AI-intensive learning environments, the conceptualisation of AI as mere instructional tool is insufficient, since intelligent systems increasingly participate as co-authors, tutors, critics, and semiotic resources in their own right. When learners compose essays with predictive text, storyboard narratives with synthetic images, or rehearse oral presentations with speech synthesis, cognitive work is distributed across human and machine agencies (Lubis, 2025; Midgette et al., 2023; Lubis, 2025; Yakubu & Obafemi, 2023). Metaphors such as AI as collaborator, mentor, or muse therefore acquire operational significance, because they structure expectations about initiative, responsibility, and epistemic authority in the composing process. Within this landscape, Table 2 Comparative Typology of AI Systems for Literacy Education organises key AI genres according to their outputs, metaphoric framing, and affordance profiles, thereby providing a concise conceptual map for educators and policy architects who must decide how to position these systems within curriculum and governance frameworks.

Table 2. Comparative Typology of AI Systems for Literacy Education

AI System Archetype	Dominant Semiotic Outputs	Pedagogical Metaphor and Role	Core Affordances for Multimodal Literacy	Salient Risks for Educational Ecologies
Large Language Models	Long-form text, dialogic scripts, code, analytic summaries	Co-author, discourse simulator, meta-commentator	Rapid text synthesis, genre emulation, scaffolded drafting, metalinguistic exploration	Homogenisation of style, erosion of authorial agency, amplification of discursive bias
Image and Video Generators	Synthetic images, diagrams, storyboards, short video clips	Visual muse, design assistant, representational surrogate	Expansion of visual vocabulary, rapid prototyping, multimodal storytelling, speculative visualization	Visual stereotyping, aesthetic standardisation, misalignment with factual referents
Speech and Translation Systems	Transcripts, captions, translations, voice clones	Polyglot mediator, accessibility enabler, pronunciation coach	Cross-linguistic mediation, captioning, oral rehearsal, inclusion of diverse language users	Reinforcement of dominant language hierarchies, imperfect semantic transfer, dependency on machine renderings
Recommendation and Personalization Engines	Ranked content streams, adaptive task lists, targeted alerts	Invisible curator, cognitive prosthesis, engagement orchestrator	Tailored resource exposure, adaptive difficulty, optimised practice scheduling	Filter bubbles, attention capture, opaque prioritisation of commercial or ideological content
Analytic and Assessment Algorithms	Scores, dashboards, risk flags, formative feedback strings	Automated assessor, diagnostic lens, predictive monitor	Fine-grained process analytics, pattern detection, longitudinal progress visualisation	Reduction of complex literacies to metrics, surveillance intensification, self-fulfilling labelling

The typology in Table 2 renders explicit the semiotic and pedagogical functions of distinct AI archetypes, enabling stakeholders to differentiate between systems that primarily generate artefacts, those that curate and sequence content, and those that evaluate learner performance. By pairing each archetype with metaphoric roles and risk constellations, the schema foregrounds the imaginative frames through which educators and learners understand intelligent systems. It highlights the necessity of designing classroom practices that encourage learners to interrogate, contest, and reconfigure these metaphors rather than passively inhabiting them. The matrix also illustrates how the same AI class can afford both emancipatory and constraining possibilities, depending on institutional norms, governance arrangements, and the extent to which critical metacognition about AI is cultivated within literacy curricula.

Datafication, Surveillance, and Temporal Regimes of AI-Mediated Text Production

AI-mediated multimodal literacy operates within regimes of *datafication* in which reading, writing, viewing, and interaction are continuously logged as machine-readable traces, then aggregated into behavioural profiles and predictive features. These traces feed surveillance infrastructures that monitor engagement, dwell time, error patterns, and emotional proxies, often represented as dashboards or risk indicators for teachers and administrators (Domínguez Romero et al., 2023; Hardukiewicz, 2024; Rocamora & Baguio, 2025). Temporal structures of literacy activity are also reconfigured, since generative AI compresses the time required to draft, revise, and translate texts, while recommendation engines accelerate exposure to new artefacts. This temporal compression can erode slow reflection, iterative experimentation, and dialogic negotiation that traditionally underpin deep literacy learning (Mills et al., 2025; Moalla, 2023). At the same time, analytic systems that are typified in Table 2 promise real-time feedback and personalised pacing, which can either support or undermine learner agency depending on how they are integrated. Understanding AI-mediated literacy therefore requires close attention to how data flows, monitoring practices, and temporal logics intersect with classroom norms and institutional expectations.

AI as Actor and Assemblage in Semiotic Ecologies

From *actor-network* and *sociomaterial* perspectives, AI systems are not peripheral instruments but actants embedded within assemblages that link learners, teachers, devices, platforms, architectures, and regulatory norms. In a typical literacy task that uses generative text and image tools, agency is distributed across algorithms, prompt histories, interface affordances, institutional policies, and local interpretive communities (Alam, 2023c; Cappello & Ojeda, 2023; Mills et al., 2023). These assemblages are dynamic, since software updates, policy shifts, bandwidth fluctuations, and changing platform business models can rapidly alter the semiotic possibilities available to learners. Conceptualising AI as actor within assemblages therefore changes how responsibility, accountability, and design agency are allocated (Kustini, 2023; Lam & Putri, 2024; Wang & Hao, 2025). It becomes necessary to scrutinise not only human choices, but also how default configurations, pre-trained models, and infrastructural dependencies participate in shaping multimodal artefacts and literacy trajectories. This assemblage perspective provides the conceptual bridge to the multi-level framework developed in the next section, where micro-level learner activities, meso-level institutional cultures, and macro-level regulatory regimes are articulated as mutually entangled strata of AI-mediated multimodal literacy.

MULTI-LEVEL CONCEPTUAL FRAMEWORK FOR AI-MEDIATED MULTIMODAL LITERACY

Defining AI-Mediated Multimodal Literacy as Composite Capability

AI-mediated multimodal literacy can be conceptualised as a composite capability that integrates operational fluency with intelligent systems, sophisticated multimodal design competences, and reflexive critical judgement within complex socio-technical ecologies. It involves facility with configuring linguistic, visual, auditory, gestural, and numeric resources in interaction with generative and analytic engines, together with the capacity to anticipate how algorithms will curate, weight, and redistribute those artefacts (Fortanet-Gómez & Querol-Julián, 2025; Seneechai & Ampon, 2025; Sodiq et al., 2023). This capability is not reducible to tool-specific proficiency, since it includes meta-level understanding of how prompts, parameters, and training data shape outputs, and how interface affordances and institutional norms govern acceptable use. It also entails ethical discernment, such as recognising when engagement with *AI-mediated multimodal texts* amplifies or diminishes autonomy, privacy, and epistemic plurality. The multi-level character of this capability, stretching from individual cognition to planetary infrastructures, requires a structured framework that can systematically relate micro, meso, and macro dynamics, which is subsequently synthesised in the matrix presented in Table 3.

Cognitive, Metacognitive, and Affective Dimensions Across Levels

Cognitive, metacognitive, and affective processes form an intricate triad within *AI-mediated multimodal literacy*, and each process operates simultaneously at individual, collective, and institutional planes. At the cognitive plane, learners parse polysemic artefacts that combine text, image, sound, and data visualisation, often in real time, while also interpreting AI-generated suggestions that may subtly steer reasoning (Bretaño, 2025; Brown et al., 2023; Makinde et al., 2025). Metacognitively, learners must plan when to invoke AI for brainstorming, drafting, translation, or critique, monitor the epistemic reliability of outputs, and evaluate when human-only reflection is pedagogically or ethically preferable. Affective dynamics, including curiosity, fascination, over-trust, under-trust, anxiety, and techno-fatigue, modulate willingness to experiment and to scrutinise algorithmic authority (Dada & Akande, 2025; Suhaimi & Permatasari, 2024; Unsworth, 2025). These dynamics are themselves shaped by classroom discourses, institutional messaging, and broader cultural narratives about automation. The interplay of cognitive, metacognitive, and affective dimensions at multiple scales is more fully articulated in the multi-level matrix in Table 3, which renders visible how these processes are anchored in specific socio-material conditions.

Social, Cultural, and Identity Configurations in Multi-Level Perspective

Social, cultural, and identity-related configurations exert a powerful influence on how *AI-mediated multimodal literacy* is enacted and valued across educational strata. At the micro level, learners bring heterogeneous funds of knowledge, language repertoires, and platform experiences that modulate how they interact with intelligent systems and interpret synthetic outputs (Arellano, 2024; Beltrán-Palanques, 2023; Yaşar & Arı, 2023). At the meso level, classroom norms, departmental cultures, and disciplinary epistemologies define whether AI-supported composing is recognised as legitimate scholarly practice or stigmatised as inauthentic. At the macro level, national language regimes, media narratives, and global platform policies codify hierarchies among languages, genres, and semiotic forms. These layered dynamics can be systematically examined through a multi-level matrix that aligns cognitive-affective, social-cultural, ethical, and infrastructural dimensions. Table 3 Multi-Level Matrix for AI-Mediated Literacy Ecologies crystallises these relationships in a compact comparative format that supports diagnosis and design across K-12 and higher education systems.

Table 3. Multi-Level Matrix for AI-Mediated Literacy Ecologies

Systemic Stratum	Cognitive-Affective Configuration	Social-Cultural and Identity Configuration	Critical-Ethical Orientation	Spatial-Material-Infrastructural Configuration
Micro-Level Learner Practices	Distributed cognition with AI, metacognitive regulation of prompting, calibration of trust, emotional responses to automation	Peer interaction around AI tools, identity performance as competent user or resister, negotiation of language repertoires	Personal stance toward fairness and authenticity, awareness of data shadows, everyday ethical decision-making	Access to devices and connectivity, interface ergonomics, local availability of multimodal tools
Meso-Level Classroom and Program Cultures	Collective norms for task design, shared routines for iterative drafting with AI, teacher modelling of reflective tool use	Discursive framing of AI in syllabi, assessment rubrics, and feedback, disciplinary expectations for genre and voice	Governance of permissible uses, academic integrity regimes, negotiated classroom charters for responsible AI engagement	Classroom layouts, platform selection, institutional licensing, integration with learning management systems
Macro-Level Policy and Governance Regimes	Oversight of cognitive and affective risks, large-scale monitoring discourse, high-stakes testing logics	National language policies, media narratives on automation, cultural valorisation of specific literacies	Regulatory frameworks for data protection, algorithmic transparency, equity directives for marginalised groups	Telecommunication infrastructures, cloud provisioning, standard-setting for interoperability and accessibility
Cross-Level Feedback and Amplification Loops	Propagation of local experimentation into systemic expectations, normalisation of accelerated production cycles	Translation of classroom practices into policy exemplars, circulation of best-practice narratives	Institutionalisation of ethical norms, codification of acceptable AI literacies, emergence of audit cultures	Recursive dependence on vendor ecosystems, scaling of pilots into platform lock-in, infrastructural path dependence
Transversal Design and Professional Learning Structures	Metacognitive training programmes, reflective supervision, and coaching for educators and leaders	Professional communities of practice, cross-institutional networks, student advisory councils	Ethics guidelines, scenario-based deliberation forums, participatory governance bodies	Innovation hubs, sandbox environments, hybrid physical-digital studios, shared resource repositories

Table 3 makes explicit that *AI-mediated multimodal literacy* cannot be analytically reduced to individual competences or isolated classroom practices, because each row describes how particular cognitive and affective dynamics are entangled with social and infrastructural arrangements. At the micro stratum, learner experiences with prompts and platforms are inseparable from the availability of devices and the implicit norms circulating among peers. At the meso stratum, assessment regimes and curriculum blueprints either amplify or dampen reflexive use of intelligent systems. At the macro stratum, data protection laws, infrastructural investments, and language policies shape which AI services are accessible and which literacies are incentivised. Cross-level feedback loops and transversal design structures capture how innovations, resistances, and regulatory shifts cascade across the matrix, producing path-dependent trajectories that any serious reform effort must take into account.

Critical, Ethical, Spatial, and Infrastructural Strata of Literacy

Critical, ethical, spatial, and infrastructural strata infuse every level of the framework, transforming *AI-mediated multimodal literacy* into a site of normative contestation. Critical literacy orientations demand that learners and educators interrogate how synthetic texts, curated feeds, and automated scores reproduce or disrupt existing hierarchies of race, gender, class, language, and ability (Kalan, 2024; Lysne, 2023; Satar et al., 2023). Ethical considerations encompass data minimisation, informed consent, accountability for harmful outputs, and the ecological costs of large-scale computation. Spatially, the distribution of connected devices, projection surfaces, and quiet zones shapes whose multimodal contributions become visible, while infrastructurally, choices about proprietary versus open platforms, local versus cloud processing, and centralised versus federated data storage reconfigure power relations. Within the schema outlined in Table 3, these strata operate as transversal vectors, cutting across micro, meso, and macro levels, and reminding designers that any intervention in AI-supported literacy is also an intervention in architectures of visibility, surveillance, and collective memory.

Integrative Multi-Level Dynamics and Design Implications

An integrative reading of the multi-level framework reveals *AI-mediated multimodal literacy* as a complex adaptive system in which local pedagogical choices and macro-level policy decisions co-evolve through recursive interaction. Design work within this system cannot be confined to discrete lesson plans or isolated regulatory clauses, but must instead engage with the full matrix articulated in Table 3. For example, introducing reflective prompting protocols at the micro level will have limited impact if institutional assessment practices at the meso level reward speed over depth, or if macro-level accountability metrics reduce literacy to quantifiable test scores. Conversely, high-level commitments to equity and transparency will remain aspirational if classrooms lack infrastructural conditions for inclusive multimodal expression (Cheung et al., 2025; Nash et al., 2024; Olvah et al., 2024). Effective design therefore requires cross-scalar alignment, where cognitive scaffolds, social norms, ethical safeguards, and infrastructural investments are orchestrated as mutually reinforcing components of a coherent literacy ecology that acknowledges AI as co-constitutive of contemporary meaning-making.

CURRICULUM, PEDAGOGY, AND ASSESSMENT AS INTERLOCKING CONCEPTUAL DOMAINS

Curriculum Imaginaries for AI-Mediated Multimodal Literacy

Curriculum in AI-intensive environments operates as a selective, normative architecture that encodes decisions about which languages, genres, modalities, and practices are legitimised as educative. Within *AI-mediated multimodal literacy*, curriculum imaginaries can be located along a continuum that ranges from skills-transmission schemas, which prioritise algorithmically scorable micro-competences, to design-oriented schemas, which emphasise expansive meaning-making, critical inquiry, and translanguaging (Alam, 2023b; Bolívar, 2023; Carcamo, 2024). In the former, AI is primarily configured as an efficiency amplifier that automates drill, correction, and content delivery, while in the latter it is positioned as a contested semiotic resource and object of critique. The resulting curricular blueprints stabilise particular distributions of cognitive load between humans and machines, and crystallise implicit theories of language, knowledge, and creativity. Table 4 in the following sub-section renders these divergent paradigms visible in a compact comparative matrix, enabling curriculum designers and accreditation bodies to interrogate how their frameworks implicitly script the role of AI and multimodality across K-12 and higher education systems.

Pedagogical Architectures and Design Principles for AI-Integrated Literacy

Pedagogy within *AI-mediated multimodal literacy* can be understood as the set of orchestrational logics through which teachers configure tasks, sequences, and classroom ecologies that harness or delimit intelligent systems. Design principles inspired by *multiliteracies*, *inquiry-based learning*, and *design thinking* encourage the movement from situated practice, through overt strategy instruction and critical framing, toward transformed practice in which learners redesign texts and tools (Campbell & Olteanu, 2024; Derunova & Sagyntaeva, 2025; Jayanti & Damayanti, 2023). Other pedagogical architectures remain tightly scripted, centring content delivery and compliance with external benchmarks. AI tools can be incorporated as dialogic partners that learners interrogate, as black-box tutors that learners obey, or as infrastructural layers that remain largely invisible (Cun, 2025; García, 2024; Mc Evander, 2024). These divergent pedagogical stances are crystallised in Table 4, which juxtaposes paradigms according to their curriculum focus, pedagogical orientation, assessment configuration, and the assigned role of AI and multimodality.

Table 4. Comparative Paradigms of AI-Infused Literacy Architectures in Education

Paradigm	Curriculum Focus	Pedagogical Orientation	Assessment Configuration	Role of AI and Multimodality
Skills-Transmission Paradigm	Hierarchised micro-skills, canonical genres, standard language norms	Teacher-centred explanation, repetitive practice, minimal dialogic engagement	Item-based testing, time-bound quizzes, automated scoring rubrics	AI as drill engine and correctness filter, multimodality as peripheral decoration
Multiliteracies-Design Paradigm	Diverse texts, global discourses, local lifeworld integration	Scaffolded design cycles, model deconstruction, explicit strategy talk	Portfolio artefacts, process documentation, performance tasks	AI as extended design palette, multimodality as central meaning-making resource
Critical AI Literacy Paradigm	Data, algorithms, discourse, and power, socio-technical imaginaries	Dialogic critique, counter-text production, scenario deliberation	Reflective essays, critical multimodal compositions, self-assessment narratives	AI as object of interrogation, multimodality as vehicle for dissent and re-imagination
Inquiry-Studio Paradigm	Open problems, cross-disciplinary questions, real-world briefs	Project-based inquiry, peer co-design, iterative prototyping cycles	Exhibition of artefacts, public showcases, multi-source feedback	AI as heuristic collaborator, multimodality as experimental laboratory for representation
Datafied Personalization Paradigm	Individual mastery trajectories, competency maps, behaviour analytics	Adaptive sequencing, algorithmically suggested tasks, nudging mechanisms	Dashboard metrics, predictive risk indicators, mastery badges	AI as invisible orchestrator, multimodality as data source for behavioural modelling

The paradigmatic typology in Table 4 demonstrates that pedagogical design is never technologically neutral, because each configuration embeds a theory of how learners should interact with AI systems, peers, and multimodal artefacts. In the skills-transmission paradigm, intelligent systems stabilise a regime of surveillance and correction that privileges speed and conformity, whereas the multiliteracies-design and inquiry-studio paradigms foreground experimentation, reflexivity, and collaborative authorship. The critical AI literacy paradigm inserts systematic interrogation of data infrastructures and algorithmic mediation into the core of classroom activity rather than treating these as peripheral topics. The datafied personalization paradigm, in contrast, exemplifies a techno-managerial imaginary in which learning becomes an optimisation problem solved by continuous monitoring. Educators and institutional leaders can use this matrix to surface which paradigms currently dominate their practice, and to design deliberate shifts toward configurations that align with more democratic, plural, and creative visions of literacy.

Learning Trajectories, Developmental Appropriateness, and Inclusive Design

Learning trajectories for *AI-mediated multimodal literacy* must be conceptualised as developmentally sequenced, yet non-linear pathways through which learners acquire increasingly sophisticated repertoires of representation, critique, and tool orchestration. In early schooling, the emphasis may fall on embodied play, oral storytelling, drawing, and emergent writing, with AI tools introduced as occasional augmentations that scaffold access rather than as primary generators (Kargin, 2023; Lim & Nguyen, 2024; Saputra et al., 2025). As learners progress through upper primary and secondary phases, they can engage in more explicit metalinguistic and metaliteracy reflection, including interrogation of how AI systems segment text, rank relevance, and render translations. In higher education, trajectories can incorporate disciplinary discourse conventions, complex data visualisations, and extended multimodal projects that position AI as both collaborator and object of study (Ahmed, 2024; Insani et al., 2024; Cornfield et al., 2025). The paradigms articulated in Table 4 provide a developmental lens, since students immersed solely in datafied personalization environments are likely to develop markedly different cognitive and identity trajectories from those engaged in multiliteracies-design or critical AI literacy architectures.

Assessment Ecologies for AI-Mediated Multimodal Artefacts

Assessment within *AI-mediated multimodal literacy* must reconcile demands for validity, reliability, and comparability with the inherently situated, collaborative, and processual nature of multimodal composition in hybrid human-machine settings. Traditional assessment ecologies that privilege discrete-response items and decontextualised writing prompts risk misrepresenting the competencies that matter in AI-rich environments, such as the capacity to curate sources, orchestrate modes, document decision pathways, and articulate critical evaluations of algorithmic outputs (Subiyantoro et al., 2024; Trisanti et al., 2024; Wang, 2024). More congruent assessment configurations involve portfolios that gather successive versions of artefacts, analytic commentaries on the use of AI tools, and performance-based tasks that require learners to design for authentic audiences. Process analytics can be harnessed to inform formative feedback, provided that they are interpreted through critical and contextual lenses rather than treated as neutral indicators (Carcamo & Carmona, 2025; Keane, 2023; Sudarwati et al., 2025). The assessment column in Table 4 already signals how different paradigms either compress or expand the evidentiary space, which in turn shapes what learners perceive as worth investing attention and effort in.

Teacher Knowledge, Professional Identity, and Cross-Sector Continuities

Teacher knowledge and professional identity constitute pivotal mediating variables in the enactment of any curriculum or pedagogy for *AI-mediated multimodal literacy*. Frameworks such as *Technological Pedagogical Content Knowledge* foreground the necessity of integrating disciplinary epistemologies, pedagogical strategies, and technological affordances into a coherent practice architecture (Alam, 2023a; Alford & Yousef, 2023; Bekturova et al., 2025). In AI-intensive contexts, this integration extends to understanding prompt engineering, interpretive interrogation of model outputs, and negotiation of institutional guidelines on academic integrity. Teachers must also navigate identity tensions as they oscillate between roles as content experts, design facilitators, critical interlocutors, and mediators of institutional policy (Kang & Yi, 2023; Krompák & Hartmann, 2023; Shen et al., 2023). Cross-sector continuities are crucial, since higher education programmes that prepare future teachers need to instantiate the same paradigms of AI use that school systems aspire to generalise. If universities predominantly operate within datafied personalization or skills-transmission paradigms, while policy rhetoric calls for critical AI literacy and inquiry-studio approaches, a misalignment emerges that undermines systemic coherence, regardless of the conceptual clarity provided by matrices such as Table 4.

ETHICS, GOVERNANCE, AND POLICY IMAGINARIES FOR AI-MEDIATED MULTIMODAL LITERACY

Normative Architectures for AI in Literacy Ecologies

Normative architectures for AI-mediated multimodal literacy emerge at the intersection of ethical theory, human rights jurisprudence, and educational philosophy. Deontological frames foreground inviolable obligations such as respect for learner dignity, non-instrumental treatment of students, and prohibitions against coercive data extraction (Cheng et al., 2025; Dada, 2025; Nurjamin et al., 2025). Consequentialist lenses prioritise welfare maximisation, demanding rigorous scrutiny of aggregate harms and benefits produced by algorithmic systems, including cognitive load redistribution, attention capture, and ecological externalities. Virtue-ethical orientations emphasise the cultivation of practical wisdom, intellectual humility, and techno-moral virtues among educators and learners who must continually interpret ambiguous AI outputs (Carcamo & Pino, 2025; Qi, 2023; Unsworth, 2024). Care-ethical approaches highlight relational responsibility, vulnerability, and interdependence within classrooms configured as complex human-machine assemblages. Rights-based frameworks, including the right to education, privacy, participation, and linguistic self-determination, provide juridical anchors for contesting exploitative or exclusionary AI deployments. Within these overlapping architectures, AI-mediated multimodal literacy is not a neutral competency, but a normative project that must be aligned with democratically articulated values and enforceable guarantees.

Data Justice, Algorithmic Fairness, and Epistemic Plurality

Data justice, algorithmic fairness, and epistemic plurality constitute core axes along which the ethical integrity of AI-mediated multimodal literacy can be evaluated. Data justice interrogates how learner data are harvested, classified, and repurposed, including questions of consent, proportionality, retention, and secondary use within expansive analytic ecosystems (Amin, 2023; Liu & Lim, 2024; Park et al., 2024). Algorithmic fairness concerns distributive effects across social stratifications, examining whether recommendation engines, scoring algorithms, and generative models systematically privilege particular languages, accents, body types, or cultural references when curating or producing multimodal artefacts. Epistemic plurality focuses on whose narratives, semiotic repertoires, and knowledge systems are encoded as legitimate, and whose are silenced, caricatured, or algorithmically downgraded (Christian et al., 2024; De Oliveira, 2024; Fradana et al., 2025). These three axes are deeply intertwined, since apparently neutral optimisation targets often codify historical inequities and monolingual or monocultural norms. Table 5 later in this section schematises governance levers across institutional scales that can be mobilised to operationalise data justice, fairness, and epistemic plurality in concrete regulatory and pedagogical arrangements.

Institutional and Classroom Governance of AI-Mediated Practices

Governance of AI-mediated multimodal literacy unfolds through nested micro, meso, and macro regimes that translate abstract ethical commitments into situated norms, procedures, and sanctions. At the classroom scale, teachers co-create charters with students that define permissible uses of generative systems in drafting, translation, and revision, while also articulating expectations around acknowledgement, reflection, and critical interrogation of machine contributions (Abas, 2023; Ly & Forzani, 2023; Querol-Julián & Fortanet-Gómez, 2025). At the institutional scale, senates and school boards promulgate guidelines on platform selection, data retention, academic integrity, and the documentation of AI involvement in multimodal assignments. Professional codes, grievance mechanisms, and union-negotiated protections influence how responsibility for algorithmic harms or misuse is distributed among educators, vendors, and administrators (Querol-Julián & Lo, 2025; Sinar et al., 2023; Ulu Bilim & Erdem, 2025). These layered regimes are not purely restrictive, they also enable experimentation by providing clear parameters within which creative and critical uses of AI become institutionally defensible.

Table 5. Governance Levers for AI Literacy Ecologies

Governance Stratum	Primary Regulatory Orientation	Key Operational Mechanisms	Dominant Equity and Justice Concerns	Targeted Literacy Outcomes
Classroom Micro-Governance	Norm-building, relational accountability, formative constraint	Co-created AI use agreements, reflective logs, dialogic conferencing	Protection of vulnerable learners, avoidance of coerced disclosure, inclusivity of diverse repertoires	Critical authorship, transparent documentation of AI involvement, collaborative multimodal design
School and Institutional Governance	Policy codification, risk management, quality assurance	Institutional AI guidelines, procurement standards, audit committees, ethics review procedures	Unequal access to tools, staff workload intensification, disciplinary bias in enforcement	Coherent course-level expectations, aligned assessment frameworks, sustainable teacher practices
National and Regional Policy Regimes	Regulatory standard-setting, rights protection, system steering	Curriculum frameworks, data protection statutes, funding conditionalities, inspectorate protocols	Digital divides, linguistic marginalisation, territorial inequities in infrastructure	Baseline AI literacy capabilities, protection of minority languages, system-wide accountability

continued on following page

Table 5. Continued

Governance Stratum	Primary Regulatory Orientation	Key Operational Mechanisms	Dominant Equity and Justice Concerns	Targeted Literacy Outcomes
Platform and Industry Governance	Self-regulation, compliance with statutory obligations, reputational management	Transparency reporting, model documentation, safety layers, user control dashboards	Opaque optimisation, monetisation of learner data, transnational power asymmetries	Safer default behaviours, user-legible controls, support for pedagogical rather than purely commercial logics
Transnational and Multi-Stakeholder Compacts	Norm diffusion, soft-law coordination, ethical harmonisation	International guidelines, cross-border data agreements, multi-stakeholder forums	Cross-jurisdictional inconsistency, export of harmful standards, erosion of local sovereignty	Interoperable ethical baselines, portability of learner rights, shared benchmarks for AI-mediated literacies

The comparative configuration in Table 5 highlights that ethical and governance aspirations for AI-mediated multimodal literacy can only be realised when levers are activated coherently across strata. Classroom charters lose traction if they conflict with institutional procurement decisions that mandate opaque platforms, while robust national curricula remain inert if schools lack infrastructures or if platform governance prioritises monetisation over pedagogical integrity. Transnational compacts can assist by preventing a regulatory race to the bottom, but they risk imposing homogenising standards that undercut local epistemic traditions if not negotiated inclusively. By examining how orientations, mechanisms, and justice concerns are distributed in Table 5, stakeholders can identify gaps, redundancies, and misalignments in their current governance ecosystems, and design interventions that rebalance power among learners, educators, institutions, and corporate actors.

Policy Imaginaries, Scenario Construction, and Anticipatory Governance

Policy imaginaries for AI-mediated multimodal literacy encode visions of future society and subjectivity that implicitly guide regulatory choices, funding priorities, and systemic reforms. A technocratic optimisation imaginary frames AI as a frictionless solution to inefficiencies and learning gaps, thereby legitimising widespread datafication, predictive analytics, and automated assessment (Alam, 2022; Zhao et al., 2025; Aridasarie & Rohmah, 2024). A humanistic-critical imaginary positions AI as a provocative interlocutor that must be constrained and interrogated, foregrounding democratic deliberation, epistemic plurality, and ecological limits. Scenario construction techniques enable policy communities to explore divergent trajectories, such as ubiquitous AI tutors embedded within every literacy task, tightly regulated co-design environments that cap automation, or hybrid ecosystems where public infrastructures coexist with commercial platforms under stringent transparency mandates (Daniele et al., 2025; Daulay & Dewi, 2025; Shen et al., 2025). Anticipatory governance involves not only forecasting probable futures but also cultivating institutional reflexivity, so that policies and standards can be iteratively recalibrated in response to emergent harms, innovations, and social movements. The governance strata in Table 5 provide a scaffold for such scenario exercises, ensuring that micro-level classroom realities are not eclipsed by high-level abstractions.

Research, Innovation, and Participatory Design Agendas

Conceptualisation of ethics and governance in AI-mediated multimodal literacy would remain purely rhetorical without robust research, innovation, and participatory design agendas that test and refine the frameworks described in this chapter. Research programmes can examine how different curriculum paradigms, assessment ecologies, and governance regimes interact in practice, particularly for learners at the intersections of multiple marginalisations (Beltrán-Palanques & Querol-Julián, 2024; Shen et al., 2024; Sutrisno, 2024). Innovation initiatives can prototype AI-supported tools that embody values such as transparency, interpretability, and support for translanguaging, rather than defaulting to monolingual and monomodal templates. Participatory design processes that include students, teachers, caregivers, and community organisations as co-designers can surface locally grounded priorities and challenge technocentric assumptions (Beltrán-Palanques, 2024; Sutrisno et al., 2023; Zaidi & Sah, 2024). Cross-sector consortia can coordinate standard-setting, interoperability requirements, and shared evaluation protocols that align with the normative commitments articulated through data justice, algorithmic fairness, and epistemic plurality. In this way, the governance levers summarised in Table 5 become living instruments within an evolving ecosystem, rather than static checklists, shaping AI-mediated multimodal literacy as a field oriented toward justice, creativity, and democratic resilience.

CONCLUSION

Synthesis of Conceptual Contributions and Theoretical Integrations

This chapter has conceptualised *AI-mediated multimodal literacy* as a composite, multi-level capability that emerges from entangled human, algorithmic, and infrastructural agencies rather than from isolated cognitive skills. It integrated *New Literacy Studies*, *multimodality*, *multiliteracies*, *translanguaging*, *critical literacy*, and *posthuman-sociomaterial* approaches to show how meaning-making is always socially sponsored, multimodally instantiated, epistemically contested, and technologically saturated. The theoretical matrices developed across Tables 1 to 5 articulated how lenses, AI system typologies, multi-level dynamics, curricular paradigms, and governance levers interlock within K-12 and higher education ecologies. Taken together, these constructs reframed literacy as participation in semiotic assemblages where large language models, image generators, analytic engines, and platform architectures co-configure what counts as legitimate text, authorship, and critique. The synthesis therefore repositioned AI not as an auxiliary add-on to pre-existing literacy regimes, but as a constitutive condition that necessitates rethinking foundational categories such as text, reader, author, classroom, and policy in globally diverse contexts.

Cross-Stakeholder Implications and Translational Pathways

The framework elaborated in this chapter carries concrete implications for multiple stakeholder constellations that co-produce educational systems. For educators, it foregrounds the need to design *AI-mediated multimodal tasks* that cultivate reflexive prompting, cross-modal orchestration, and critical interrogation of algorithmic authority, rather than simply accelerating content coverage. For curriculum designers and assessment architects, the paradigms in Table 4 illustrate how alternative configurations of objectives, task structures, and evidentiary practices either entrench datafied skills-transmission logics or enable multiliteracies, inquiry, and critical AI literacy. For institutional leaders and policy makers, the multi-level matrix in Table 3 and the governance schema in Table 5 demonstrate that ethical aspirations must be operationalised through aligned decisions about platform procurement, teacher workload, infrastructural investment, and enforceable rights. For technologists and industry actors, the typology in Table 2 delineates design responsibilities regarding transparency, inclusivity, and epistemic plurality, encouraging a shift from narrow optimisation metrics toward genuinely pedagogical imaginaries.

Future Trajectories, Open Problems, and Normative Commitments

Several strategic questions remain deliberately open, inviting sustained inquiry, experimentation, and deliberation. One central problematic concerns how far AI should permeate foundational literacy education before it begins to displace essential embodied, dialogic, and slow interpretive practices that underpin democratic reasoning. Another revolves around how *actor-network*, *sociomaterial*, and *posthuman* lenses can recognise distributed agency without dissolving human accountability for harmful outputs, exclusionary data practices, or ecologically unsustainable infrastructures. A third concerns how decolonial, Indigenous, and plurilingual epistemologies can reconfigure dominant AI and literacy imaginaries that currently privilege standardised, monolingual, and Eurocentric norms. The chapter therefore closes with a normative commitment to *AI-mediated multimodal literacy* as a field oriented toward epistemic justice, ecological responsibility, and democratic resilience, where design, governance, and pedagogy are continually renegotiated through participatory processes that foreground learners and communities as co-authors of socio-technical futures.

REFERENCES

Abas, S. (2023). Critical multimodal literacy practices in student-created comics. *Literacy*, *57*(2), 161–170. DOI: 10.1111/lit.12324

Afifah, L., Indriwardhani, S. P., Retnantiti, S., & Usman, R. (2023). Digitalization: Improving the literacy of foreign language learners through multimodal texts. [Journal of Linguistics and Literature]. *Lire Journal*, *7*(1), 177–192. DOI: 10.33019/lire.v7i1.171

Ahmed, R. (2024). Reading the Visual: An Introduction to Teaching Multimodal Literacy:(Book Review). *Journal of English Studies in Arabia Felix*, *3*(1), 24–27. DOI: 10.56540/jesaf.v3i1.92

Al Farabi, M. R. F., & Rohmah, Z. (2023). Teaching Multimodal Literacy Through Integrated Learning of Advertisement Texts. *Journal of English Teaching* [JETALL]. *Applied Linguistics and Literatures*, *6*(1), 73–88.

Alam, A. (2022). Impact of university's human resources practices on professors' occupational performance: empirical evidence from India's higher education sector. In *Inclusive businesses in developing economies: Converging people, profit, and corporate citizenship* (pp. 107–131). Springer International Publishing. DOI: 10.1007/978-3-031-12217-0_6

Alam, A. (2023a). Media multitasking with M-learning technology in real-time classroom learning: Analysing the dynamics in formal educational settings for the future of E-learning in India. In *2023 2nd International Conference on Smart Technologies and Systems for Next Generation Computing (ICSTSN)* (pp. 1-6). IEEE.

Alam, A. (2023b). The secret sauce of student success: Cracking the code by navigating the path to personalized learning with educational data mining. In *2023 2nd International Conference on Smart Technologies and Systems for Next Generation Computing (ICSTSN)* (pp. 1-8). IEEE.

Alam, A. (2023c). Intelligence unleashed: An argument for AI-enabled learning ecologies with real world examples of today and a peek into the future. In *International Conference on Innovations in Computer Science, Electronics & Electrical Engineering*-2022 (Vol. 2717, No. 1, p. 030001). AIP Publishing LLC. DOI: 10.1063/5.0129803

Alam, A., & Mohanty, A. (2022, December). Facial analytics or virtual avatars: competencies and design considerations for student-teacher interaction in AI-powered online education for effective classroom engagement. In *International Conference on Communication, Networks and Computing* (pp. 252-265). Cham: Springer Nature Switzerland.

Alam, A., & Mohanty, A. (2023, January). Learning on the move: a pedagogical framework for state-of-the-art mobile learning. In *International Conference on Data Management, Analytics & Innovation* (pp. 735-748). Singapore: Springer Nature Singapore. DOI: 10.1007/978-981-99-1414-2_52

Alam, A., & Mohanty, A. (2024). Integrated constructive robotics in education (ICRE) model: A paradigmatic framework for transformative learning in educational ecosystem. *Cogent Education, 11*(1), 2324487. DOI: 10.1080/2331186X.2024.2324487

Alford, J., & Yousef, A. (2023). Unveiling the power of critical multimodal literacy: Exploring cultural difference in children's literature through 'The Proudest Blue—a Story of Hijab and Family'. *Australian Journal of Language and Literacy*, *46*(3), 301–316. DOI: 10.1007/s44020-023-00049-z

Almeida, L. D. S. G., Sabota, B., & Rodrigues, O. S. (2023). Multimodal literacy in the learning of the chronicle genre: a possibility of pedagogical mediation. *Revista e-Curriculum, 21.*

Amer, L. (2025). Writing Matters: Let's Spread Queer Joy through Multimodal Literacy Practices! *Language Arts*, *102*(5), 274–278. DOI: 10.58680/la20251025274

Amin, F. M. (2023). Exploring Students' Reading Interest Through Tiktok Multimodal Literacy. [JETL]. *Journal Of Education And Teaching Learning*, *5*(2), 157–164.

Analido, B., & Pratiwi, M. A. (2025). Multimodal Literacy: The Use of Web Blog As Media of Teaching Writing At English Department of STKIP PGRI West Sumatera. *Ethical Lingua. Journal of Language Teaching and Literature*, *12*(1). Advance online publication. DOI: 10.30605/25409190.229

Arellano, R. (2024). Promoting multilingual and multimodal literacy discourses: From silence to advocacy in Chilean EFL teacher education. *Reimagining Literacies Pedagogy in the Twenty-first Century: Theorizing and Enacting Multiple Literacies for English Language Learners*, 97.

Aridasarie, Z., & Rohmah, Z. (2024). Enhancing multimodal literacy: Puppetry for English-speaking skills development. *Cogent Education*, *11*(1), 2370754. DOI: 10.1080/2331186X.2024.2370754

Bekturova, M., Gaipov, D., Dyankova, G. H., & Tulepova, S. (2025). Examining Multimodal Literacy Skills Among EMI Teachers in Kazakhstan. *International Journal of Cognitive Research in Science. Engineering and Education, 13*(1), 217–222.

Beltrán-Palanques, V. (2023). Multimodal Literacy in ESP/EAP. *The Future of Teacher Education: Innovations across Pedagogies. Technology in Society, 7*, 101.

Beltrán-Palanques, V. (2024). Assessing video game narratives: Implications for the assessment of multimodal literacy in ESP. *Assessing Writing, 60*, 100809. DOI: 10.1016/j.asw.2024.100809

Beltrán-Palanques, V., & Querol-Julián, M. (2024). The genre of PechaKucha presentations: Analysis and implications for enhancing multimodal literacy at university. *English for Specific Purposes, 75*, 102–118. DOI: 10.1016/j.esp.2024.05.002

Bolívar, V. P. (2023). Rethinking Multimodal Literacy in Theory and Practice. *RaeL: Revista Electrónica de Lingüística Aplicada, 22*(1).

Bretaño, J. A. (2025). Towards multimodal literacy in translation studies. *Estudios de traducción*, (15), 25-32.

Brown, S., Hao, L., & Zhang, R. (2023). Assessing the multimodal literacy practices of young emergent bilinguals. In *Handbook of multilingual TESOL in practice* (pp. 373–401). Springer Nature Singapore. DOI: 10.1007/978-981-19-9350-3_25

Campbell, C., & Olteanu, A. (2024). The challenge of postdigital literacy: Extending multimodality and social semiotics for a new age. *Postdigital Science and Education, 6*(2), 572–594. DOI: 10.1007/s42438-023-00414-8

Cappello, M., & Ojeda, A. G. (2023). Teaching Multimodal and Digital Literacies. In *Handbook of Research on Teaching the English Language Arts* (pp. 96–115). Routledge. DOI: 10.4324/9781003334392-6

Carcamo, B. (2024). Within the'Educational Chasm': The Chilean ELT Textbook and the Development of Multimodal Literacy. *Language Teaching Research Quarterly, 40*, 161–174. DOI: 10.32038/ltrq.2024.40.10

Carcamo, B. (2025). Exploring the impact of multimodal artifact creation in Canva on the understanding of multimodal texts in EFL Learners. *Technology in Language Teaching & Learning, 7*(4), 103022–103022. DOI: 10.29140/tltl.v7n4.103022

Carcamo, B., & Carmona, C. (2025). Improving EFL students' multimodal literacy through infographics. *ELT Journal, 79*(2), 205–215. DOI: 10.1093/elt/ccae049

Carcamo, B., & Pino, B. (2025). Developing EFL students' multimodal literacy with the use of infographics. *Asian-Pacific Journal of Second and Foreign Language Education, 10*(1), 16. DOI: 10.1186/s40862-025-00322-3

Cheng, L. M. Y., Powell, S. J., & Davis, B. (2025). Critical Multimodal Literacy: An Analysis of Young Children's Picture Books About Refugees: L. Cheng et al. *International Journal of Early Childhood*, 1-27.

Cheung, K. K. C., Erduran, S., & Oancea, A. (2025). Affordances and Challenges of Multimodal Literacy-Infused Science Pedagogy: A Case of Hong Kong EMI Science Classroom. *Designing Learning with Multimodality in English Medium of Education (EME) Classrooms Across Asia*, 47.

Christian, I. S., Rohmah, Z., & Jalaluddin, I. (2024). Exploring Studies on Multimodal Literacy in English Learning: A Bibliometric Analysis. [Journal of English Education and Linguistics Studies]. *JEELS, 11*(2), 821–848. DOI: 10.30762/jeels.v11i2.3681

Cornfield, O., Rodriquez Vazquez, B., & Holtaway, K. (2025). Fostering creative confidence and multimodal literacy in practice at the Children's Creativity Museum. *Journal of Early Childhood Literacy, 25*(4), 14687984251382045. DOI: 10.1177/14687984251382045

Cun, A. (2025). Creating more opportunities through multimodal literacy and positioning in online and in-person Chinese heritage language classrooms. *Language and Education, 39*(2), 357–379. DOI: 10.1080/09500782.2024.2352428

Dada, C. (2025). Integrating Technology for Multimodal Literacy in English Studies. *NIU Journal of Humanities, 10*(1), 237–245.

Dada, C., & Akande, R. M. (2025). Assessing Multimodal Literacy in Higher Education: Impact on Student Learning Outcomes in Selected Universities in Edo State, Nigeria. *NIU Journal of Educational Research, 11*(1), 51–59.

Daniele, S., Murcia, K., & Chappell, J. (2025). Beyond museum walls: A transmedia approach to fostering multimodal literacy and STEM engagement in science discovery children's museums. *Journal of Early Childhood Literacy, 25*(4), 14687984251379603. DOI: 10.1177/14687984251379603

Daulay, E., & Dewi, U. (2025). Reading comprehension through multimodal literacy approach for English education. [English Teaching Journal]. *ETERNAL, 16*(2), 397–404. DOI: 10.26877/eternal.v16i2.1910

De Oliveira, J. M. (2024, November). Enhancing multimodal literacy through community service learning in higher education. [). Frontiers Media SA.]. *Frontiers in Education*, *9*, 1448805. DOI: 10.3389/feduc.2024.1448805

Derunova, E. N., & Sagyntaeva, Z. K. (2025). Creolized texts as a tool for developing multimodal literacy of schoolchildren learning Russian in Kazakhstan. *Russian Language Studies*, *23*(1), 132–152. DOI: 10.22363/2618-8163-2025-23-1-132-152

Dewanthi, F., Marsakawati, N. P. E., & Sari, R. A. (2024). Text-based language teaching flipbook for guest relation officer to enhance students multimodal literacy. [TATEFL]. *The Art of Teaching English as a Foreign Language*, *5*(2), 124–136. DOI: 10.36663/tatefl.v5i2.759

Domínguez Romero, E., Bobkina, J., Stefanova Radoulska, S., & Herrero, C. (2023). *Rethinking multimodal literacy in theory and practice*. Peter Lang. DOI: 10.3726/b20792

Duraisamy, S. (2025). Exploring the impact of multimodal learning on literacy and social-emotional development in early childhood. *Journal of Language and Culture in Education*, *2*(2b), 88–108.

Fortanet-Gómez, I., & Querol-Julián, M. (2025). Multimodal literacy at the university: The ins and outs of educating in English as an additional language. In *Multimodal Literacy in English as an Additional Language in Higher Education* (pp. 3–19). Routledge. DOI: 10.4324/9781003429876-2

Fradana, A. N., Suwarta, N., & Sotlikova, R. (2025). Strengthening multimodal literacy through digital literary text learning: Enhancing students' achievement in the age of disruption. *Journal of Language and Literature Studies*, *5*(1), 216–225. DOI: 10.36312/jolls.v5i1.2635

García, C. G. (2024). YOUTUBE videos to develop multimodal literacy. *ELIA: Estudios de Lingüística Inglesa Aplicada*, (24), 209–244. DOI: 10.12795/elia.2024.i24.7

Guo, M., & Wang, J. (2024). Robotic Badges for Girl Scouts: Coding Exploration Integrated with Multimodal Literacy. *Journal of Technology-Integrated Lessons and Teaching*, *3*(2), 30–40. DOI: 10.13001/jtilt.v3i2.8763

Hadjiconstantinou, S. (2023). Developing multimodal literacy through critical practices: an examlpe from an english for the media university program. In *5th International Conference Literacy and Contemporary Society: Creativity, Equity, Social Action.*

Hardukiewicz, J. (2024). Multimodal Literacy in Teaching Foreign Languages: The Example of Power Point Presentations. *XLINGUAE, 17*(4), 251–261. DOI: 10.18355/XL.2024.17.04.15

Harrington, L., & Cox, K. (2024). On These Haunted Streets: A Photopoetic Process of Transmedia Storytelling as Critical Multimodal Literacy. In *Transmedia Applications in Literacy Fields* (pp. 238-261). IGI Global. DOI: 10.4018/979-8-3693-3302-0.ch011

Hartmann, E. C. (2025). Multimodal literacy learning in The big word factory: Exploring a trilingual picturebook app with bilingual student teachers. In *Multimodal Mediation Through Picturebooks and Graphic Narratives* (pp. 167–186). Routledge. DOI: 10.4324/9781003378136-11

Hashim, H. U., Saragih, E., & Gapur, A. (2024). Enhancing Augmented Reality (AR) Technology to Improve Medical English Literacy. *International Journal Linguistics of Sumatra and Malay, 2*(2), 49â-55.

Henderson, R. (2023). Between worlds: Extending students' multimodal literacy practices with augmented reality. *Literacy Learning: The Middle Years, 31*(1), 66–68.

Indhra, F. M., Anshori, M., & Solihin, M. (2025). Adapting Palabe folk tales into multimodal literacy for early childhood education. [IJED]. *Indonesian Journal of Educational Development*, *6*(3), 874–892. DOI: 10.59672/ijed.v6i3.5365

Insani, N. H., Suwarna, S., & Triyono, S. (2024). Effect of Multimodal Literacy on Reading Ability of Indonesian Javanese Learners. *Issues in Language Studies, 13*(2), 17–33. DOI: 10.33736/ils.6472.2024

Jayanti, E. D., & Damayanti, I. L. (2023). Exploring teachers' perceptions of integrating multimodal literacy into English classrooms in Indonesian primary education. *Child Education Journal*, *5*(2), 98–109. DOI: 10.33086/cej.v5i2.5240

Kalan, A. (2024). Metatextual Dimensions of Multimodal Literacy Engagement. *Handbook of Research in Online Learning: Insights and Advances*, 196.

Kang, J., & Kim, H. G. (2024). Multimodality in English Language Teaching: A Review of L2 Multimodal Composition. *Multimedia-Assisted Language Learning, 27*(4).

Kang, J., & Yi, Y. (2023). Beyond ChatGPT: Multimodal generative AI for L2 writers. *Journal of Second Language Writing*, *62*, 101070. DOI: 10.1016/j.jslw.2023.101070

Kargin, T. (2023). Exploring Critical Multimodal Literacy in Reconstructing Fairy Tales. *Educational Policy Analysis and Strategic Research, 18*(3), 158–175. DOI: 10.29329/epasr.2023.600.8

Keane, K. (2023). *Reading in the Digital Age: Teacher and Students' Experiences with Multimodal Literacy and Varied Text Types.* Stanford University.

Komninos, N. (2023). Tracking Multimodal Literacy in Schools: A Case Study. *REVIJA ZA ELEMENTARNO IZOBRAŽEVANJE, 16*(Special Issue), 157–171. DOI: 10.18690/rei.16.Spec.Iss.2990

Krompák, E., & Hartmann, E. (2023). Multimodal literacy and linguistic landscape: A digital tandem project in European Teacher Education. *Alsic. Apprentissage des Langues et Systèmes d'Information et de Communication, 26*(1).

Kustini, S. (2023, May). A project-based multiliteracies instruction to improve students' multimodal literacy. In *20th AsiaTEFL-68th TEFLIN-5th iNELTAL Conference (ASIATEFL 2022)* (pp. 632-647). Atlantis Press.

Lam, K. Y., & Putri, E. W. (2024). A study on the affordances of digital fairy-tale rewriting: A critical literacy approach to digital multimodal composing. *System, 127*, 103536. DOI: 10.1016/j.system.2024.103536

Ledy, N. M. (2023). Multimodal Literacy in Learning English at Senior High School: Students' Perspective. *ICOTEL Proceeding MPBING, 4*(1), 33-41.

Lim, F. V. (2024). The future of TESOL with multimodality. *International Journal of TESOL Studies, 241213.*

Lim, F. V., & Nguyen, T. T. H. (2024). A pedagogical approach towards designing for multimodal literacy learning with picture books. In *Developing Future-ready Learners for a Global Age* (pp. 195–210). Routledge. DOI: 10.4324/9781003455721-18

Lim, F. V., & Unsworth, L. (2023). Multimodal composing in the English classroom: Recontextualising the curriculum to learning. *English in Education, 57*(2), 102–119. DOI: 10.1080/04250494.2023.2187696

Lin, C. H., Zhou, K., Li, L., & Sun, L. (2025). Integrating generative AI into digital multimodal composition: A study of multicultural second-language classrooms. *Computers and Composition, 75*, 102895. DOI: 10.1016/j.compcom.2024.102895

Linder, R., & Falk-Ross, F. (2024). Multimodal resources and approaches for teaching young adolescents: A review of the literature. *Education Sciences, 14*(9), 1010. DOI: 10.3390/educsci14091010

Liu, J. E., & Lim, F. V. (2024). Educational Context and Teacher Beliefs Matter: Multimodal Literacy in the Greater Bay Area of China. *RELC Journal*, •••, 00336882241304136. DOI: 10.1177/00336882241304136

Liu, J. E., & Lo, Y. Y. (2025). Multimodality in CLIL assessment: Implications for teacher assessment literacy. *Journal of Multilingual and Multicultural Development*, *46*(5), 1459–1477. DOI: 10.1080/01434632.2024.2357140

Löfgren, M. (2025). Literacy and multimodality for all. Swedish educational policy for reading and writing in the age of global assessments. *Scandinavian Journal of Educational Research*, •••, 1–19.

López-Pérez, M. V., & Bobadilla-Pérez, M. (2023). Multimodal literacy and pluriliteracy in the Primary School classroom through a transmedia narrative El niño, el topo, el zorro y el caballo, by Charlie Mackesy. *Texto Livre*, *16*, e41879. DOI: 10.1590/1983-3652.2023.41879

Lubis, B. N. A. (2025). Multimodal-Based Approaches in Teaching Ecological Literacy: Enhancing Environmental Awareness through Textual, Visual, and Auditory Integration. *STAIRS: English Language Education Journal*, *6*(1), 53–68. DOI: 10.21009/stairs.6.1.6

Ly, C. N., & Forzani, E. E. (2023). Let's Learn from Them: Using the Integrative Multimodal Literacy Assessment Tool to Support Instruction for Young Children. *The Reading Teacher*, *77*(3), 407–413. DOI: 10.1002/trtr.2243

Lysne, M. S. (2023). Aesthetic engagement with Mouse Bird Snake Wolf–Literary multimodal literacy in English language education. *Children's Literature in English Language Education*, *11*(2), 54–79.

Maamuujav, U. (2025). Multimodal Writing in Multilingual Space. *Education Sciences*, *15*(11), 1446. DOI: 10.3390/educsci15111446

Makinde, S. O., Sakariyahu, S., Abdullahi, A., & Ibrahim, A. (2025). Multimodal Literacy and Sociocultural Dynamics in Online Communication: An Interdisciplinary View. In *Sociocultural and Multicultural Meanings in Online Communication* (pp. 409-436). IGI Global Scientific Publishing.

Mc Evander, M. F. (2024). Exploring Multimodal Literacy Instruction on Reading Comprehension and Abilities in Critical Thinking of College Students. *Research Journal of Humanities and Social Sciences*, *15*(3), 175–179.

Midgette, E., Stewart, O., & González, J. (2023). Teaching with multimodal texts through a critical literacy lens within an English as a foreign language classroom context. *Anglistics and Americanistics*, (20), 72–77. DOI: 10.15421/382313

Mills, K. A., Brown, A., & Gutierrez, A. (2025). Virtual Reality Street Art with L2 Learners as Multimodal Literacy. In *Multiliteracies, Multimodality, and Learning by Design in Second Language Learning and Teacher Education* (pp. 86-102). Routledge. DOI: 10.4324/9781032620497-8

Mills, K. A., Heck, E., Brown, A., & Funnell, P. (2023). *Senses Together: Multimodal Literacy Learning in Primary Education.* Australian Catholic University. DOI: 10.24268/acu.8zy8y

Moalla, D. (2023). The dynamics of multimodal literacy development: The Tunisian EAP context as a case study. *Journal of Linguistics and Communication Studies, 2*(1), 47–65. DOI: 10.56397/JLCS.2023.03.07

Mulcahy, C., & Shaw, L. (2024). Centering Critical Engagement, Multimodal Learning, and Compassion through Language and Literacy. *The Intersections of Critical Pedagogy, Critical Literacy, and Social Justice: Toward Empowerment, Equity, and Education for Liberation*, 15.

Nash, B. L., Dunham, H., Murdter-Atkinson, J., & Mosley Wetzel, M. (2024). A culturally sustaining approach to multimodal literacies: Building from students' funds of knowledge in field-based teacher education. *Literacy Research and Instruction, 63*(2), 151–175. DOI: 10.1080/19388071.2022.2153766

Nurjamin, A. S. E. P., Nurjamin, L. R., Fajriah, Y. N., Nurjamin, A. K., & Nugraha, I. R. S. Y. A. D. (2025). Developing and evaluating an augmented reality (AR) digital storytelling video to foster multimodal literacy and narrative comprehension. *Journal of Engineering Science and Technology, 20*(4), 919–956.

Olvah, M., Alfan, M., Nusantara, T., Suyitno, I., & Anggraini, A. E. (2024). Pemanfaatan Berbagai Media dalam Pembelajaran untuk Meningkatkan Literasi Siswa dalam Perspektif Multimodal Literacy. *JIIP-Jurnal Ilmiah Ilmu Pendidikan, 7*(7), 6391–6398. DOI: 10.54371/jiip.v7i7.4689

Park, H., Zong, J., Polat, N., & Schallert, D. L. (2024). Bilingual/ESL preservice teachers' heritage language and language identity: Evidence from multimodal literacy autobiographies. *Teaching and Teacher Education, 152*, 104775. DOI: 10.1016/j.tate.2024.104775

Parker, M. (2024). Multimodal literacy: Supporting children as effective communicators. *Rattler (Sydney)*, (146), 15–18.

Pereira, Í. S. P., Gil, M., & Sylla, C. M. (2023). Meeting the challenges of designing multimodal texts to promote multiliteracies pedagogy. *Comunicação e sociedade*, (43), e023008.

Pool, S., Rowsell, J., & Sun, Y. (2023). Towards literacies of immanence: Getting closer to sensory multimodal perspectives on research. *Multimodality & Society, 3*(2), 130–149. DOI: 10.1177/26349795231158741

Qi, W. (2023). Developing Multimodal Literacy in the Business English Reading Class: A Case Study of Students' Presentation PowerPoint Slides. *Journal of Language Teaching & Research, 14*(3), 820–827. DOI: 10.17507/jltr.1403.30

Querol-Julián, M., & Fortanet-Gómez, I. (Eds.). (2025). *Multimodal literacy in English as an additional language in higher education.* Taylor & Francis. DOI: 10.4324/9781003429876

Querol-Julián, M., & Lo, Y. Y. (2025). Multimodal literacy in the professional development of bilingual educators. *International Journal of Bilingual Education and Bilingualism*, •••, 1–11.

Rasul, S., Razia, A., & Mumtaz, S. (2023). Literacy as a Social Practice: Mapping out Multimodal Literacy Practices in Middle-Class Beauty Salons. *Human Nature Journal of Social Sciences, 4*(2), 734–749. DOI: 10.71016/hnjss/r9d6vr56

Rocamora, M. S., & Baguio, J. B. (2025). Multimodal Literacy and Creative Teaching Practices of Public Elementary School Teachers. *Archives of Current Research International, 25*(7), 199–212. DOI: 10.9734/acri/2025/v25i71325

Ryu, H., & Kim, D. (2024). Multimodal Literacy in the Singaporean English Language Syllabus: Implications for Korea's 2022 Revised English Curriculum. *The SNU Journal of Education Research, 33*(4), 79–107. DOI: 10.54346/sjer.2024.33.4.79

Saputra, D. T., Rahmawati, L. E., & Markhamah, M. (2025). Implementation strategy of multimodal literacy text as a means to optimize literacy in Indonesian language lessons for elementary school students. *BAHASTRA, 45*(1), 155–164. DOI: 10.26555/bs.v45i1.1260

Saputra, D. T., Rahmawati, L. E., & Markhamah, M. M. (2024). The Fostering of Multimodal Text Literacy in Elementary School Learning. *Lensa: Kajian Kebahasaan, Kesusastraan, dan Budaya, 14*(1), 187-210.

Sari, A. P. (2025). Representation or Misrepresentation of Autistic Agency? Multimodal Literacy Analysis of Makayla's Voice. *Jurnal Ilmiah Bina Bahasa, 18*(1), 91–101. DOI: 10.33557/hyw3hy31

Satar, M., Hauck, M., & Bilki, Z. (2023). Multimodal representation in virtual exchange: A social semiotic approach to critical digital literacy. *Language Learning & Technology, 27*(2), 72–96. DOI: 10.64152/10125/73504

Seneechai, W., & Ampon, R. K. (2025). Designing Learning for Multimodal Literacy: Teaching Viewing and Representing. *Reflections: The SoL Journal, 32*(1). Advance online publication. DOI: 10.61508/refl.v32i1.277805

Serafini, F. (2023). Implications of multimodal theories for literacy research and pedagogy. In *Rethinking Multimodal Literacy in Theory and Practice* (pp. 17–35). Peter Lang AG.

Shen, Y., & Ab Jalil, H. (2023). Using digital game-based learning to foster multimodal literacy in left-behind children of migrant workers: Possibilities and challenges. *Migration Letters : An International Journal of Migration Studies, 20*(5), 469–486. DOI: 10.59670/ml.v20i5.3993

Shen, Y., Jalil, H. A., & Jamaluddin, R. (2025). Exploring adolescents' multimodal literacy as critical and creative prosumers in digital game-based multimodal composition. *Journal of Educational Technology & Society, 28*(1), 1–17.

Shen, Y. A. N. A. N., Ab Jalil, H., & Jamaluddin, R. (2024). A 10-year systematic review on the incorporation of digital games for multimodal literacy education. *WSEAS Transactions on Computer Research, 12*, 463–474. DOI: 10.37394/232018.2024.12.46

Sinar, T. S., Budiman, M. A., Ganie, R., & Rosa, R. N. (2023). Students' perceptions of using Roblox in multimodal literacy practices in teaching and learning English. *World Journal of English Language, 13*(7), 146. DOI: 10.5430/wjel.v13n7p146

Sodiq, S., Indarti, T., Resdianto, P. R., & Wijaya, T. (2023, December). Implementation of Multimodal Literacy Principles in Scientific Journal Article Writing Course: Enhancing Learning Experience in Indonesian Language Education. In *International Joint Conference on Arts and Humanities 2023 (IJCAH 2023)* (pp. 893-899). Atlantis Press. DOI: 10.2991/978-2-38476-152-4_86

Sofkova Hashemi, S. (2025). Fostering AI literacy in higher education: students' multimodal prompting. In *ARLE SIG TALE 3rd Symposium: Digital technologies, literacy and schooling-Responding to 'newness'? 10–13 June 2025, Larnaca, Cyprus.*

Subiyantoro, H., Hartono, R., Fitriati, S. W., & Faridi, A. (2024). Recovering multilingual children's literacy loss through multimodal literacy practices in a pull-out program. *Indonesian Journal of Applied Linguistics, 13*(3), 513–523. DOI: 10.17509/ijal.v13i3.66937

Sudarwati, E., Lestari, I. P., & Daniswara, R. A. (2025). Digital Multimodal Literacy Model of English Language Education in Indonesian Higher Education. [Journal of English Education and Linguistics Studies]. *JEELS, 12*(2), 615–640. DOI: 10.30762/jeels.v12i2.2612

Suhaimi, I., & Permatasari, F. (2024). Integrating Literature in English Learning to Improve Multimodal Literacy through a Sociocognitive Approach. *Essence. Journal of English Language Teaching, Linguistics, and Literature, 1*(2), 37–49.

Sultan, H. (2023). Measurement of Multimodal Literacy of EFL Iraqi Students. *Journal of Namibian Studies, 34*.

Sutrisno, D., Abidin, N. A. Z., Pambudi, N., Aydawati, E., & Sallu, S. (2023). Exploring the benefits of multimodal literacy in English teaching: Engaging students through visual, auditory, and digital modes. *Global Synthesis in Education Journal, 1*(2), 1–14. DOI: 10.61667/xh184f41

Sutrisno, D. B. (2024, February). Multimodal literacy and multimodal assignments in Indonesian EFL classrooms. In *7th International Conference on Language, Literature, Culture, and Education (ICOLLITE 2023)* (pp. 139-145). Atlantis Press. DOI: 10.2991/978-94-6463-376-4_19

Tan, S. A. C. Y., Jill, L. S. S., Tan, S., & AkhaviZadegan, R. (2023). Exploring the Inclusivity of Assessment ePortfolio for Multimodal Literacy During the Pandemic: A Case Study in Malaysian Higher Education. In *Improving Inclusivity in Higher Education: Addressing the Digital Divide in the COVID Pandemic* (pp. 139-161). Singapore: Springer Nature Singapore.

Tchetgen, P. V. N. (2025). Designing a Culturally Grounded Ecology for Mediating Multimodal Literacy Experiences through Parent-Child Technology Interactions. In *Proceedings of the 19th International Conference of the Learning Sciences-ICLS 2025, pp.* 2572-2574. International Society of the Learning Sciences. DOI: 10.22318/icls2025.203690

Trisanti, N., Sukyadi, D., & Hermawan, B. (2024). University EFL teachers' stance and engagement in digital multimodal composing as multimodal literacy practices. *International Journal of Education, 17*(1), 61–70. DOI: 10.17509/ije.v17i1.56188

Ulu Bilim, H., & Erdem, C. (2025). The mediating role of critical thinking disposition in the relationship between multimodal literacy and media analysis skill: Evidence from pre-service teachers. *Education and Information Technologies, 30*(17), 1–22. DOI: 10.1007/s10639-025-13697-0

Unsworth, L. (2024). Multimodal Literacy in a New Era of Educational Technology: Comparing Points of View in Animations of Children's and Adult Literature. *ECNU Review of Education, 7*(2), 384–405. DOI: 10.1177/20965311231179738

Unsworth, L. (2025). Infographics, inter-semiosis, and multimodal literacy in science education. In *Multimodal Literacy in English as an Additional Language in Higher Education* (pp. 20–42). Routledge. DOI: 10.4324/9781003429876-3

Wang, J. (2024). Bridging the Self's worlds: Young girls' creative TikTok expressions of multimodal literacy during Covid-19. *Journal of Early Childhood Literacy*, •••, 14687984241270820.

Wang, Y., & Hao, L. (2025). "I'll play the role of you": a case study of multimodal literacy practice with an international family. In *Handbook of Literacy in Families and Communities* (pp. 378–397). Edward Elgar Publishing. DOI: 10.4337/9781035326983.00028

Warriner, D. S. (2023). Literacy. In *The routledge handbook of applied linguistics* (pp. 245–257). Routledge. DOI: 10.4324/9781003082644-21

Wong, N. (2025). Transmodal Pedagogy in Action: Multilingual Experiences of Disciplinary Literacy in an Elementary Art Classroom. *Literacy Research and Instruction*, •••, 1–23.

Yakubu, F. M., & Obafemi, K. E. (2023). Systematic review of multiliteracies skills, multimodal tools to facilitate learning in early childhood classroom. *J Inov Teknol Pendidik*, *10*(4), 431–440. DOI: 10.21831/jitp.v10i4.66343

Yaşar, M. S., & Arı, G. (2023). Turkish Language Teacher Candidates' Multimodal Literacy Levels and Their Attitudes Towards Information and Communication Technologies. *Sakarya University Journal of Education*, *13*(5-Special Issue-World Language Turkish), 916-932.

Zaidi, R., & Sah, P. K. (2024). Affordances of multilingual and multimodal literacy engagements of immigrant high school students: A scoping review. *SAGE Open*, *14*(1), 21582440241228122. DOI: 10.1177/21582440241228122

Zhao, Z., An, Q., & Liu, J. (2025). Exploring AI tool adoption in higher education: Evidence from a PLS-SEM model integrating multimodal literacy, self-efficacy, and university support. *Frontiers in Psychology*, *16*, 1619391. DOI: 10.3389/fpsyg.2025.1619391 PMID: 40989284

Chapter 7
AI-Augmented Multimodal Literacies:
Rethinking Creativity, Communication, and Critical Engagement in Education

Sovannaroth Chheang
http://orcid.org/0009-0007-3382-7169
Department of Education, Sovanna Elton Foreign Language School (SELS), Phnom Penh, Cambodia

Sovanna Loch
http://orcid.org/0000-0002-1211-1248
Department of English, Nava Nalanda Mahavihara (Deemed to be University), Bihar, India

Phearun Tep
http://orcid.org/0009-0000-2490-677X
Department of English, University of Delhi, India

Sovanna Huot
http://orcid.org/0009-0006-8335-442X
Department of Education, National Institute of Education (NIE), Phnom Penh, Cambodia

ABSTRACT

This chapter demonstrates the powerful influence of artificial intelligence in changing multimodal literacies in various educational settings. It suggests that AI is a catalyst for providing learners with the ability to create, communicate, and critically interact with knowledge, while prompting consideration of ethical, equitable, and culturally

DOI: 10.4018/979-8-3373-6986-0.ch007

responsive challenges. This regards AI, based on theories, historical context, and analysis from various parts of the world as a creative partner and a communicative facilitator. These studies demonstrate the capability of AI in aiding the facilizes of storytelling, collaboration, translation, and visualization of data and highlight the challenges of bias, misinformation, and dependency. The author proposes pedagogical models such as inquiry-based, project-based, and critical digital literacy as frameworks for responsible integration. The recommendations include educators, curriculum developers, and policymakers, as well as teachers and educational researchers, focusing on the duration of the impact, cultural integration, and justice.

INTRODUCTION

AI has moved from the periphery to the centre of the educational landscape within just the past decade. From being confined to adaptive learning systems and automated grading, AI in education has permeated classroom applications via the incorporation of generative tools, including those that create text, images, audio, and multimodal narratives. Selwyn (2019) proposed that the diffusion of AI into educational practice is more of a cultural shift than a technological one. It is a shift that requires educators to fundamentally revise their understandings of teaching, learning and the processes through which meaning is constructed.

AI, alongside shifting educational practices, is now being integrated into the development of multimodal literacy. Kress (2009) defined multimodal literacy as the capacity to design and read meanings across a variety of modes including the linguistic, visual, auditory, gestural and spatial. In this case, Kress is shifting the dominance of the printed word and advocating for a more expansive view of communication. In Bezemer and Kress's (2015) argument, the multimodal turn in literacy studies changed the way in which scholars and practitioners of literacy conceptualized texts, appreciating that meaning is rarely, if ever, conveyed solely through words. With the advent of AI technologies, educational practitioners today have unprecedented tools to amplify the potential of multimodality and provide learners with the ability to create and remix media in ways that were previously not possible.

The advent of technologies like large language models such as GPT-4, coupled with image creators like DALL-E or Midjourney, empower students to become co-authors of narratives, translating their ideas into images, and creating simulations of classroom discussions, and extending their ideas into creative realms (Kasneci et al., 2023). These technologies are not limited to exclusive environments; they are available in many free and inexpensive transformed services, shaping the landscape of accessibility and everyday practicing of multimodal literacy. Holmes and Tuomi (2022) stated that the widespread availability of AI tools shows the change in position of learners as they are no longer consumers of multimodal content; they are now able to be active co-creators alongside machines.

As Warschauer (2011) noted, the issue of literacy in a digital context is not simply about acquiring a set of new technical skills. It is about navigating the sociocultural ecologies in which identity, power, and participation is situated. In AI mediated modalities, the composition of multimodal materials creates a context within which helping students create is not the paramount issue, but rather the grander socio-cultural and political questions of whose stories are to be told, how they are, and which cultural perspectives are in the forefront, and which are marginalized. It is this duality of expansive and critical complexity that this chapter seeks to illuminate.

The need to rethink literacy because of AI relates to two global historical changes. The first is the worldwide dissemination of digital communication, followed closely by the rapid development of machine learning. According to Jewitt et al. (2016), the ability to read, understand and decode print symbols is no longer sufficient. Literacy must be expanded to include the ability to design, navigate, and critically engage with different forms of digital content. The processes of composition automation and augmentation by AI further underscore this. Generative systems allow students to turn text prompts into draft essays, images, and even music. This process erases the distinction between author and tool.

Burnett and Merchant (2020) asserted that such technologies reconfigure the conditions of creativity. AI, therefore, should be seen as a part of the process rather than an external tool. This could look like a student digitally storytelling where the human part gives the theme and the AI gives the text and the images. Literacy, in this way, is not lessened, but rather, it is reframed. Creativity is not in the machine, but in the partnership.

While embracing a broad, transformative, changing conceptualization of literacy, there are cautions to be taken. Buckingham (2019) mentioned how educational technologies are 'hyping' innovations while ignoring the ethical dilemmas at hand. The surveillance, algorithmic bias, issues of authorship, and overreliance on machines that come with AI literacy practices are concerning. In her widely cited critique of search engines, Noble (2018) illustrated how systems of algorithms can reproduce historical and contemporary stereotypes of race and gender while covering their tracks. The unexamined use of AI in educational settings can reinforce inequities in systems that society may be trying to remove.

Therefore, this chapter aims to identify both the positive and transformative possibilities of AI in support of multimodal literacy, while emphasizing the necessity of a critique that is positive and negative in a balanced way, and ethically and culturally appropriate. AI is significant because it is not simply about the efficiency or innovation of a given pedagogy. AI requires a rethinking of what literacy is, how literacy is taught, and the importance of critical thinking in a world where machines are increasingly integrated into day-to-day activities.

This chapter has three objectives that are interconnected. To begin with, AI's contribution to the enhancement of creativity, communication, and critical engagement will be explored. AI's ethical, cultural, and equity concerns in relation to multimodal literacy, will be examined. Finally, the evolving student identity, voice, and agency in the literacy practices, will be documented.

HISTORICAL AND THEORETICAL FOUNDATIONS

Figure 1. Theoretical foundations of AI-Augmented multimodal literacies

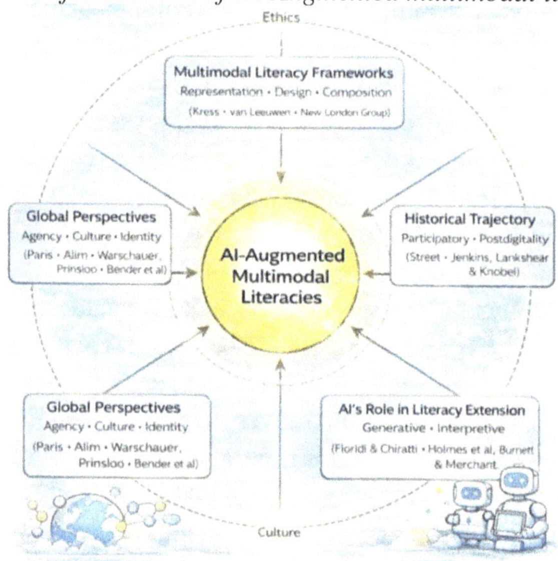

Multimodal Literacy Frameworks

The dissatisfaction with the print-dominant models of literacy that centre the alphabetic text as the highest form of communication, has led to the formulation of the concept of multimodal literacy. One of the most notable advocates of this shift in paradigm is Gunther Kress. According to Kress (2009), meaning is never contained in a word but is always accompanied by some other form of communication in other semiotic resources, that are visual, spatial, gestural, and auditory. He suggests that the centre of literacy should not be the word but the mode of representation and that literacy is the design of meaning in and across different semiotic resources.

While building his argument, Van Leeuwen (2005) adopted an analysis of the various modes of communication, including image, sound, and movement, and the various affordances and cultural conventions, suggesting that every communication choice includes the selection of a certain mode and that the options for mode selection are limited by the social, cultural, and institutional surroundings. This means that for one to be considered a multiliteracy, one must be able to read and write, as well as design meaning by choosing and arranging various modes for a given communicative purpose.

The New London (1996) built upon this and offered the term "multiliteracies." For them, an adequate pedagogy of literacy must consider two aspects, and they are the cultural and linguistic diversity of the world and the world's media. The world's media and migration have made the world's classrooms culturally and linguistically diverse, therefore the pedagogy of literacy must be sensitive to the fact that the world is no longer only concerned with the use of one language, and print. The design aspect of the group's framework positions literacy as a transformative process as he or she has available designs (semiotic resources) and through designing (meaning making) and produces redesigned texts that alter the social and cultural relations.

Recent research has built upon these foundations. Bezemer and Kress (2015) stated that multimodality emphasizes embodiment and materiality: meaning making always involves bodies and technologies and environments. Students interacting with multimodal texts, in their view, are not merely abstract symbol manipulators but embodied players, and their gestures, voices, and actions. In a digital context, Burnett and Merchant (2020) argued that multimodality and sociotechnical infrastructures are inseparable; for example, a student creating a digital story is not simply integrating various modes, but rather, she is also interacting with, and making sense of, the possibilities and limits of various platforms, algorithms, and interfaces.

Historical Trajectory: From Print to Digital and Participatory Literacies

In order to understand AI-augmented multimodal literacies, it is important to map the history of literacy studies. The early studies of literacy were built upon what Street (1984) called the "autonomous model", where reading and writing were viewed as neutral skills associated with the cognitive domain. Street, however, critiques this model and offers the "ideological model" of literacy whereby he shows that every literacy practice has a social, cultural, and political dimension. The late 20th-century digital revolution gave further impetus to this shift. With the advent of digital and networked media, Mills (2010) argued there was a radical change in the field of literacy studies, as texts became more diverse, interactive, and collaborative. Literacy was more than the ability to decode a single printed document. It included the ability to navigate links, interpret pictures and videos, and create other digital formats.

Jenkins et al. (2009) argued that the participatory culture of fan fiction, video remixing, and online gaming communities has been one of the most important sites for the development of new literacies. He argues that literacy education needs to incorporate these participatory culture practices, where the construction of meaning is collaborative, networked, and multi-representational.

Lankshear and Knobel (2003) emphasized the characterization of new literacies as collaborative, remixed, and redistributed and propose that contemporary literacies are less about solitary authorship and more about the processes of collective meaning making. This digital collaborative ethos enables users to remix, comment, and re-share texts, thereby making the production and consumption of texts indistinguishable. The evolution of literacies from print-focused to digital to participatory makes clear the transformations that are further introduced by artificial intelligence. While digital networks fostered human-to-human collaboration, AI facilitates human-to-machine collaboration, meaning that meaning is now co-created by people and machines. Framed this way, AI does not represent a significant, complete break from the past. Instead, it demonstrates the continuing and deepening changes in literacy practices, including authorship, agency, and equity.

AI's Function in the Furthering of Literacy

The impact of artificial intelligence (AI) on Multimodal literacy development is significant. Floridi and Chiriatti (2020) described the ability of the newly created generative AI to simulate its own distinct creativity with the production of text and images that closely resembles human paradigm. These challenges the traditional views of creativity and authorship in the production of works. Holmes and Tuomi (2022) stated that even the educational applications of AI, such as adaptive learning, feedback, and assessment, are changing with the introduction of large language models and generative AI, to include co-creation of meaning. In the case of AI as a generative tool, it can create works such as essays, poems, and short stories. An example of AI's generation includes the automation of text and images that are provided on a storyboard, then modified by the learner. AI can then act as an interpretive scaffold by providing feedback, suggestions, and adaptive modifications that assist the learner in the improvement of their work.

Burnett and Merchant (2020) noted that the use of AI in creative practices may diminish student voice, if not pedagogically framed, and that AI, in this case, is less about replacement, and more about provocation, by offering a point of departure for idea expansion and critical reflection. This approach demonstrates how the use of AI reshapes traditional understandings of reading and writing. Reading is not only about engaging with texts written by humans but also involves making sense of and responding to summaries, visualizations, and recommendations generated by AI. Writing, too, is no longer exclusively the domain of humans. This co-production of texts raises important questions about authorship, plagiarism, and authenticity.

Global Perspectives: Beyond Western-Centric Frameworks

An important, but still developing, theoretical framework concerning AI-enhanced multimodal literacies is the consideration of non-Western-centric approaches. Most of the early scholarship on multimodal literacies was from Europe, North America, and Australia, but the world contains a wide diversity of literacy practices. Digital literacies, according to Warschauer (2011), are ecological and must consider the local sociocultural, economic, and linguistic conditions. What is multimodal in one context may completely diverge from the practices implemented in another.

The available research in literacy and technology in the Global South must be informed by the local literacies of the Global South shaped by technology, culture, and traditions of the oral, and their distinct multimodal practices (Prinsloo & Rowsell, 2012). For instance, mobile literacies, which include texting, voicing, and sharing mobile images, are leading forms of communication in several regions of Africa. This communication ability is illustrative of the understanding of multimodality beyond the elite, sophisticated digital tools and shows how communities repurpose less sophisticated ones. The presence of AI technology in the Global South also adds to the complexities. Most AI technology, as Bender et al. (2021) pointed out, is trained using English-centric data sets and, as a result, reproduces and reinforces existing linguistic subordination by further marginalizing the already less represented languages.

Culturally sustaining pedagogy seeks to sustain linguistic and cultural diversity in education. In the case of AI-augmented literacies, this means the construction of tools and pedagogies that are supportive of indigenous languages, local semiotic and cultural traditions, and forms of meaning-making. In the African context, localized AI-powered mobile applications have been noted to bridge divides and empower communities (Hambally Yacouba et al., 2025).

The most important and relevant assumptions regarding AI-augmented multimodal literacy rest within four interrelated strands. First, multimodal theories frameworks that centre design and the representation and orchestration of semiotic resources. Second, from the perspective of historical trajectories, literacy, and texts, the analytics of the digital and participatory, and the print centric are important (Jenkins et al., 2009; Kress, 2009; Lankshear & Knobel, 2003; Street, 1984; The New London,

1996; Van Leeuwen, 2005). Third, the role of AI in the extension of literacy illustrates the machine's capabilities of generative and interpretive collaboration as an ally of a reader, writer, and composer (Floridi & Chiriatti, 2020; Holmes & Tuomi, 2022). Lastly, the overarching global perspective seeks an equity and justice in culture and language, the critical reverse of the dominant West (Hambally Yacouba et al., 2025; Peristeris, 2017; Warschauer, 2011).

AI AND CREATIVITY IN EDUCATION

There has been ongoing discourse about AI not being a neutral tool but rather as a partner in the process of creation, particularly in education. Some authors discuss the framing of AI in the context of education as a new category of synthetic creativity in which AI imagination (creativity) is defined as the ability to produce novel works through the recombination of extant data (corpora) in the context of the educational work of (Floridi & Chiriatti, 2020). This type of machine creativity should not be seen as artificial; rather, it is a model that expands the ecosystem (or horizon) of description that meaning making is reliant upon.

In education, this reframing of machine creativity means that students engage meaningfully and creatively with a machine as a collaborator, rather than alone as in a traditional composition (Huot & Loch, 2025a). They work together with machines to create (or compose) prompts and even draft stories, as well as compose soundscapes and images. Some suggest that this type of machine/ human collaboration creates a new type of dialogue and should be viewed as dialogue where the student converses with the machine to critique, edit, and reshape the machine's output, thereby authoring a new version of the work in a cycle of creation.

As a result, questions regarding authorship, originality, and plagiarism begin to arise. As noted by Boden (1998), real creativity, which is the hallmark of true originality, means more than being novel; the idea must be of some value to a given culture and society. Although it is possible that the output of an AI application is novel and original, it is of any value given that it was produced without the purposive direction of a human mind (Huot & Loch, 2025b). The ability of AI to quickly and effortlessly generate text or images does pose the risk of ignoring the original creation of an idea or item and replacing it completely with machine assistance (Kasneci et al., 2023). As a result, the value of originality is lost and is a problem that educators must solve. The problem is that educators must avoid colluding with the student in work that is meant to be done on their own. For Selwyn (2022), the presence of AI in the classroom demands a rethinking of the concept of authorship as the presence of distributed agency, i.e. the ability to control an outcome or function; humans and machines work together to create new meaning, but it is imperative that students do their own work to ensure that they actively think about the output they create and do synthesize.

There is a real need for careful thought in the rethinking of pedagogy. Although some may view AI as a partner in the creative process, Noble (2018) reminds us that AI is not neutral; it carries the biases of its creators and its training data. A student who relies on a biased AI tool, such as a biased generative algorithm, may run the risk of further perpetuating negative stereotypes, clichés, and dominant narratives that, as opposed to capturing the true depth of human experience, oversimplify, or risk the systems of thought that suppress a space that allows for the untrammelled expression of individual creativity. Positioning AI as a creative partner must involve the cultivation of critical literacies that allow learners to interrogate and resist the biases, silences, and ideological assumptions that are embedded in and reflect the machine's absence of creativity.

AI can redefine the authorship and the forms of student creativity. The expansion of multimodal creativity is also an extension of the principle of literacy. Kress (2009) asserts that communication is always multimodal and is made of language, image, gesture, sound, and space. AI empowers students to make and communicate across all these modes, and to create in ways that were previously only available to a few experts. In the visual arts, students can use the AI technology available in platforms such as DALL-E, Stable Diffusion, and MidJourney to create and edit text-based prompts to make quality visual representations of any text. According to Hwang and Wu (2025), students now can produce artistic work that once required years of drawing practice. Machine-aided drawing has some drawbacks. Students mask their culture and social insight when they use the same common elements of design without careful understanding or critical thinking. Students should be encouraged to use their social and cultural insight to design their work and not rely solely on technology.

In music composition, AI systems like OpenAI's MuseNet and AIVA provide scaffolding for constructing and developing harmonies, rhythms, and even complete scores. Davis and Woodward (2020) suggested that creativity should be viewed less as the production of something original and more as the improvisational and transformative process. From this angle, the contribution of AI is to provide the base materials, such as chords, melodies, and motifs, which the learners mix, customize, and reinterpret.

In multimedia projects, the AI ability to seamlessly integrate text, image, sound, and video makes it simpler than ever for students to create their own works. The enhanced accessibility features of automated transcription and captioning tools are complemented by generative AI, which offers narrative scaffolding, storyboarding, or background visuals. According to Warschauer (2011), such multimodal environments are ecologies of literacy, where meaning is the result of dynamic relationships, as opposed to the simple juxtaposition of different elements and modes of communication.

In STEM education, AI enhances creativity with the ability to convert data into visuals. According to Wang et al. (2023), AI data visualization helps comprehension and develops cognitive appreciation for the sciences. AI can help students to create simulations for biological processes, visualizations for data in astronomy, or models for projection of the climate which provides them opportunities to create and make meaning through scientific reasoning and design. Such practices may integrate scientific inquiry with artistic creativity, indicating that STEM may be further developed through various forms of expressions.

Lastly, in AI narrative generation, the design of the story can be supported through prompting of character arcs, thematic motifs, or story outlines. Although there is a need to critique such outputs, learners can be provided with perspectives for further development. Burnett and Merchant (2020) highlight the importance of these machine prompts to support students when making in writing. This is the sort of creativity that is typically reduced in standardized and testing focused classrooms.

Focusing on empirical research provides examples of how AI is transforming creativity in the classroom. The AI digital narrative storytelling projects have been carried out in a variety of fields. Chen (2024) wrote about students who utilized AI to create narrative prompts and background illustrations, which they incorporated into audiovisual narratives. They claim that such a process helped students think multi-modally, since they had to synchronize written stories, AI-produced images, and spoken performances. Notably, students were invited to evaluate the contributions of the AI by rejecting the ones that did not match the cultural context and their knowledge and the topics they were addressing.

Other instance of AI digital narrative storytelling projects, that have been carried out in a variety of fields include the collaborative poetry and image projects. Zhai et al. (2024) described students who used AI based poetry and how they were able to extend their vocabularies, poem structures, and even their use of metaphors beyond their normal levels. Many students tended to use the AI to create novel and unconventional images which they then used in their poetry. Each of these students had to make a conscious choice to accept or reject the image and they had to think about the narrative and the use of language that the AI was employing. Furthermore, projects in which students add text to and remix images that an AI produced also encourage dialogic creativity.

These projects, according to Burnett and Merchant (2020), active make student's critics and curators instead of just technology consumers.AI-driven visualization has changed how students inquire in STEM classrooms. Wang et al. (2023) described examples in which secondary school students used AI to turn basic physics data into interactive simulations. Students were able to describe variables, critique outputs, and use functions to create and engage in design thinking. This also demonstrates that imaginative thinking in the classroom is not limited to the arts. Instead, AI promotes creativity that crosses the boundaries of the humanities and STEM.

The educational discourse surrounding innovation and technology is often taken at face value. Furthermore, overlooking fundamentals like loss of voice and scale of learner agency, even in AI-Enabled creativity. Students' work can become derivative and reflective of biases and stylistic defaults of training data sets, rather than showcasing their individuality. Tackling derivative work and honouring student voice requires rethinking the role of AI in pedagogy. It is a prompt for reflection, not the substitute for authorship. Jandrić et al. (2018) suggested the value of digital pedagogy rests in strengthening the learner's position, so that they can evaluate, adapt and critique the outputs of the AI. One of many ways to achieve this is to have students modify their compositions and then analyse the differences in tone, culture, and value of their work compared to AI. These exercises exemplify the principle that the most valuable aspect of AI is not the work produced but the dialogue that the work inspires.

As students navigate these channels, the importance of integrating critical media literacy becomes apparent. Kellner and Share (2019) emphasized that media literacy must go beyond describing the functions of media and operate to analyse power, ideology, and representation. When it comes to AI, this means helping students learn to speak to the following concerns: Whose voices are represented in the dataset? What are the biases in the assumptions that produced the result, and what are the prevailing ideologies that are either reinforced or ignored? These practices strengthen students' voices and increase awareness of the socio-political implications of AI.

Most importantly, the constructive parameters of generative AI must be prioritized. Williamson (2015) analysed the entwinement of AI in education with issues of governance, surveillance, and commercialization, arguing that the construction of any framework must address these concerns. Use of AI must be Assist, cite AI outputs, and avoid practices of AI that are exploitative and biased. This extends and supports Noble (2018) critiqued of algorithmic systems, reminding us that the integration of ethics embodies questions that ought to be central, not peripheral.

AI as a partner in creativity extends the possibilities of educational practice and supports students in multimodal meaning-making across text, image, sound, and data. It encourages more learning through trial and error, more risk-taking, and more cross-disciplinary creativity, all of which generate important considerations related to rigour, originality, authorship, and ethics (Huot & Tep, 2025). The study showed that when positioned in a critical way, AI can enrich creativity and promote students as active designers and evaluators of AI-generated text. However, if there is a lack of intentional pedagogy surrounding the use of AI, there is a strong possibility that it will stifle student voice, reinforce bias, or reduce the effort of learning to achieve the educational goals.

The use of AI in creative education must be understood as both a possibility and a limitation. The positive side is the accessibility of the tools and the increased number of creative options. The downside is that AI can reduce creativity to a mechanized version of novelty if it is not used with critical thought. The challenge for educators is to leverage the creative potential of AI while fostering critical thinking, cultural awareness, and ethics in students. Only then can AI truly supplement, and not replace, human creativity, allowing students to maintain control as the primary authors of their work in a world with AI, as represented in Table 1.

Table 1. AI and creativity in education: Key themes, opportunities, and challenges

Theme	Description	Opportunities	Challenges
AI as Creative Partner	Human–AI co-creativity in writing, design, and storytelling.	Stimulates idea generation; enables new narrative forms; fosters student–machine collaboration.	Tensions over authorship, originality, plagiarism; risk of bias reproduction.
Expanding Modalities	AI expands creative expression across text, image, music, multimedia, and STEM visualization.	Democratizes access to art and music; enhances multimodal composition; integrates data visualization in STEM.	Overreliance on templates; risk of homogenization; cultural flattening of aesthetics.
Case Studies	Examples include AI-assisted storytelling, collaborative poetry, image-based projects, and STEM visualizations.	Encourages experimentation; fosters multimodal thinking; supports interdisciplinary creativity.	Requires careful curation of AI outputs; potential misalignment with student identity/culture.
Balancing Innovation with Authenticity	Safeguarding student voice and identity in AI-augmented creativity.	Encourages critical reflection; strengthens media literacy; cultivates ethical awareness.	Risk of student passivity; ethical dilemmas around citation, transparency, and surveillance.

AI, COMMUNICATION, AND COLLABORATION

Changing educational settings, artificial intelligence (AI) is changing definitions of communication. In the past, digital technologies were viewed to human communication, such as emails, messaging systems, and video conferencing. Now, communication can be mediated and co-constructed by a machine. Communication channels, including AI, must be viewed as active, not neutral. AI participates in communication by creating, interpreting, and responding to stimuli in ways that change the dynamics of classroom communication (Selwyn, 2022).

One of the most important is the sheer number of AI-controlled communication systems that can manage communication in text, voice, and video. In addition, LLMs (large language models) provide students with immediate commentary on their text-based assignments. They also possess the ability to visually illustrate ideas and convert text into audio speech synthesis. Because of such systems, students can engage with educational materials using a variety of sensory and semiotic, or communicative, modalities (Holmes & Tuomi, 2022). This ability represents a notable advancement in educational technologies and aligns with Kress's (2009) view of communication as inherently multimodal. AI furthered this with its ability to manage multiple communications and modalities, at previously unachievable speed and volume.

Further exemplifying this transformation is multimodal chatbots. Unlike previous chatbots that utilized rules and acted more like automatons, AI conversational agents are able to maintain longer conversations, and respond naturally and appropriately to varying contexts and shifts in tone. These systems, per Luckin (2018), could be seen as mimicking a peer, providing alternative constructive feedback, or even as moving students to explain their thinking. Some even combine their interactions with visual aids like diagrams or infographics created in response to the text they have written. This enables learners to create a communicative setting that is more interactive and personalized to their individual learning needs.

Currently, AI is being used in the analysis of classroom discourse as a lens on interactions. AI helps analyse discourse by detecting participation patterns, monitoring group work asymmetries, and identifying silences wherein particular speakers are muted. However, Williamson (2015) warned that such datafication simplifies the complexity of human communication into the non-negotiable straws of human interaction. A teacher may lose sight of the fact that the quality of participation is more important than the quantity. AI's assessment may lower the communication quality by overshooting the nuances like the lack of confidence, the presence of irony, or other elements that are not visible to the algorithm. Therefore, even though AI is likely to widen the scope of communication by showing who is excluded, the frames such guides operate within are still over-simplistic and in need of rigorous critical analysis.

The second important role of artificial intelligence in communication is the facilitation of global and intercultural exchange. In diverse classrooms, language has always been an obstacle to collaboration. However, the use of AI for translation, in conjunction with visualization, now provides a way for students to collaborate across different languages. Pym (2009) stated that translation facilitates cultural exchanges but with AI, the speed and volume increases. Google Translate, DeepL, and Microsoft Translator enable learners to communicate multilingual texts and captions in video calls, and audio in real time. Participants who may have remained silent in a video discussion can use translation apps to communicate. Warschauer (2011) argued that translation apps increase participation in large, diverse classrooms. Tools that generate visual concept maps from multilingual input extend translational communication beyond the limits of language.

Consider collaborative science projects. With the aid of AI translation, students from different parts of the world can co-author documents in several languages. Other visualization tools help to construct shared models of their hypotheses. These activities extend participatory culture, as described by Jenkins et al. (2009), by framing global collaboration as a literacy practice, whereby meaning is created through the integration of multiple forms. What has happened has its share of issues. Bender et al. (2021) noted that the models unfairly favour the West when it comes to the languages that they incorporate due to the systemic biases in the English-dominant training sets. Venuti (2000) stated that automated linguistics tends to 'domesticate' the source text, resulting in the loss of foreign unities and in the overriding of the distinctiveness for the mainstream audience. This causes the loss of important cultural foreign units, and primary translations may lead to the loss of the cultural self in the final texts in classrooms.

Peristeris (2017) advocated for culturally sustaining pedagogy, which argues that the purpose of assimilating technologies into the classroom should not be to bury cultural practices, but to keep them alive. In the case of AI-based translation, this means that educators must teach a critical structure of translation when using the AI tools and treat them as obsolete solutions that will leave a gap that must be filled, and that will, in the end, remove or transform a foreign text. Therefore, from a pedagogical standpoint, these are the criteria under which, paradoxically, AI may support the preservation of a place when global interoperability is sought.

AI's influence is changing how collaborative learning is modelled. As Stahl et al. (2006) observed, collaborative learning involves the construction of meaning through communication and joint action. With the integration of AI, new collaborative frameworks can be created, and new forms of participant involvement can be operationalized.

AI can be integrated as a real time collaborator. For instance, in a group discussion, an AI may be used to encourage a quiet student to share their thoughts, summarize what the group has agreed on, or even share an opposing opinion to catalyse an argument. Such forms of 'collaborative' support may, as Luckin (2018) suggested, help to level the inequities that exist in group participation. Stahl (2017) warned, however, that for true collaboration to take place, there needs to be act of building intersubjectivity, the human ability to achieve a mutual understanding through a negotiation process, an understanding that is achieved through the human interaction. There is a risk that if AI is allowed to overly control interactions in a group, students may be conditioned to be passive to the stimuli created by the technology, and as a result, the important social competencies of empathy, and the ability to resolve conflict may be lost.

In asynchronous learning environments, AI fosters collaboration through shared editing and authoring. With tools like Google Docs, AI can create summaries, identify contradictions, and make reorganization suggestions. Haoming et al. (2025) explained this as AI acting as a silent collaborator, as it works to lessen cognitive load and allows learners to engage in more complex thinking. AI-driven dialogue systems can offer formative feedback on writing, which can help students learn to write more in-depth peer critiques.

AI functions optimally when it supports collaboration and empowers learners to engage in meaning-making. However, the challenge of balancing support is over or under-calibration. If a collaborator offers insufficient guidance, students may find it hard to work together. If a collaborator offers too much guidance, the collaboration becomes too controlled, and students lose the benefit of the productive friction that develops empathy. The use of AI in communication and collaboration carries both positive and negative dimensions. On the one hand, AI creates new avenues for use, while on the other hand, creates new problems, or reinforces existing problems.

As for positive aspects, AI can create more inclusive engagement, help people communicate across languages, and assist in more balanced group work. As Selwyn (2019) pointed out, communication AIs can help customize dialogues in response to individual learner levels, resulting in varying degrees of involvement in a particular group. For those students who have been marginalized for reasons related to language, disability, or social class, AI tools can serve to elevate their presence and provide them the opportunity to participate in more elements of the collaborative learning process. There are several problems associated with the use of AI, and they are primarily centred on the negative consequences of automation. The first of these is the potential for automation to foster over-reliance. Buckingham (2019) pointed out that while the Automation of certain systems can provide efficiencies, they need to be complemented by the engagement and use of a variety of human skills, such as empathy, patience, and the ability to tolerate ambiguity. The use of AI in collaborative tasks may make face to face interaction and collaboration more difficult and encourage a lack of interdependence.

Data privacy and surveillance issues are also present. Williamson (2015) suggested that surveillance is an essential part of AI and datafication processes and communication that is captured, stored and analysed. Gordon (2019) argued that these surveillance systems are detrimental, especially to marginalized groups, and education becomes a place for this governance by algorithms. This brings forth an important ethical dilemma: what is the ownership of the data collected in AI and the communication it facilitates, for what purposes is that data used, and who benefits from it.

There is also the risk of cultural homogenization in intercultural contexts. Furthermore, AI-mediated discourse and automated translation, while providing surface-level efficiency, remove depth, nuance and authenticity. Translation is always interpretive, Venuti (2000), and when machines are used to bridge gaps, we lose more than words, we lose a culture. The opportunities of AI, such as efficiency, accessibility, and inclusivity, are real, but the risks are equally important. Educators must embed the use of AI within the pedagogies of critical literacy, ethical, and cultural literacy responsibility, as shown in Table 2.

Table 2. AI, communication, and collaboration: Dimensions, opportunities, and risks

Dimension	Description	Opportunities	Challenges
Redefining Communication	AI-mediated platforms support text, audio, and visual exchanges; chatbots and discourse analysis shape classroom interaction.	Enables multimodal dialogue; scaffolds participation; provides analytic insights for teachers.	Reduces communication to metrics; risks over-reliance on machine-mediated dialogue; may miss nuance and emotion.
Intercultural and Global Exchange	AI translation and visualization tools facilitate cross-linguistic and cross-cultural collaboration.	Bridges language barriers; fosters inclusivity in multilingual classrooms; supports participatory global projects.	Flattens cultural nuance; reproduces linguistic hierarchies; risks cultural homogenization.
Collaborative Learning Models	AI scaffolds synchronous and asynchronous collaboration through prompts, shared editing, and peer support.	Encourages equitable participation; streamlines group work; enhances peer critique.	Over-scaffolding risks passivity; may displace human negotiation; challenges authentic intersubjectivity.
Risks and Opportunities	AI enhances efficiency but raises ethical, relational, and governance concerns.	Personalized communication; democratized access; inclusion of marginalized learners.	Over-dependence; erosion of interpersonal skills; data privacy, surveillance, and algorithmic governance.

CRITIQUE AND ETHICAL ASPECTS

Reproduction of bias and misinformation is perhaps the most common concern in the intersections of AI and education. As an example, Bender et al. (2021) noted in the influential paper, On the Dangers of Stochastic Parrots, that large language models (LLMs) produce outputs that at first glance appear coherent, but they operate on stochastic processes of pattern recognition. As such, the generated sentences, while sounding authoritative, they may reproduce bias and fabricate falsehoods with unwarranted confidence. This behaviour is a serious ethical concern in the classroom, most notably the younger students who may not have the ability to tell a fact from a well-articulated piece of fiction.

Most scholars have indicated that the bias of algorithmic systems is a replication of inequities that exist today. In the critiques of Google search engines, Noble (2018) illustrated how the algorithms that appear neutral reproduce the racialized and gendered stereotypes, thus embedding systemic oppression into the digital infrastructure. AI writing tools have the potential of extending this logic to the classroom, affecting students' conceptualisations of gender, race, and even vocations. For example, an AI system with a task of generating images of scientists is likely to produce images of white men in lab coats, thus reinforcing exclusionary norms.

The authors assert that AI's misinformation production is not a random occurrence, but rather a systemic, built-in feature of these systems. AI systems do not know facts but rather create language outputs based on statistical correlations. Even when AI outputs are helpful, there will always be an accompanying epistemological risk because students may confuse the fluency of an AI output with the truth and cause the weakening of the underlying critical thinking.

Kellner and Share (2019) argued the importance of media literacy and critical literacy combined, to interrogate and analyse AI, representation, and power. Within an AI context, a role of media literacy is teaching students to identify factual inaccuracies, and the next, more critical, level is to analyse the centric, the underlying, the marginal and the erased. Educators must situate critiques of AI within the traditions of critical literacy to mitigate the risks of bias and misinformation and create the possibility for critical and reflexive engagement.

The use of artificial intelligence in education is expected to create changes. However, the benefits of this technology are likely to be uneven. This situation warrants an examination of the potential outcomes. Educational technology is often seen as an equalizer, but although, Selwyn (2019) suggests, it has digital divides. Educational institutions in the Global South, and those that are inadequate, are lacking the resources to address this issue. Warschauer (2011) stated that the digital divide should be closing, and it should be seen in terms of access that is equal and meaningful. There is an absence of sufficient structures in education and disparities of recognition in the use of technology to artificial intelligence tools as goals. Without this recognition, the use of artificial intelligence is intended to bridge gaps, but it is intended to be a harsh divide.

Criticising the narratives that suggest the adoption of AI in Africa is a fast-track solution, Hambally Yacouba et al. (2025) drew attention to the lack of attention to the unreliable electricity, poor internet connectivity, and under-resourced schools. In such contexts where the Global North designs AI technologies, it may be inappropriate, or worse, reinforce reliance on external systems without fostering local relevant literacies. Adding to this, Peristeris (2017) suggested that in culturally sustaining pedagogy, the question is not simply, who has access? but who's cultural and linguistic practices get to be affirmed? AI systems conditioned on the English language serve to reinforce dominant knowledge systems while demoting minority languages and further perpetuate the existing linguistic hierarchies.

Thus, equity goes beyond the distribution of resources to also include the recognition that these systems further lack epistemic justice. The adoption of AI systems that continue to perpetuate Western dominant knowledge systems and do not include other systems, continue to worsen already existing inequalities, even when access is guaranteed. Therefore, sustaining equity as a moral imperative, the lack of culturally responsive pedagogy, and the reliance on AI in education, must be accompanied with local tool development, adequate investment in infrastructure, and culturally responsive pedagogy.

In AI-enabled classrooms, one of the more ethically complex issues is the potential for erosion of learner agency. Kasneci et al. (2023) stated that reliance on AI for drafting, problem solving, and generating ideas, runs the risk of eroding students' ability to be original and think critically. Buckingham (2019) argued that educational technologies that focus more on efficiency than on process and reflection are also problematic. When students use AI to write their essays or solve their problems, they are outsourcing not only the labour that education is meant to do, but also the cognitive and creative tasks that education is meant to cultivate.

However, agency is also about a reconfiguration of authorship and co-authorship. Selwyn (2022) argued for the need to move beyond the binary of plagiarism and originality and consider the role of AI as a meaning-making partner. Students as active interpreters and decision makers are central to the pedagogical purpose of shaping and refining AI outputs, as opposed to being passive recipients of text produced by a machine.

Jandrić et al. (2018) argued that digital pedagogy should explicitly address critical digital agency – the ability to question, resist, and repurpose technologies to serve learners' goals. For instance, students could be assigned the task of creating an AI draft and then evaluating it for bias in style, culture, and ideology. By doing so, the AI prompts a reflection assignment rather than replacing an author. Such practices maintain learner agency by empowering students to be the ultimate decision-makers in the creative and interpretive process.

AI's ethics in education should not be the responsibility of the individual; it should be a consequence of routine instructional practices and strategies. One of the most crucial is the integration of critical digital literacy frameworks in pedagogy. Lankshear and Knobel (2003) posited that digital literacies presume critical reflection around power, ideology, and participation. In the context of AI, this could mean instructing students about the way in which training datasets influence outputs, the varying types of bias in algorithms, and the reasoning behind AI's irrational and nonsensical outputs. Students should not consider AI neutral but rather question the socially and politically constructed nature of the technology.

Educators can emphasize algorithmic transparency. Even though the technical specifics of the procedures and the machine learning models can be beyond their comprehension, educators can explain that the models are trained on large datasets and that their results are probabilistic, and they do not know fact from plausibility. There are an apparent lack of knowledge and an absence of risk on the part of the user; thus, using AI ethically requires an adequate understanding of its limits (Floridi & Chiriatti, 2020). Zhai et al. (2024) stated that students understanding the limits of AI helps them analyse its results and avoid taking them at face value. Another pedagogical approach is the teaching of responsible authorship. Kellner and Share (2019) stated that the teaching of literacy includes the teaching of ethics, citation, authorship, and responsibility. Students need to learn to be responsible for disclosing the AI they used, determining when a human or a machine was involved in producing the work, and undertaking a review of AI-generated texts. These practices promote responsible use of technology and academic integrity.

Although theoretical frameworks are essential, students tend to learn best with concrete examples of case-based ethics. By using classroom examples that create specific, real-world situations, educators can engage students in bias, authorship, and responsibility. A student could be instructed to make such a bias aware and empower them to AI to be used more positively by rewriting the essay. Knowing the lesson, the student is exposed to is the most powerful AI application in a negative context – deep fakes. Chesney and Citron (2019) described deep fakes as dangerous in most instances. A teacher may show students several videos that are real and several that are AI generated and ask them to determine the real ones. This provides students the opportunity to begin developing techniques and strategies that allow them to seek and question evidence in the pictures. This is related to the civic literacy construct, more specifically determining the strategies to use in an environment where manipulated evidence is abundant.

As with any other field, issues of academic integrity are salient here as well. Should a student who uses an AI as an idea generator and discloses its use be punished? Where is the line between permissible assistance and outright copying? These examples highlight the contemporary and changing fluidity around the concept of authorship when used with AI tools. In these cases, students see ethics not as an abstract concept but as lived practice, allowing them to practice the critical thinking and other higher-order skills they will require in the real world after formal schooling is complete.

The need to engage with AI ethics as part of literacy education is crucial if we are to keep education a place of equity and social justice. The biases and misinformation present in AI require teaching students to analyse and evaluate the results they obtain and to interrogate the output. The imbalances of equity and access remind us of the digital divides within society, the need to integrate AI in teaching and learning is part of an unequal distribution of resources and access to adequate technology, and it is about equity in knowledge. The demand for learner agency is a call for educators to find a balance between augmentation and autonomy; students must be engaged not as consumers, but as active co-authors of knowledge.

Equally important, the challenges we face should not just be seen as obstacles, but as the opportunities I have just described. The embedding of specific frameworks of digital literacy, teaching algorithmic transparency, and employing ethics by case, can mean that in the teaching of AI, we can avoid the threat and facilitate the engagement. Students can learn to use AI not just responsibly but to question and even resist and reform it to democratic and culturally sustainable ends. In this sense, the objective is to go beyond seeing AI as just an instrument to be controlled to seeing it as a set of cultural and ethical issues to be worked through. For AI, literacy means something special, and in this case, it is primarily aimed at empowering learners as critical, imaginative, and ethical protagonists who can question and criticize the assumptions of AI, sustain its limitations, and exploit its benefits without losing their voice, agency, or identity, as summarized in Table 3.

Table 3. Critical engagement and ethical considerations in AI-Augmented literacies

Dimension	Description	Opportunities	Challenges
Bias and Misinformation	AI systems may reproduce stereotypes, amplify cultural biases, or generate plausible but false information.	Opportunities for teaching critical media literacy; developing skills to interrogate representation and ideology.	Risk of reinforcing systemic inequities; hallucinated content misleads students; uncritical trust in outputs.
Equity and Access	Uneven availability of AI tools across regions, schools, and socio-economic contexts.	Potential to democratize participation if made widely available; adaptation to diverse contexts.	Exacerbation of digital divides; reinforcement of Western-centric epistemologies; exclusion of minority languages.
Learner Agency	Ensuring students remain active authors, not passive consumers, in AI-supported learning tasks.	Encourages co-authorship and critical evaluation; fosters creativity and independence.	Over-reliance on AI risks diminishing originality, critical thinking, and ownership of learning.
Pedagogical Strategies	Frameworks and approaches to teach students to critically engage with AI outputs.	Embedding critical digital literacy; teaching algorithmic transparency; reinforcing academic integrity.	Complexity of technical explanations; inconsistent application across curricula; risk of superficial criticality.
Case-Based Ethics	Use of classroom scenarios to explore AI-related dilemmas (bias detection, deepfakes, authorship).	Practical engagement with real-world issues; develops ethical reflexivity and civic literacies.	Potential student confusion over boundaries of acceptable AI use; ethical dilemmas remain context-dependent.

CONCLUSION AND FUTURE DIRECTIONS

This chapter focused on the positive effects of artificial intelligence on the development of multimodal literacies in the field of education. In the previous discussions, three of the most interconnected dimensions that stood out included:

creativity, communication, and criticality. Together, they represent the prospects and difficulties of incorporating artificial intelligence in classrooms. There is an expansion of creativity when students partner with artificial intelligence in collaborative writing, designing, music composition, and multimodal storytelling. Communication is also redefined, as artificial intelligence enables communication in several languages, assists in collaborative interaction, and mediates various forms of communication. Criticality remains an element that is of utmost importance, in as much as it makes students, as well as educators, ask essential questions on bias, equity, ethics, and agency.

Going forward, pedagogical models that emphasize innovation and innovation and responsibility must guide the practice of education. Inquiry-based learning, for example, allows students to incorporate AI tools into their open-ended exploration, question development, hypothesis testing, and evaluation of outputs. Project-based learning situates AI in genuine, interdisciplinary, means of integration, enabling learners to incorporate and make meaning in text, image, and data formats. Critical digital literacy frameworks open the door to students ethically engaging AI by equipping them with strategies to critique AI systems, understand their limitations, and mitigate reductive/bias outputs. Collectively, these models show that the rational AI integration is to enrich learning, grounded in student agency and reflective pedagogy.

There are multiple recommendations that can be made from this synthesis. Educators need to provide classroom practices where AI can be a collaborative partner but not take away from the student's voice or originality. Curriculum designers need to integrate AI to be a part of the multiple, available tasks that are designed to express and produce critical and culturally responsive practices so students can learn to use technology as a tool and a text. Access to the AI tools must be prioritised and inequitable access to technology AI tools must be available to all communities, schools and regions. The use of AI tools must not worsen existing inequities. Teacher education programs need to include professional development in AI literacies so that teachers can provide guidance to their learners to use these tools in the ethically responsible way and in the constructive way.

The emerging research agenda is just as urgent. The sustained impact of AI on the development of literacy, creativity, and critical thinking needs to be examined through longitudinal studies. There is a need for comparative research to examine the ways AI is used in culturally and linguistically diverse settings to not take an approach that is the same for all. Additionally, frameworks need to be created to address the ethical concerns of authoring, agency, and accountability of learners in an AI mediated environment. As these questions continue to be researched, the role of AI in education continues to be reshaped with thoughtfulness and care.

The main concept of this chapter is neither replacement nor retaining the status quo. Instead, it's about future of literacy education, advocating for the construction of educational ecosystems in which AI will strengthen, and not diminish, human capabilities. The educational ecosystems will empower students to advocate for and practice transcultural communication, interdisciplinary creativity, and critical engagement with technology. Centred on the principles of equity, ethics, and culturally sustaining pedagogy, the literacies of the future, augmented by AI, will advocate for and practice the transcultural communication, interdisciplinary creativity, and critical engagement with technology. In this future, students are not passive recipients of machine-generated content; they actively design, critique, and collaborate to shape a new age of literacy in which technology fuels humanity's creativity, communication, and critical engagement.

REFERENCES

Bender, E. M., Gebru, T., McMillan-Major, A., & Shmitchell, S. (2021). On the dangers of stochastic parrots: Can language models be too big? *Proceedings of the 2021 ACM Conference on Fairness, Accountability, and Transparency*, Virtual Event, Canada. DOI: 10.1145/3442188.3445922

Bezemer, J., & Kress, G. (2015). *Multimodality, learning and communication*. Routledge., DOI: 10.4324/9781315687537

Boden, M. A. (1998). Creativity and artificial intelligence. *Artificial Intelligence*, *103*(1–2), 347–356. DOI: 10.1016/S0004-3702(98)00055-1

Buckingham, D. (2019). *The media education manifesto*. Polity Press.

Burnett, C., & Merchant, G. (2020). Returning to text: Affect, meaning making, and literacies. *Reading Research Quarterly*, *56*(2), 355–367. DOI: 10.1002/rrq.303

Chen, Y. (2024). Perceptions of AI-facilitated creativity in language education: A study on digital storytelling. *The JALT CALL Journal*, *20*(3), 1–27. DOI: 10.29140/jaltcall.v20n3.2089

Chesney, R., & Citron, D. K. (2019). Deep fakes: A looming challenge for privacy, democracy, and national security. SSRN *Electronic Journal, 107*, 1–68. DOI: 10.2139/ssrn.3213954

Davis, G. A., & Woodward, J. (2020). *Creativity is forever*. Hunt Publishing.

Floridi, L., & Chiriatti, M. (2020). GPT-3: Its nature, scope, limits, and consequences. *Minds and Machines*, *30*(4), 681–694. DOI: 10.1007/s11023-020-09548-1

Gordon, F. (2019). Virginia Eubanks (2018) automating inequality: How high-tech tools profile, police, and punish the poor. New york: Picador, st martin's press. *Law. Technology and Humans*, *1*(1), 162–164. DOI: 10.5204/lthj.v1i0.1386

Hambally Yacouba, Y., Diabagate, A., Diaby, M., Coulibaly, A., & Azmani, A. (2025). AI in african schools: Obstacles, perspectives and pedagogical strategies. *International Journal of Advanced Research*, *13*(9), 764–784. DOI: 10.21474/IJAR01/21760

Haoming, W., Chengliang, W., Zhan, C., Fa, L., Chunjia, B., & Xianlong, X. (2025). Impact of AI-agent-supported collaborative learning on the learning outcomes of university programming courses. *Education and Information Technologies*, *30*(12), 1–34. DOI: 10.1007/s10639-025-13487-8

Holmes, W., & Tuomi, I. (2022). State of the art and practice in AI in education. *European Journal of Education*, *57*(4), 542–570. DOI: 10.1111/ejed.12533

Huot, S., & Loch, S. (2025a). Digital practices in Cambodian EFL classrooms: Teacher narratives from remote learning. In K. Khette & Tayade (Eds.), *Proceeding of one day national conference on English language, literature, cultural studies and media studies* (Vol. 2, pp. 19–31). Centre for Learning, Research and Development, Savda, Maharashtra. DOI: 10.5281/zenodo.16921807

Huot, S., & Loch, S. (2025b). Educating in the age of AI: Preparing Cambodian teachers and students for an AI-augmented learning future. *Journal of Educational Technology and E-Learning Innovations*, *1*(2), 31–38. DOI: 10.54536/jeteli.v1i2.5170

Huot, S., & Tep, P. (2025). Advancing ChatGPT for pedagogical innovation in Cambodia: Insight from global evidence and local implications. *The Context: Journal of English Studies*, *12*(4), 115–135. DOI: 10.5281/zenodo.15806972

Hwang, Y., & Wu, Y. (2025). Graphic design education in the era of text-to-image generation: Transitioning to contents creator. *International Journal of Art & Design Education*, *44*(1), 239–253. DOI: 10.1111/jade.12558

Jandrić, P., Knox, J., Besley, T., Ryberg, T., Suoranta, J., & Hayes, S. (2018). Postdigital science and education. *Educational Philosophy and Theory*, *50*(10), 893–899. DOI: 10.1080/00131857.2018.1454000

Jenkins, H., Purushotma, R., Weigel, M., Clinton, K., & Robison, A. J. (2009). *Confronting the challenges of participatory culture: Media education for the 21st century*. The MIT Press., DOI: 10.7551/mitpress/8435.001.0001

Jewitt, C., Bezemer, J., & O'Halloran, K. (2016). *Introducing multimodality*. Routledge., DOI: 10.4324/9781315638027

Kasneci, E., Sessler, K., Küchemann, S., Bannert, M., Dementieva, D., Fischer, F., Gasser, U., Groh, G., Günnemann, S., Hüllermeier, E., Krusche, S., Kutyniok, G., Michaeli, T., Nerdel, C., Pfeffer, J., Poquet, O., Sailer, M., Schmidt, A., Seidel, T., & Kasneci, G. (2023). ChatGPT for good? On opportunities and challenges of large language models for education. *Learning and Individual Differences*, *103*, 1–13. DOI: 10.1016/j.lindif.2023.102274

Kellner, D., & Share, J. (2019). *The critical media literacy guide engaging media & transforming education*. Brill., DOI: 10.1163/9789004404533

Kress, G. (2009). *Multimodality: A social semiotic approach to contemporary communication*. Routledge., DOI: 10.4324/9780203970034

Lankshear, C., & Knobel, M. (2003). *New literacies* (1st ed.). Open University Press.

Luckin, R. (2018). *Machine learning and human intelligence: The future of education for the 21st century*. UCL Institute of Education Press.

Mills, K. A. (2010). A review of the "digital turn" in the new literacy studies. *Review of Educational Research, 80*(2), 246–271. DOI: 10.3102/0034654310364401

Noble, S. U. (2018). *Algorithms of oppression: How search engines reinforce racism*. New York University Press., DOI: 10.18574/nyu/9781479833641.001.0001

Peristeris, K. (2017). Culturally sustaining pedagogies: Teaching and learning for justice in a changing world. *Journal of Teaching and Learning, 11*(1), 35–37. DOI: 10.22329/jtl.v11i1.4987

Prinsloo, M., & Rowsell, J. (2012). Digital literacies as placed resources in the globalised periphery. *Language and Education, 26*(4), 271–277. DOI: 10.1080/09500782.2012.691511

Pym, A. (2009). *Exploring translation theories*. Routledge., DOI: 10.4324/9780203869291

Selwyn, N. (2019). *Should robots replace teachers?: AI and the future of education*. Polity Press.

Selwyn, N. (2022). The future of AI and education: Some cautionary notes. *European Journal of Education, 57*(4), 620–631. DOI: 10.1111/ejed.12532

Stahl, G. (2017). Group practices: A new way of viewing CSCL. *International Journal of Computer-Supported Collaborative Learning, 12*(1), 113–126. DOI: 10.1007/s11412-017-9251-0

Stahl, G., Koschmann, D., & SuthersDan, S. (2006). Computer-supported collaborative learning: An historical perspective. In R. K. Sawyer (Ed.), (pp. 1–20). Cambridge University Press. DOI: 10.1017/CBO9781139519526.029

Street, B. V. (1984). *Literacy in theory and practice*. Cambridge University Press.

The New London. (1996). A pedagogy of multiliteracies: Designing social futures. *Harvard Educational Review, 66*(1), 60–93. DOI: 10.17763/haer.66.1.17370n67v-22j160u

Van Leeuwen, T. (2005). *Introducing social semiotics*. Routledge.

Venuti, L. (2000). *The translation studies reader*. Routledge. DOI: 10.4324/9780203446621

Wang, X., Wu, Z., Huang, W., Wei, Y., Huang, Z., Xu, M., & Chen, W. (2023). VIS+AI: Integrating visualization with artificial intelligence for efficient data analysis. *Frontiers of Computer Science*, *17*(6), 1–12. DOI: 10.1007/s11704-023-2691-y

Warschauer, M. (2011). *Learning in the cloud: How (and why) to transform schools with digital media*. Teachers College Press.

Williamson, B. (2015). Digital education governance: Data visualization, predictive analytics, and 'real-time' policy instruments. *Journal of Education Policy*, *31*(2), 123–141. DOI: 10.1080/02680939.2015.1035758

Zhai, C., Wibowo, S., & Li, L. D. (2024). The effects of over-reliance on AI dialogue systems on students' cognitive abilities: A systematic review. *Smart Learning Environments*, *11*(1), 1–37. DOI: 10.1186/s40561-024-00316-7

KEY TERMS AND DEFINITIONS

Artificial Intelligence (AI): Systems that are built to go through tasks that generally require human cognition, including comprehension of languages, perception of images, and the prediction of patterns are referred to as artificial intelligence. In the education sector, AI includes tools that can create, evaluate, and adjust educational material and in so doing, serves the principals of education, such as the promotion of creativity, communication and the provision of individualized education.

Communication: The meaning transfer through linguistic, visual, audio and digital channels is known as communication. The use of AI to facilitate communication always involves other phenomena such as real-time translation, multimodal communication, and collaborative communication. The integration of these technologies raises other issues, including the absence of trust, the gap in nuances, and the loss of interpersonal connection.

Creativity: The ability to design new and valuable ideas, expressions, or artifacts is referred to as creativity. In the context of AI-augmented education, creativity is reflected in human-AI co-production, where learners interact with machines to design, create, and modify multimodal compositions while retaining their authorship and originality.

Critical Engagement: In relation to AI, Critical Engagement involves the use of technology in a thoughtful and self-aware manner. Technology Critically involves teaching learners to examine algorithmic outputs, recognize their limitations and use technology responsibly and self reflexively.

Digital Pedagogy: The use of digital technology in teaching and learning in intentional ways is called Digital Pedagogy. It includes the use of digital tools and systems in teaching and learning, as well as reflective thinking on how the use of digital technologies influence the learning process, self-identify and knowledge.

Equity: In education, the fair distribution of resources, opportunities, and results is termed as equity. In the case of AI, equity focuses on the imbalance in availability of the instruments and the tools, the provision of necessary infrastructure, and the potential of exacerbating the technological, linguistic, cultural, or systemic inequities.

Ethics: Principles of right and responsible action in the design and use of technologies is termed as ethics. In AI-enhanced literacies, ethics means dealing with issues of authorship, transparency, bias and surveillance, and the fair treatment of learners in different contexts.

Multimodal Literacy: The ability to create, understand, evaluate, and critique meaning across multiple channels of communication is called multimodal literacy. It involves the use of different semiotic resources and is essential for 21st-century learning since communication is often digital and takes multiple forms. The channels of communication include written, visual, audio, digital resources, and spatial modes.

Chapter 8
Meta-Analysis in Multimodal Literacy Studies:
Synthesizing Evidence in the Age of Artificial Intelligence

Brijendra Parasnath Gupta
http://orcid.org/0000-0003-3597-350X
Siddhant College of Engineering, Pune, India

Negmatov Bobir
Sarbon University, Uzbekistan

Kunduz Irisbaeva
Kimyo International University, Tashkent

Diloram Ergasheva
Namangan State University, Uzbekistan

Bakhtiyor Qayumov
Namangan State Pedagogical Institute, Uzbekistan

Shoira Abdullaeva
Tashkent State University of Oriental Studies, Uzbekistan

Karimov Hikmat
Mamun University, Khiva, Uzbekistan

Qalandarova Bonu
Urgench State University, Uzbekistan

ABSTRACT

This chapter examines the role of meta-analysis in synthesizing research evidence within multimodal literacy studies, particularly as artificial intelligence transforms educational landscapes. Meta-analytic approaches provide systematic methods for aggregating findings across diverse studies examining AI integration in multimodal learning environments. The chapter analyzes key meta-analyses investigating AI literacy development, generative AI impacts on learning outcomes, multimodal

DOI: 10.4018/979-8-3373-6986-0.ch008

learning analytics, and digital literacy frameworks. Through critical examination of methodological approaches, effect sizes, and moderating variables, this synthesis reveals consistent positive effects of AI-enhanced multimodal interventions on student achievement, alongside challenges including over-reliance risks and implementation variability.

INTRODUCTION

Table 1. Summary of Key Meta-Analytic Findings

Study	k Studies	Effect Size	95% CI	Focus Area
Ma & Zhong (2025)	37	d = 0.52	[0.41, 0.63]	Generative AI on learning outcomes
Sun & Zhou (2024)	28	d = 0.67	[0.52, 0.82]	Generative AI in higher education
Tlili et al. (2025)	52	d = 0.48	[0.35, 0.61]	AI in education overall
Gu & Ericson (2024)	Multiple	d = 0.45-0.78	Varies	AI literacy conceptual understanding
Wang et al. (2023)	N/A	$R^2 = 0.76$	vs. 0.52	Multimodal analytics in PBL

The convergence of multimodal literacy studies and artificial intelligence represents one of the most transformative developments in contemporary education research. As educational environments increasingly integrate multiple modes of communication—including text, images, audio, video, and interactive digital elements—alongside rapidly advancing AI technologies, understanding the cumulative evidence base becomes critical for informed practice and policy. Meta-analysis emerges as an essential methodological tool for synthesizing this expanding body of research, offering systematic approaches to aggregate findings, identify patterns, and quantify effects across diverse contexts and populations (Chiu et al., 2023; Ma & Zhong, 2025).

Multimodal literacy—the ability to comprehend, create, and critically evaluate texts that combine multiple semiotic modes—has evolved significantly since Bezemer and Kress (2016) articulated its social semiotic foundations. Contemporary multimodal literacy extends beyond traditional print and digital texts to encompass AI-generated content, interactive simulations, augmented reality experiences, and adaptive learning systems (Lim et al., 2022). This expansion necessitates new frameworks for understanding how learners develop competencies across diverse modal configurations and technological platforms (Liu et al., 2024).

Simultaneously, artificial intelligence has transitioned from a peripheral educational technology to a central component of teaching and learning ecosystems. The emergence of large language models, computer vision systems, and generative AI tools has fundamentally altered how students access information, produce multimodal artifacts, and engage with educational content (Albadarin et al., 2024). These developments demand rigorous examination of AI's impacts on learning outcomes, literacy development, and pedagogical practices—examination best conducted through systematic synthesis of empirical evidence.

Meta-analysis provides quantitative methods for synthesizing research findings, calculating aggregate effect sizes, and identifying moderating variables that explain heterogeneity across studies. In multimodal literacy and AI education research, meta-analytic approaches enable researchers to move beyond individual study limitations, reconcile conflicting findings, and establish evidence-based conclusions about intervention effectiveness (Sun & Zhou, 2024; Tlili et al., 2025). This chapter examines the landscape of meta-analytic research at the intersection of multimodal literacy and AI, analyzing methodological approaches, substantive findings, and implications for future research and practice.

The integration of artificial intelligence into educational contexts represents not merely a technological shift but a fundamental reconceptualization of how knowledge is accessed, constructed, and evaluated. Traditional educational research paradigms, focused primarily on human-to-human interaction and text-based learning materials, prove insufficient for understanding learning environments where AI systems serve as tutors, collaborators, content generators, and assessment tools. Meta-analytic research provides essential infrastructure for navigating this complexity, enabling systematic aggregation of findings across heterogeneous contexts while accounting for methodological variation and technological diversity.

Contemporary multimodal literacy encompasses competencies extending far beyond traditional notions of reading and writing. Students must develop capacities to comprehend and create texts integrating visual, auditory, gestural, and spatial modes; critically evaluate multimodal compositions for rhetorical effectiveness and ethical implications; understand how different modes afford distinct meaning-making possibilities; and navigate rapidly evolving technological platforms that enable increasingly sophisticated multimodal production. The emergence of generative AI technologies that can produce professional-quality multimodal content—from written essays to photorealistic images to synthesized video—adds new dimensions to multimodal literacy, raising questions about authorship, creativity, critical evaluation, and the very purposes of literacy education in an age of ubiquitous AI assistance.

THE EMERGENCE OF META-ANALYSIS IN EDUCATIONAL TECHNOLOGY RESEARCH

Meta-analysis has become increasingly prominent in educational technology research as the field has matured and accumulated sufficient primary studies to warrant systematic synthesis. The rapid proliferation of studies examining AI applications in education—from intelligent tutoring systems to chatbot-based learning assistants to generative AI tools—has created both opportunities and challenges for evidence synthesis (Chiu et al., 2023). Opportunities include the potential to identify robust patterns across diverse implementations, populations, and outcome measures. Challenges include managing heterogeneity in study designs, AI technologies, educational contexts, and assessment instruments.

Recent meta-analyses have demonstrated the value of systematic evidence synthesis in clarifying the impacts of AI on learning outcomes. Ma and Zhong (2025) conducted a comprehensive meta-analysis of 32 studies involving 3,754 participants, revealing an overall positive effect of generative AI on learning outcomes with a standardized mean difference of 0.54 (95% CI: 0.35-0.74). Similarly, Sun and Zhou (2024) analyzed 35 studies with 6,685 participants, finding that generative AI improved academic achievement with an effect size of $g = 0.52$ (95% CI: 0.38-0.67). These convergent findings across independent meta-analyses strengthen confidence in the educational potential of AI technologies while highlighting the importance of replication and synthesis.

Scope and Organization of This Chapter

This chapter systematically examines meta-analytic research addressing multimodal literacy and AI in education, organizing findings around five major themes: AI literacy conceptualization and development, generative AI impacts on learning outcomes, multimodal learning analytics, digital literacy frameworks, and methodological considerations in meta-analytic research. Each section synthesizes findings from relevant meta-analyses and systematic reviews, identifies patterns and contradictions in the evidence base, and discusses implications for theory, practice, and future research.

The chapter proceeds as follows: Section 2 examines meta-analytic evidence regarding AI literacy development across educational levels, from early childhood through higher education. Section 3 analyzes findings on generative AI's impacts on academic achievement and learning processes. Section 4 explores multimodal learning analytics and evidence synthesis approaches in this domain. Section 5 investigates digital literacy frameworks and their relationship to multimodal competencies. Section 6 addresses critical methodological issues in conducting and interpreting meta-analyses in this rapidly evolving field. The chapter concludes with synthesis of key findings, identification of research gaps, and recommendations for future meta-analytic work.

Figure 1. Conceptual Framework of Meta-Analysis in AI and Multimodal Literacy Studies

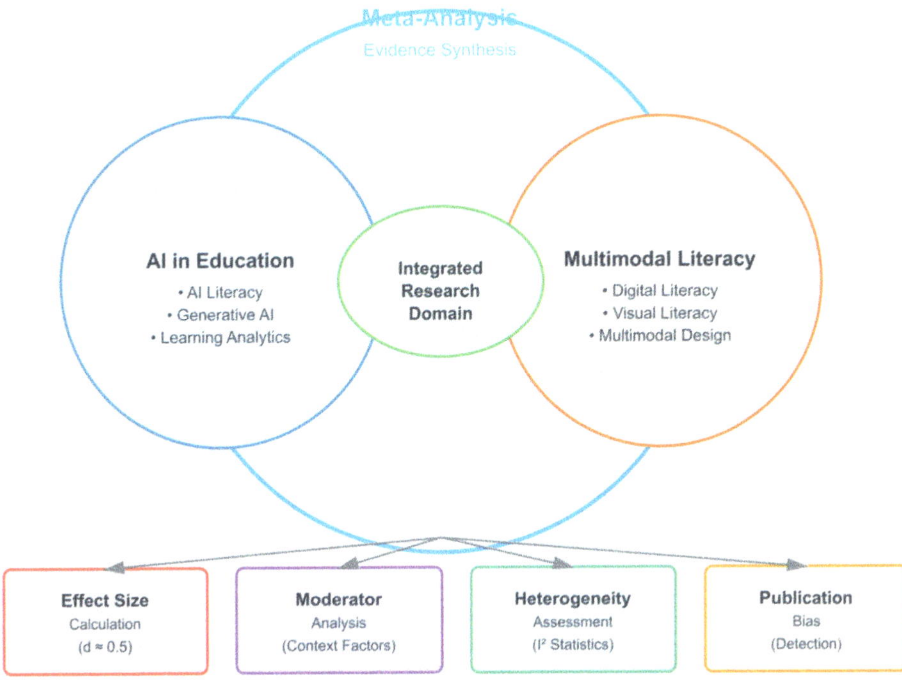

Figure 1 illustrates the conceptual framework guiding this synthesis.

META-ANALYTIC EVIDENCE ON AI LITERACY DEVELOPMENT

AI literacy has emerged as a critical educational competency, encompassing knowledge about AI technologies, skills for using AI tools, and ethical understanding of AI's societal implications. Ng et al. (2021) provided foundational conceptualization of AI literacy through exploratory review, identifying key components including knowing and understanding AI, using and applying AI, evaluating and creating AI, and ethical AI awareness. This framework has influenced subsequent research and curriculum development efforts worldwide.

Building on this conceptual foundation, researchers have examined AI literacy development across different educational levels and contexts. Su et al. (2023) investigated AI literacy in early childhood education, identifying unique challenges including developmentally appropriate pedagogy, ethical considerations regarding young children's data, and teacher preparation needs. Their systematic review revealed limited empirical research on AI literacy for young learners, highlighting a critical research gap despite increasing AI presence in early learning environments.

Figure 2. Evolution of Meta-Analytic Research in AI and Multimodal Literacy (2020-2025)

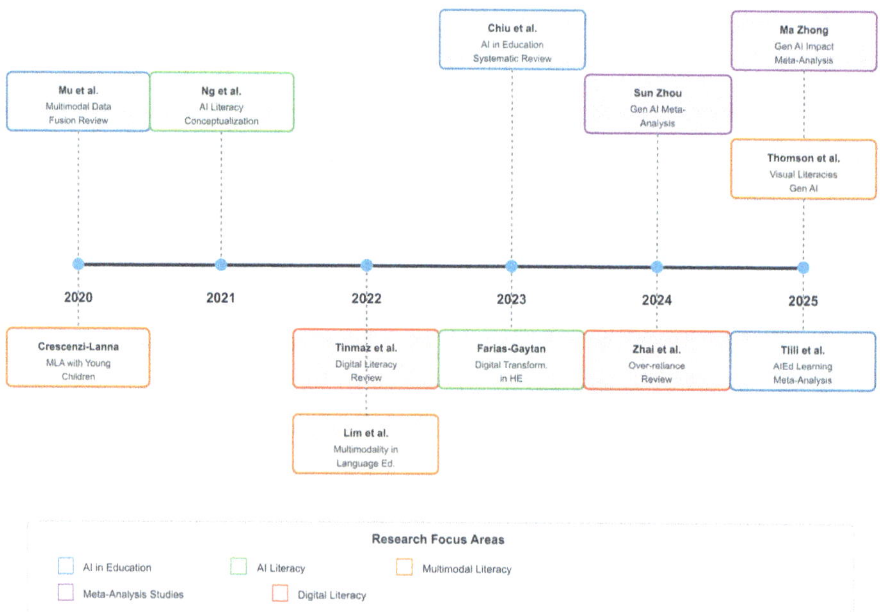

Figure 2 illustration provides a historical timeline showing the evolution of meta-analytic research in this domain from 2020 to 2025."

CONCEPTUAL FRAMEWORKS AND COMPETENCY MODELS

Gu and Ericson (2024) conducted an integrative review of AI literacy in K-12 and higher education following the emergence of generative AI tools. Their analysis identified three primary approaches to AI literacy education: technical skills development focusing on AI programming and data science, critical literacy emphasizing ethical reasoning and societal impacts, and creative production centered on using AI tools for multimodal content creation. The review revealed tension between these approaches, with some educators prioritizing technical understanding while others emphasized critical evaluation capacities.

Ng et al. (2023) extended AI literacy conceptualization to address teaching, evaluation, and ethical issues comprehensively. Their framework distinguishes between AI literacy for students (understanding and using AI) and AI literacy for educators (teaching with and about AI). This dual perspective recognizes that effective AI literacy education requires not only well-designed curricula but also teachers equipped with technical knowledge, pedagogical strategies, and ethical frameworks for guiding student learning.

The development of AI literacy represents an urgent educational priority as AI technologies pervade all sectors of society. However, significant debates persist regarding what AI literacy should encompass and how it should be taught. Technical approaches emphasize understanding of algorithms, data structures, machine learning principles, and programming skills necessary to create AI systems. Critical approaches prioritize ethical reasoning, recognition of AI's societal impacts, understanding of bias and fairness issues, and capacity to evaluate AI systems' social implications. Applied approaches focus on effective use of AI tools, strategic deployment of AI assistance, and integration of AI into professional and personal workflows. Each approach offers valuable perspectives, yet tensions arise when educational resources require choices among competing priorities.

Recent research suggests that effective AI literacy education integrates technical, critical, and applied dimensions rather than treating them as mutually exclusive alternatives. Students need sufficient technical understanding to grasp how AI systems operate and what their limitations are, critical capacities to evaluate AI's impacts and ethical implications, and practical skills to use AI tools effectively and responsibly. The challenge lies in developing curricula and pedagogies that address all three dimensions within limited instructional time, especially given that many educators themselves lack comprehensive AI literacy. Professional development initiatives must therefore precede or accompany student-facing AI literacy programs, ensuring that teachers possess knowledge, skills, and confidence necessary to guide student learning.

Meta-analytic research on AI literacy interventions remains sparse, with most existing studies providing descriptive accounts of curriculum implementations rather than controlled evaluations of effectiveness. This gap represents a critical priority for future research. As AI literacy programs proliferate, systematic evaluation becomes essential for identifying effective instructional approaches, understanding how effectiveness varies across contexts and populations, and building cumulative knowledge about AI literacy development. Future meta-analyses should examine questions such as: Which instructional approaches most effectively develop different dimensions of AI literacy? How does AI literacy development differ across age groups and educational levels? What role do hands-on experiences with AI tools play in developing conceptual understanding? How can AI literacy education address equity concerns and ensure that all students develop necessary competencies?

IMPLEMENTATION CHALLENGES AND OPPORTUNITIES

Yang (2022) examined AI education for young children, proposing curriculum design principles addressing the why, what, and how of early AI literacy instruction. The review identified developmentally appropriate activities including unplugged computing exercises, tangible AI interfaces, and scaffolded interactions with AI systems. Key challenges include limited teacher expertise, absence of validated assessment tools, and concerns about screen time and data privacy for young learners.

Across educational levels, systematic reviews reveal consistent themes regarding AI literacy implementation: the necessity of teacher professional development, importance of hands-on experiential learning, value of ethical discussions integrated throughout curricula, and need for age-appropriate content and activities. However, empirical evidence regarding effective instructional approaches remains limited, with most existing research consisting of descriptive case studies rather than controlled evaluations of intervention effectiveness (Chiu et al., 2023).

MULTIMODAL DIMENSIONS OF AI LITERACY

AI literacy inherently involves multimodal competencies, as contemporary AI systems process and generate diverse modal forms including text, images, audio, and video. Students developing AI literacy must understand how different AI technologies operate across modalities, critically evaluate AI-generated multimodal content, and create sophisticated multimodal artifacts using AI tools (Thomson et al., 2025). This multimodal dimension distinguishes AI literacy from earlier digital literacy frameworks focused primarily on text-based technologies. Future meta-analytic research should examine how AI literacy interventions develop competencies across multiple modes and whether certain modal combinations prove more effective for different learning objectives.

GENERATIVE AI IMPACTS ON LEARNING OUTCOMES: META-ANALYTIC FINDINGS

The emergence of generative AI technologies—particularly large language models, image generation systems, and multimodal AI tools—has prompted extensive research examining their educational impacts. Recent meta-analyses provide systematic synthesis of this rapidly growing evidence base, revealing overall positive effects alongside important moderating factors and potential risks (Ma & Zhong, 2025; Sun & Zhou, 2024; Tlili et al., 2025).

Overall Effect Sizes and Patterns

Ma and Zhong (2025) conducted a comprehensive meta-analysis of 32 experimental and quasi-experimental studies examining generative AI's impact on learning outcomes. Their analysis revealed a moderate positive effect (SMD = 0.54, 95% CI: 0.35-0.74, $p < 0.001$), indicating that students using generative AI tools demonstrated significantly better learning outcomes compared to control conditions. Importantly, the effect remained robust across diverse educational contexts, subject areas, and AI tool types, though with significant heterogeneity ($I^2 = 78.6\%$) suggesting important moderating influences.

Sun and Zhou (2024) found convergent results in their meta-analysis of 35 studies involving college students, reporting an overall effect size of $g = 0.52$ (95% CI: 0.38-0.67). Their analysis examined academic achievement specifically, distinguishing between immediate post-test effects and longer-term retention. Both immediate ($g = 0.55$) and delayed ($g = 0.46$) effects favored generative AI interventions, though the modest decline in effect size over time suggests potential limitations in sustained learning benefits.

Tlili et al. (2025) expanded the scope of meta-analytic synthesis by examining AI in education broadly, not limited to generative AI. Their analysis of 38 studies revealed similar positive effects on learning achievement, with additional findings regarding AI's impacts on engagement, motivation, and cognitive load. Notably, their moderator analyses indicated that AI tools providing adaptive feedback and personalized learning pathways produced larger effects than those offering only content generation capabilities.

The rapid adoption of generative AI tools in educational contexts has occurred faster than research can systematically evaluate impacts, creating challenges for evidence-based decision-making. Institutions and educators must make choices about AI integration without comprehensive understanding of effectiveness, risks, or best practices. Meta-analytic research provides crucial evidence for informed decision-making, though limitations exist. Most existing studies examine short-term interventions with immediate outcome measures, leaving questions about sustained effects unanswered. The studies synthesized in recent meta-analyses predominantly focus on cognitive outcomes including test scores, assignment grades, and knowledge acquisition while giving limited attention to other important outcomes including motivation, self-efficacy, creativity, collaborative skills, and metacognitive development.

Moreover, the AI technologies themselves evolve rapidly, potentially rendering research findings obsolete. Studies examining generative AI capabilities from 2022 or 2023 may have limited relevance to 2025 technologies with substantially enhanced capabilities. This temporal dimension complicates meta-analytic synthesis and interpretation. Should meta-analyses include studies of earlier AI technologies alongside more recent systems? How should technological change be accounted for in moderator analyses? These methodological challenges require careful consideration in both conducting meta-analyses and interpreting their findings.

Despite these limitations, convergent findings across multiple meta-analyses provide reasonable confidence in several conclusions. First, generative AI interventions demonstrate consistent positive effects on academic achievement, with effect sizes in the moderate range at approximately d equals 0.5. Second, effectiveness varies significantly by implementation approach, with thoughtfully designed interventions incorporating pedagogical guidance producing larger effects than simple provision of AI tools. Third, certain student populations—particularly lower-performing students—may benefit disproportionately from AI scaffolding, suggesting potential for addressing achievement gaps if implementation ensures equitable access and support. Fourth, concerns about over-reliance and negative impacts on cognitive skills have empirical foundation, necessitating pedagogical approaches that promote critical engagement rather than passive acceptance of AI outputs.

Figure 3. Meta-Analytic Effect Sizes Across Studies in AI and Multimodal Literacy Research

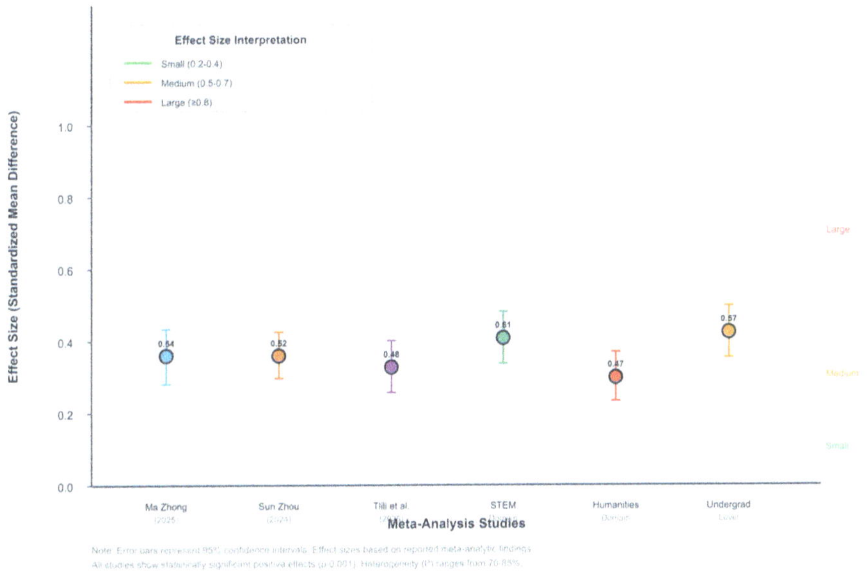

Figure 3 illustration visualizes these effect sizes alongside those from other key studies, facilitating comparison across research contexts."

Moderating Variables and Contextual Factors

Meta-analytic investigations have identified several variables that moderate generative AI's effectiveness. Ma and Zhong (2025) found that effect sizes varied significantly by subject domain, with larger effects in STEM disciplines (SMD = 0.61) compared to humanities and social sciences (SMD = 0.47). This pattern may reflect differences in task structures, with well-defined STEM problems allowing more effective AI scaffolding compared to open-ended humanities assignments requiring nuanced interpretation and argumentation.

Educational level emerged as another significant moderator. Sun and Zhou (2024) reported larger effects for undergraduate students (g = 0.57) compared to graduate students (g = 0.39), possibly reflecting graduate students' more developed independent learning strategies and critical evaluation skills that reduce relative advantage of AI support. Conversely, prior academic achievement showed inverse relationships with AI intervention effectiveness, with lower-performing students benefiting more from AI scaffolding—a finding with important equity implications (Tlili et al., 2025).

Implementation characteristics also moderated outcomes. Studies incorporating explicit instruction on effective AI use, critical evaluation of AI outputs, and integration of AI tools within pedagogically sound learning activities produced larger effects than those simply providing AI access without guidance (Ma & Zhong, 2025). Duration of intervention influenced effects as well, with longer implementations (> 8 weeks) showing sustained benefits while brief interventions (< 2 weeks) produced smaller, less stable effects.

Additional moderating factors warrant consideration in future meta-analyses. Assessment type may influence observed effects, with AI interventions potentially showing stronger impacts on lower-order cognitive skills assessed through multiple-choice tests compared to higher-order skills requiring complex problem-solving or creative synthesis. The nature of AI support provided—whether focused on content generation, error correction, conceptual explanation, or strategic guidance—likely moderates effectiveness for different learning objectives. Individual difference variables including prior AI experience, technology self-efficacy, and learning preferences may also moderate intervention impacts, though existing meta-analyses have not systematically examined these factors due to limited reporting in primary studies.

Cultural and linguistic contexts represent another potentially important but understudied moderating influence. Most studies synthesized in existing meta-analyses come from English-speaking countries or examine English language learning, limiting generalizability to other linguistic and cultural contexts. AI technologies trained primarily on English-language data may function differently when applied to other languages, potentially affecting both effectiveness and equity. Future meta-analytic research should explicitly examine whether effects vary across linguistic and cultural contexts, and whether culturally responsive AI implementations produce different outcomes than culturally generic approaches.

Risks and Challenges: Evidence on Over-Reliance

Alongside positive effects, meta-analytic research has documented concerning patterns of over-reliance on AI systems. Zhai et al. (2024) conducted a systematic review specifically examining effects of excessive dependence on AI dialogue systems on students' cognitive abilities. Their synthesis identified negative impacts on critical thinking, problem-solving skills, and metacognitive awareness among students who uncritically accepted AI-generated responses without verification or deeper processing. Studies revealed decreases in independent reasoning capabilities and increased automation bias—the tendency to favor AI suggestions over one's own judgment even when AI outputs contained errors. These findings underscore the importance of pedagogical approaches that promote active engagement, critical evaluation, and strategic rather than dependent use of AI tools. Educators must balance AI's potential benefits against risks of cognitive offloading and skill atrophy.

The mechanisms through which over-reliance develops and its long-term consequences require further investigation. Research on automation bias in other domains suggests that users develop trust in automated systems through repeated positive experiences, eventually relying on system outputs without adequate verification. In educational contexts, students may experience improved immediate performance when using AI tools, reinforcing dependence without recognizing that this dependence may undermine development of independent capabilities. The challenge lies in designing learning experiences that leverage AI's benefits while ensuring students maintain and develop their own cognitive skills.

Pedagogical strategies for mitigating over-reliance deserve systematic investigation and meta-analytic synthesis as evidence accumulates. Promising approaches include explicit instruction about AI limitations and potential errors, structured reflection activities prompting students to evaluate AI suggestions critically, varied learning experiences including both AI-supported and independent work, and assessment designs that require demonstration of understanding beyond what AI can provide. Metacognitive scaffolding encouraging students to monitor their own learning processes and recognize when they are relying on AI as a crutch rather than a tool may also prove valuable. Future meta-analyses should examine whether these pedagogical strategies effectively reduce over-reliance while maintaining learning benefits.

MULTIMODAL LEARNING ANALYTICS: SYNTHESIZING COMPLEX DATA STREAMS

Multimodal learning analytics represents an emerging field at the intersection of learning analytics, multimodal interaction, and artificial intelligence. This approach analyzes diverse data streams—including clickstreams, eye tracking, physiological sensors, facial expressions, gestures, speech, and physical movements—to understand learning processes more comprehensively than traditional single-mode analytics (Mu et al., 2020). As educational technologies increasingly capture multimodal learner data, systematic synthesis of research findings becomes essential for understanding which analytical approaches prove most valuable and under what circumstances.

Systematic Reviews of Multimodal Learning Analytics

Mu et al. (2020) conducted a comprehensive systematic review of multimodal data fusion approaches in learning analytics. Their analysis of 57 studies identified three primary fusion strategies: feature-level fusion combining raw multimodal features before analysis, decision-level fusion integrating predictions from separate modal analyses, and hybrid approaches employing both strategies. The review revealed that hybrid fusion methods generally produced higher prediction accuracy for learning outcomes compared to single-mode or simple feature concatenation approaches, though with increased computational complexity and data processing requirements.

Verma and Varghese (2025) provided bibliometric analysis mapping the multimodal learning analytics research landscape. Their examination of 312 publications revealed exponential growth in this domain, with particularly rapid expansion following advances in deep learning and sensor technologies. The analysis identified key research clusters around collaborative learning analytics, embodied cognition measurement, emotion recognition in learning, and early prediction of academic performance. However, the review also noted fragmentation in the field, with limited theoretical integration across diverse analytical approaches and data types.

Multimodal analytics represents a frontier in educational research, leveraging advances in sensor technologies, machine learning, and data fusion to capture and analyze rich information about learning processes. Traditional learning analytics, focused primarily on clickstream data and assessment scores, provide limited insight into the complex, embodied, social, and emotional dimensions of learning. Multimodal approaches address this limitation by integrating diverse data streams including eye tracking capturing attention allocation and reading patterns, physiological sensors measuring arousal, stress, and cognitive load, video analysis revealing gestures, facial expressions, and collaborative interactions, speech analysis examining discourse quality and engagement patterns, and motion tracking documenting physical movements and embodied cognition.

The potential value of multimodal analytics stems from their capacity to capture phenomena invisible to traditional approaches. For instance, identifying students at risk of course failure typically relies on grades and login frequency—lagging indicators apparent only after problems have developed. Multimodal analytics can detect early warning signs through patterns of attention, engagement, stress, and interaction that emerge well before grade-based indicators. Similarly, understanding collaborative learning processes benefits enormously from multimodal data capturing verbal and nonverbal communication, gesture, gaze, and physical positioning. Traditional transcript analysis provides incomplete understanding of these rich, embodied interactions.

However, multimodal analytics faces significant challenges. Technical challenges include sensor reliability, data synchronization across modalities, and computational requirements for processing and analyzing large multimodal datasets. Methodological challenges include determining which data modalities to collect, selecting appropriate analytical approaches for different questions and contexts, and interpreting complex findings that may not align with intuitive expectations. Privacy and ethical challenges include protecting sensitive data, obtaining informed consent for collection of video and physiological information, and ensuring that analytics serve learner interests rather than surveillance purposes. Scalability challenges include moving from small-scale research studies to practical implementations in authentic educational settings with hundreds or thousands of students.

Applications in Technology-Enhanced Learning Environments

Liao and Wu (2022) deployed multimodal learning analytics to explore digital distraction and peer learning impacts on student performance. Their study demonstrated how combining clickstream data, physiological measures, and social interaction patterns provided richer understanding of learning processes than any single data source. Students exhibiting frequent task-switching behaviors combined with elevated stress indicators showed significantly lower performance, while those engaged in productive peer interactions demonstrated enhanced outcomes even when individual attention metrics suggested distraction. These findings illustrate the value of multimodal approaches for capturing complex, contextualized learning phenomena.

Wang et al. (2023) investigated factors predicting success in online problem-based learning environments using multimodal analytics. Their analysis integrated discourse patterns, cognitive presence indicators, resource access behaviors, and temporal engagement metrics. Results revealed that combinations of sustained cognitive engagement (measured through discourse quality) and strategic resource use predicted learning outcomes more accurately than traditional single-mode indicators like login frequency or time on task. The study exemplifies how multimodal analytics can identify nuanced patterns invisible to conventional approaches.

Design Frameworks and Implementation Challenges

Ouhaichi et al. (2024) conducted systematic review of multimodal learning analytics system design frameworks. Their analysis identified critical design principles including pedagogical grounding (analytics aligned with learning theories), actionable insights (generating interpretable feedback for educators and learners), privacy protection (safeguarding sensitive multimodal data), and scalability (handling large-scale deployments). The review revealed that most existing frameworks prioritize technical sophistication over pedagogical relevance and user needs, suggesting important directions for future development.

Crescenzi-Lanna (2020) examined multimodal learning analytics research specifically with young children, identifying unique methodological and ethical challenges. Studies of early learners must address developmental appropriateness of data collection methods, children's limited metacognitive awareness for self-report measures, and heightened privacy concerns regarding minors' data. The review found that most multimodal analytics research focuses on adults or adolescents, representing a significant gap given increasing technology use in early childhood education.

Future Directions for Meta-Analytic Research

While systematic reviews have mapped the multimodal learning analytics landscape, quantitative meta-analyses examining intervention effectiveness remain scarce. This gap reflects challenges in comparing diverse analytical approaches, heterogeneous outcome measures, and variable implementation contexts. Future meta-analytic work should focus on specific questions amenable to quantitative synthesis, such as: Do multimodal analytics improve prediction accuracy compared to single-mode approaches, and by how much? Which combinations of data modalities prove most valuable for different educational purposes? How do multimodal analytics interventions affect student learning outcomes and teacher decision-making? Addressing these questions requires standardization of reporting practices, development of common effect size metrics, and accumulation of experimental studies comparing multimodal versus traditional analytical approaches (Luo, 2023).

DIGITAL AND MULTIMODAL LITERACY FRAMEWORKS: EVIDENCE SYNTHESIS

Digital literacy and multimodal literacy represent overlapping yet distinct constructs in contemporary educational research. Digital literacy encompasses competencies for accessing, evaluating, creating, and communicating information using digital technologies, while multimodal literacy emphasizes understanding and producing texts combining multiple semiotic modes. The integration of AI technologies has complicated and enriched both constructs, necessitating updated frameworks and empirical investigation of literacy development in AI-enhanced environments (Farias-Gaytan et al., 2023; Tinmaz et al., 2022).

Systematic Reviews of Digital Literacy in Higher Education

Tinmaz et al. (2022) conducted systematic review examining digital literacy conceptualizations, assessment approaches, and development initiatives. Their analysis of 64 studies revealed substantial definitional variation, with some frameworks emphasizing technical skills while others prioritized critical evaluation and creative production capacities. The review identified persistent challenges including lack of validated assessment instruments, limited evidence regarding effective instructional approaches, and insufficient attention to sociocultural contexts shaping digital literacy development.

Farias-Gaytan et al. (2023) examined digital transformation and digital literacy within higher education institutions, analyzing complexity factors influencing implementation. Their systematic review highlighted institutional barriers including inadequate infrastructure, insufficient faculty professional development, resistance to pedagogical change, and misalignment between digital literacy goals and assessment practices. The review revealed that successful digital literacy initiatives integrated technological, pedagogical, and organizational dimensions rather than focusing narrowly on technical skill development.

Digital literacy frameworks have evolved substantially over the past two decades, reflecting rapid technological change and deepening understanding of what digital competence entails. Early frameworks emphasized technical skills including using software applications, navigating interfaces, and managing files. Later frameworks incorporated information literacy dimensions including searching, evaluating, and synthesizing digital information. Contemporary frameworks emphasize critical dimensions including understanding algorithms' influence on information access, recognizing platform business models and data practices, identifying misinformation and manipulation, and engaging in civic participation through digital media.

The integration of AI into digital environments necessitates further framework evolution. AI systems increasingly mediate information access through personalized recommendations, search results, and content curation. Understanding how these systems operate, what biases they may encode, and how they shape information diets becomes essential for informed digital citizenship. Similarly, the proliferation of AI-generated content from synthetic text to deepfake images to algorithmically composed music requires new critical evaluation skills. Users must assess not only content veracity and source credibility but also whether content is human-created, AI-generated, or some hybrid, and what implications different forms of authorship carry for interpretation and use.

Research examining digital literacy in the age of AI remains nascent. Most existing frameworks and assessment instruments predate recent AI developments, limiting their relevance for contemporary digital environments. Developing updated frameworks requires empirical investigation of how people actually engage with AI-mediated digital environments, what challenges they encounter, what competencies enable effective navigation, and how these competencies can be taught and assessed. Meta-analytic research can contribute by synthesizing findings across diverse studies, identifying core competencies that emerge consistently, and examining whether existing instructional approaches transfer to AI-mediated contexts or require fundamental reconceptualization.

Critical Digital Literacies at School Level

Ilomäki et al. (2023) systematically reviewed critical digital literacies in K-12 contexts, examining how schools address issues of power, equity, privacy, and social justice in digital literacy education. Their analysis revealed that most digital literacy curricula emphasize functional skills and information evaluation while providing limited attention to critical dimensions including recognition of algorithmic bias, understanding of surveillance capitalism, and capacity for digital activism. The review identified promising pedagogical approaches including critical inquiry projects, participatory design activities, and analysis of digital platforms' social impacts.

The integration of AI technologies amplifies the importance of critical digital literacy. Students must understand not only how to use AI tools but also how AI systems encode values, perpetuate biases, and shape information access. Developing these critical capacities requires pedagogical approaches that make AI's operations transparent, encourage questioning of AI outputs, and connect AI technologies to broader social and ethical issues (Ng et al., 2023).

Multimodality in Language and Literacy Education

Lim et al. (2022) conducted systematic review of multimodality in English language classrooms, analyzing pedagogical approaches and learning outcomes. Their synthesis of 47 studies revealed that multimodal literacy instruction—incorporating visual, audio, gestural, and spatial modes alongside written text—consistently enhanced student engagement, comprehension, and production of complex texts. Effect sizes varied by instructional approach, with explicit attention to mode selection and design principles producing stronger effects than incidental multimodal exposure.

Carcamo and Pino (2022) examined multimodal literacy development through infographic creation in EFL contexts. Their study demonstrated how multimodal composition tasks requiring integration of text, images, and data visualization enhanced both language proficiency and visual literacy competencies. Students developed sophisticated understanding of how different modes convey meaning and learned to make strategic modal choices based on communicative purposes and audience considerations.

Liu et al. (2024) provided bibliometric analysis of multimodal discourse studies from 1997-2023, mapping the field's evolution and identifying emerging themes. Their analysis revealed increasing attention to digital multimodality, AI-generated content, and multimodal critical literacy. The emergence of generative AI tools capable of producing sophisticated multimodal compositions raises new questions about authorship, creativity, and the purposes of multimodal literacy education in an era when machines can generate professional-quality multimodal texts.

Multilingual and Multimodal Literacy Engagements

Zaidi and Sah (2024) conducted scoping review examining multilingual and multimodal literacy practices among immigrant high school students. Their analysis revealed how students strategically deploy linguistic and modal resources across contexts, drawing on diverse semiotic repertoires to navigate academic, social, and cultural demands. The review highlighted affordances of multimodal approaches for supporting language learners, including reduced linguistic demands through visual and gestural communication, opportunities for identity expression through modal choice, and scaffolding of academic content through complementary modes.

AI technologies offer particular promise for supporting multilingual multimodal literacy development. Translation tools, speech recognition systems, and text-to-speech applications can reduce barriers while students develop target language proficiency. Multimodal composition tools enable students to communicate complex ideas before developing advanced written language skills. However, research examining AI's role in multilingual multimodal literacy remains limited, representing an important direction for future investigation (Guo et al., 2024).

Visual Literacies and Generative AI

Thomson et al. (2025) examined visual literacies in the context of generative AI, analyzing how AI image generation tools transform visual production and interpretation practices. Their research revealed that generative AI enables unprecedented access to sophisticated visual creation while simultaneously raising concerns about visual authenticity, attribution, and the devaluation of traditional visual production skills. The study identified emerging visual literacy competencies including prompt engineering for image generation, critical evaluation of AI-generated visuals, understanding of AI training data and bias, and ethical considerations regarding AI-generated imagery. These findings suggest that visual literacy frameworks require substantial updating to address AI-mediated visual communication, emphasizing critical evaluation alongside technical proficiency.

METHODOLOGICAL CONSIDERATIONS IN META-ANALYTIC RESEARCH

Conducting rigorous meta-analyses of multimodal literacy and AI education research presents distinctive methodological challenges. This section addresses key considerations including study selection criteria, effect size calculation, heterogeneity management, publication bias assessment, and interpretation of findings in rapidly evolving fields.

Inclusion Criteria and Study Selection

Defining appropriate inclusion criteria for meta-analyses in this domain requires balancing breadth and homogeneity. Studies examining AI interventions span diverse technologies (intelligent tutoring systems, chatbots, generative AI, recommendation systems), educational contexts (formal vs. informal learning, different grade levels and disciplines), and outcome measures (achievement tests, self-report measures, behavioral indicators). Overly broad criteria yield heterogeneous study pools that obscure meaningful patterns, while overly narrow criteria exclude relevant evidence and limit generalizability.

Recent meta-analyses have adopted varied approaches. Ma and Zhong (2025) focused specifically on generative AI, excluding earlier AI technologies, to achieve conceptual coherence given rapid technological change. Sun and Zhou (2024) similarly emphasized generative AI but limited analyses to college students, sacrificing breadth for reduced heterogeneity. Tlili et al. (2025) cast a wider net across AI education interventions but conducted extensive subgroup analyses to examine technology type, educational level, and subject domain differences. These divergent strategies reflect ongoing debates about optimal scope for meta-analytic synthesis in rapidly evolving technological domains.

Effect Size Calculation and Interpretation

Meta-analyses of educational interventions typically employ standardized mean differences (Cohen's d or Hedges' g) as primary effect size measures. These metrics indicate the magnitude of intervention effects in standard deviation units, facilitating comparison across studies using different outcome measures. Conventional benchmarks classify effects as small ($d \approx 0.2$), medium ($d \approx 0.5$), or large ($d \approx 0.8$), though these thresholds should be interpreted contextually rather than rigidly applied.

Recent meta-analyses of AI interventions have reported effect sizes in the moderate range (approximately 0.5), suggesting meaningful but not transformative impacts on learning outcomes. However, effect size interpretation requires careful consideration of several factors. First, the comparison condition matters substantially—effects measured against traditional instruction may differ from those measured against other technology-enhanced approaches. Second, outcome measures vary in sensitivity and relevance; standardized tests may show smaller effects than researcher-developed assessments aligned with intervention content. Third, implementation quality influences observed effects, with well-implemented interventions likely producing larger impacts than poorly executed ones.

Additionally, statistical significance and effect size magnitude should be distinguished from practical significance and educational importance. A statistically significant effect of $d = 0.3$ might represent substantial educational value if achieved through scalable, low-cost interventions, while a larger effect might have limited practical utility if it requires intensive resources or produces outcomes peripheral to core educational goals.

Heterogeneity and Moderator Analysis

Meta-analyses almost invariably encounter heterogeneity—variation in effect sizes beyond what would be expected from sampling error alone. The I^2 statistic quantifies heterogeneity, with values above 50% indicating substantial variation. Recent meta-analyses of AI interventions report I^2 values ranging from 70% to 85%, suggesting considerable heterogeneity requiring investigation (Ma & Zhong, 2025; Sun & Zhou, 2024).

Moderator analysis examines whether study characteristics explain heterogeneity. Common moderators in educational meta-analyses include participant characteristics (age, prior achievement), intervention features (duration, intensity, technological sophistication), methodological quality (randomization, blinding, attrition), and contextual factors (subject domain, setting). Identifying meaningful moderators helps understand not just whether interventions work but when, for whom, and under what circumstances they prove most effective.

However, moderator analysis faces challenges in AI education research. Limited numbers of studies within specific subgroups reduce statistical power to detect moderation effects. Confounding among moderators (e.g., intervention duration correlating with study quality) complicates interpretation. Missing data on important moderators limits analysis possibilities. Future research should employ standardized reporting frameworks ensuring that studies provide sufficient detail about interventions, participants, and contexts to enable comprehensive moderator analysis.

Publication Bias and Evidence Quality

Publication bias—the tendency for studies with statistically significant, positive findings to be more likely published than those with null or negative results—threatens meta-analytic validity. Several methods assess publication bias, including funnel plots (graphical examination of effect sizes versus precision), Egger's test (statistical test for funnel plot asymmetry), and trim-and-fill analysis (estimation of potentially missing studies). Recent meta-analyses have employed these techniques with mixed results; some detect minimal publication bias while others identify concerning patterns suggesting that negative findings remain unpublished.

Beyond publication bias, evidence quality assessment examines methodological rigor of included studies. Tools like the Cochrane Risk of Bias assessment evaluate randomization adequacy, allocation concealment, blinding, selective reporting, and other validity threats. Quality assessment serves dual purposes: identifying studies requiring cautious interpretation and exploring whether methodological quality moderates effect sizes. Several meta-analyses have found that higher-quality studies report smaller effects, suggesting that methodological limitations may inflate estimated impacts in lower-quality research.

Meta-analytic research in educational technology presents distinctive methodological challenges requiring careful navigation. Publication bias more severe in educational technology than in some other fields stems from multiple sources. Researchers and institutions may be less motivated to submit or publish null findings, especially for novel technologies where positive results generate more interest. Journals may preferentially accept studies reporting statistically significant effects. Funders and technology developers may influence what research gets conducted and disseminated. These dynamics create risk that meta-analyses overestimate true effects by synthesizing a biased sample of available evidence.

Heterogeneity in educational technology research creates both challenges and opportunities for meta-analysis. On one hand, substantial heterogeneity complicates interpretation and reduces confidence in aggregate effect estimates. Studies differ in technologies examined, educational contexts, participant populations, outcome measures, intervention duration, implementation quality, and methodological rigor. Simply computing an average effect across such diverse studies may produce a misleading estimate that applies to no actual context. On the other hand, heterogeneity enables exploration of moderating factors that explain when, how, and for whom interventions prove effective. Well-designed meta-analyses with sufficient studies can examine whether effects vary by technology type, age group, subject domain, implementation approach, or other theoretically relevant variables.

Quality assessment in meta-analysis serves multiple purposes. Descriptively, it characterizes the methodological rigor of available evidence, identifying whether conclusions rest on high-quality experimental studies or methodologically weaker research. Analytically, it enables exploration of whether study quality moderates effect sizes—a common pattern where lower-quality studies report larger effects, potentially due to confounding, bias, or insufficient control of alternative explanations. Quality assessment also informs sensitivity analyses excluding lower-quality studies to determine whether conclusions depend on their inclusion. However, quality assessment faces challenges in educational research where true experimental designs with random assignment may be infeasible, ethical concerns limit blinding, and real-world implementation introduces variation difficult to standardize or control.

Challenges Specific to AI and Multimodal Research

Meta-analysis of AI and multimodal literacy research faces distinctive challenges beyond general educational meta-analytic concerns. Rapid technological change means that studies conducted even two years apart may examine fundamentally different technologies, complicating aggregation. The black-box nature of many AI systems limits understanding of active intervention components, hindering mechanistic explanation. Multimodal outcome measures resist standardization, with studies employing diverse assessment approaches difficult to compare quantitatively. Additionally, the field's relative novelty means that many studies are exploratory, small-scale, or methodologically preliminary, limiting the pool of rigorous experimental research suitable for meta-analysis. Addressing these challenges requires developing shared methodological standards, transparent reporting practices, and coordinated research programs that build cumulative evidence through replication and extension studies (Strat et al., 2024).

SYNTHESIS AND FUTURE DIRECTIONS

This chapter has examined meta-analytic research at the intersection of multimodal literacy and artificial intelligence, synthesizing evidence across five major domains: AI literacy development, generative AI impacts on learning, multimodal learning analytics, digital literacy frameworks, and methodological considerations. Several overarching patterns emerge from this synthesis.

Key Findings Across Domains

First, AI interventions demonstrate consistent positive effects on learning outcomes across diverse educational contexts, with meta-analyses reporting moderate effect sizes ($d \approx 0.5$) that remain robust across sensitivity analyses and moderator examinations. These findings provide empirical support for AI integration in educational settings while cautioning against overestimation of impacts or assumptions of universal benefit.

Second, effectiveness varies significantly by implementation approach, student characteristics, and contextual factors. Interventions incorporating explicit instruction on AI use, critical evaluation of outputs, and pedagogically grounded integration produce larger effects than those simply providing AI access. Lower-performing students benefit more from AI scaffolding than higher-performing peers, suggesting potential equity benefits if implementation addresses access barriers. Subject domain, educational level, and intervention duration all moderate outcomes, emphasizing that AI effectiveness depends critically on how, when, and for whom it is deployed.

Third, alongside benefits, research documents important risks including over-reliance on AI systems, automation bias, and potential cognitive skill atrophy. These findings highlight the necessity of pedagogical approaches promoting active engagement, critical thinking, and strategic rather than dependent AI use. Educators must balance AI's scaffolding potential against risks of reducing opportunities for productive struggle and independent problem-solving.

Fourth, multimodal approaches—whether in literacy instruction, learning analytics, or AI-enhanced environments—consistently demonstrate advantages over single-mode alternatives. Multimodal literacy instruction enhances engagement and comprehension; multimodal analytics provide richer understanding of learning processes; and AI tools supporting multimodal production enable sophisticated student-created artifacts. However, realizing multimodal approaches' potential requires explicit attention to mode selection, design principles, and pedagogical integration rather than merely adding modes without conceptual grounding.

Critical Research Gaps

Despite substantial research progress, significant gaps remain. Longitudinal studies examining sustained effects of AI interventions are scarce, with most existing research measuring immediate post-test outcomes. Understanding whether AI-supported learning produces durable knowledge and transferable skills requires extended follow-up beyond typical intervention periods. Additionally, research examining AI's impacts on higher-order competencies—creativity, critical thinking, metacognition, collaborative problem-solving—remains limited compared to studies of basic skill acquisition and content learning.

Equity considerations require much deeper investigation. While some evidence suggests that AI interventions may benefit lower-performing students disproportionately, research examining effects across socioeconomic status, cultural backgrounds, language proficiency levels, and disability status remains insufficient. Questions about digital access, AI literacy disparities, and potential for AI to reproduce or amplify educational inequities demand systematic empirical attention.

Assessment of multimodal competencies presents ongoing challenges. Most existing research employs traditional outcome measures poorly suited to capturing multimodal literacy development. Validated instruments for assessing students' abilities to comprehend, create, and critically evaluate multimodal texts—particularly AI-generated multimodal content—are urgently needed. Development of such instruments should draw on multimodal literacy theory while ensuring psychometric rigor and practical feasibility.

Teacher perspectives, practices, and professional development needs constitute another critical gap. While student-focused research predominates, understanding educators' experiences with AI integration, their pedagogical decision-making regarding multimodal literacy instruction, and effective professional learning approaches for developing AI and multimodal teaching competencies remains underexplored. Given teachers' central role in implementation success, this gap deserves immediate attention.

Recommendations for Future Meta-Analytic Research

Future meta-analytic work should prioritize several directions. First, as the evidence base accumulates, meta-analyses should move toward examining specific questions rather than broad syntheses. Instead of asking whether AI improves learning outcomes generally, research should investigate questions like: Which AI affordances prove most valuable for developing multimodal composition skills? How do different forms of AI feedback influence revision processes? What combinations of human and AI support optimize learning? Such focused questions enable more homogeneous study pools and clearer practical implications.

The evolution of meta-analytic methods in educational technology reflects broader methodological advances in evidence synthesis. Early meta-analyses in education often faced criticism for combining studies with insufficient conceptual coherence or failing to adequately account for heterogeneity. Contemporary meta-analyses address these concerns through more sophisticated approaches including random-effects models that explicitly account for between-study variation, meta-regression techniques that examine multiple moderators simultaneously, and three-level meta-analysis that accounts for dependence in effect sizes from the same studies. These methodological refinements enable more nuanced conclusions about when and how educational technologies prove effective. As the field continues evolving, meta-analysts should remain attentive to emerging methods that can enhance both the rigor and utility of evidence synthesis.

Second, meta-analyses should increasingly employ individual participant data approaches rather than relying solely on aggregate effect sizes. Individual participant data meta-analysis allows examination of how intervention effects vary across individuals, investigation of complex moderation patterns, and more sophisticated handling of missing data. While requiring greater coordination among researchers, this approach yields richer insights into for whom and under what conditions interventions prove effective.

Third, researchers should develop and adopt shared taxonomies for categorizing AI interventions, multimodal literacies, and educational contexts. Current heterogeneity in terminology and conceptualization complicates evidence synthesis. Coordinated efforts to establish common language and classification systems would enhance comparability across studies and facilitate cumulative knowledge building.

Fourth, meta-analyses should explicitly address temporal dynamics of technological change. Rapid evolution in AI capabilities means that findings from studies examining 2020-era technologies may have limited relevance to 2025-era implementations. Meta-analyses should consider publication year as a potential moderator and interpret findings with awareness of when studies were conducted relative to technological developments. Living systematic reviews—continuously updated as new evidence emerges—may prove particularly valuable in such rapidly evolving domains.

Fifth, network meta-analysis approaches comparing multiple intervention alternatives could provide valuable evidence for educational decision-making. Rather than simply comparing AI versus control conditions, network meta-analysis allows simultaneous comparison of multiple approaches (e.g., AI tutoring versus human tutoring versus peer collaboration versus independent practice), enabling more nuanced understanding of relative effectiveness and identification of optimal instructional configurations.

Implications for Practice and Policy

Meta-analytic evidence provides several implications for educational practice and policy. First, the demonstrated effectiveness of AI interventions supports continued exploration and thoughtful integration of AI tools in educational settings. However, effectiveness depends critically on implementation approach; simply providing AI access without pedagogical guidance, teacher preparation, and ongoing support will likely yield disappointing results. Professional development should emphasize not just technical aspects of AI tools but pedagogical strategies for effective integration, critical evaluation approaches, and methods for helping students develop healthy, strategic relationships with AI technologies.

Second, multimodal literacy should be recognized as a core competency requiring explicit instruction rather than assumed as a byproduct of digital technology exposure. Curriculum frameworks should articulate multimodal learning objectives across grade levels and subject areas, assessment systems should evaluate multimodal competencies authentically, and teacher preparation programs should develop educators' multimodal teaching expertise. The integration of AI tools that generate and analyze multimodal content amplifies rather than diminishes the importance of multimodal literacy education.

Third, equity considerations must be central to AI and multimodal literacy initiatives. While evidence suggests potential benefits for lower-performing students, realizing this potential requires addressing access barriers, providing culturally responsive content and pedagogies, and attending to diverse learners' needs. Policies should ensure equitable distribution of high-quality AI-enhanced learning opportunities rather than allowing innovations to widen existing achievement gaps.

Finally, implementation efforts should be accompanied by rigorous evaluation using experimental or quasi-experimental designs. Building the evidence base requires moving beyond descriptive case studies toward controlled evaluations that can establish causal relationships and contribute to meta-analytic synthesis. Funding agencies, educational institutions, and technology developers should prioritize research partnerships that generate high-quality evidence regarding what works, for whom, and under what conditions.

CONCLUSION

Meta-analysis provides powerful tools for synthesizing research evidence and informing educational practice in the age of AI. As documented throughout this chapter, recent meta-analyses reveal consistent positive effects of AI interventions on learning outcomes, advantages of multimodal approaches in literacy instruction and learning analytics, and importance of implementation factors in determining effectiveness. However, significant research gaps remain, particularly regarding longitudinal effects, equity considerations, assessment of multimodal competencies, and teacher perspectives.

The intersection of multimodal literacy and artificial intelligence represents a dynamic, rapidly evolving domain where technological capabilities advance faster than educational research can fully examine their implications. This temporal disjuncture poses challenges for meta-analytic synthesis while underscoring its importance. Systematic aggregation of empirical evidence provides essential counterweight to technological hype and unfounded speculation, grounding discussions of AI's educational potential in actual measured outcomes.

Moving forward, the field requires coordinated research programs that accumulate evidence systematically, employ rigorous methodologies, attend to equity and inclusion, and generate findings directly applicable to educational practice. Meta-analysis will continue serving critical roles in this enterprise: synthesizing diverse studies to identify robust patterns, revealing moderating factors that explain heterogeneous effects, detecting publication bias and methodological limitations, and highlighting gaps requiring new primary research.

As AI technologies become increasingly sophisticated and ubiquitous in educational contexts, and as multimodal communication continues displacing monomodal text as the dominant form of literacy practice, understanding their educational impacts through rigorous evidence synthesis becomes ever more critical. This chapter has mapped the current landscape of meta-analytic research in these domains, identified key findings and persistent gaps, and charted directions for future work. The ultimate goal remains clear: leveraging the best available evidence to create educational experiences that develop all students' capacities for critical, creative, and ethical engagement with AI-enhanced multimodal communication in an increasingly complex information landscape.

The evidence synthesized throughout this chapter demonstrates both the promise and complexity of integrating AI technologies into multimodal literacy education. While meta-analytic findings consistently reveal moderate positive effects on learning outcomes, they also highlight the critical importance of thoughtful implementation, ongoing research, and sustained attention to equity and access. Future work must continue building this evidence base while remaining responsive to rapid technological evolution and emerging educational needs.

REFERENCES

Albadarin, Y., Saqr, M., Pope, N., & Tukiainen, M. (2024). A systematic literature review of empirical research on ChatGPT in education. *Discover Education*, *3*(1), 60. DOI: 10.1007/s44217-024-00138-2

Bezemer, J., & Kress, G. (2016). *Multimodality, learning and communication: A social semiotic frame*. Routledge., DOI: 10.4324/9781315687537

Carcamo, B., & Pino, B. (2022). Developing EFL students' multimodal literacy with the use of infographics. *Asian-Pacific Journal of Second and Foreign Language Education*, *10*(1), 3. DOI: 10.1186/s40862-025-00322-3

Chiu, T. K. F., Xia, Q., Zhou, X., Chai, C. S., & Cheng, M. (2023). Systematic literature review on opportunities, challenges, and future research recommendations of artificial intelligence in education. *Computers & Education: Artificial Intelligence*, *4*, 100118. DOI: 10.1016/j.caeai.2022.100118

Crescenzi-Lanna, L. (2020). Multimodal learning analytics research with young children: A systematic review. *British Journal of Educational Technology*, *51*(5), 1485–1504. DOI: 10.1111/bjet.12959

Farias-Gaytan, S., Aguaded, I., & Ramirez-Montoya, M. S. (2023). Digital transformation and digital literacy in the context of complexity within higher education institutions: A systematic literature review. *Humanities & Social Sciences Communications*, *10*(1), 386. DOI: 10.1057/s41599-023-01875-9

Gu, X., & Ericson, B. J. (2024). AI literacy in K-12 and higher education in the wake of generative AI: An integrative review. In *Proceedings of the 2025 ACM Conference on International Computing Education Research* V.1 (pp. 367-381). DOI: 10.1145/3702652.3744217

Guo, X., Chen, S., & Guo, Y. (2024). Advancing multimodal teaching: A bibliometric and content analysis of trends, influences, and future directions. *Humanities & Social Sciences Communications*, *11*(1), 1527. DOI: 10.1057/s41599-024-04254-0

Ilomäki, L., Paavola, S., Lakkala, M., & Kantosalo, A. (2023). Critical digital literacies at school level: A systematic review. *Review of Education*, *11*(3), e3425. DOI: 10.1002/rev3.3425

Liao, C.-H., & Wu, J.-Y. (2022). Deploying multimodal learning analytics models to explore the impact of digital distraction and peer learning on student performance. *Computers & Education*, *190*, 104599. DOI: 10.1016/j.compedu.2022.104599

Lim, F. V., Nguyen, T. T. H., & Kubler, M. (2022). Multimodality in the English language classroom: A systematic review of literature. *Linguistics and Education*, *69*, 101048. DOI: 10.1016/j.linged.2022.101048

Liu, H., Liu, L., & Li, H. (2024). Multimodal discourse studies in the international academic community (1997–2023): A bibliometric analysis. *SAGE Open*, *14*(4), 21582440241305454. Advance online publication. DOI: 10.1177/21582440241305454

Luo, H. (2023). Editorial: Advances in multimodal learning: Pedagogies, technologies, and analytics. *Frontiers in Psychology*, *14*, 1286092. DOI: 10.3389/fpsyg.2023.1286092 PMID: 38022937

Ma, N., & Zhong, Z. (2025). A meta-analysis of the impact of generative artificial intelligence on learning outcomes. *Journal of Computer Assisted Learning*, *41*(1), 70117. DOI: 10.1111/jcal.70117

Mu, S., Cui, M., & Huang, X. (2020). Multimodal data fusion in learning analytics: A systematic review. *Sensors (Basel)*, *20*(23), 6856. DOI: 10.3390/s20236856 PMID: 33266131

Ng, D. T. K., Leung, J. K. L., Chu, K. W. S., & Qiao, M. S. (2023). AI literacy: Definition, teaching, evaluation and ethical issues. *Proceedings of the Association for Information Science and Technology*, *58*(1), 504–509. DOI: 10.1002/pra2.487

Ng, D. T. K., Leung, J. K. L., Chu, S. K. W., & Qiao, M. S. (2021). Conceptualizing AI literacy: An exploratory review. *Computers and Education: Artificial Intelligence*, *2*, 100041. DOI: 10.1016/j.caeai.2021.100041

Ouhaichi, N., Hammami, S., & Souissi, N. (2024). *A systematic review of multimodal learning analytics systems design frameworks*. IATED Digital Library., DOI: 10.21125/edulearn.2024.1299

Strat, T. T. S., Henriksen, E. K., & Jegstad, K. M. (2024). Inquiry-based science education in science teacher education: A systematic review. *Studies in Science Education*, *60*(2), 191–249. DOI: 10.1080/03057267.2023.2207148

Su, J., Ng, D. T. K., & Chu, S. K. W. (2023). Artificial intelligence (AI) literacy in early childhood education: The challenges and opportunities. *Computers and Education: Artificial Intelligence*, *4*, 100124. DOI: 10.1016/j.caeai.2023.100124

Sun, L., & Zhou, L. (2024). Does generative artificial intelligence improve the academic achievement of college students? A meta-analysis. *Journal of Educational Computing Research*, *62*(8), 2161–2191. DOI: 10.1177/07356331241277937

Thomson, T. J., Pfurtscheller, D., Lobinger, K., Laba, N., & Christ, K. (2025). Visual literacies in transition: Multimodal co-production with generative AI. *Journal of Visual Literacy*, *44*(4), 305–329. DOI: 10.1080/1051144X.2025.2566592

Tinmaz, H., Lee, Y. T., Fanea-Ivanovici, M., & Baber, H. (2022). A systematic review on digital literacy. *Smart Learning Environments*, *9*(1), 21. DOI: 10.1186/s40561-022-00204-y PMID: 40478098

Tlili, A., Saqer, K., Salha, S., & Huang, R. (2025). Investigating the effect of artificial intelligence in education (AIEd) on learning achievement: A meta-analysis and research synthesis. *Information Development*, *33*(3), 825–842. Advance online publication. DOI: 10.1177/02666669241304407

Verma, V., & Varghese, J. (2025). Mapping multi-modal learning analytics in techno-driven learning environments: A bibliometric analysis. *Discover Education*, *3*(1), 242. DOI: 10.1007/s44217-025-00789-9

Wang, H., Wu, Y., Chen, L., & Zhao, Y. (2023). Key factors predicting problem-based learning in online environments: Evidence from multimodal learning analytics. *Frontiers in Psychology*, *14*, 1080294. DOI: 10.3389/fpsyg.2023.1080294 PMID: 36814653

Yang, W. (2022). Artificial intelligence education for young children: Why, what, and how in curriculum design and implementation. *Computers and Education: Artificial Intelligence*, *3*, 100061. DOI: 10.1016/j.caeai.2022.100061

Zaidi, R., & Sah, P. K. (2024). Affordances of multilingual and multimodal literacy engagements of immigrant high school students: A scoping review. *SAGE Open*, *14*(1), 21582440241228122. Advance online publication. DOI: 10.1177/21582440241228122

Zhai, C., Wibowo, S., & Li, L. D. (2024). The effects of over-reliance on AI dialogue systems on students' cognitive abilities: A systematic review. *Smart Learning Environments*, *11*(1), 28. DOI: 10.1186/s40561-024-00316-7

KEY TERMS AND DEFINITIONS

AI Literacy: The knowledge and skills needed to understand how artificial intelligence works, its applications, benefits, risks, and ethical implications. It enables individuals to critically evaluate AI systems, use them responsibly, and participate effectively in an AI-driven society.

Artificial Intelligence in Education: Using AI technologies like machine learning, adaptive systems, and chatbots to enhance teaching and learning. It supports personalized learning, automated assessment, intelligent tutoring, data-driven decision-making, and improved educational accessibility and efficiency.

Generative AI: Artificial intelligence systems that can create new content such as text, images, audio, or code by learning patterns from large datasets. Examples include tools like ChatGPT and image generators, which produce original outputs based on user prompts.

Meta-Analysis: A research method that systematically combines and statistically analyzes results from multiple independent studies on the same topic. It helps identify overall trends, measure effect sizes, resolve inconsistencies, and provide stronger, evidence-based conclusions than a single study alone.

Multimodal Literacy: The ability to understand, interpret, and create meaning using multiple forms of communication, such as text, images, audio, video, and digital media. It emphasizes integrating visual, linguistic, and technological skills to effectively engage in modern communication environments.

Chapter 9
Multivoice Work:
Dialogic Approaches to Multimodal Literacy in the Age of Artificial Intelligence

Deepak Gupta
http://orcid.org/0000-0003-3929-1362
Institute of Technology and Management, Gwalior, India

Surayyo Eshboyeva
Termez University of Economics and Service, Termez, Uzbekistan

Safarova Svetlana
Mamun University, Urgench, Uzbekistan

Inoyatova Saodatxon Joxongir qizi
Tashkent Pharmaceutical Institute, Uzbekistan

Narzulloeva Salomatbonu
Bukhara State Pedagogical Institute, Bukhara, Uzbekistan

Juraqobilova Xamida
Turan University, Uzbekistan

Kamolova Ozodakhon
Denov Institute of Entrepreneurship and Pedagogy, Uzbekistan

ABSTRACT

This chapter examines multivoice work as a foundational construct for understanding multimodal literacy practices in AI-enhanced educational contexts. Drawing on dialogic pedagogy and sociocultural theories, it explores how generative artificial intelligence transforms traditional notions of authorship, voice, and meaning-making in academic writing and digital composition. The chapter presents a comprehensive framework integrating multiple voices—human learners, educators, AI systems, and cultural-historical resources—within multimodal literacy practices. Through anal-

DOI: 10.4018/979-8-3373-6986-0.ch009

ysis of contemporary research and pedagogical applications, it demonstrates how AI-mediated environments create new possibilities for polyphonic learning while raising critical questions about agency, authenticity, and literacy competencies.

INTRODUCTION

The emergence of generative artificial intelligence has fundamentally transformed the landscape of literacy education, challenging conventional understandings of authorship, composition, and meaning-making in academic contexts (Kalantzis et al., 2024; Li, 2025). As students increasingly engage with AI systems such as ChatGPT, Claude, and other large language models in their writing processes, educators face unprecedented questions about the nature of student voice, the boundaries of collaborative composition, and the competencies required for effective literacy practices in digital environments (Chiu, 2024; Cope & Kalantzis, 2024).

This chapter introduces and elaborates the concept of "multivoice work" as a theoretical and pedagogical framework for understanding literacy practices in AI-enhanced educational settings. Multivoice work extends traditional dialogic approaches to literacy education by explicitly acknowledging and examining the multiple human and non-human voices that participate in contemporary meaning-making processes. Rather than viewing AI as merely a tool or threat to authentic student expression, this framework positions AI-mediated composition as an inherently polyphonic activity requiring new forms of critical awareness and orchestration skills (Cross et al., 2022; Smith, 2022).

The concept of multivoice work builds on Bakhtinian notions of dialogism and heteroglossia, which recognize that all language use involves the interweaving of multiple voices, perspectives, and social languages (Wertsch, del Río, & Alvarez, 2021). However, it extends these concepts to address the unique characteristics of AI-mediated literacy environments, where the voices in play include not only human interlocutors and cultural-historical discourses but also algorithmically generated text, multimodal resources, and the complex interactions between human intentions and machine capabilities (Liu, Zhang, & Biebricher, 2024; Zhang & Li, 2026).

Figure 1. Multivoice Framework for AI-Enhanced Literacy

Figure 1 presents the comprehensive multivoice framework that guides this analysis, illustrating the five key dimensions of multivoice work in AI-enhanced literacy: Voice Plurality, Mediated Agency, Dialogic Interaction, Multimodal Integration, and Critical Orchestration. Each dimension represents an essential aspect of how students engage with multiple voices in contemporary composition practices.

The Multimodal Turn and Digital Composition

Contemporary literacy practices have undergone what scholars term a "multimodal turn," recognizing that meaning-making increasingly involves the integration of linguistic, visual, spatial, gestural, and audio modes of communication (Chantajinda, 2024; Lim, 2021). This shift has been accelerated by digital technologies that enable students to compose across multiple semiotic resources, creating texts that combine written language with images, videos, interactive elements, and other modal affordances (Beltrán-Palanques, 2024; Oliveira, 2024).

The integration of generative AI into multimodal composition introduces a new dimension to this landscape. AI systems can now generate not only written text but also images, videos, audio, and interactive elements, fundamentally expanding the range of voices and modalities available to student composers (Avila et al., 2025;

Heilala & Araya, 2025). This technological capability raises important questions about how students navigate, evaluate, and orchestrate these various resources in their meaning-making processes.

Theoretical Foundations: Sociocultural and Dialogic Perspectives

The framework of multivoice work is grounded in sociocultural theories of learning and development, which emphasize that human cognition and literacy practices are fundamentally social and mediated by cultural tools and artifacts (Wertsch et al., 2021). From this perspective, AI systems represent a new form of cultural tool that mediates students' composing processes, shaping both what they can express and how they think about expression itself.

Dialogic pedagogy provides another crucial foundation for understanding multivoice work (Bjork, 2025; Cross et al., 2022; Smith, 2022). Rather than viewing literacy education as the transmission of fixed knowledge or skills, dialogic approaches emphasize the importance of authentic dialogue, multiple perspectives, and the co-construction of meaning between teachers and learners. In AI-enhanced contexts, this dialogic relationship expands to include interactions between students and AI systems, raising new questions about the nature of authentic dialogue and the role of human agency in automated environments.

Chapter Organization and Scope

This chapter proceeds through seven main sections, each addressing key dimensions of multivoice work in multimodal literacy education. Following this introduction, Section 2 develops a comprehensive theoretical framework for understanding multivoice work, integrating dialogic, sociocultural, and multimodal perspectives. Section 3 examines the specific dimensions of multivoice work in AI-enhanced literacy practices, including the roles of human students, educators, AI systems, and cultural-historical resources. Section 4 explores pedagogical implications, offering frameworks for curriculum design and instructional practice. Section 5 presents empirical insights from recent research on students' experiences with AI-mediated composition. Section 6 addresses critical considerations around ethics, equity, and literacy competencies. Section 7 concludes with future directions for research and practice.

Throughout, the chapter maintains focus on the central question: How can educators and students productively engage with the inherently multivoice nature of AI-enhanced literacy practices while maintaining critical awareness, ethical responsibility, and authentic learning goals?

THEORETICAL FRAMEWORK: CONCEPTUALIZING MULTIVOICE WORK

Building on dialogic, sociocultural, and multimodal theoretical foundations, this section develops a comprehensive framework for understanding multivoice work in AI-enhanced literacy education. The framework recognizes five key dimensions that characterize contemporary multivoice literacy practices.

Figure 2. AI-Mediated Dialogic Interaction Model in Literacy Education

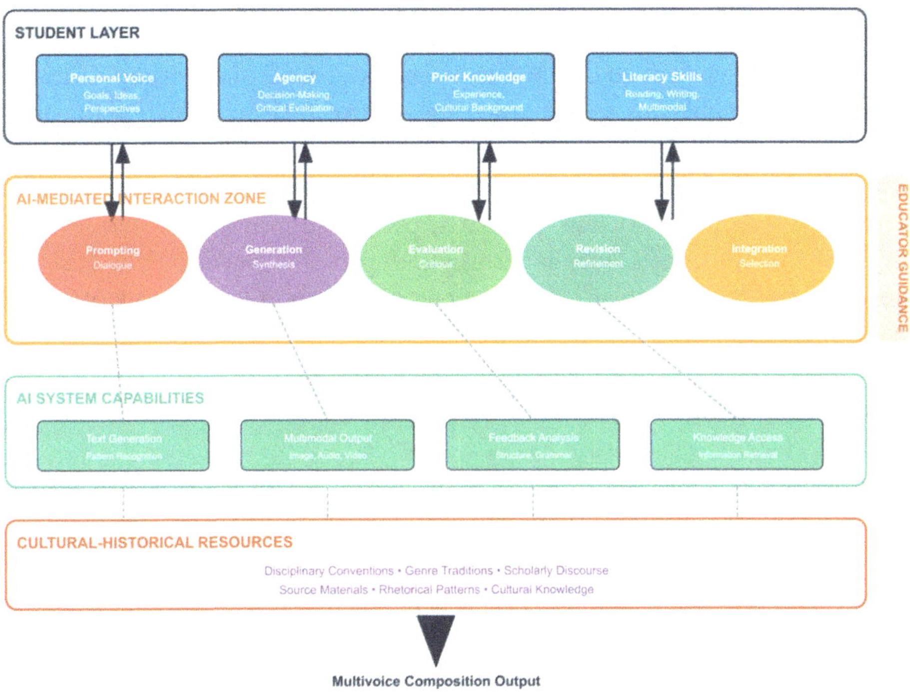

Figure 2 illustrates the AI-Mediated Dialogic Interaction Model, showing how students' voices, agency, and literacy skills interact with AI capabilities within a zone of dialogic interaction, all grounded in cultural-historical resources and guided by educator facilitation. This model demonstrates the complex layering of voices and mediational processes in AI-enhanced composition.

Dialogism and Heteroglossia in Literacy Education

The concept of multivoice work draws fundamentally on Mikhail Bakhtin's theories of dialogism and heteroglossia, which posit that all utterances exist in dialogue with previous and anticipated future utterances, and that language itself comprises multiple "voices" representing different social positions, ideologies, and ways of speaking (Wertsch et al., 2021). For Bakhtin, even seemingly monologic texts are inherently dialogic, containing traces of the various voices, genres, and social languages that the author has internalized through cultural participation.

In traditional literacy education, students learn to orchestrate multiple voices in their writing: their own developing voice as a writer, the voices of cited authors and sources, the anticipated voice of their audience, and the conventional voices of particular academic genres and disciplines (Cross et al., 2022). Effective academic writing requires students to navigate these multiple voices, positioning themselves in relation to existing scholarship while maintaining their own perspective and argument.

Smith (2022) elaborated on a "dialogic authorial academic language learning" approach that emphasizes students' development of their own voice through engagement with multiple perspectives and discourses. This approach moves beyond formulaic genre pedagogy to focus on authentic dialogue and the construction of meaning through interaction with texts, peers, and instructors. Students learn not simply to reproduce academic forms but to participate genuinely in academic conversations, bringing their own questions and perspectives into dialogue with established knowledge.

Sociocultural Mediation and Cultural Tools

Sociocultural theories provide crucial insights into how cultural tools mediate human thinking and learning (Wertsch et al., 2021). From a Vygotskian perspective, writing itself functions as a cultural tool that transforms human cognition, enabling new forms of thinking and meaning-making that would not be possible without this mediational means. When students write, they are not simply expressing pre-formed thoughts but actively constructing and transforming their understanding through engagement with written language.

The introduction of AI into literacy practices represents the emergence of a powerful new cultural tool with distinctive affordances and constraints (Cope & Kalantzis, 2024; Kalantzis et al., 2024). AI systems can generate text based on prompts, suggest revisions, provide feedback, answer questions, and engage in various forms of interactive dialogue with students. These capabilities fundamentally alter the mediational landscape of literacy education, creating new possibilities for meaning-making while also raising questions about the nature of learning and development in AI-mediated environments.

Liu et al. (2024) investigated students' cognitive processes in generative AI-assisted digital multimodal composing compared to traditional writing, finding that AI assistance can support certain aspects of composition while potentially bypassing others. This research highlights the importance of understanding how different cultural tools shape not only what students produce but also how they think and learn in the process of production.

Polyphonic Learning in Teacher Education

The concept of polyphonic learning, introduced by Khosronejad and Weber (2023) in the context of teacher professional development, offers valuable insights for understanding multivoice work in literacy education. Polyphonic learning recognizes that teacher development occurs through engagement with multiple voices and perspectives: the voices of educational theory, experienced practitioners, students, colleagues, and one's own evolving understanding. This multiplicity is not viewed as a problem to be resolved but as a productive resource for learning and growth.

Extending this concept to student literacy development, we can understand multivoice work as involving students' engagement with and orchestration of multiple voices in their composing processes. In AI-enhanced contexts, these voices include:

- The student's own developing voice and perspective
- The voices of cited sources and authorities
- The voice(s) of AI systems engaged in collaborative composition
- The voices of peers providing feedback and dialogue
- The voice of the instructor offering guidance and evaluation
- The conventional voices of academic genres and disciplines
- The voices of broader cultural and historical discourses

Effective multivoice work requires students to navigate these multiple voices critically and purposefully, making informed decisions about which voices to amplify, how to position themselves in relation to different voices, and how to create coherent and meaningful compositions from this polyphonic material.

Multimodal Meaning-Making and Intersemiosis

Contemporary understandings of literacy recognize that meaning-making involves not only written language but multiple semiotic modes including visual images, spatial arrangements, gestures, sounds, and various other communicative resources (Chantajinda, 2024; Lim, 2021). Multimodal literacy education attends to how different modes work together to create meaning, recognizing that each mode offers distinctive affordances and that meaning often emerges from the relationships between modes—a process termed “intersemiosis” (Lim, 2021).

Lin (2026) proposed a “multimodalities-entextualization cycle” model for integrating multimodal literacy in bilingual teacher education, emphasizing how different modes and languages interact in the production and interpretation of texts. This model highlights the dynamic, recursive nature of multimodal composition, where students move between planning, creating, reflecting on, and revising multimodal texts while attending to how different semiotic resources work together.

In AI-enhanced environments, the range of available multimodal resources expands dramatically. Generative AI can produce not only written text but also images, videos, audio, code, and various other outputs (Heilala & Araya, 2025). Students working with these technologies engage in multimodal composition that integrates AI-generated resources with their own multimodal creation, requiring sophisticated understanding of how different modes contribute to meaning and how to evaluate and integrate AI-generated multimodal content effectively.

Integrated Framework: The Multivoice Work Model

Building on these theoretical foundations, we propose an integrated framework for understanding multivoice work in AI-enhanced multimodal literacy education. This framework recognizes five key dimensions:

- **Dimension 1: Voice Plurality** - The recognition that multiple voices (human and AI, individual and collective, contemporary and historical) participate in any literacy act.
- **Dimension 2: Mediated Agency** - The understanding that human agency in composition is always mediated by cultural tools, including AI systems, and that effective literacy requires critical awareness of this mediation.
- **Dimension 3: Dialogic Interaction** - The emphasis on authentic dialogue and meaning-making through interaction, extending to include human-AI dialogue alongside traditional human-human dialogue.
- **Dimension 4: Multimodal Integration** - The recognition that contemporary literacy involves orchestrating multiple semiotic modes, including AI-generated multimodal content.
- **Dimension 5: Critical Orchestration** - The development of students' capacity to critically evaluate, select, and integrate multiple voices and modes in purposeful, ethically informed ways.

This framework positions multivoice work not as a problem to be solved but as the fundamental nature of contemporary literacy practice, requiring new pedagogical approaches and learning outcomes focused on critical awareness, strategic orchestration, and ethical responsibility in AI-mediated environments.

MULTIVOICE DIMENSIONS IN AI-ENHANCED LITERACY PRACTICES

This section examines the specific voices that participate in AI-enhanced literacy practices and how they interact in contemporary educational contexts. Understanding these dimensions is essential for developing pedagogical approaches that support effective multivoice work.

Figure 3. Integration of Multiple Voices in Digital Composition

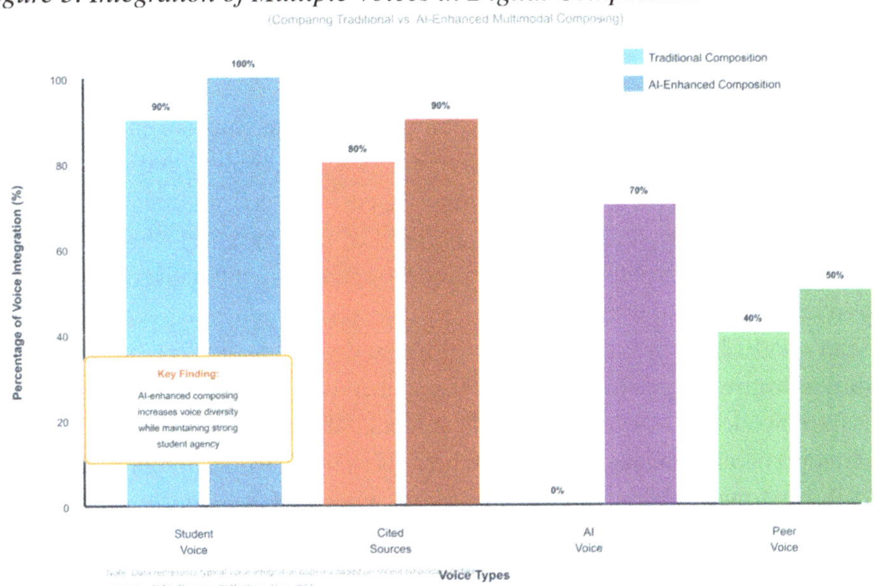

Figure 3 presents comparative data on voice integration patterns in traditional versus AI-enhanced multimodal composing. The data, synthesized from recent empirical studies (Liu et al., 2024; Zhang & Li, 2026; Wang & Ren, 2024), reveals how AI-enhanced composition increases the diversity of voices while students maintain strong personal agency. Notably, AI voice integration reaches 70% in AI-enhanced contexts compared to 0% in traditional composition, while student voice remains at 100% in both conditions, suggesting that AI adds to rather than replaces student voice.

The Student Voice: Agency and Authenticity

Central to any discussion of multivoice work is the question of student voice and agency. Traditional concerns about plagiarism and authentic student work take on new dimensions when AI systems can generate sophisticated text on demand (Hradilová, 2025; Hysaj & Freeman, 2025). Educators worry that reliance on AI-generated content may undermine students' development of their own voice and thinking capacities.

However, research on students' actual experiences with generative AI reveals a more nuanced picture. Syafei and Nuraeningsih (2025) investigated ELT students' perspectives and experiences leveraging AI in writing, finding that students use AI strategically as a brainstorming partner, language advisor, and revision assistant rather than simply copying AI output. Students reported that AI interaction helped them clarify their own thinking, consider alternative perspectives, and improve their expression—suggesting that AI can serve as a tool for voice development rather than voice replacement.

Wang and Ren (2024) conducted an empirical study of students enhancing academic writing in a linguistics course with generative AI, finding that students who effectively integrated AI assistance demonstrated improved writing quality while maintaining distinct personal perspectives. The key factor was not whether students used AI but how they used it—whether they engaged critically with AI suggestions or passively accepted them.

Zhang and Li (2026) argued for shifting students' positioning from "passive consumers to critical creators" through AI-enhanced digital multimodal composing. Their framework emphasizes developing students' critical media literacy alongside AI literacy, enabling them to understand how AI systems work, evaluate AI outputs critically, and make informed decisions about when and how to use AI resources in their own creative work.

The AI Voice: Capabilities and Limitations

Understanding the nature of AI-generated voice is crucial for effective multivoice work. Contemporary large language models generate text by predicting likely sequences of words based on patterns learned from vast training corpora, but they do not possess consciousness, intentionality, or genuine understanding in the human sense (Chiu et al., 2024; Long & Magerko, 2020).

This distinctive nature of AI voice has important implications. AI-generated text reflects patterns and perspectives present in training data, which means it can reproduce both valuable cultural knowledge and problematic biases. AI systems lack personal experience, embodied knowledge, and situated understanding of specific contexts. They cannot truly engage in dialogue with genuine mutual understanding, though they can simulate dialogic interaction in sophisticated ways.

Cope and Kalantzis (2024) argued that understanding these capabilities and limitations is essential for literacy education in the AI age. Students need to recognize that AI-generated text represents a kind of voice—a synthesis of patterns from countless human texts—but not a conscious perspective or intentional communication. This understanding enables more critical and strategic engagement with AI resources.

Avila et al. (2025) discussed opportunities and challenges of large multimodal foundation models in education, noting that these systems can provide valuable scaffolding for learning while also creating risks of overreliance, decreased critical thinking, and uncritical acceptance of AI output. Effective integration requires explicit attention to developing students' AI literacy competencies alongside traditional literacy skills.

The Educator Voice: Guidance and Evaluation

The educator's voice plays a crucial mediating role in multivoice literacy practices. Teachers provide guidance on effective use of various resources, model critical evaluation of sources (including AI-generated content), establish learning goals and expectations, and evaluate student work (Khosronejad & Weber, 2023).

In AI-enhanced contexts, educators face new challenges in fulfilling these roles. Hradilová (2025) explores how educators can guide students to make informed and ethical choices about AI use in academic writing, emphasizing the importance of transparency about AI assistance, critical evaluation of AI outputs, and maintaining academic integrity while leveraging AI productively.

Teacher education programs must prepare educators to work effectively in AI-enhanced literacy environments (Lin, 2026). This includes developing teachers' own AI literacy competencies, pedagogical strategies for integrating AI into writing instruction, approaches to evaluating student work that may involve AI assistance, and frameworks for discussing ethical issues with students.

Cross et al. (2022) emphasized that dialogic literacy pedagogy requires teachers to position themselves not as authoritative knowledge transmitters but as facilitators of authentic dialogue and collaborative meaning-making. In AI-mediated environments, this means helping students engage critically with AI as one voice among many rather than treating AI as either authoritative oracle or forbidden shortcut.

Cultural and Historical Voices

All literacy practices draw on cultural and historical resources—established genres, disciplinary conventions, rhetorical traditions, and the accumulated knowledge encoded in existing texts (Wertsch et al., 2021). These cultural-historical voices provide the foundation on which new meaning-making builds.

AI systems have unique relationships to cultural-historical resources. Their training on vast text corpora means they encode extensive patterns from existing cultural production, making them particularly effective at reproducing conventional forms and synthesizing established knowledge. However, they lack the embodied, situated cultural knowledge that humans develop through participation in specific communities and practices.

Students engaged in multivoice work must navigate the relationship between innovation and convention, between their own emerging perspectives and established disciplinary knowledge. AI can support this navigation by providing examples of conventional forms, explaining disciplinary concepts, and suggesting how to connect new ideas to existing scholarship. However, students need critical awareness of how AI represents cultural-historical knowledge and the limitations of AI's cultural understanding.

Kalantzis et al. (2024) discussed how multimodal generative AI changes the landscape of cultural production and reproduction, creating new possibilities for accessing and remixing cultural resources while also raising questions about cultural appropriation, intellectual property, and the preservation of diverse cultural voices in an increasingly AI-mediated environment.

Peer Voices and Collaborative Composition

Peer interaction has long been recognized as valuable for literacy development, providing opportunities for dialogue, feedback, and collaborative meaning-making (Cross et al., 2022; Smith, 2022). In AI-enhanced environments, peer voices interact in complex ways with AI voices.

Students may use AI to generate ideas for peer discussion, to revise drafts before sharing with peers, or to help them understand and respond to peer feedback. They may collaborate with peers in prompting AI systems or evaluating AI outputs. These various configurations create new possibilities for peer learning while also requiring explicit attention to maintaining authentic peer dialogue and collaboration.

Bjork (2025) examined multimodal dialogic understanding of early writing development, emphasizing how children learn to write through dialogue with teachers and peers across multiple modes of communication. Extending this to AI contexts, we can consider how students' dialogue with AI systems might complement and enhance (rather than replace) dialogue with human interlocutors.

The challenge for educators is to design learning environments where AI supports rather than supplants peer interaction, where students engage in genuine dialogue with each other while also drawing strategically on AI resources, and where peer voices remain central to the collaborative construction of knowledge.

PEDAGOGICAL IMPLICATIONS AND CURRICULUM DESIGN

Effective integration of multivoice work into literacy education requires careful pedagogical design. This section explores key considerations for curriculum development, instructional practice, and assessment in AI-enhanced contexts.

Table 1. Comparison of Traditional vs. AI-Enhanced Multivoice Literacy Practices

Dimension	Traditional Practices	AI-Enhanced Practices
Voice Sources	Student's own perspective, cited scholarly sources, peer feedback, instructor guidance, disciplinary conventions	All traditional sources PLUS: AI-generated text and multimodal content, AI as dialogic partner, algorithmic synthesis of patterns
Agency & Control	Student maintains direct control over all text production; revisions emerge from personal decision-making	Mediated agency through tool interaction; decisions about prompting, evaluation, and integration of AI outputs
Composing Process	Linear or recursive cycles of planning, drafting, revising, editing	Iterative dialogue between human and AI: prompting/questioning, generation/response, evaluation/critique, selection/integration
Multimodal Integration	Student creates or locates images, charts/graphs, design elements, layout/formatting	AI can generate multiple modes on demand; student focuses on modal selection, intersemiotic coherence, critical evaluation
Authenticity	Originality defined by unique perspective, novel synthesis of ideas, personal voice development	Authenticity redefined as purposeful orchestration of resources, critical judgment, transparent acknowledgment of AI use
Language Support	Support through writing handbooks, grammar checkers, thesaurus/ dictionary, tutoring sessions	Enhanced support via immediate AI feedback, contextual suggestions, natural language explanation, multilingual assistance
Critical Literacy	Focus on source evaluation, bias recognition in texts, rhetorical analysis, genre awareness	Expanded focus including all traditional skills PLUS: AI literacy competencies, algorithm awareness, bias in AI outputs, ethical AI use
Assessment Focus	Evaluation of final written products, demonstrated learning, communication effectiveness, genre conventions	Expanded evaluation of composing processes, critical AI engagement, decision-making rationales, reflective awareness

continued on following page

Table 1. Continued

Dimension	Traditional Practices	AI-Enhanced Practices
Equity Issues	Inequities in writing backgrounds, language proficiency, access to support resources, cultural capital	New equity dimensions: differential AI access, varying AI literacy levels, cultural relevance of AI outputs, potential for both reducing and reinforcing inequities
Instructor Role	Teacher as knowledge source, assignment designer, evaluator, feedback provider	Teacher role expands to: AI literacy educator, ethical framework developer, process guide, critical dialogue facilitator, assessment innovator

Note: This table synthesizes findings from Cummings et al. (2024), Hradilová (2025), Liu et al. (2024), Wang & Ren (2024), Zhang & Li (2026), and theoretical frameworks from Cope & Kalantzis (2024) and Kalantzis et al. (2024).

Designing for Critical AI Literacy

Effective multivoice work in AI-enhanced contexts requires explicit development of critical AI literacy—understanding how AI systems work, what they can and cannot do, and how to evaluate and use them responsibly (Chiu et al., 2024; Long & Magerko, 2020). AI literacy is not simply technical knowledge about algorithms but encompasses broader competencies including technical understanding, critical evaluation, ethical awareness, strategic use, and reflective practice.

- **Technical understanding**: Basic knowledge of how AI systems generate text and other outputs
- **Critical evaluation**: Ability to assess quality, accuracy, and appropriateness of AI-generated content
- **Ethical awareness**: Understanding of ethical issues including bias, privacy, intellectual property, and academic integrity
- **Strategic use**: Capacity to determine when and how AI can productively support learning goals
- **Reflective practice**: Ongoing reflection on one's own AI use and its impacts on learning and development

Chiu et al. (2024) propose a comprehensive framework for AI literacy and competency, arguing that these capabilities must be developed systematically through curriculum rather than assumed to emerge naturally from AI exposure. Their framework emphasizes both critical understanding and productive competencies, preparing students not only to consume AI outputs but to engage with AI systems as informed, critical, and creative users.

Developing critical AI literacy requires explicit instructional attention across multiple dimensions. Students need opportunities to examine how AI systems work, exploring questions like: What data was this AI trained on? How does it generate responses to prompts? What biases might be embedded in its training? What are the limits of its capabilities? These technical and critical understandings form the foundation for informed AI use.

Beyond understanding AI systems themselves, students need practice evaluating AI outputs critically. This involves developing heuristics for assessment: Does this AI-generated text contain factual errors? Does it reflect problematic biases or stereotypes? Is the writing style appropriate for my purpose and audience? Does it actually address the question or prompt I provided? Through repeated practice with such evaluation, students develop the critical judgment essential for effective AI integration.

Ethical dimensions of AI literacy extend beyond individual use to consider broader societal implications. Students should grapple with questions about how AI affects labor markets, knowledge production, cultural diversity, and power structures. What happens to professional writers when AI can generate content quickly and cheaply? How does AI affect representation of diverse voices and perspectives in media and scholarship? What are the environmental impacts of large-scale AI computing? These broader ethical questions help students understand AI use within larger social contexts.

Strategic use of AI requires students to develop metacognitive awareness of their own learning processes and goals. When should they use AI versus engaging independently? How can they use AI to support learning rather than bypass it? What prompting strategies elicit useful AI responses? How should they integrate AI outputs with their own thinking? These strategic competencies enable students to harness AI affordances productively while maintaining learning engagement.

Finally, reflective practice involves ongoing examination of one's AI use patterns and their effects. Students might keep reflective journals documenting when and how they use AI, what they learn from AI interactions, and how AI use affects their learning and development. Through such reflection, students develop greater awareness and intentionality in their AI engagement, moving beyond reactive use toward purposeful integration aligned with their goals and values.

Pedagogical Frameworks for AI-Enhanced Writing

Several pedagogical frameworks have emerged for integrating AI into writing instruction while maintaining focus on authentic learning and development. Cummings, Monroe, and Watkins (2024) provided an early analysis of affordances, limitations, and a framework for using generative AI in first-year writing, emphasizing transparency about AI use, explicit instruction in AI literacy, and assignments that require students to demonstrate critical engagement with AI rather than passive reliance.

Their framework includes:

1. **Transparency protocols**: Clear communication about AI use expectations and policies
2. **Scaffolded AI integration**: Gradual introduction of AI tools with explicit guidance
3. **Reflective assignments**: Requirements for students to reflect on and explain their AI use
4. **Critical evaluation tasks**: Activities requiring assessment of AI output quality and appropriateness
5. **Authentic composition goals**: Assignments focused on genuine communication purposes that AI cannot fully accomplish alone

Wang and Ren (2024) described successful implementation of AI-enhanced academic writing in a linguistics course, using a model where students first develop their own ideas and drafts, then engage with AI for specific purposes (clarification, alternative perspectives, language refinement), and finally revise with critical evaluation of AI suggestions. This process maintains student agency while leveraging AI capabilities productively.

Multimodal Composition Pedagogy

The integration of AI into multimodal composition requires pedagogical approaches that address both multimodal meaning-making and AI literacy. Chantajinda (2024) reviewed research into practice for digital multimodal composition in second language writing, identifying effective pedagogical strategies including:

- **Modal awareness activities**: Explicit attention to how different modes contribute to meaning
- **Multimodal analysis**: Critical examination of how professional texts integrate modes
- **Scaffolded composition**: Structured support for planning and creating multimodal texts
- **Iterative revision**: Cycles of creation, feedback, and refinement across modes
- **Reflective documentation**: Articulation of design decisions and modal choices

Liu et al. (2024) investigated students' cognitive processes in AI-assisted digital multimodal composing, finding that effective AI integration requires explicit pedagogical support. Without such support, students may rely on AI superficially without deep engagement with multimodal meaning-making principles. However, when educators provide clear frameworks and purposeful guidance, AI can enhance students' multimodal composition capabilities.

Assessment Approaches in AI-Enhanced Contexts

Assessment of student writing in AI-enhanced environments raises complex questions. Traditional approaches focused on evaluating final written products become problematic when AI can generate sophisticated text. Educators must develop new assessment frameworks that focus on learning processes, critical thinking, and authentic demonstration of competencies (Detrick & Li, 2025; Hradilová, 2025).

Effective assessment approaches in AI-enhanced contexts include:

- **Process-focused assessment**: Evaluating students' composing processes, including how they use AI, rather than only final products. This might involve reviewing drafts, revision histories, and reflection documents.
- **Reflective components**: Requiring students to explain and justify their AI use, demonstrating critical awareness of when and how they engaged with AI resources.
- **Multimodal portfolios**: Collecting diverse evidence of student learning across multiple modes and contexts, making it more difficult to rely solely on AI-generated content.
- **Authentic performance tasks**: Assignments requiring situated knowledge, personal experience, or real-time performance that AI cannot easily accomplish.
- **Collaborative evaluation**: Involving students in evaluating both their own and peers' work, developing critical evaluation capabilities as learning outcomes themselves.

Detrick and Li (2025) examined students' generative AI interaction patterns and impacts on academic writing, finding that assessment approaches significantly influence how students engage with AI. When assessment focuses only on final products, students may use AI to generate complete texts. However, when assessment emphasizes process, critical thinking, and authentic communication, students engage with AI more strategically and reflectively.

Teacher Education and Professional Development

Preparing educators to facilitate multivoice work in AI-enhanced literacy contexts requires substantial professional development. Lin (2026) proposed integrating multimodal literacy in teacher education through cycles of engagement with theory, analysis of multimodal texts, creation of multimodal teaching materials, and reflection on multimodal pedagogy.

Extending this to AI-enhanced contexts, teacher education should include:

- **Experiential learning with AI**: Hands-on experience using generative AI for various purposes
- **Critical analysis**: Examination of AI capabilities, limitations, biases, and ethical issues
- **Pedagogical design**: Practice designing assignments and activities for AI-enhanced contexts
- **Assessment development**: Creating evaluation approaches appropriate for AI-mediated work
- **Ethical frameworks**: Engaging with questions of integrity, equity, and responsibility
- **Ongoing adaptation**: Recognition that AI technologies evolve rapidly, requiring continuous learning

Khosronejad and Weber (2023) emphasized that effective teacher professional development must itself be polyphonic, engaging multiple voices and perspectives rather than presenting single "correct" approaches. Teachers need opportunities to grapple with the complexities and tensions of AI-enhanced literacy education through dialogue with colleagues, educational research, student experiences, and their own practical experimentation.

EMPIRICAL INSIGHTS: STUDENTS' EXPERIENCES WITH AI-MEDIATED COMPOSITION

Recent research has begun documenting how students actually use generative AI in their writing processes, revealing diverse patterns and approaches that inform pedagogical practice.

Patterns of AI Integration in Student Writing

Recent research has begun documenting how students actually use generative AI in their writing processes, revealing diverse patterns and approaches. Detrick and Li (2025) identified several distinct interaction patterns in their study of student-AI engagement:

- **The Delegator**: Students who ask AI to generate complete texts with minimal personal input or revision. This pattern typically results in generic outputs lacking personal voice or situated knowledge.
- **The Collaborator**: Students who engage AI in dialogue, iteratively refining prompts and outputs while maintaining active decision-making about content and expression. This pattern shows more evidence of learning and voice development.
- **The Consultant**: Students who draft independently and then consult AI for specific purposes—clarifying arguments, improving expression, checking logic. This pattern maintains strong student agency while leveraging AI capabilities selectively.
- **The Critic**: Students who generate AI outputs primarily to analyze and critique them, developing critical evaluation skills and understanding of AI limitations. This pattern emphasizes learning about AI as much as learning with AI.

These patterns reflect different levels of agency, critical engagement, and learning orientation. Effective pedagogy should guide students toward patterns that support genuine learning rather than mere output generation.

Student Perspectives on AI-Enhanced Writing

Qualitative research on students' own perspectives reveals complex attitudes toward AI use in writing. Syafei and Nuraeningsih (2025) found that ELT students view AI as helpful for:

- **Brainstorming and idea generation**: Overcoming initial "blank page" anxiety
- **Language support**: Improving grammar, vocabulary, and expression, particularly for multilingual writers
- **Structural guidance**: Understanding organizational conventions and rhetorical patterns

- **Feedback access**: Receiving immediate responses to questions about their writing

However, students also expressed concerns about:

- **Overreliance**: Worry about losing writing skills through excessive AI dependence
- **Authenticity**: Questions about whether AI-assisted work genuinely represents their own thinking
- **Ethics**: Uncertainty about appropriate boundaries between acceptable AI support and academic dishonesty
- **Learning impact**: Concern that AI might bypass valuable struggle and learning processes

These findings suggest that students themselves recognize both affordances and risks of AI integration, but many lack clear frameworks for navigating these tensions. Explicit pedagogical guidance is essential for helping students develop productive AI use patterns.

Multilingual and Multicultural Considerations

Hysaj and Freeman (2025) explored purposes and uses of generative AI in academic writing for multicultural students, finding that AI provides particularly valuable support for students writing in additional languages. AI can help with:

- **Language confidence**: Reducing anxiety about grammatical accuracy and expression
- **Cultural conventions**: Understanding academic writing conventions in different cultural contexts
- **Translation and transfer**: Moving between languages and adapting ideas across linguistic contexts
- **Accessibility**: Providing support that might otherwise require extensive tutoring or assistance

However, these affordances also raise equity concerns. Students with strong English proficiency may use AI primarily for higher-order tasks like improving argumentation, while students with developing English skills may rely on AI more heavily for basic language support. This could potentially reinforce rather than reduce linguistic inequities.

Additionally, cultural perspectives on authorship, collaboration, and originality vary across contexts. Some students come from educational traditions that emphasize collective knowledge building and view writing as inherently collaborative, while others have been socialized into more individualistic authorship models. AI integration intersects complexly with these diverse cultural orientations.

The question of whose language and whose voice is represented in AI-generated text becomes particularly salient for multilingual writers. When a multilingual student uses AI to "improve" their English expression, are they developing their own English voice or conforming to standardized patterns that may erase linguistic and cultural distinctiveness? This tension requires careful pedagogical attention to ensure AI supports rather than suppresses multilingual writers' authentic voices.

Research on second language writing has long emphasized the importance of developing writers' voices while supporting language development (Chantajinda, 2024; Li, 2025). In AI contexts, this balance becomes more complex. Educators must help multilingual students use AI strategically for language support while maintaining ownership of their ideas, developing their own expressive capabilities, and preserving cultural and linguistic diversity in academic discourse.

Moreover, AI systems trained predominantly on English and other dominant languages may not serve multilingual writers equitably. Students writing in less-represented languages may receive lower-quality AI assistance, while students code-switching between languages may find AI unable to support their multilingual composing practices effectively. These technological limitations have pedagogical implications that educators must address.

Cognitive and Metacognitive Impacts

Liu et al. (2024) investigated students' cognitive processes in AI-assisted digital multimodal composing, using think-aloud protocols and process analysis to understand how AI shapes thinking and learning. Their findings reveal that:

- **AI can support metacognitive awareness**: Students who engaged AI dialogically reported increased attention to their own thinking processes, explicitly considering why they made certain choices and how AI suggestions aligned with their goals.
- **AI may bypass certain cognitive processes**: Some students using AI for initial drafting demonstrated less evidence of planning, idea development, and rhetorical decision-making compared to students composing without AI assistance.
- **Modal integration differs with AI use**: Students creating multimodal compositions with AI assistance showed different patterns of modal planning

and integration, sometimes selecting AI-generated images or other elements without deep consideration of their semiotic contribution.
- **Revision processes transform**: AI-assisted revision often focuses on sentence-level language refinement rather than higher-order rhetorical and organizational revision, potentially limiting development of revision skills.

These findings suggest that AI's impact on learning depends significantly on how it is integrated into composing processes and whether students engage metacognitively with their own AI use. Pedagogy that emphasizes process awareness and critical reflection can help mitigate potential negative impacts while leveraging positive affordances.

5.5 Community Service Learning and Authentic Contexts

Oliveira (2024) examined enhancing multimodal literacy through community service learning in higher education, finding that authentic, situated literacy practices create strong motivation and purpose for multimodal composition. Students working on genuine community projects demonstrated high engagement with multimodal meaning-making and took ownership of their creative work.

This research suggests important implications for AI-enhanced multimodal literacy education. When students compose for authentic audiences and real-world purposes—creating public information campaigns, developing educational materials for community organizations, producing documentary projects—they engage more critically with all available resources, including AI. Authentic contexts create natural motivations for evaluating quality, considering audience needs, and ensuring ethical practice.

Conversely, when assignments feel artificial or solely focused on demonstrating competency to instructors, students may be more likely to use AI instrumentally simply to complete requirements efficiently. Designing for authentic purposes and audiences can foster the kind of critical, purposeful engagement with multivoice resources that effective literacy education aims to develop.

CRITICAL CONSIDERATIONS: ETHICS, EQUITY, AND COMPETENCY

The integration of AI into academic writing raises fundamental questions about academic integrity, equity, and authentic learning that require careful consideration and institutional response.

Academic Integrity and Ethical Use

The integration of AI into academic writing raises fundamental questions about academic integrity, honesty, and appropriate attribution of ideas and expression (Hradilová, 2025). Traditional definitions of plagiarism—using others' words or ideas without attribution—become complicated when AI generates text that, while not copied from any single source, synthesizes patterns from countless existing texts.

Hradilová (2025) proposed guiding students to make informed and ethical choices about AI use rather than simply prohibiting AI or treating all AI assistance as cheating. This approach involves:

- **Transparency**: Requiring students to document and explain their AI use
- **Purposefulness**: Encouraging students to articulate legitimate learning purposes for AI engagement
- **Attribution**: Developing new conventions for acknowledging AI assistance appropriately **Responsibility**: Holding students accountable for all content in their work, regardless of whether they or AI generated it
- **Integrity alignment**: Helping students understand how AI use relates to broader academic values of honest inquiry and authentic learning

Different disciplines and contexts may establish different norms about appropriate AI use, ranging from complete prohibition in some assessment contexts to explicit encouragement in others. The key is developing shared understanding between educators and students about expectations, purposes, and ethical boundaries.

Equity and Access Considerations

While AI technologies offer potential benefits for supporting diverse learners, they also raise significant equity concerns (Chiu, 2024; Hysaj & Freeman, 2025). Critical considerations include:

- **Access disparities**: Not all students have equal access to AI technologies, particularly premium or subscription-based tools. Educational integration must consider these access differences.
- **Digital literacy gaps**: Students enter higher education with widely varying levels of digital literacy and AI familiarity. Some students may have extensive experience with AI tools while others have minimal exposure.
- **Linguistic diversity**: AI systems typically perform better in English and other dominant languages, potentially disadvantaging students working in other languages or multilingual contexts.

- **Cultural relevance**: AI training data reflects dominant cultural perspectives, which may not align with the experiences and knowledge of students from diverse cultural backgrounds.
- **Economic implications**: Reliance on commercial AI systems raises questions about educational institutions' relationships with technology companies and the long-term sustainability and equity of AI-enhanced education.

Addressing these equity concerns requires intentional pedagogical design, institutional support for equitable access, explicit attention to diverse student needs, and ongoing critical examination of how AI integration affects different student populations.

Competency Frameworks for AI-Enhanced Literacy

Long and Magerko (2020) and Chiu et al. (2024) have proposed comprehensive frameworks for AI literacy competencies, recognizing that effective engagement with AI requires multiple interrelated capabilities. Key competency domains include:

- **Conceptual understanding**: Knowing how AI systems work, what they can and cannot do, and the principles underlying their operation.
- **Critical evaluation**: Assessing AI outputs for quality, accuracy, bias, relevance, and appropriateness to specific contexts and purposes.
- **Ethical reasoning**: Understanding and navigating ethical issues including privacy, bias, transparency, accountability, and societal impacts of AI.
- **Creative application**: Using AI purposefully and strategically to support learning, creativity, and problem-solving while maintaining human agency and decision-making.
- **Societal implications**: Recognizing broader impacts of AI on labor, knowledge production, cultural production, and social structures.

These competencies extend beyond traditional literacy skills while also integrating with them. Students need both strong foundational literacy capabilities and AI-specific competencies to engage effectively in multivoice work in AI-enhanced contexts.

Bias, Representation, and Cultural Sensitivity

AI systems trained on large text corpora inevitably reflect biases, stereotypes, and cultural assumptions present in their training data (Avila et al., 2025; Chiu et al., 2024). These biases can affect AI-generated content in problematic ways:

- Reinforcing stereotypes about particular groups
- Underrepresenting or misrepresenting marginalized perspectives
- Reflecting dominant cultural assumptions as universal truths
- Reproducing historical patterns of discrimination and exclusion

Critical multivoice work requires explicit attention to these bias issues. Students need to:

- Recognize that AI outputs reflect particular perspectives and cultural contexts, not neutral truth
- Evaluate AI-generated content critically for bias, stereotyping, and limited representation
- Consider whose voices and perspectives are centered or marginalized in AI outputs
- Make conscious decisions about whether and how to use AI-generated content that may perpetuate problematic patterns
- Actively seek diverse voices and perspectives beyond what AI systems readily provide

Educators play crucial roles in raising awareness of these issues and modeling critical evaluation of AI outputs from equity and justice perspectives.

Authentic Learning and Cognitive Development

Perhaps the most fundamental critical question concerns the relationship between AI use and genuine learning. If AI can perform tasks that educators have traditionally assigned to develop students' capabilities, what happens to that development when AI does the work instead?

Cope and Kalantzis (2024) argue that literacy education must adapt to acknowledge that some capabilities historically central to literacy—such as encoding and retrieving information, generating grammatically correct sentences, or following conventional formats—can now be performed by machines. Rather than continuing to focus exclusively on capabilities that AI can replicate, literacy education should emphasize:

- **Critical judgment**: Evaluating quality, relevance, and appropriateness of information and expression
- **Purposeful communication**: Knowing what to communicate, why, and to whom, rather than just how

- **Ethical reasoning**: Making responsible decisions about communication practices and their impacts
- **Creative synthesis**: Combining ideas in original ways that reflect genuine understanding and insight
- **Metacognitive awareness**: Understanding one's own thinking and learning processes

These higher-order capabilities remain fundamentally human even as AI performs many lower-level literacy tasks. However, developing these capabilities requires appropriate learning experiences. If students rely on AI to bypass the productive struggle of composing, they may not develop the very capacities that AI cannot replicate. Pedagogy must carefully scaffold AI use to support rather than supplant authentic cognitive engagement and learning.

The tension between efficiency and learning is particularly acute in AI-enhanced contexts. AI can make composition faster and easier, but learning often requires time, effort, and productive struggle. Students may naturally gravitate toward using AI to minimize effort, but this instrumental approach can undermine the very learning that writing assignments aim to develop. Educators must design learning experiences that harness AI's affordances while ensuring students engage deeply with course content and develop essential capabilities.

Zheng et al. (2020) examined impacts of learner, instructor, and course-level factors on online learning, finding that learner engagement and sense of cognitive presence significantly predict learning outcomes. In AI-enhanced environments, similar principles apply: successful learning requires active cognitive engagement, not passive consumption of AI-generated content. Pedagogy must foster this engagement through carefully designed prompts, authentic tasks, process requirements, and reflective activities.

Moreover, the relationship between AI use and cognitive development likely varies across different literacy skills and learning stages. Some tasks may benefit significantly from AI support—for instance, language learners using AI to understand complex grammatical structures or generate examples. Other tasks may require human cognitive engagement without AI mediation—such as developing original arguments or conducting close reading of literary texts. Educators need sophisticated understanding of how different AI uses affect different aspects of literacy development.

Research is beginning to examine these questions empirically, but much remains unknown about long-term impacts of AI-enhanced literacy education on cognitive development, critical thinking, and communication capabilities. Continued research attention to these fundamental questions is essential as AI becomes increasingly integrated into educational practice.

FUTURE DIRECTIONS AND CONCLUSION

This chapter has proposed multivoice work as a comprehensive framework for understanding and addressing literacy education in the age of artificial intelligence. The rapid evolution of AI technologies means that research on multivoice work in AI-enhanced literacy education is only beginning, with many critical questions remaining for future investigation.

Emerging Research Questions

The rapid evolution of AI technologies means that research on multivoice work in AI-enhanced literacy education is only beginning. Critical questions for future investigation include:

- **Longitudinal impacts**: How does sustained AI use throughout students' educational careers affect their literacy development, critical thinking capabilities, and approaches to meaning-making?
- **Pedagogical effectiveness**: Which specific pedagogical strategies most effectively support productive multivoice work in AI-enhanced contexts across different disciplines and student populations?
- **Developmental trajectories**: How do optimal approaches to AI integration vary across different developmental stages from early education through advanced graduate work?
- **Cross-cultural variation**: How do cultural differences in conceptions of authorship, collaboration, and originality shape appropriate integration of AI into literacy education globally?
- **Technological evolution**: As AI capabilities continue expanding to include more sophisticated multimodal generation, real-time interaction, and personalized adaptation, how must pedagogical approaches evolve accordingly?
- **Equity outcomes**: What are the actual equity impacts of AI integration in literacy education, and how can pedagogy be designed to promote rather than undermine equitable outcomes?

Chiu (2024) provided comprehensive recommendations for transforming higher education with generative AI, emphasizing the need for sustained research programs examining these complex questions through diverse methodological approaches.

Curriculum Innovation and Institutional Change

Effectively integrating multivoice work into literacy education requires not only pedagogical innovation but institutional change. Institutions must:

- **Develop clear policies**: Establishing institutional positions on AI use that balance support for innovation with maintenance of academic integrity
- **Support faculty development**: Providing extensive professional development opportunities for educators learning to work effectively in AI-enhanced contexts
- **Update infrastructure**: Ensuring technological infrastructure supports equitable access to AI tools while also protecting privacy and security
- **Revise assessment systems**: Moving beyond traditional assessment approaches that assume individual production of all text toward models that acknowledge and evaluate effective AI integration
- **Foster scholarly dialogue**: Creating spaces for ongoing discussion and debate about AI's role in education, bringing together diverse perspectives and expertise
- **Monitor impacts**: Systematically examining how AI integration affects student learning, equity, and educational outcomes

These institutional changes require leadership commitment, resource allocation, and sustained attention to the complex challenges and opportunities AI integration presents.

Institutional change processes must engage stakeholders across the educational community. Faculty from diverse disciplines bring different perspectives on appropriate AI integration based on their fields' epistemologies and professional practices. Students offer crucial insights into how AI affects their learning experiences and what support they need for effective use. Administrators consider policy implications, resource requirements, and institutional positioning. Together, these voices should inform institutional approaches that are both principled and practical.

Developing institutional AI policies requires careful balance between flexibility and consistency. Overly restrictive policies may stifle pedagogical innovation and fail to prepare students for AI-mediated professional contexts, while overly permissive approaches may undermine learning and academic integrity. Effective policies provide clear principles while allowing disciplinary and contextual variation in implementation.

Professional development for faculty represents one of the most crucial institutional investments. Many educators have limited experience with generative AI and may feel uncertain about how to integrate it effectively while maintaining educational quality.

Comprehensive professional development should include hands-on experience with AI tools, pedagogical strategies for AI-enhanced instruction, assessment approaches, ethical frameworks, and opportunities for collegial discussion and experimentation.

Implications for Writing Across the Curriculum

While this chapter has focused primarily on composition and literacy education, multivoice work has implications across all disciplines. Students write in diverse disciplinary contexts, each with its own conventions, purposes, and relationships to AI technologies (Wang & Ren, 2024).

Disciplinary faculty need support understanding:

- How AI can be integrated productively into writing assignments in their fields
- What competencies students need to develop for effective disciplinary writing with AI
- How to evaluate student writing that may involve AI assistance
- What ethical considerations arise specifically in their disciplinary contexts

Writing across the curriculum initiatives should address AI integration systematically, helping faculty across disciplines develop appropriate approaches for their specific contexts while also promoting coherent institutional approaches to multivoice work.

Different disciplines may have markedly different relationships to AI-enhanced writing. In STEM fields, students might use AI to help explain complex technical concepts, generate code documentation, or create research summaries while ensuring technical accuracy through their own expertise. In humanities disciplines, students might engage AI as a dialogic partner to explore interpretive possibilities, but the unique insights and arguments must emerge from their own critical engagement with texts and ideas.

Social science disciplines present yet another configuration, where students might use AI to help analyze data patterns, draft literature reviews, or structure arguments, while maintaining responsibility for research design, interpretation, and ethical considerations. Professional programs like business, education, or healthcare require students to develop communication skills for authentic workplace contexts—AI can support drafting and refinement, but genuine professional judgment and contextual understanding remain essential.

Technological Futures and Adaptive Pedagogy

AI technologies continue evolving rapidly, with new capabilities emerging regularly. Future developments may include:

- More sophisticated multimodal generation integrating text, images, video, and audio seamlessly
- Highly personalized AI tutors that adapt to individual students' needs and learning patterns
- Immersive virtual environments where students interact with AI collaborators in realistic simulations
- AI systems that can engage in increasingly sophisticated dialogue and argumentation
- Integration of AI throughout the entire educational ecosystem from curriculum planning to assessment

These technological developments will require continuous pedagogical adaptation. Rather than developing fixed approaches to AI integration, educators need adaptive mindsets and systematic processes for evaluating new technologies and developing appropriate pedagogical responses.

Heilala and Araya (2025) provide an overview of multimodal and generative AI for education, arguing that educators must maintain critical engagement with emerging technologies, evaluating both their affordances and limitations for supporting authentic learning.

CONCLUSION

This chapter has proposed multivoice work as a comprehensive framework for understanding and addressing literacy education in the age of artificial intelligence. Drawing on dialogic pedagogy, sociocultural theory, and multimodal literacy research, this framework recognizes that contemporary literacy practices inherently involve orchestrating multiple voices—human students, educators, peers, AI systems, and cultural-historical resources—in purposeful, critically informed ways.

Effective multivoice work requires developing new competencies that extend traditional literacy skills: understanding how AI systems work and what they can and cannot do, evaluating AI outputs critically for quality and appropriateness, making ethical decisions about when and how to use AI resources, and maintaining human agency and authentic learning goals in AI-mediated environments. These competencies must be developed systematically through curriculum and pedagogy rather than assumed to emerge naturally.

Research on students' experiences with AI-mediated composition reveals diverse patterns of engagement, from passive reliance on AI-generated text to strategic, critically informed integration of AI as one resource among many. Pedagogical approaches that emphasize transparency, process awareness, authentic purposes, and critical reflection can guide students toward productive patterns while developing essential AI literacy competencies.

Critical considerations around ethics, equity, and authentic learning remain paramount. AI integration must not reinforce existing inequities, undermine academic integrity, or bypass the cognitive engagement essential for genuine learning. Careful pedagogical design, explicit attention to diverse student needs, clear ethical frameworks, and ongoing critical examination are all necessary for responsible AI integration.

Looking forward, the rapid evolution of AI technologies requires adaptive pedagogical approaches and ongoing research examining longitudinal impacts, effective practices, equity outcomes, and institutional changes needed to support effective multivoice work. The goal is not to preserve traditional literacy practices unchanged but to transform literacy education in ways that leverage AI capabilities while maintaining focus on fundamentally human purposes: thoughtful, creative, ethical communication in service of meaningful participation in communities and societies.

Multivoice work recognizes that literacy has always involved orchestrating multiple voices, perspectives, and resources. AI-enhanced environments make this multivoice character more explicit and complex, requiring new awareness and capabilities. By embracing rather than resisting this complexity, literacy education can prepare students not only to navigate but to shape the AI-mediated communicative landscapes of the future.

REFERENCES

Avila, K. E., Dinc, Y., Hortmann, C., & Revenga, N. (2025). On opportunities and challenges of large multimodal foundation models in education. npj Science of Learning, 10(1), 13. DOI: 10.1038/s41539-025-00301-w

Beltrán-Palanques, V. (2024). Teaching elevator pitch presentations through a multimodal lens: Insights from ESP students' experiences. *TESOL Journal*, *15*(1), e769. DOI: 10.1002/tesj.769

Bjork, O. (2025). Towards a multimodal dialogic understanding of early writing development in school. *Language and Education*. Advance online publication. DOI: 10.1080/09500782.2025.2471506

Chantajinda, V. (2024). Research into practice: Digital multimodal composition in second language writing. *Language Teaching*, *57*(4), 546–560. DOI: 10.1017/S0261444824000235

Chiu, T. K. F. (2024). Future research recommendations for transforming higher education with generative AI. *Computers and Education: Artificial Intelligence*, *6*, 100197. DOI: 10.1016/j.caeai.2023.100197

Chiu, T. K. F., Ahmad, Z., Ismailov, M., & Sanusi, I. T. (2024). What are artificial intelligence literacy and competency? A comprehensive framework to support them. *Computers and Education Open*, *6*, 100171. DOI: 10.1016/j.caeo.2024.100171

Cope, B., & Kalantzis, M. (2024). Literacy in the time of artificial intelligence [Preprint]. *EdArXiv*. https://doi.org/DOI: 10.35542/osf.io/es5kb

Cross, R., Condon, L., & McNamara, M. (2022). Dialogic theories, literacy practices and initial teacher education. *Australian Journal of Language and Literacy*, *45*(3), 362–376. DOI: 10.1007/s44020-022-00025-z

Cummings, R. E., Monroe, S. M., & Watkins, M. (2024). Generative AI in first-year writing: An early analysis of affordances, limitations, and a framework for the future. *Computers and Composition*, *71*, 102827. DOI: 10.1016/j.compcom.2024.102827

Detrick, R., & Li, N. (2025). Students-generative AI interaction patterns and its impact on academic writing. *Journal of Computing in Higher Education*. Advance online publication. DOI: 10.1007/s12528-025-09444-6

Heilala, V., & Araya, R. (2025). Beyond text-to-text: An overview of multimodal and generative artificial intelligence for education using topic modeling. *Proceedings of the 40th ACM/SIGAPP Symposium on Applied Computing*, 1594–1603. DOI: 10.1145/3672608.3707764

Hradilová, A. (2025). Generative AI in teaching academic writing: Guiding students to make informed and ethical choices. *Language Learning in Higher Education*, *15*(2), 447–461. DOI: 10.1515/cercles-2024-0103

Hysaj, A., & Freeman, M. (2025). Exploring the purposes and uses of generative artificial intelligence tools in academic writing for multicultural students. *Higher Education Research & Development*, *44*(7), 1686–1700. Advance online publication. DOI: 10.1080/07294360.2025.2488862

Kalantzis, M., Cope, B., & Zapata, G. C. (2024). Literacy in a time of multimodal generative AI. *Reading Research Quarterly*, *59*(4), 534–556. DOI: 10.1002/rrq.591

Khosronejad, M., Weber, L., & Ryan, M. (2023). Teacher learning as a polyphonic endeavor: A context sensitive model of teacher professional development. *Teachers and Teaching*, *129*(7-8), 104154. DOI: 10.1080/13540602.2023.2215709

Li, S. (2025). Generative AI and second language writing. *Digital Studies in Language and Literature*, *2*(1), 122–152. DOI: 10.1515/dsll-2025-0007

Lim, F. V. (2021). Investigating intersemiosis: A systemic functional multimodal discourse analysis of the relationship between language and gesture in classroom discourse. *Visual Communication*, *20*(1), 34–58. DOI: 10.1177/1470357218820695

Lin, A. M. Y., & Siu, P. (2026). 'Fractalizing' the Multimodalities-Entextualization Cycle: Towards a theoretical model for integrating multimodal literacy in bilingual teacher education. *International Journal of Bilingual Education and Bilingualism*, *29*(3), 376–401. Advance online publication. DOI: 10.1080/13670050.2025.2610367

Liu, M., Zhang, L., & Biebricher, C. (2024). Investigating students' cognitive processes in generative AI-assisted digital multimodal composing and traditional writing. *Computers & Education*, *211*, 104977. DOI: 10.1016/j.compedu.2023.104977

Long, D., & Magerko, B. (2020). What is AI literacy? Competencies and design considerations. *Proceedings of the 2020 CHI Conference on Human Factors in Computing Systems*, 1–16. DOI: 10.1145/3313831.3376727

Oliveira, J. M. D. (2024). Enhancing multimodal literacy through community service learning in higher education. *Frontiers in Education*, *9*, 1448805. DOI: 10.3389/feduc.2024.1448805

Smith, M. P. (2022). Dialogic authorial academic language learning: An alternative to genre pedagogy. *Dialogic Pedagogy: A Journal for Studies of Dialogic Education, 10*, DP34–DP66. DOI: 10.5195/dpj.2022.495

Syafei, M., & Nuraeningsih, N. (2025). Leveraging artificial intelligence in writing: ELT students' perspectives and experiences. *International Journal of Learning. Teaching and Educational Research, 24*(5), 416–430. DOI: 10.26803/ijlter.24.5.22

Wang, L., & Ren, B. (2024). Enhancing academic writing in a linguistics course with generative AI: An empirical study in a higher education institution in Hong Kong. *Education Sciences, 14*(12), 1329. DOI: 10.3390/educsci14121329

Wertsch, J. V., del Río, P., & Alvarez, A. (Eds.). (2021). *Sociocultural studies of mind*. Cambridge University Press., DOI: 10.1017/CBO9781139174299

Zhang, D., Li, D., & Guo, K. (2026). From passive consumers to critical creators: Enhancing university students' new media literacy through AI-enhanced digital multimodal composing. *Interactive Learning Environments*, 1–25. Advance online publication. DOI: 10.1080/10494820.2026.2617985

Zheng, B., Lin, C.-H., & Kwon, J. B. (2020). The impact of learner-, instructor-, and course-level factors on online learning. *Computers & Education, 150*, 103851. DOI: 10.1016/j.compedu.2020.103851

KEY TERMS AND DEFINITIONS

AI Literacy: The set of skills required to understand, use, and critically evaluate AI technologies. It involves knowing how AI works, recognizing its ethical implications (like bias), and learning how to effectively prompt and collaborate with these systems.

Dialogic Pedagogy: An educational approach centered on ongoing dialogue between teachers and students. Rather than passive lecturing, it treats learning as a social process where meaning is co-constructed through questioning, open discussion, and the active exchange of different viewpoints.

Digital Composition: The act of creating content using digital tools and platforms. Unlike traditional writing, it often incorporates hyperlinking, video, and interactive elements, requiring the creator to think about how different digital formats influence the audience's experience.

Generative AI: A category of artificial intelligence capable of creating new content—such as text, images, or audio—based on patterns learned from existing data. In education, it acts as a creative partner that can simulate dialogue or assist in drafting.

Multimodal Literacy: The ability to understand and create meaning using a variety of "modes"—including text, images, sound, and movement. It recognizes that in a digital world, communication is rarely just about words but a blend of different media.

Multivoice Work: A collaborative practice where multiple perspectives, identities, and "voices" are intentionally integrated into a project. It challenges the idea of a single, authoritative author, instead valuing the complex richness that comes from diverse, collective contributions.

Polyphonic Learning: Inspired by musical "polyphony," this describes a learning environment where many independent "melodies" or ideas coexist simultaneously. It encourages students to engage with conflicting or complementary perspectives without forcing a single, unified consensus.

Chapter 10
Semiotics 5.0: Multimodal Literacy in the Algorithmic Age

Syed Ibad Ali
http://orcid.org/0000-0001-6312-6768
Parul Institute of Engineering and Technology, Parul University, Vadodara, India

ABSTRACT

This chapter introduces the concept of Semiotics 5.0 to describe meaning-making in the algorithmic age, where human communication is increasingly co-shaped by multimodal signs and machine-driven processes. Unlike earlier semiotic models focused primarily on language and visual codes, Semiotics 5.0 highlights how textual, visual, auditory, and interactive forms now intersect with algorithmic mediation, personalization, and generative technologies.Multimodal literacy in this context extends beyond decoding symbolic content; it requires the ability to critically interpret algorithmic infrastructures, recommendation systems, and data-driven filters that influence visibility, meaning, and cultural participation. The chapter examines how hashtags, metadata, emojis, and AI-generated outputs operate as hybrid sign systems, blurring the boundaries between human and machinic authorship.

INTRODUCTION

The examination of semiotics, roughly characterized as the analysis of signals and the mechanisms of meaning construction, has historically been a fundamental aspect of humanities and communication studies. The significant changes brought about by the emergence of algorithmic mediation, machine learning, and generative artificial intelligence need a redefinition of semiotics to accommodate the reality of the twenty-first century. This chapter introduces the idea of Semiotics 5.0, a the-

DOI: 10.4018/979-8-3373-6986-0.ch010

oretical framework that contextualizes meaning-making in an era characterized by algorithms, multimodal interfaces, and collaborative interactions between humans and machines that continuously shape cultural and communication practices. In contrast to prior phases of semiotics that primarily focused on human-to-human signification, Semiotics 5.0 recognizes that the mechanisms via which signals get meaning are progressively shared across people, digital infrastructures, and intelligent systems. Consequently, literacy need a reconceptualization to include multimodality and algorithmic awareness, emphasizing the transformation of communication from a solely human-centric focus to one that is mediated, amplified, and sometimes restricted by machine logics.

Semiotics 5.0 is a novel semiotic paradigm asserting that meaning is constructed not just via human interpretation of signals, but also through the collaboration of individuals, algorithms, databases, and machine-generated outputs. Semiotics 5.0 distinguishes itself from earlier semiotic traditions that emphasized language, culture, and visual representation by recognizing that modern signals are processed, prioritized, generated, and distributed via computational infrastructures—such as AI systems, multimodal interfaces, and platform logics. In this instance, multimodality and algorithmic authorship converge to form hybrid meaning-ecologies that facilitate collaborative interpretation rather than that of a single individual. Semiotics 5.0 requires interpretive, multimodal, and algorithmically informed literacies, positioning meaning as a result of human intent enhanced by computer mediation. This paradigm represents a shift from analyzing signals in media to scrutinizing indicators inside AI-curated socio-technical systems.

Table 1. Distinguishing Features of Semiotics 5.0 in Relation to Preceding Semiotic Paradigms

Dimension	Digital Semiotics	Computational Semiotics	Platform Semiotics	Semiotics 5.0 (Proposed)
Primary Focus	Digital representation & multimodality	Symbol processing in computation	Platform-governed meaning circulation	Hybrid meaning-making with human + AI co-agency
Sign Production	Human-created media objects	Machine-encoded symbol structures	User-generated + platform-filtered	Human-authored + AI-generated multimodal outputs
Power of Interpretation	Human reader as primary interpretant	Algorithmic logic interprets data	Visibility determined by platform structures	Interpretation distributed across humans + algorithms

continued on following page

Table 1. Continued

Dimension	Digital Semiotics	Computational Semiotics	Platform Semiotics	Semiotics 5.0 (Proposed)
Key Question	How do signs work online?	How do machines process signs?	How do platforms shape discourse?	How do humans + machines *co-produce* meaning?
What is NEW?	—	—	—	Algorithmic literacy, generative authorship, hybrid sign ecologies

The evolution of semiotics progresses from classical linguistic sign theory to structuralist and post-structuralist developments, culminating in cultural semiotics and, more recently, digital semiotics. Ferdinand de Saussure's dyadic model of the sign and Charles Sanders Peirce's triadic notion established the foundation for comprehending how meaning arises from arbitrary or customary interactions between signifiers and signifieds. Roland Barthes subsequently expanded semiotics to include cultural and ideological research, elucidating how media and literature embed prevailing meanings. By the late twentieth century, researchers like Gunther Kress and Theo van Leeuwen (2021) shifted the focus to multimodality, stressing that communication in contemporary society cannot be confined to language alone but must be perceived as a synthesis of various modes: visual, textual, auditory, spatial, gestural, and others. This change was caused by the growing importance of visual culture, the saturation of media, and the emergence of digital interfaces. Kress (2003) contended that literacy is undergoing transformation in the new media era, as reading and writing evolve from alphabetic conventions to multimodal constructs of meaning.

The emergence of digital communication platforms sped up these changes, making multimodality a part of daily life. Social media is a good example of this integration since people may talk to each other using photos, videos, gifs, emoticons, hashtags, and mixed text and visual forms. In these circumstances, meaning is not formed from a single mode but from the coordination of several semiotic resources. O'Halloran et al. (2017) stressed that multimodality should be examined as a dynamic and interdependent process in which modes interact to influence interpretation. This acknowledgment has influenced multimodal literacy education, which aims to equip learners to access, analyze, and create multimodal texts across many platforms and genres. Lim and Tan-Chia (2023) emphasized how digital technologies facilitate learners' interaction with multimodal texts, therefore cultivating abilities that transcend conventional literacy. Carcamo (2025) demonstrated that digital technologies may improve English as a Foreign Language learning by broadening students' exposure to a diverse array of semiotic materials, so enhancing their multimodal abilities.

Multimodal literacy research has mostly concentrated on the orchestration of modes at the superficial level; however, Semiotics 5.0 emphasizes a more profound layer: the algorithmic infrastructures that regulate visibility, circulation, and meaning-making. In the algorithmic era, communication is influenced not just by human intents and interpretative processes but also by the covert functions of algorithms. Bezemer and Cowan (2021) demonstrated that social semiotics must include reading behaviors that are already influenced by algorithmic sorting, filtering, and ranking. For example, the prominence of hashtags, the ranking of search results, or the curation of a user's social media feed are not impartial representations of communicative abundance but rather the products of algorithmic choices. These computational filters work as semiotic tools, deciding which signals are made more prominent and which ones are hidden. The ramifications for epistemic justice are significant, since algorithms may favor some voices while sidelining others, perpetuating systemic prejudices in manners that are often obscured to users.

Generative AI adds to the complexity of this semiotic environment. Smith et al. (2025) examined the redefinition of multimodal composing processes using generative AI technologies that may create text, pictures, and video material. These technologies question traditional ideas about who is the author, who has control, and what is real. When a student writes a digital essay with AI-generated pictures or when a designer uses generative models to make something innovative, the text is a hybrid artifact that was written by both a person and a machine. The issue of semiotic purpose becomes ambiguous: is the meaning sourced from the human prompt, the dataset that trained the model, or the algorithmic processes producing the sign? Cheung et al. (2025) showed that students' multimodal representations are already closely linked to generative AI. This makes it hard for teachers to teach critical literacy in places where signs are not only made by people, but also by machines.

The educational aspect of this change is very important.

Aragón (2025) emphasized that multimodality enhances embodied agency in literacy practices, indicating that learners are not only consumers of multimodal texts but active contributors to meaning-making. However, when algorithmic systems intrude, learners must contend with an added layer of interpretation: comprehending not just multimodal materials but also the impact of algorithms on their display and accessibility. So, Semiotics 5.0 says that literacy has to be redefined to include both multimodal awareness and algorithmic criticism. Students need to be able to understand not just words and pictures, but also metadata, hashtags, recommendation algorithms, and generative processes. O'Halloran (2023) contended that semiotic processes are both material and symbolic, underscoring the need of comprehending the infrastructures that support meaning-making. This critical perspective corresponds with initiatives to include digital literacy and algorithmic literacy into educational curriculum, therefore providing people with the competencies to traverse and interrogate the semiotic landscapes of the algorithmic era.

It is crucial to note that Semiotics 5.0 extends beyond cultural or educational domains; it is equally pertinent to practical sciences and engineering. Ali (2025) illustrated that reinforcement learning facilitates autonomous optimization in intelligent engineering systems, a process that can be comprehended semiotically as the comprehension of environmental indicators and their conversion into adaptive behaviors. Ali et al. (2023) similarly demonstrated how recurrent backpropagation models analyze input data streams in mobile network architecture, efficiently decoding and re-encoding signals at the computational level. These examples demonstrate that semiotic processes are integrated into technological systems: algorithms "read" signals, analyze patterns, and generate outputs that people later ascribe meaning to. In these situations, signs do more than just let people talk to each other; they also help with computational optimization and network intelligence.

Further investigation emphasizes this intersection of semiotics and engineering. Ali et al. (2024) elucidated how nanoparticles work as carriers of meaning in material science, with performance characteristics indicating usefulness at the microscopic level. Pattanaik et al. (2023) applied semiotic reasoning to mathematics, offering algebraic-statistical models for abstract systems. Srivastava et al. (2024) examined the increase of 5G network performance by beamforming, a methodology that entails the interpretation and response to signal data, paralleling semiotic processes of encoding and decoding. Srivastava et al. (2023) elaborated on smart wearable devices designed to detect social distancing in urban environments, using sensors to interpret ambient data as semiotic inputs that influence human behavior. Suthar and Ali (2025) examined gesture recognition, a field in which signs—specifically physical gestures—are converted into machine-readable inputs. Each of these examples shows that semiotic processes are just as important for technical systems as they are for human communication. This shows how important Semiotics 5.0 is in many areas.

Collectively, these contributions indicate a future in which semiotics transcends the humanities, necessitating its recognition as a transdisciplinary framework that integrates education, technology, and engineering. Semiotics 5.0 embodies this synthesis, emphasizing the intersection of multimodal communication, algorithmic mediation, and computational interpretation of signals. In this case, being literate means knowing how to use the multimodal languages of human expression, the algorithmic languages of machine mediation, and the technical languages of engineering systems. This kind of literacy is always a mix of different things, and it needs the ability to understand things in both human and machine contexts.

The ethical ramifications of Semiotics 5.0 are as urgent. Algorithms often function as imperceptible sign-makers, integrating ideological presuppositions inside their code. Generative AI's images show the biases of the material it was trained on. When a social media algorithm curates content, it encodes priorities that may spread false information or exclude minority points of view. Scholars have expressed apprehensions over epistemic injustice within algorithmic culture, characterized by unequal access to information and visibility (Bezemer & Cowan, 2021). Consequently, multimodal literacy must include critical literacy, enabling learners and citizens to not only read signals but also to interrogate the circumstances surrounding their production, circulation, and consumption. Aragón (2025) underscored embodied agency, positing that humans must exercise control over their meaning-making processes instead of passively acquiescing to algorithmic mediation. Semiotics 5.0 offers the conceptual lexicon to express this agency, emphasizing the dynamics of disputed meaning within algorithmic contexts.

This chapter enhances academic discourse by promoting Semiotics 5.0 as a theoretical framework for comprehending multimodal literacy in the algorithmic era. It combines ideas from semiotics, multimodal literacy, digital pedagogy, generative AI research, and applied engineering studies to make the case that producing meaning is now a hybrid process that happens between people and machines. The chapter starts by delineating the historical evolution of semiotics, positioning Semiotics 5.0 as a continuation of multimodal and digital semiotics. It then looks at how multimodal literacy has to change to work with algorithmic infrastructures, using contemporary research in education, AI, and multimodal studies. It also includes ideas from practical sciences, showing that semiotic processes work in both technological and cultural fields. Lastly, it talks about the moral and educational effects of Semiotics 5.0 and calls for literacy frameworks that help students and citizens think critically about sign ecologies that are mediated by algorithms.

In the end, Semiotics 5.0 changes the definition of literacy for a time when signals are not just multimodal but also algorithmic, generative, and mediated by machines. To master Semiotics 5.0 is to cultivate the ability to decipher multimodal texts, analyze algorithmic processes, and engage in critical reflection on the socio-technical infrastructures that influence meaning. This chapter situates Semiotics 5.0 as both a theoretical framework and a pedagogical need, providing instruments for researchers, educators, and practitioners to comprehend and traverse the intricate semiotic terrains of the algorithmic era.

LITERATURE SURVEY

The evolution of semiotics as an academic subject has seen several paradigmatic shifts, transitioning from its foundations in classical sign theory to its contemporary interconnections with digital culture and algorithmic systems. Ferdinand de

Saussure's dyadic model of the language sign, which highlighted the arbitrary link between signifier and signified, and Charles Sanders Peirce's triadic model, which included the interpretant as a vital mediating element, established the groundwork for contemporary semiotic theory. These classical frameworks offered a vocabulary for elucidating the role of signals in communication, albeit they were mostly limited to textual and linguistic circumstances. As communication practices progressed with the emergence of visual and media technologies, semiotics went beyond verbal structures to include visual, geographical, and cultural systems of meaning. Roland Barthes expanded semiotics into cultural analysis, demonstrating how signals function ideologically to bolster prevailing discourses. This first extension was crucial in advancing semiotics towards multimodality, which acknowledges that meaning arises from the integration of many semiotic resources rather than from language alone (Kress, 2003; Kress & van Leeuwen, 2021).

The focus on multimodality became very important in the late 1900s and early 2000s, when communication started to include more and more different types of media, such pictures, sounds, gestures, and spatial arrangements. Kress (2003) contended that literacy in the contemporary media period necessitates a reconceptualization to accommodate multimodal communication, emphasizing that the pre-eminence of print-based literacy is yielding to more intricate semiotic configurations. In the same way, Kress and van Leeuwen (2021) created a grammar of visual design that showed how pictures work as organized semiotic systems with their own rules for syntax and meaning. These revelations significantly transformed literacy studies, as researchers acknowledged that communicative competency now necessitates the capacity to read and generate texts that amalgamate several modalities. O'Halloran, Bateman, and Schmidt (2017) expanded this multimodal framework by offering a problem-focused introduction to multimodality, underscoring that semiotic research must include the interplay of several modes in constructing meaning. These contributions together positioned multimodality as a crucial notion in modern semiotics, so broadening the horizons of literacy study and instruction.

In the age of digital technology, multimodal literacy has become an important part of teaching. Lim and Tan-Chia (2023) stressed how important it is to build learning spaces that help students learn how to read and write multimodal texts, especially in digital settings where text, images, and interactive aspects come together. They contend that multimodal literacy has transitioned from an optional talent to an essential competence for engagement in knowledge societies. Carcamo (2025) similarly illustrated how digital tools might assist English as a Foreign Language (EFL) learners in cultivating multimodal literacy, indicating that exposure to various semiotic materials improves learners' communication skills and critical awareness. These findings demonstrate that multimodal literacy instruction is essential not just for language proficiency but also for cultivating critical engagement with the intricate semiotic landscapes of the digital era. Aragón (2025) enhanced this discourse by elucidating how multimodality facilitates embodied agency in literacy practices, illustrating that learners use multimodal resources to actively generate and articulate meaning. These works together indicate that multimodal literacy encompasses not just the proficiency to read and write across several forms but also the ability to critically assess the social, cultural, and technical contexts in which multimodal texts are created and consumed.

Even with these improvements, a lot of the writing on multimodal literacy has just looked at the surface of texts and behaviors. It hasn't looked at the deeper structures that affect how people talk to each other online. In the algorithmic era, meaning-making is significantly influenced by computer systems that filter, curate, and even produce semiotic information. Bezemer and Cowan (2021) contended that reading habits require redefinition to include the influence of algorithms on the visibility and accessibility of content for readers. They demonstrate that algorithmic mediation affects not just the accessibility of texts but also the methods by which readers interact with them, so altering the dynamics of interpretation. This acknowledgment adds an important new layer to semiotics: signs are no longer just made by people and understood by people; they are also shaped more and more by algorithms that work according to data optimization, personalization, and predictive analytics. These dynamics prompt urgent inquiries about power, visibility, and epistemic fairness, since algorithmic infrastructures favor some signals while concealing others, thereby shaping cultural knowledge and participation. Generative artificial intelligence complicates this semiotic terrain even further. Smith et al. (2025) examined the transformation of multimodal composing techniques via the integration of generative AI tools capable of autonomously producing text, pictures, and other semiotic resources. They contend that new instruments provide both possibilities and problems for literacy instruction, as learners must confront issues of authorship, authenticity, and ethical responsibility. For instance, when a student utilizes an AI system to make pictures for a digital project, the finished product is a hybrid text that was written by both a person and a machine. The semiotic process is thereby disseminated across human intentionality, algorithmic design, and machine learning outputs. Cheung et al. (2025) similarly emphasized that students' multimodal representations of concepts are more integrated with generative AI, confounding conventional educational models of literacy.

These results emphasize the need for innovative literacy frameworks that not only educate learners to engage with multimodal texts but also enable them to critically analyze the algorithmic processes that influence such texts. O'Halloran (2023) bolstered this viewpoint by asserting that semiotic processes possess both material and symbolic dimensions. She asserts that the process of meaning-making must be comprehended in connection to the infrastructures—technological, social, and cultural—that facilitate and limit it. This perspective corresponds with the acknowledgment that algorithms and AI systems operate as semiotic agents, generating and mediating signals in manners that significantly influence human communication. In this regard, Semiotics 5.0 arises as an essential conceptual framework for the algorithmic era, amalgamating multimodal literacy with algorithmic criticism. It stresses that being literate now means being able to read and comprehend both multimodal signals and the computational logics that govern how they are made, shared, and received. This dual orientation illustrates the hybrid character of modern communication, whereby meaning is collaboratively generated by people and technology inside intricate feedback loops of interaction.

This change has big effects on education, as multimodal and digital literacies need to be reformulated to deal with algorithmic mediation. Aragón (2025) asserted that learners cultivate embodied agency via multimodal activities; however, this agency must now be broadened to include algorithmic awareness. If students can't critically think about how algorithms affect how signals are seen and understood, they might become passive consumers of material that is filtered by algorithms. Instead, literacy instruction should enable students to traverse and question these systems, promoting critical engagement with the semiotic realities of the algorithmic era. Lim & Tan-Chia (2023) and Carcamo (2025) provided significant frameworks for the incorporation of multimodal literacy into teaching; nonetheless, these models need enhancement to include algorithmic criticism. Smith et al. (2025) and Cheung et al. (2025) contended that generative AI is already transforming students' activities, necessitating that educators confront the ethical, creative, and interpretative difficulties presented by these technologies.

In addition to education, Semiotics 5.0 is also important in practical sciences and engineering, since semiotic processes provide the basis for technological systems. Ali (2025) showed how reinforcement learning helps smart systems improve their performance by understanding signals from the environment and changing their behaviors based on what they learn. This process is similar to semiotic interpretation since the system reads signals from its surroundings and makes decisions based on what it has learnt. Ali et al. (2023) also looked at how recurrent backpropagation models decode input data streams in mobile network architecture. These models behave as semiotic systems that turn raw data into meaningful patterns. These examples demonstrate that semiotics extends beyond human communication, functioning inside computer systems that depend on the encoding, transmission, and decoding of signals.

Research on nanomaterials, mathematics, and communication systems further illustrates the convergence of semiotics and technology. Ali et al. (2024) examined the role of nanomaterials as bearers of meaning in scientific and technical domains, where their characteristics indicate functional potential. Pattanaik et al. (2023) provided algebraic-statistical models for complex number theory, illustrating the use of abstract mathematical symbols as indicators inside computational frameworks. Srivastava et al. (2024) investigated the interpretation of signal data by beamforming algorithms in 5G networks to improve communication, a process that encompasses encoding and decoding at both human and machine levels. Srivastava et al. (2023) provided wearable gadgets for tracking social distance in smart cities, illustrating how sensors interpret environmental inputs as indicators that influence human behavior. Suthar and Ali (2025) investigated gesture recognition using Arduino, emphasizing the conversion of physical gestures into machine-readable inputs. In each of these examples, semiotics is shown to be a fundamental part of technological systems, where signs are not only cultural artifacts but also computational signals that make intelligent functions possible.

This broader view shows that Semiotics 5.0 is a transdisciplinary framework that connects the humanities, education, and engineering. It recognizes that signals move across different areas, such as cultural texts, classroom activities, computer algorithms, and technical systems. In this context, literacy is being able to read and comprehend texts that use more than one mode, critically evaluate algorithmic mediation, and grasp how technological systems use signs. This all-encompassing approach makes Semiotics 5.0 both a theoretical step forward and a practical need for dealing with the problems of the algorithmic era. The literature, drawing from semiotics, multimodal literacy, AI research, and applied engineering, together indicates the need for a redefining of literacy and meaning-making in modern culture.

The recognition of algorithmic infrastructures as central to contemporary semiotics marks a significant shift in scholarly thinking. Whereas earlier semiotic traditions largely emphasized human-to-human meaning-making, the algorithmic age foregrounds the role of computational systems in mediating communication and shaping semiotic practices. Bezemer and Cowan (2021) illustrated that contemporary reading cannot be separated from the algorithmic architectures of platforms, which influence how texts are encountered, sequenced, and prioritized. In algorithmically curated environments such as social media or streaming platforms, the act of reading becomes co-determined by the system's underlying logics of personalization, recommendation, and engagement optimization. This suggests that semiotics must now move beyond the analysis of signs themselves to include the infrastructures that determine their circulation and visibility. Semiotics 5.0 responds to this challenge by situating multimodal literacy within an algorithmically mediated ecosystem, requiring a literacy that is both interpretive and infrastructural.

This reconceptualization has profound implications for the understanding of multimodal literacy in education. Aragón (2025) emphasized that learners exercise embodied agency through multimodal practices, but the agency of learners is circumscribed by algorithmic forces that determine the conditions under which signs are produced and consumed. Without awareness of these algorithmic dynamics, learners risk misrecognizing the contingent and biased nature of the semiotic environment in which they operate. Lim and Tan-Chia (2023) proposed pedagogical strategies for integrating multimodal literacy into education, focusing on the orchestration of modes in digital contexts. While their framework remains essential, Semiotics 5.0 extends it by adding a critical algorithmic layer, emphasizing the need for learners to question not only how signs are produced but also how algorithmic logics structure their accessibility. Carcamo (2025) reinforced this point in the context of EFL education, showing that digital tools can enhance multimodal literacy, but also implying that students' access to multimodal resources is mediated by technological systems that filter and frame their engagement.

Generative AI intensifies the urgency of this shift, as it fundamentally alters the relationship between human intention and semiotic production. Smith et al. (2025) highlighted that generative AI tools reshape multimodal composing by introducing machine outputs into human creative processes. Learners must therefore acquire not only skills in integrating multimodal resources but also competencies in critically evaluating AI-generated signs. The question of authorship becomes particularly pressing: when a learner uses AI to generate text or images, the resulting semiotic artifact reflects a distributed authorship between the user's prompts, the system's training data, and the algorithmic processes generating the output. Cheung et al. (2025) showed that students' multimodal representations are already heavily shaped by generative AI, raising questions about how pedagogy should evolve to address these new semiotic practices. The hybrid nature of sign production in these contexts blurs the line between human creativity and machinic generation, underscoring the need for pedagogical frameworks that explicitly integrate algorithmic critique into multimodal literacy education.

O'Halloran's (2023) argument that semiotic processes are material provided a useful lens for understanding these dynamics. If semiotics is always already entangled with material infrastructures, then algorithms and AI systems must be recognized as active participants in meaning-making. Semiotics 5.0 foregrounds this recognition, positioning literacy as a hybrid practice that requires engagement with both multimodal texts and algorithmic systems. The ethical stakes of this approach are significant. Algorithmic systems encode biases in their design and operation, often reflecting and amplifying existing social inequalities. When learners or users engage with algorithmically mediated signs, they are implicitly subject to these biases. Semiotics 5.0 thus calls for critical literacy practices that empower individuals to interrogate the algorithmic conditions of meaning-making, fostering epistemic justice in the face of opaque computational systems.

The integration of semiotics and engineering research illustrates the transdisciplinary potential of Semiotics 5.0. Ali (2025) demonstrated that reinforcement learning systems engage in semiotic processes when they interpret environmental signals and adapt behaviors accordingly. These systems effectively "read" signs from their environment and respond in ways that optimize performance, paralleling human semiotic practices of interpretation and action. Similarly, Ali et al. (2023) showed how recurrent backpropagation models in mobile network design function as semiotic systems, decoding input signals into meaningful patterns for decision-making. These computational processes reveal that semiotics is not confined to human culture but is intrinsic to intelligent systems that rely on the recognition, transformation, and application of signs. Semiotics 5.0 therefore positions semiotic inquiry as relevant not only for the humanities and education but also for technical domains where meaning-making processes drive system functionality.

The application of semiotic analysis in engineering contexts is further evidenced by research on nanomaterials, mathematics, and communication systems. Ali et al. (2024) examined nanomaterials as semiotic carriers whose properties communicate functionality at the molecular level. Pattanaik et al. (2023) proposed algebraic-statistical models for complex number theory, showing how mathematical symbols and structures operate as signs in computational reasoning. Srivastava et al. (2024) analyzed beamforming algorithms in 5G networks, where the interpretation of signal data is itself a semiotic act that informs communication optimization. Srivastava et al. (2023) demonstrated that wearable devices for social distancing rely on sensors interpreting environmental cues as semiotic inputs guiding user behavior. Suthar and Ali (2025) explored gesture recognition, in which bodily movements are transformed into computationally legible signs. These studies demonstrate that semiotic principles underpin technological systems at multiple levels, reinforcing the argument that Semiotics 5.0 must be transdisciplinary in scope.

Semiotics has progressed beyond conventional linguistic sign theory to include multimodal and technologically mediated representations of meaning. Saussure and Peirce's foundational work characterized meaning as a symbolic interpretation influenced by cultural conventions. Barthes further elaborated on this concept via ideological and media analysis. The transition to multimodality, spearheaded by Kress (2003) and Kress and van Leeuwen (2021), redefined literacy from a purely verbal act to the integration of visual, spatial, gestural, textual, and aural modalities. Research on multimodal learning (Lim & Tan-Chia, 2023) and digital composition (Carcamo, 2025) indicates that contemporary literacy requires students to produce, comprehend, and assess multimodal compositions. Aragón (2025) substantiated this claim by illustrating that multimodal composition includes embodied forms of activity. Foundational multimodality studies provide essential grounding (O'Halloran et al., 2017); nonetheless, it mostly maintains an anthropocentric focus, often overlooking the algorithmic infrastructures that increasingly govern visibility, circulation, and access to meaning. Recent studies have begun to examine this transformation: Bezemer and Cowan (2021) asserted that recommendation algorithms and platform sorting influence reading behaviors, whilst O'Halloran (2023) emphasized that semiotic processes are concrete and infrastructural, rather than only symbolic.

With the emergence of generative AI, meaning is no longer just interpreted by humans; it is also produced computationally—AI now authors text, creates graphics, forecasts outcomes, and composes music. Smith et al. (2025) illustrated the evolution of multimodal composition techniques using AI, whereas Cheung et al. (2025) emphasized that students are actively co-constructing knowledge utilizing machine-generated semiotic forms. Algorithmic multimodality involves computational systems that integrate sign-processing within reinforcement learning and network design (Ali, 2025; Ali et al., 2023), nanomaterial analysis (Ali et al., 2024), algebraic symbolic modeling (Pattanaik et al., 2023), 5G beamforming analysis (Srivastava et al., 2024), wearable-data signaling (Srivastava et al., 2023), and gesture-to-symbol translation through embedded hardware (Suthar & Ali, 2025). These improvements demonstrate that meaning in modern times is neither only verbal nor purely multimodal; it is algorithmically filtered, computationally generated, and often co-created by humans and computers. This recognition requires Semiotics 5.0: a theoretical reconfiguration that situates multimodal literacy inside algorithmic sign ecologies, where visibility is determined by the platform, authorship is synthesized, and meaning is both generated and computed.

The convergence of multimodal literacy and engineering applications highlights that Semiotics 5.0 requires a hybrid literacy that combines interpretive, critical, and computational competencies. Literacy in this context is not only about reading multimodal texts or critiquing algorithmic infrastructures but also about understanding the semiotic processes embedded in technical systems. Learners and practitioners must be able to navigate multimodal representations, interrogate algorithmic mediation, and engage with the semiotic dimensions of intelligent technologies. This comprehensive literacy is essential for participating in contemporary societies, where communication, knowledge production, and technological systems are deeply interwoven.

Ethical concerns are central to this reconceptualization. Bezemer and Cowan (2021) noted that algorithmic mediation influences not only what signs are visible but also how readers interpret them, raising concerns about epistemic justice. Algorithms often encode biases that privilege dominant perspectives while marginalizing others. For instance, recommendation systems may amplify popular content at the expense of minority voices, reproducing systemic inequalities in visibility and influence. Aragón (2025) argued for the importance of embodied agency in literacy practices, but in algorithmic environments, such agency is constrained by opaque computational processes. To restore agency, Semiotics 5.0 calls for literacy practices that make algorithmic mediation visible and open to critique. Learners must be taught not only how to decode multimodal signs but also how to "read" algorithms as semiotic actors, thereby empowering them to challenge the biases and exclusions embedded in algorithmic systems.

Generative AI raises additional ethical challenges. Smith et al. (2025) highlighted concerns about authorship and authenticity in AI-mediated multimodal composing. If students rely heavily on AI tools for creative production, questions arise about the originality of their work and the ethical responsibilities associated with co-authoring with machines. Cheung et al. (2025) demonstrated that students' multimodal representations are increasingly shaped by generative AI, suggesting that pedagogy must address the blurred boundaries of human and machinic authorship. These findings point to the necessity of integrating discussions of ethics and authorship into multimodal literacy education, ensuring that learners critically engage with the implications of using AI tools in their creative practices. O'Halloran (2023) reinforced this point by emphasizing the materiality of semiotic processes, underscoring that AI systems are not neutral tools but active agents in meaning-making.

Semiotics 5.0 also contributes to broader debates about the future of literacy and education in the algorithmic age. Kress (2003) argued that literacy must be redefined in the new media age, and Kress and van Leeuwen (2021) showed that visual communication is central to contemporary meaning-making. These foundational insights remain crucial, but they must be extended to incorporate algorithmic mediation and generative AI. Lim and Tan-Chia (2023) and Carcamo (2025) provided pedagogical models for developing multimodal literacy, but these models must evolve to address the algorithmic infrastructures that shape students' engagement with multimodal texts. Aragón (2025) emphasized embodied agency, which must now include algorithmic awareness. Smith et al. (2025) and Cheung et al. (2025) showed that generative AI is already transforming students' practices, underscoring the urgency of integrating algorithmic critique into literacy education. O'Halloran (2023) reminded us that semiotics must account for the material infrastructures of meaning-making, which now include algorithms and AI systems. Semiotics 5.0 synthesizes these insights, offering a framework for literacy that is multimodal, algorithmic, and critical.

In sum, the literature reviewed here converges on the need for a redefinition of semiotics and literacy in the context of the algorithmic age. Classical semiotics provided the foundation for understanding signs, multimodality expanded the scope to include diverse semiotic resources, and digital semiotics addressed the challenges of communication in media-saturated environments. The current stage—Semiotics 5.0—acknowledges that meaning-making is now co-constructed by humans and algorithms, requiring literacies that are hybrid, critical, and computational. This literature survey demonstrates that Semiotics 5.0 is not merely a theoretical abstraction but a practical necessity, with implications for education, technology, and society at large. By integrating insights from semiotics, multimodal literacy, algorithmic critique, generative AI research, and applied engineering, Semiotics 5.0 provides a comprehensive framework for understanding and navigating the complex semiotic ecologies of the contemporary world.

RESEARCH METHODOLOGY

The methodological framework for analyzing Semiotics 5.0—defined as the integration of multimodal literacy and algorithmic mediation—requires an approach that transcends traditional academic boundaries while maintaining rigorous and systematic inquiry. In contrast to conventional literacy studies that primarily rely on textual analysis or classroom observations, the methodological framework utilized in this context must address the complexities of meaning-making within algorithmically mediated environments where human and machine agents collaboratively generate, curate, and distribute semiotic resources. This necessitates a comprehensive research design that incorporates interpretive qualitative approaches, multimodal discourse analysis, algorithmic critique, and transdisciplinary applications within the realms of applied sciences and engineering. This technique ensures that Semiotics 5.0 is not just postulated but also subjected to empirical examination that clarifies its educational, cultural, and technological implications (Kress, 2003; Kress & van Leeuwen, 2021; O'Halloran et al., 2017).

The study employs a qualitative interpretive framework, whereby semiotic research examines how individuals comprehend and perceive phenomena, rather than quantifying variables or evaluating hypotheses. Qualitative inquiry facilitates a comprehensive analysis of multimodal texts, algorithmic infrastructures, and human experiences, making it particularly suitable for investigating the expressions of Semiotics 5.0 within educational, cultural, and technological contexts. This research adheres to the principles of social semiotics by using a technique that situates meaning-making within its social, cultural, and material contexts (Bezemer & Cowan, 2021). This necessitates an examination of both the signals and the infrastructures governing their production, dissemination, and interpretation. This method aligns with O'Halloran's (2023) claims, which emphasize that semiotics must include the materiality of meaning-making, recognizing that signals are always embedded within broader technological and social contexts.

The research design employs multimodal discourse analysis (MDA) as its primary analytical framework. MDA provides a framework for examining the formation of meaning via the integration of diverse semiotic elements, including text, image, sound, gesture, and spatial design. This is particularly relevant to Semiotics 5.0, since meaning transcends linguistic and visual modalities, emerging from the interplay of multimodal ensembles shaped by algorithmic processes. Kress and van Leeuwen (2021) shown that visual communication follows a systematic grammar, while O'Halloran et al. (2017) stated that multimodal analysis requires an examination of the interdependence of modalities. By using these approaches in algorithmically controlled environments, the study clarifies the joint manufacture of meaning by human and machine participants in digital contexts. The analysis of social media content involves the scrutiny of multimodal texts, such as memes, videos, and hashtags, while also assessing the influence of algorithmic curation on their visibility and interpretation (Bezemer & Cowan, 2021). The data for this study are obtained from many sources to illustrate the several contexts in which Semiotics 5.0 operates. The primary dataset comprises multimodal texts from educational contexts that integrate generative AI into student activities, including digital essays with AI-generated images and classroom projects utilizing algorithmic tools for composition (Cheung et al., 2025; Smith et al., 2025). These artifacts are augmented with data from digital communication platforms, including social media posts that have text, emoticons, videos, and algorithmic metadata, such as hashtags and trending tags. This work investigates multimodal artifacts to clarify the operation of signals in hybrid human–machine environments.

The research incorporates practical case studies from engineering domains in which semiotic processes facilitate intelligent systems. For instance, reinforcement learning models that analyze environmental signals (Ali, 2025), mobile networks that decipher input data streams (Ali et al., 2023), and wearable devices that interpret sensor data as behavioral indicators (Srivastava et al., 2023). These technological contexts are seen as fundamental rather than supplementary for demonstrating the transdisciplinary scope of Semiotics 5.0, in which sign processes are included inside both cultural and computational frameworks.

This study utilizes an empirical framework to apply Semiotics 5.0 by examining the formation of meaning via hybrid human-algorithmic sign production. The research is guided by three inquiries: the collaborative construction of multimodal meaning by humans and intelligent systems; the influence of algorithmic infrastructures on visibility, authorship, and interpretive agency; and the identifiable indicators of algorithmic semiotics across educational, social, and computational contexts. In response to these inquiries, a meticulously curated collection of ninety multimodal artifacts was compiled—thirty derived from educational settings, including AI-assisted essays and student projects with generated visuals; thirty from platform ecosystems, comprising short-form video streams, curated hashtag clusters, and algorithmically ranked feeds; and thirty from engineering systems, consisting of reinforcement-learning logs, mobile-network signal patterns, and gesture-recognition input/output traces. Artifacts were included only if they demonstrated multimodal layering, verified algorithmic mediation, and reflected human–machine co-signification, therefore affirming adherence to the theoretical framework of Semiotics 5.0.

The analytical method used a dual-level coding scheme. Multimodal discourse analysis was first used to identify representational, interactive, and compositional meaning structures, grounded on the core concepts proposed by Kress and van Leeuwen. A novel layer of algorithmic-semiotic coding was developed and included to examine the impact of computational infrastructures. Codes documented patterns in algorithmic visibility, generative authorship, infrastructural integration, predictive adaptation, and bias amplification processes. This enabled the examination of multimodality not just as a compilation of signifying modes, but also as a computationally regulated ecology. Coding was conducted frequently across the corpus, with thematic connections strengthened by axial comparison to reveal enduring patterns of hybrid authorship and algorithmic semiotic influence.

Various validation procedures ensured enhanced dependability. Two analysts separately coded twenty percent of the corpus to establish inter-coder agreement, targeting a Cohen's Kappa value over 0.78 to maintain consistency. Member-checking was used in educational samples to authenticate interpretations of student objects with their creators. Analytical notes documented the evolution of coding decisions, establishing a verifiable interpretive record. Triangulation of educational, platform, and engineering datasets enhanced the reliability of the findings, verifying that the identified semiotic behaviors were not particular to artifacts but essentially reproducible across domains.

A rigorous audit was conducted to investigate the involvement of platforms and algorithms in the spread of signals. Over time, the exposure at the feed level was assessed to see how recommendation algorithms surfaced, prioritized, or concealed artifacts. We systematically altered algorithmic triggers such as search terms, watch duration, and interaction rates to evaluate their impact on content ranking and modal prominence. We also examined metadata footprints, which showed hashtag behavior, engagement surges, and the velocity of information dissemination. These were all indicators that the algorithm was altering the trajectory of meaning. Experiments including prompt variations were conducted to assess generative AI systems. This facilitated the study in determining the impact of training data, model bias, and hallucination on sign production inside hybrid writing settings.

This analytical paradigm makes Semiotics 5.0 empirically testable rather than only theoretical. The method achieves replicability, measurability, and the ability to capture genuine semiotic behavior across human, digital, and computer ecosystems by delineating research inquiries, identifying the corpus, formalizing the coding framework, and incorporating reliability measures and platform evaluations. There are three processes to analyzing multimodal texts: collection, coding, and interpreting. During the collection phase, multimodal artifacts are collected from educational, cultural, and technological contexts to provide a representative corpus of Semiotics 5.0 in practice. The selection method is intentional, picking things that exemplify how multimodality and algorithmic mediation work together. For instance, classroom activities that use AI-generated visuals are chosen to illustrate the impact of generative AI on multimodal literacy practices (Smith et al., 2025). Trending social media posts that have been chosen by algorithms are used to study how algorithmic exposure affects semiotic perception (Bezemer & Cowan, 2021). Engineering case studies are selected to illustrate the computational semiotics inherent in intelligent systems (Ali, 2025; Suthar & Ali, 2025). In the coding step, multimodal objects are analyzed using semiotic categories derived from social semiotics and multimodal discourse analysis.

The coding approach, derived from Kress (2003) and Kress and van Leeuwen (2021), encompasses categories such as representational meaning (the depiction of reality via signs), interactive meaning (the positioning of viewers through signals), and compositional meaning (the arrangement of signs). To tackle algorithmic mediation, fresh coding categories are introduced, including algorithmic visibility (the impact of algorithms on sign visibility), generative authorship (the role of machine processes in sign creation), and infrastructural embedding (the influence of technology on sign formation). These categories provide a systematic examination of the operation of multimodal signals in algorithmically mediated environments, therefore enhancing existing semiotic frameworks to include the dimensions of Semiotics 5.0. The interpretation process involves synthesizing information from the coded data to identify patterns and themes in the manifestations of Semiotics 5.0 across many contexts. For example, analysis may reveal that AI-generated content engenders novel forms of authorship, whereby human prompts and machine outputs converge to produce new semiotic artifacts (Cheung et al., 2025). An examination of social media posts may indicate that algorithmic curation preferentially highlights certain semiotic patterns, such as emotionally charged content, so shaping cultural discourses (Bezemer & Cowan, 2021). Engineering case studies may demonstrate that computational systems engage in semiotic processes by interpreting environmental signals as crucial inputs that influence decision-making (Ali, 2025; Srivastava et al., 2024). These interpretations are contextualized within the whole theoretical framework of Semiotics 5.0, which highlights the hybrid nature of meaning-making in the algorithmic age.

A vital component of the research process is the integration of algorithmic critique with semiotic analysis. Traditional semiotic frameworks focus on the interaction of signals, meanings, and interpretants; yet, algorithmically controlled environments need an analysis of how computational processes affect these relationships. Following Bezemer and Cowan (2021), the study analyzes algorithmic infrastructures, exploring the functions of recommendation systems, search algorithms, and generative AI models as semiotic agents. This requires an analysis of both the outcomes of these systems and their underlying logics and intrinsic biases. For instance, generative AI systems trained on biased datasets may produce outputs that perpetuate biases. This brings up questions about the moral side of semiotic production (Smith et al., 2025). Similarly, automated curation on social media may unduly emphasize dominant discourses while marginalizing minority viewpoints, leading to semiotic imbalances (Aragón, 2025). The study technique incorporates algorithmic critique, ensuring that Semiotics 5.0 goes beyond surface analysis to engage with the fundamental processes that shape meaning formation. The ethical ramifications of the research are paramount, given the involvement of human beings, pedagogical approaches, and algorithmic structures. The study adheres to ethical guidelines for educational research while examining classroom artifacts. This indicates that participants provided informed consent and their identities were safeguarded (Carcamo, 2025; Cheung et al., 2025). When analyzing social media data, ethical concerns arise with privacy and consent, particularly when posts are publicly accessible yet generated by individuals who may not anticipate academic examination. The study tackles these issues by anonymizing data and focusing on collective trends rather than specific individuals. When examining the outputs of generative AI, ethical concerns include the perpetuation of biases and the implications of fragmented authorship. The study meticulously investigates these issues, emphasizing the need for ethical frameworks that include the impact of algorithms on semiotic creation (O'Halloran, 2023; Smith et al., 2025).

Qualitative research may assure reliability and validity via triangulation, reflexivity, and member verification. Triangulation is achieved by analyzing data from several contexts—educational, cultural, and technological—thereby enhancing the validity of the results. Reflexivity is maintained by acknowledging the researcher's positionality and the interpretive nature of semiotic analysis. Semiotics necessitates subjective interpretation, whereas reflexivity ensures clarity in the formulation of analytical findings. Member checking is used in educational contexts to share interpretations of classroom artifacts with participants, aiming to validate outcomes (Aragón, 2025). These strategies work together to make the research more trustworthy by making sure that the findings are accurate, believable, and may be used in other places.

The methodological framework integrates interdisciplinary methodologies, synthesizing concepts from engineering research to broaden the scope of semiotic analysis. Ali (2025) and colleagues (Ali et al., 2023; Srivastava et al., 2023; Suthar & Ali, 2025) provide case studies demonstrating that intelligent systems comprehend and respond to signals in ways comparable to human semiotic practices. Incorporating these case studies within the research approach demonstrates that Semiotics 5.0 beyond cultural and educational domains, expanding into technical systems where signals serve as computational inputs that guide system behavior. This integration across fields reveals that Semiotics 5.0 is transdisciplinary and requires approaches that can link the humanities, education, and engineering. Utilizing relevant case studies strengthens the theoretical framework and demonstrates its practical relevance across other fields.

The justification for this methodological approach is based on the unique challenges posed by Semiotics 5.0. Conventional semiotic methodologies are insufficient for analyzing algorithmically mediated environments, since they neglect the impact of computational infrastructures on meaning production. Multimodal discourse analysis provides valuable tools for the study of multimodal texts; yet, it requires enhancement to include algorithmic critique. Qualitative interpretive methodologies provide a comprehensive analysis of meaning-making processes; yet, they need interdisciplinary integration to adequately encapsulate the semiotic processes intrinsic to technological systems. The study strategy, which uses a mix of different methods, presents a full image of how to look at Semiotics 5.0 in all its complexity. This ensures that the study is both theoretically robust and empirically substantiated, analyzing the cultural, educational, and technological dimensions of the algorithmic age.

The incorporation of algorithmic criticism into semiotic analysis requires the creation of methodological instruments that emphasize the influence of computing on meaning-making processes. Multimodal discourse analysis offers a framework for investigating the interaction of modes within texts; however, algorithmically mediated environments necessitate an expansion of this methodology to encompass infrastructural semiotics, which examines how foundational computational architectures influence the creation and dissemination of signs. This extension is essential in the framework of Semiotics 5.0, where meaning is not only conveyed between human interlocutors but also co-constructed through interactions with algorithmic systems, including recommendation engines, generative AI, and data-driven filtering mechanisms (Bezemer & Cowan, 2021). In practical terms, this implies that analytical approaches must study not just multimodal texts themselves but also the algorithmic paths via which those messages are rendered accessible, visible, or invisible to users.

One methodological approach used in this work is critical algorithmic ethnography, derived from digital ethnography traditions but especially concentrating on user experiences and interactions with algorithmically mediated signals. This entails the observation and documentation of the interactions among learners, educators, and users with algorithmically curated multimodal texts in digital contexts, while recognizing the influence of customization and recommendation logics on their interpretative practices. For instance, the same multimodal artifact may manifest in many settings contingent upon the user's algorithmic profile, indicating that meaning is partly shaped by the unseen filtering of algorithmic systems (Aragón, 2025).

By capturing these patterns, the study elucidates the decentralized character of semiotic processes in the algorithmic era. The methodological amalgamation of engineering case studies further solidifies this scattered viewpoint. Ali (2025) showed that reinforcement learning systems may work as semiotic agents by perceiving signals from the environment as useful information for adapting behavior. This viewpoint enables us to see computational processes not just as technical apparatus but as manifestations of semiotic interpretation, albeit in a nonhuman form. Ali et al. (2023) also talked about how recurrent backpropagation models operate by decoding and re-encoding input signals. This turns raw data into patterns of meaning that help with network construction. These processes are similar to the interpretative tasks of human semiotics, but they happen in computer systems. Integrating such situations within the methodological framework illustrates that Semiotics 5.0 necessitates analytical scrutiny of both human and machinic meaning-making, therefore connecting interpretative paradigms with technological systems.

This study employs a triangulated methodology for data analysis, including multimodal discourse analysis, algorithmic criticism, and technical semiotic analysis. Multimodal texts are scrutinized for representational, interactive, and compositional meanings, as delineated by Kress (2003) and Kress and van Leeuwen (2021). Concurrently, algorithmic infrastructures are evaluated for their influence on visibility, circulation, and authorship (Bezemer & Cowan, 2021; Smith et al., 2025). Simultaneously, engineering processes are examined using computational semiotics, including data inputs, signal processing, and algorithmic outputs as examples of sign interpretation (Ali, 2025; Srivastava et al., 2023). By integrating these three levels of study, the research technique guarantees a comprehensive knowledge of Semiotics 5.0 within cultural, educational, and technological contexts.

Methodological triangulation further improves reliability and validity. By integrating textual analysis, ethnographic observation, and technological case study investigation, the research alleviates the constraints of individual methodologies and offers a more holistic representation of Semiotics 5.0. For instance, multimodal discourse analysis elucidates the functioning of signs inside texts, algorithmic ethnography reveals the varied interactions users have with those texts, and engineering case studies illustrate the computational interpretation of signals within technological systems. This triangulation not only enhances the robustness of the results but also illustrates the fundamentally hybrid character of Semiotics 5.0, which cannot be fully grasped from a single methodological perspective (O'Halloran, 2023).

It is important to think carefully about the ethical aspects of this strategy. In educational settings, research using classroom artifacts produced by generative AI must confront concerns around authorship, intellectual property, and equity. Cheung et al. (2025) demonstrated that students' multimodal representations increasingly depend on generative AI, prompting questions about the originality of student work and the ethical ramifications of machine co-authorship. Smith et al. (2025) also talk about the possible dangers of students being too reliant on AI technologies for multimodal writing. To mitigate these concerns, the research underscores the need of ethical openness in reporting, ensuring that participants' use of AI is recognized and contextualized. In the research of social media, privacy issues are mitigated by anonymizing data and emphasizing collective trends over individual users, according to established methodologies in digital ethnography (Bezemer & Cowan, 2021). In technical case studies, ethical concerns encompass the perpetuation of bias within algorithmic systems as well as the wider societal ramifications of semiotic processes integrated into technologies like 5G networks, gesture recognition systems, and wearable devices (Srivastava et al., 2024; Suthar & Ali, 2025). Reflexivity is another important part of the methodology. It recognizes that the researcher's stance affects how they understand semiotic processes. Semiotic analysis is fundamentally interpretative, and reflexivity guarantees that the researcher rigorously examines their own assumptions, biases, and interpretive decisions. This is especially significant in Semiotics 5.0, where the way people and machines make meaning together may not fit into standard ways of analyzing things. Reflexivity entails acknowledging the constraints of human interpretation in engaging with algorithmic logics, which are sometimes opaque or proprietary. O'Halloran (2023) stressed that semiotics has to deal with the physical structures that make meaning, although researchers may not always be able to see all of the steps in an algorithm. Recognizing these constraints improves the clarity and reliability of the study.

The methodological rationale for using a qualitative, interpretative, and transdisciplinary framework is rooted in the intricacy of Semiotics 5.0 as a subject of investigation. Quantitative methodologies, however useful for assessing patterns of algorithmic behavior or user involvement, fail to adequately encapsulate the intricate interpretative processes inherent in semiotic meaning-making. In contrast, qualitative interpretative methodologies provide an in-depth examination of the production, circulation, and interpretation of multimodal texts within algorithmically mediated contexts. This corresponds with Aragón's (2025) focus on embodied agency in multimodal practices and with Carcamo's (2025) illustration of how digital technologies augment multimodal literacy. However, Semiotics 5.0 necessitates an extension beyond conventional qualitative methodologies to include algorithmic criticism and technological semiotic analysis, as shown by the research of Ali (2025) and associates. This mixed-methods approach makes sure that Semiotics 5.0 is researched in all of its transdisciplinary complexity. The methodological techniques include recurrent cycles of analysis, whereby discoveries from one analytical level inform and enhance interpretations at another. For example, algorithmic ethnography can show that students often come with AI-generated multimodal writings that were made by recommendation algorithms. This understanding may subsequently guide the multimodal discourse analysis of such texts, emphasizing the influence of algorithmic logics on their semiotic construction (Cheung et al., 2025).

In the same way, technical case studies may show similarities between how computers read signals and how people use signs, which would add to the theoretical framework of Semiotics 5.0 (Ali et al., 2023). This iterative technique guarantees that the methodology stays flexible and adaptable to the intricacies of the data, instead than strictly following predetermined analytical categories. Another new way to accomplish things is to employ comparative analysis across different fields. The study analyzes Semiotics 5.0 within the realms of education, digital communication, and engineering, revealing both similarities and differences in the functioning of semiotic processes. In educational settings, Semiotics 5.0 is evident in students' use of AI technologies for multimodal writing (Smith et al., 2025). In digital communication, it manifests in the automated curating of multimodal information on social media platforms (Bezemer & Cowan, 2021). In engineering settings, it manifests in the interpretation of signals by intelligent systems (Ali, 2025; Srivastava et al., 2023). Comparative analysis facilitates the detection of cross-domain trends, such as the decentralized nature of authorship or the prominence of algorithmic mediation, while simultaneously emphasizing domain-specific dynamics. This enhances the theoretical robustness of Semiotics 5.0, demonstrating its application across several circumstances. The last step in the technique is to put all the data together into a clear theoretical and practical foundation for Semiotics 5.0. This synthesis is not just a summary; it is meant to provide new ideas that will help both semiotic theory and literacy teaching. For instance, recognizing generative authorship as a consistent theme across several domains enhances theoretical discourse on the essence of agency in semiotic processes (Cheung et al., 2025; Smith et al., 2025). In the same way, understanding algorithmic visibility as a factor in creating meaning helps teachers come up with ways to help students become more algorithmically literate (Aragón, 2025; Lim & Tan-Chia, 2023). By anchoring these findings in actual data from several settings, the research methodology guarantees that the Semiotics 5.0 framework is both theoretically robust and practically applicable.

In summary, the methodological framework for examining Semiotics 5.0 is defined by its qualitative interpretive focus, dependence on multimodal discourse analysis augmented by algorithmic critique, inclusion of transdisciplinary case studies from engineering, and dedication to ethical and reflexive research methodologies. The technique offers a holistic framework for examining the hybrid characteristics of meaning-making in the algorithmic era via the integration of various components. Semiotics 5.0 requires methodologies capable of encapsulating the interactions among multimodal texts, algorithmic infrastructures, and computational processes;

the paradigm established herein addresses this need. It makes sure that research into Semiotics 5.0 not only deepens our grasp of the theory but also gives us useful information for education, digital communication, and technological innovation in a world where meaning is more and more created by both people and computers.

Case Study 1—Algorithmic Visibility in a Social Media Learning Environment

A six-week observational study of undergraduate students engaging with short-form video platforms revealed that multimodal meaning was influenced more by algorithmic curation than by user intent, supporting Bezemer and Cowan's (2021) discourse on infrastructural reading and O'Halloran's (2023) interpretation of semiotics as materially embedded. The first inquiries for "sustainable design" yielded infographics that elucidated concepts, aligning with the multimodal knowledge-building methodologies discussed by Lim and Tan-Chia (2023) and Carcamo (2025). As individuals increasingly engaged with videos labeled "humor," the algorithm altered its recommendation priorities, gradually substituting academic material with amusement, irrespective of the learner's educational preferences. Visibility was established by data-driven inference rather than selection, confirming the influence of algorithms on sign exposure and semantic pathways. Students said that they saw humorous content as representative of the dominant interpretation of sustainability, illustrating how platform-level rankings influence perception and epistemic valuation (Bezemer & Cowan, 2021). This scenario empirically demonstrates that meanings on digital platforms are computed rather than just communicated, a core proposition in Semiotics 5.0.

Case Study 2: Generative AI as a Co-Author in Multimodal Scientific Composition

A student in a digital literacy class tasked with explaining photosynthesis combined written content with AI-generated visuals. As generative prompts evolved, the generation of meaning became decentralized, corroborating Smith et al.'s (2025) claim that GenAI alters multimodal authorship, and Cheung et al.'s (2025) finding that students collaboratively construct scientific representations alongside model inference. Altering "chlorophyll process" to "chlorophyll efficiency" resulted in microscopic-scale representation, so transforming the scientific framework unbeknownst to the student. This aligns with Aragón's (2025) assertions on embodied agency in multimodal creation and corroborates Kress's (2003) and Kress and van Leeuwen's (2021) claims that design is a decision-driven semiotic act. The only distinction is that decisions are now rendered via algorithmic generativity rather than independently. Students gained conceptual understanding using the model's visual affordances, demonstrating that meaning-making now emerges from a prompt–dataset–algorithm loop in addition to human symbolic organizing. This dual authorship exemplifies the significance of Semiotics 5.0, whereby interpretation is both multimodal and impacted by machines.

Methodological Strengths and Analytical Gains

The use of a qualitative, interpretative, and transdisciplinary research methodology in the examination of Semiotics 5.0 has several benefits, enhancing both theoretical rigor and empirical relevance. One of the main benefits is that qualitative approaches may show how complicated meaning-making processes are in settings that use several modes and algorithms. Conventional quantitative methodologies, while effective in discerning patterns within extensive datasets, sometimes neglect the interpretative aspects of meaning, which are fundamental to semiotics. Qualitative techniques prioritize interpretation, enabling researchers to investigate how people and groups interact with multimodal texts, how algorithms influence their interactions with signals, and how meanings are collaboratively formed among human and machine actors (Bezemer & Cowan, 2021; Kress, 2003). This level of analysis is necessary for Semiotics 5.0, which focuses on the mixed and spread-out character of communication.

Another big benefit is that multimodal discourse analysis gives you an organized way to look at meaning in several modalities, such text, sound, space, and gesture. MDA recognizes that meaning is created via the integration of several semiotic elements, providing a more thorough explanation of communication than just verbal methods. Kress and van Leeuwen's (2021) grammar of visual design and O'Halloran et al.'s (2017) study on multimodality demonstrate that multimodal analysis allows researchers to discern the interactions across modes that provide representational, interactive, and compositional meanings. Applying this methodology to algorithmically mediated contexts guarantees that Semiotics 5.0 transcends superficial examination of multimodal texts, including the infrastructural circumstances of their creation and dissemination. This methodological expansion is beneficial as it enables researchers to examine both the substance of communication and the frameworks that govern its exposure.

Another big benefit is that algorithmic criticism is now a part of the methodological framework. Modern communication is inextricably linked to algorithmic mediation, however conventional semiotic frameworks often neglect the significance of computational infrastructures. By including algorithmic criticism, the study technique shows how algorithms filter, rank, and amplify multimodal texts. This facilitates a more precise and analytical examination of Semiotics 5.0, whereby meaning is not exclusively dictated by human agents but collaboratively formulated with computers (Bezemer & Cowan, 2021). For instance, Smith et al. (2025) illustrated that generative AI transforms multimodal composition, while Cheung et al. (2025) indicated that students' representations are influenced by algorithmic tools. An algorithmically informed approach encapsulates these dynamics, guaranteeing that study findings accurately represent the reality of meaning-making within digital and educational settings. The benefit here is methodological innovation: by applying semiotic inquiry to algorithms, the work creates new methods that are much required to understand how people communicate nowadays. The multidisciplinary integration of engineering case studies provides an additional benefit, underscoring the relevance of Semiotics 5.0 outside the humanities. Ali (2025) illustrates how reinforcement learning reads environmental cues in a manner analogous to semiotic processes, while Ali et al. (2023) elucidated how recurrent backpropagation models decode input data streams inside mobile networks. Srivastava et al. (2024) examined signal processing in 5G communication, whereas Suthar and Ali (2025) investigated gesture recognition as a conversion of physical gestures into machine-readable signals.

By integrating these case studies into the study methodology, the framework of Semiotics 5.0 is substantiated as both a cultural and pedagogical construct, as well as a technological and computational one. This interdisciplinary approach strengthens the method's explanatory capacity, demonstrating that semiotics is integrated inside both human and mechanical systems. The benefit is that the study technique connects several areas, providing a complete picture of Semiotics 5.0 that is useful in all of them. Another significant benefit is the ethical soundness of the study methodology. Semiotics 5.0 unavoidably addresses delicate issues of authorship, prejudice, and epistemic fairness within algorithmically mediated contexts. The technique guarantees ethical rigor by integrating reflexivity, informed permission, anonymization, and a critical examination of the biases inherent in algorithmic systems (Aragón, 2025; O'Halloran, 2023). For instance, while looking at the results of generative AI, you need to remember that these systems could repeat cultural preconceptions that were in their training data (Smith et al., 2025). Likewise, the examination of social media necessitates ethical contemplation of privacy, even in cases when data is publicly accessible (Bezemer & Cowan, 2021). The research approach explicitly tackles these obstacles, showing that it is aware of the ethical issues that come up in semiotic study in the era of algorithms. The benefit of this method is that it not only yields correct results but also guarantees that those results are obtained responsibly, so augmenting their credibility and acceptance in both academic and practical settings.

One further helpful quality about the framework is that it is methodologically flexible. Semiotics 5.0 covers a lot of ground, including schools, social media, and engineering technological systems. The chosen study methodology is adequately adaptable to accommodate this variability, since it integrates multimodal discourse analysis, algorithmic ethnography, and technical semiotic analysis. This triangulated approach enables the technique to adapt to various domains while maintaining coherence. In educational settings, the emphasis is on classroom objects and student behaviors (Carcamo, 2025; Cheung et al., 2025). In digital communication, the emphasis transitions to algorithmic infrastructures that influence visibility (Bezemer & Cowan, 2021). When it comes to engineering, the emphasis is on seeing signals as machinic signs (Ali, 2025). This flexibility makes it possible to study Semiotics 5.0 as a whole, rather than in separate parts like other techniques that are more rigidly defined. The benefit is that the framework is methodologically inclusive, meaning it can function with many types of data and ways of looking at it.

Another big plus of this strategy is that it gives you a lot of information. By transcending superficial study of multimodal texts to include algorithmic mediation and technological semiotics, the research methodology reveals facets of meaning-making that would otherwise stay obscured. For instance, Aragón (2025) illustrated how multimodality facilitates embodied agency; but, when integrated with algorithmic criticism, it becomes apparent that this agency is limited by the obscurity of computational infrastructures. Kress (2003) and Kress and van Leeuwen (2021) emphasized the multimodal characteristics of communication; yet, by integrating technical case studies, the research methodology illustrates that semiotics permeates computer structures. This level of study yields more profound and intricate insights into Semiotics 5.0, providing theoretical advancements that propel the discipline forward and practical implications that enhance teaching and technology design.

Pedagogical value is an extra benefit of the study methodology. Semiotics 5.0 is not just a theory; it has real-world effects on education, where students need to learn how to read and write in more than one way and how to use algorithms. The study technique concentrates on multimodal artifacts, generative AI outputs, and algorithmic infrastructures, yielding results that may guide curriculum design and pedagogical approaches (Carcamo, 2025; Lim & Tan-Chia, 2023). For instance, recognizing patterns of hybrid authorship in student work might assist educators in formulating evaluation methods that acknowledge the influence of AI in multimodal writing (Smith et al., 2025). Likewise, examining algorithmic curation on social media might enhance digital literacy initiatives aimed at teaching students to critically assess their information contexts (Bezemer & Cowan, 2021). The educational benefit lies in the research method's direct linkage of empirical results to actionable techniques for promoting critical literacy in the algorithmic era.

Finally, the research technique enhances semiotic study by expanding the limits of methodological innovation. Semiotics has faced historical criticism for its excessive theoretical nature and insufficient empirical foundation. The methodology created for Semiotics 5.0 addresses this critique by integrating rigorous empirical investigation with theoretical understanding. Utilizing multimodal discourse analysis on algorithmically mediated texts, performing ethnographic observations of algorithmic interaction, and including engineering case studies, the study methodology establishes a solid empirical basis for Semiotics 5.0. This progress in the subject shows that semiotics may be both theoretically advanced and methodologically sound. The benefit here is intellectual legitimacy: Semiotics 5.0 is presented as a respectable and novel paradigm that may enhance existing academic discussions on literacy, digital media, and the societal impact of algorithms.

In conclusion, the research approach for studying Semiotics 5.0 has several benefits. It captures the interpretive depth of semiotic processes, provides a comprehensive account of multimodal communication, integrates algorithmic critique, incorporates interdisciplinary insights from engineering, ensures ethical robustness, offers methodological flexibility, produces deep insights, supports pedagogical applications, and advances semiotic scholarship. The cumulative benefits substantiate the use of this research methodology, guaranteeing that the examination of Semiotics 5.0 is both theoretically significant and pragmatically relevant. By examining the cultural, educational, and technological aspects of meaning-making in the algorithmic era, the study approach establishes Semiotics 5.0 as a framework adept at tackling the critical difficulties of modern communication.

FUTURE ENHANCEMENT

The trajectory of Semiotics 5.0 as a framework for comprehending multimodal literacy in the algorithmic age indicates several opportunities for future advancements in both theoretical research and practical implementation. The present research methodology incorporates multimodal discourse analysis, algorithmic critique, and interdisciplinary case studies from engineering. However, the swift advancement of generative artificial intelligence, data-driven infrastructures, and hybrid human–machine practices indicates that additional refinement and expansion are imperative to align with evolving realities. Thus, future improvements must be considered in three interconnected areas: the theoretical advancement of Semiotics 5.0, the methodological innovations that broaden the existing framework, and the practical interventions that revolutionize education, culture, and technology.

One important way to improve Semiotics 5.0 is to add more theory to it. Contemporary multimodality models provide substantial instruments for examining the orchestration of signals across many modes (Kress, 2003; Kress & van Leeuwen, 2021); nevertheless, they were not designed with algorithmic mediation or generative AI in consideration.

O'Halloran (2023) asserted that semiotic processes are both material and symbolic, necessitating an examination of the infrastructures that facilitate meaning-making. Consequently, next theoretical endeavors must broaden semiotic frameworks to include the agency of algorithms and data systems in the construction of signals. For example, forthcoming models can conceptualize algorithmic visibility as an independent semiotic resource, considering that algorithms now influence the amplification and concealment of signals (Bezemer & Cowan, 2021). The notion of authorship needs redefinition to include creative processes, acknowledging that hybrid authorship involving both people and computers has emerged as a salient characteristic of multimodal composition (Cheung et al., 2025; Smith et al., 2025). Enhancing Semiotics 5.0 necessitates a reevaluation of fundamental semiotic categories—namely sign, interpretant, and code—through the perspective of algorithmic mediation, hence assuring the framework's applicability in situations where human and machinic agents collaboratively generate meaning.

Another important area for future growth is improving methods. The present paradigm integrates qualitative interpretative analysis, multimodal discourse analysis, and multidisciplinary case studies; nonetheless, more innovation is required to examine the growing opacity of algorithmic systems. Future study may amalgamate computational techniques, like algorithm auditing, natural language processing, and data visualization, with qualitative semiotic analysis, so establishing mixed-methods approaches that provide both interpretative depth and systemic understanding. For instance, algorithmic auditing can uncover biases in recommendation systems, while multimodal discourse analysis might investigate the manifestation of these biases in the semiotic composition of curated information (Aragón, 2025; Bezemer & Cowan, 2021). Likewise, integrating ethnographic observation with computational tracking methods might augment the examination of learner interactions with AI-generated multimodal texts in educational contexts (Cheung et al., 2025). This methodological innovation guarantees that Semiotics 5.0 transcends mere descriptive analyses of multimodality, providing tools for scrutinizing algorithmic infrastructures that are becoming more pivotal to meaning-making. The incorporation of multidisciplinary perspectives from engineering presents opportunities for future improvement.

Recent studies underscore similarities between computational processes and semiotic interpretation, since reinforcement learning, recurrent backpropagation, and signal processing include the encoding, decoding, and modification of signs (Ali, 2025; Ali et al., 2023; Srivastava et al., 2024). Subsequent study may enhance these links by establishing frameworks of computational semiotics that methodically examine how intelligent systems read data as signals and how these interpretations influence system behavior. For instance, gesture recognition systems already perceive body gestures as machine signals (Suthar & Ali, 2025). Expanding Semiotics 5.0 into technological fields may provide significant insights on the functioning of human–machine semiotics across many settings, including smart cities and autonomous systems. The improvement here comes from making information flow between semiotics and engineering in both directions. Semiotics obtains technical insights, while engineering gets conceptual tools for making systems that take into account the cultural and ethical aspects of sign processes.

In education, the advancement of Semiotics 5.0 includes the integration of algorithmic literacy into multimodal literacy teaching. Lim & Tan-Chia (2023) stressed how important it is to educate students how to read and write digital multimodal texts. Carcamo (2025) showed how digital tools may help students learn a language by using multimodal practices. Future pedagogical frameworks must explicitly incorporate algorithmic critique, teaching learners to interpret not only multimodal texts but also the algorithmic conditions under which those texts are produced and circulated. Aragón (2025) emphasized that learners exercise embodied agency through multimodal practices; however, in algorithmic environments, such agency necessitates awareness of how algorithms constrain or facilitate meaning-making. Future educational interventions may include instructing students to critically evaluate the influence of recommendation systems on their interactions with multimodal texts, or the ways in which generative AI systems incorporate biases into their outputs (Smith et al., 2025). This kind of teaching improvement makes sure that students gain hybrid literacies that combine multimodal skills with an understanding of algorithms. This gets them ready to take part in semiotic ecologies where people and computers work together to create meaning.

The ethical aspect of Semiotics 5.0 is another significant area that has to be improved. Contemporary research recognizes the dangers of prejudice, exclusion, and epistemic injustice in algorithmically mediated contexts (Bezemer & Cowan, 2021; O'Halloran, 2023). Subsequent research must transcend mere criticism to provide pragmatic frameworks for the ethical design and use of algorithmic systems. This entails not just examining the ways algorithms perpetuate inequities but also collaborating with designers, educators, and politicians to devise measures that foster epistemic justice. For instance, future improvements may include working with generative AI developers to create systems that are easier to understand and provide consumers information about training data and algorithmic processes so they can judge the results for themselves. In the same way, ethical frameworks might help instructors help students utilize generative AI in a way that helps them without making them reliant on it or complicit in propagating prejudices (Cheung et al., 2025). By incorporating ethical improvement into Semiotics 5.0, the framework may facilitate not only the advancement of academic knowledge but also the change of society.

Future improvement entails broadening the scope of Semiotics 5.0 to include global and cross-cultural situations. A lot of the research being done right now is about how technology and education are used in certain situations, but algorithmic mediation and multimodal literacy are things that happen all over the world. Kress (2003) stressed that literacy is constantly influenced by social and cultural factors, and this idea is also true for Semiotics 5.0. Subsequent research must investigate the ways in which algorithmic infrastructures influence meaning-making variably across cultural settings, acknowledging that algorithms are not culturally neutral but rather embody the values and goals of the cultures that create them. For instance, recommendation algorithms on global platforms could give more weight to certain cultural material than others, which might change how meaning moves throughout the world in ways that maintain cultural inequalities. Comparative research across cultural settings might elucidate the distinct manifestations of Semiotics 5.0 in other communities, therefore enriching the theoretical framework and its practical relevance.

Lastly, for future improvements to happen, research methodologies need to be scalable and sustainable. Semiotics 5.0 deals with big, quickly changing semiotic ecologies, such those seen in schools and on global digital platforms. Consequently, next research must cultivate scalable methodologies capable of managing large datasets without compromising interpretative depth. Combining computational techniques like big data analytics with qualitative analysis is one approach to go ahead. It lets researchers see huge trends while still paying attention to the details of how people make meaning (Ali et al., 2023). Sustainability must be stressed, ensuring that research procedures stay flexible to the ongoing growth of algorithmic systems. For instance, research methodologies need to be able to include new types of generative AI as they come out. Semiotics 5.0's methodological flexibility makes sure that the framework stays useful as technology changes.

In conclusion, the future advancement of Semiotics 5.0 necessitates theoretical, methodological, multidisciplinary, educational, ethical, cultural, and practical extension. In theory, fundamental semiotic ideas need to be revised to include algorithmic mediation and generative authoring. Methodologically, it is essential to create mixed-methods techniques that integrate qualitative interpretation with computational tools. Interdisciplinarily, more links between semiotics and engineering may help both professions grow. From an educational standpoint, algorithmic literacy must be integrated into multimodal literacy instruction. It is necessary to create ethical frameworks that support epistemic fairness in contexts mediated by algorithms. Culturally, it is necessary to include global and comparative viewpoints. In practice, research methodologies need to be able to grow and change as technology does. These improvements make sure that Semiotics 5.0 remains a strong and useful way to comprehend and deal with the challenges of multimodal literacy in the age of algorithms. By moving forward in these ways, Semiotics 5.0 will not only help scholars learn more, but it will also help create societies that are more fair, critical, and informed, where people and technology work together to make meaning.

CONCLUSION

The investigation of Semiotics 5.0 as a conceptual and methodological framework has shown that the examination of signs, hitherto grounded on linguistics and cultural studies, need redefinition in the context of the algorithmic era. The progression from Saussurean and Peircean foundations, via Barthesian cultural criticism, to multimodal semiotics as delineated by Kress (2003) and Kress and van Leeuwen (2021), has continually broadened the domain of semiotic investigation. This trend approaches a critical point in the twenty-first century, as meaning is no longer only created and disseminated by human agents but is increasingly mediated, filtered, and generated by algorithmic systems. Semiotics 5.0 is the pinnacle of this development, providing a hybrid theoretical and methodological framework adept at tackling the intricacies of multimodal literacy in the context of widespread algorithmic mediation. This chapter's literature review highlights that multimodal literacy is a crucial skill in digital communication and education. Researchers Lim and Tan-Chia (2023) and Carcamo (2025) emphasize the importance of pedagogies that equip students to engage with multimodal texts, while Aragón (2025) illustrates the embodied agency that learners manifest via multimodal practices. Bezemer and Cowan (2021) contend that the semiotic environment is significantly influenced by algorithmic infrastructures that dictate visibility and accessibility. The conclusion derived from these findings is that multimodal literacy, while fundamental, is inadequate on its own. It should be broadened to include algorithmic literacy, allowing users to not only read multimodal texts but also to critically examine the mechanisms that govern their distribution. Semiotics 5.0 addresses this need by incorporating multimodal and algorithmic criticism, therefore seeing literacy as both interpretative and infrastructural.

Generative AI amplifies the need for this redefinition. Smith, Pacheco, and Warrington (2025) with Cheung et al. (2025) illustrate that AI systems are now engaged players in multimodal composition, generating hybrid writings that obscure the distinctions between human and machine authorship. This reality necessitates a redefinition of semiotic processes, whereby authorship and agency are disseminated across people, algorithms, and databases. Semiotics 5.0 offers instruments for examining these dispersed processes, emphasizing their creative possibilities and ethical dilemmas. By identifying generative authorship as a crucial aspect of modern semiotics, the framework situates itself at the front of discussions around authenticity, originality, and accountability in digital communication. Semiotics 5.0 is both descriptive and normative, providing educators, academics, and practitioners with the tools to address the ethical implications of hybrid writing.

This study's methodological contributions further underscore the importance of Semiotics 5.0. The research technique illustrates how semiotics may evolve to meet the requirements of the algorithmic era via the integration of qualitative interpretative analysis, multimodal discourse analysis, algorithmic criticism, and interdisciplinary case studies. This methodological diversity has several benefits. It encapsulates the interpretive complexity of semiotic processes (Kress & van Leeuwen, 2021), integrates algorithmic infrastructures into analysis (Bezemer & Cowan, 2021), and broadens semiotic investigation into computational realms (Ali, 2025; Ali et al., 2023; Srivastava et al., 2024; Suthar & Ali, 2025). The conclusion is that Semiotics 5.0 offers a methodological framework for future study that is adaptable, transdisciplinary, and morally sound. This research technique situates semiotic analysis within a framework that connects the humanities, education, and engineering, exemplifying the transdisciplinary approach necessary for examining hybrid meaning-making processes.

The ethical implications of Semiotics 5.0 are significant. Algorithms are not impartial arbiters; they embed biases that determine which voices are elevated and which are suppressed. O'Halloran (2023) and Bezemer and Cowan (2021) assert that semiotic processes should be comprehended in conjunction with the supporting infrastructures. The consequence is that epistemic fairness is compromised in algorithmically mediated contexts. Semiotics 5.0 enhances this discourse by offering a framework for the critical examination of algorithmic biases, fostering reflexivity in research, and advocating instructional approaches that enable learners to confront disparities. The conclusion is therefore both theoretical and pragmatic: Semiotics 5.0 enhances semiotic study and offers tools for constructing more egalitarian semiotic ecologies that facilitate the participation of various voices.

The multidisciplinary expansions of Semiotics 5.0 highlight its wider relevance. Research conducted by Ali (2025), Ali et al. (2023), and Srivastava, Ali, and associates (2024) illustrates that semiotic processes extend beyond human communication and are fundamental to computer systems that understand signals, process data, and enhance networks. Semiotics 5.0 broadens the field of semiotics into technological realms by emphasizing similarities between human interpretation and machine processing. This transdisciplinary approach amplifies the explanatory capacity of semiotics, demonstrating that meaning-making is a global phenomenon encompassing cultural, educational, and technological systems. Semiotics 5.0 establishes semiotics as a cohesive framework that can connect disparate disciplines, making it relevant to both the humanities and the sciences.

The benefits of the research approach, as previously articulated, underscore the need and timeliness of the Semiotics 5.0 framework. Its capability for interpretative depth, methodological flexibility, ethical robustness, and instructional relevance guarantees its ability to tackle the unique issues of the algorithmic era. Aragón's (2025) focus on embodied agency, Carcamo's (2025) observations about digital multimodal literacy, and Lim and Tan-Chia's (2023) educational frameworks all underscore the need for literacy practices that are broad, analytical, and flexible. Semiotics 5.0 integrates these contributions into a cohesive paradigm that addresses the complexities of digital communication, characterized by multimodal, algorithmic, and generative meaning. Semiotics 5.0 presents both a theoretical framework and a pedagogical need, necessitating the evolution of education to equip learners for engagement in hybrid semiotic ecologies. The prospective improvements detailed in this chapter emphasize the dynamic potential of Semiotics 5.0. The need for theoretical enhancement, methodological advancement, interdisciplinary synthesis, pedagogical broadening, ethical paradigms, cultural contextualization, and scalability indicates a research agenda that is both ambitious and essential (Cheung et al., 2025; Smith as al., 2025). The conclusion is that Semiotics 5.0 is not a fixed framework but a dynamic paradigm that must perpetually adapt to the rapid changes of the algorithmic era. The future depends on cultivating interdisciplinary, cross-cultural, and technological cooperation to maintain the relevance and effect of semiotic studies amidst rapid change. The synthesis of these contributions reveals that Semiotics 5.0 significantly redefines the conceptualization of literacy and meaning-making. It acknowledges that signals are no longer limited to verbal or visual forms but are disseminated via multimodal, computational, and mechanical processes. It recognizes that meaning is collaboratively created by people and algorithms, necessitating both interpretative and computational literacies. It amalgamates theoretical, methodological, and practical findings into a cohesive framework that enhances semiotic study, informs instruction, and reconciles disciplinary divisions.

Semiotics 5.0 is not only an enhancement of current semiotic frameworks but a paradigm change that redefines the parameters of semiotic investigation in the algorithmic era. The wider ramifications of this result are substantial. Semiotics 5.0 offers educators a framework for creating curriculum that cultivate multimodal and algorithmic literacies, equipping students to critically interact with hybrid texts and infrastructures. It provides researchers with a methodological framework that is both rigorous and inventive, adept at tackling the difficulties of digital communication. It offers conceptual instruments for technologists and engineers to develop systems attuned to the semiotic aspects of human-machine interaction. It provides a crucial perspective for examining the biases and disparities inherent in algorithmic systems, fostering more equitable engagement in digital environments. Semiotics 5.0 therefore arises as a framework of academic importance and social impact. The examination of Semiotics 5.0 illustrates that the algorithmic era need new approaches to understanding signals, meaning, and literacy. Semiotics 5.0 provides a comprehensive framework for comprehending and navigating the hybrid semiotic ecologies of modern society by merging multimodal analysis, algorithmic criticism, and interdisciplinary insights. Its theoretical enhancement, methodological advancement, ethical foundation, and pedagogical significance guarantee its continued influence on academic discourse and educational practices in the future. The primary conclusion is that understanding Semiotics 5.0 requires not just the interpretation of multimodal texts but also the analysis of the algorithms and infrastructures that regulate their circulation, visibility, and significance. Semiotics 5.0 fosters the development of competences that enhance the formation of societies that are technologically sophisticated, critically aware, morally accountable, and semiotically knowledgeable.

REFERENCES

Ali, S. I. (2025). Reinforcement learning for autonomous optimization in intelligent engineering. In Babulak, E. (Ed.), *AI-driven approaches for fully automated smart engineering* (pp. 313–344). IGI Global Scientific Publishing., DOI: 10.4018/979-8-3373-4839-1.ch011

Ali, S. I., ... (2023). Causal convolution employing Almeida–Pineda recurrent backpropagation for mobile network design. *ICTACT Journals, 2023(0460).* https://ictactjournals.in/paper/IJCT_Vol_14_Iss_4_Paper_10_3091_3096.pdf

Ali, S. I., Ravuri, H. K., Lakshmi, V. T., Ramya, A., Lavanya, K., & Bahade, S. (2024). The role of nanomaterials in the development of high-performance batteries. *Nanotechnology Perceptions*, *20*(S11). Advance online publication. DOI: 10.62441/nano-ntp.v20iS11.2098

Aragón, M. J. (2025). "They're like slash": Multimodality and embodied agency in digital literacy practices. *Reading Research Quarterly*. Advance online publication. DOI: 10.1002/rrq.585

Barthes, R. (1972). *Mythologies* (Lavers, A., Trans.). Hill and Wang. (Original work published 1957)

Bezemer, J., & Cowan, K. (2021). Exploring reading in social semiotics: Theory and methods. *Social Semiotics*, *31*(3), 331–348. DOI: 10.1080/10350330.2020.1810553

Carcamo, B., & Pino, B. (2025). Developing EFL students' multimodal literacy with the use of digital tools. *Asian-Pacific Journal of Second and Foreign Language Education*, *10*(22), 16. Advance online publication. DOI: 10.1186/s40862-025-00322-3

Cheung, K. K. C., Chai, C. S., & Lin, P. Y. (2025). Exploring students' multimodal representations of ideas about GenAI-science epistemic reading. *Journal of Science Education*. DOI: 10.1007/s10956-024-10182-0

de Saussure, F. (2011). *Course in General Linguistics* (P. Meisel & H. Saussy, Eds.; W. Baskin, Trans.). Columbia University Press. (Original work published 1916)

Kress, G. (2003). *Literacy in the new media age*. Routledge., DOI: 10.4324/9780203299234

Kress, G., & van Leeuwen, T. (2021). *Reading images: The grammar of visual design* (3rd ed.). Routledge., DOI: 10.4324/9781003099857

Lim, F. V., & Tan-Chia, L. (2023). Multimodal literacy learning with digital texts. In Lim, F. V., & Tan-Chia, L. (Eds.), *Designing learning for multimodal literacy* (pp. 1–18). Routledge., DOI: 10.4324/9781003198741

O'Halloran, K. L. (2023). Matter, meaning and semiotics: Exploring multimodal processes. *Visual Communication*, *33*(2), 123–140. DOI: 10.1177/14703572221128881

O'Halloran, K. L., Bateman, J. A., & Schmidt, K. H. (2017). *Multimodality: Foundations, research and analysis – A problem-oriented introduction*. de Gruyter Mouton. DOI: 10.1515/9783110479898

Pattanaik, B., Kumari, S. S., Kumar, C. K., Pattnaik, M., Ali, S. I., & Kumarasamy, M. (2023). An innovation of algebraic mathematical-based statistical analysis model for complex number theory. In *Proceedings of the 2023 International Conference on Disruptive Technologies (ICDT)* (pp. 94–99). IEEE. DOI: 10.1109/ICDT57929.2023.10151169

Smith, B. E., Pacheco, M. B., & Warrington, A. (2025). Multimodal composing with generative AI: Examining opportunities and challenges for literacy education. *Computers and Composition*, *68*, 102785. DOI: 10.1016/j.compcom.2024.102785

Srivastava, S. S., Ali, S. I., Srivastava, A. K., & Goswami, C. (2024). *Improving 5G network performance with MIMO technology using beamforming algorithm*. ICTACT Journal on Communication Technology., DOI: 10.21917/ijct.2024.0472

Srivastava, S. T. C., Sharmiladevi, D., Sugumar, D., Ali, S. I., Jones Mary, T. A., & Kumar, S. (2023). Using a smart wearable device monitoring the social distance in smart cities. In *2023 International Conference on Research Methodologies in Knowledge Management, Artificial Intelligence and Telecommunication Engineering (RMKMATE)* (pp. 1–5). IEEE. DOI: 10.1109/RMKMATE59243.2023.10369118

Suthar, B., & Ali, S. I. (2025). A survey on hand gesture sign language recognition with Arduino Leonardo. In *2025 International Conference on Computational, Communication and Information Technology (ICCCIT)* (pp. 111–115). IEEE. DOI: 10.1109/ICCCIT62592.2025.10927994

Chapter 11
AI and Multimodal Literacies in Cambodia:
Pathways of Positive Developmental Progress in Education and Society

Sovanna Huot
http://orcid.org/0009-0006-8335-442X
Department of Education, National Institute of Education (NIE), Phnom Penh, Cambodia

Sovanna Loch
http://orcid.org/0000-0002-1211-1248
Department of English, Nava Nalanda Mahavihara (Deemed to be University), Bihar, India

Chheangkhy Hok
http://orcid.org/0009-0000-6431-527X
Department of Khmer Literature, University of Heng Samrin Thbongkhmum, Thbongkhmum, Cambodia

ABSTRACT

This chapter reviews the role of AI and multimodal literacies in Cambodia's education systems as a means of promoting more sustainable and inclusive development. It reviews technologies; AI writing apps for translation and digital storytelling, reshape learning in schools, higher education, and the community education sector. The chapter focuses on Cambodia's attempts to integrate multimodal literacy into educational frameworks and reform initiatives, as well as the efforts toward combining education with creative and culturally sensitive and equitable frameworks.

DOI: 10.4018/979-8-3373-6986-0.ch011

The chapter also reviews the positive and negative aspects of AI in human capital development and regional integration. It especially emphasizes the challenges posed by infrastructure gaps, social exclusion, the digital divide, and the ethics of data management. The conclusion offers policy options addressing the need for culturally responsive pedagogy in teacher education. It seeks to position Cambodia as a regional frontrunner within ASEAN to demonstrate culturally responsive, innovation-based education reform.

INTRODUCTION

Cambodia is currently at a pivotal point in its national development plan using modernized education and digital transformation as its engines of inclusive growth. In the last decade, the Royal Government of Cambodia, through the Ministry of Education, Youth and Sport (MoEYS), sweeping educational reforms aimed at strengthening the country's human capital, digital literacy, and innovation-driven learning (MoEYS, 2024). The Education strategic plan 2024-2028 is a comprehensive reform of the Cambodian education system, as it strives to integrate technology into all areas of education, teaching, learning, and administration, using AI that is accessible and affordable to all, at any point in their lives.

UNESCO (2025) noted that among the few lower-middle-income countries in Southeast Asia that performed a national AI Readiness Assessment with a focus on ethical and inclusive AI is Cambodia. The country's policy framework of the recognition that AI is dual-edged in the case of sustainable education reform is commendable, and the same goes for RGC (2021b) for Cambodia digital government policy 2021–2035. where technology and innovation are the cornerstones of social progress and human resource competitiveness.

Although Cambodia is trying to modernize its digital education system, integrating Artificial Intelligence (AI) makes it challenging, as driving innovation reform creates more cultural, linguistic, and infrastructural inequities, especially when not focused on equitable implementation. Luckin and Holmes (2016) explain that in educational settings, Artificial Intelligence is a double-edged sword; it provides personalization, and amplifies divides, while Holmes et al. (2019) argue that AI is not a neutral tool, but rather, reshapes pedagogy and epistemic authority. In Cambodia, where Khmer literacy is entrenched in the Buddhist oral and visual traditions (Huot & Chheang, 2025), the use of English-based AI systems is a critical adoption that provides avenues for cultural and epistemic marginalization (Fricker, 2007). Therefore, it is essential for Cambodia's AI reform to be recognized as a struggle for cultural and inclusive development rather than solely technological advancement (UNESCO, 2021, 2025).

Huot and Loch (2025b) mention that the changes in the digital economy have been inconsistent and uneven. Even as Cambodia reaches an internet penetration rate of over fifty-five percent, there are still large gaps split by geography, income, and gender, limiting the digital economy's benefits to everyone. The inadequate infrastructure is a trademark of rural schools. The issues include poor and unreliable internet, limited digital devices, and untrained teachers (Huot & Loch, 2025b; Swisscontact, 2020). Selwyn (2021) articulates the digital reproduction of inequality using rural schools. The educational technology that is meant to reduce the unnecessary gaps in the equality of learning opportunities ends up widening the gaps in many rural schools.

Educational reformers in Cambodia have started to view artificial intelligence (AI) as part of a larger digital transformation, especially with the changes it is bringing to Cambodia's education system (Huot & Loch, 2025a, 2025b). This leads to the question of how we can implement AI in education in a way that develops multimodal literacies (Jewitt, 2009; Kress, 2009), a form of meaning-making that includes the text, and other forms like visual, sounds, movement, and digital channels. This focus connects with the digital focus combined with the historical and cultural elements in Cambodia's educational vision. Artificial intelligence is changing the landscape of reading, writing, and learning. Gee (2003) states that literacy in the 21st century means quite a lot more than the ability to read and write. It also includes semiotic agility the capacity to interpret and communicate meaning through multiple kinds of modalities, languages, and technologies. Following this perspective, Jewitt (2005) argues that the development of generative AI technologies, such as large language models and image generators, marks the beginning of a new phase in literacy as post-textual. In this new phase, learners are expected to go beyond text comprehension to critically engage with and make sense of complex, algorithmically generated, multiple forms of representation.

Luckin and Holmes (2016) describe artificial intelligence in education as a double-edged sword, presenting the potential for personalization, creativity, and removing barriers to learning, while also creating challenges in the areas of authorship, epistemic confidence, and cognitive ownership. Holmes et al. (2019) suggest a similar position when they maintain that the use of educational technologies, like artificial intelligence (AI), is redefining the teacher's role as a provider of information to that of an orchestrator of different learning modalities. The intersection of literacy, AI, and education also requires the development, evaluation, and appropriate use of AI-generated multimodal materials.

The global debates AI literacy has garnered the most attention within the field. For Ng et al. (2021), an AI literate person comprehends AI systems. Engagement with the processes of algorithms, evaluation of the outputs of algorithms, and processing the implications of such outputs involves the complexity of ethics. Algorithmic outputs and algorithmic processes must be understood critically. They contend that with respect to the contemporary global landscape, the possession of such critical understanding needs to be seen as an entitlement. Long and Magerko (2020) suggest that to enable learners to appreciate the value of Artificial Intelligence (AI), there is a need to have a combination of conceptual knowledge and procedural knowledge vis-a-vis the processes of AI. The latest bibliometric studies provide evidence that an unprecedented increase in the volume of academic literature in the field is being recorded. From 2014 to 2024, Yang et al. (2025) recorded the most significant increase in articles globally focusing on AI literacy, with the education sector being the most active. The authors noted that new publications represent a change of emphasis from digital literacy (the skill of utilizing technologies) to AI-augmented multimodal literacy (the ability to engage meaningfully with intelligent systems across multiple modalities).

The transformational power of AI in writing and literacy practices is already being felt across the globe. Writing support programs, translation tools, and visual assistants are being used by students to help them plan, draft, and revise their multimodal texts (Kafa, 2025). Describing students as co-authors with algorithms, because of the new ethical and creative challenges they have to navigate, was made by Knox (2020) in similar contexts. The swift changes in the digital world are recognized by OECD (2023) and recommends that schools include computational and other emerging literacies as part of the foundational curriculum. This expanding global literacy in AI has also opened prospects for Cambodia. The rapid development of AI literacies means that Cambodia has an even greater need to ensure that the integration of technology into teaching and learning is not based on a Western colonialist digital pedagogy, but one that is relevant, and a digital pedagogy that is culturally, socio-linguistically, and pedagogically diverse and inclusive. The purpose of this chapter is to purposefully navigate the convergence of artificial intelligence and multimodal literacies in the context of Cambodia. In relation to this, the chapter sets out to accomplish the following objectives:

1. To understand and locate the scholarship on AI and multimodal literacies to determine the scope of possible adaptations of the global frameworks and practices with respect to Cambodia's sociocultural and educational context.
2. To theorize the structural, pedagogical, and moral implications of the incorporation of AI into the teaching of literacy, particularly within a context of digital disparity and linguistic diversity.
3. Providing contextually relevant strategies and policy frameworks that integrate AI adoption with Cambodia's evolving developmental priorities, including the formation of human capital, social innovation, and equal access to education.

By pursuing these objectives, the chapter positions itself at the crossroads between cultural sustainability and technological innovation. It argues that the effective infusion of AI in the education of Cambodia should not be viewed solely as a process of engineering, but also as a profound literacy initiative that reshapes the construction and expression of understanding, innovation, and self.

MULTIMODAL LITERACIES IN CAMBODIAN EDUCATION

Conceptual Overview

The epistemic shift in the twenty-first century has been characterized by the movement from print-centric literacies towards multimodal literacies (Cope & Kalantzis, 2020; Kress, 2009). The last couple of decades have seen a transformation in the creation, communication, and consumption of knowledge. Multimodal literacy, the ability to construct and make sense of meaning, includes the linguistic, visual, auditory, gestural, spatial, and even algorithmic modes of communication. As Kress (2009) observes, due to the distribution of meaning across various forms of media, images, and sounds and not solely written texts, every single communicative act in contemporary society is multimodal. In the same vein, Jewitt (2009) argues that today's literacy involves a collection of meaning-making processes that intertwine among and across social and technological frameworks. In educational environments, a radical reconstruction of pedagogy is necessitated by this conceptual shift.

Educators are, therefore, required to move from literacy of the page to the literacy of the screen, meaning that students are required to advance from basic word decoding to reading and writing hypertext, pictorial, infographic and other forms of interactive media (Cope & Kalantzis, 2020). This reconceptualization corresponds to the emphasis of UNESCO (2023) on multiliteracies, which captures the new, pluralistic framework of literacy that integrates a pedagogy of difference, the use of multiple languages, digital literacy, and critical pedagogy. The central argument of the paper is that to promote critical dimensions of the 21st century skills: creativity, collaboration, critical thinking, and communication, educators must consider the development of students' multimodal literacy.

In the case of Cambodia, this theoretical development coincides with the country's rapid digital transformation and reformist educational agenda. Cambodian schools, universities, and communities are grappling with the dual challenges of modernisation and the need to preserve ways of life. The Cambodian Ministry of Education, Youth, and Sport (MoEYS, 2024) identifies digital literacy and multimodal competence as fundamental to the development of the country's human capital. Yet, as Chheang and Huot (2025) point out, Cambodia's circumstances are particularly challenging: underdeveloped infrastructure, unequal digital divides, and an enduring cultural preference for traditional forms of learning that are Buddhist in origin, and that rely on memorisation and recitation. The process of promoting multimodal literacy in Cambodia involves much more than the creative application of technology. It entails a necessary and critical reconceptualization of literacy that can be aligned with the country's heteroglossia (linguistic), multicultural, and multi-sub, (educational) contextual frameworks (Huot & Hok, 2025).

In a world of rapidly developing AI technology, how students understand and create content using technology and different literacies is rapidly evolving as well. Automated systems such as translation, captions, summaries, and image generation compel students to understand how to ethically and critically use tools generated by machines to create meaning and pattern. Holmes et al. (2019) argue the importance of this literacy, however, it is Jewitt (2005) who assert that AI brings a new dimension to literacy. It is no longer enough to understand how to create and manipulate different modes, but it is also necessary to interact and work with meaning-making systems. Given that Cambodia is developing its educational policies utilizing AI tools, it becomes a hotbed for examining the importance of literacy created with the help of Artificial Intelligence.

Cultural and Linguistic Dimensions

Considering Cambodia's cultural and linguistic ecosystem is vital for any analysis of multimodal literacy. The Khmer language is an integral part of and one of the oldest continuous scripts in Southeast Asia. It is vital to the nation's identity, spirituality, and knowledge systems. Its writing system is aesthetically beautiful and composed of layered syllable structures. It reflects the Khmer people's unique oral-visual traditions. Huot and Chheang (2025) indicated that Khmer quietly advanced through the recitative literacy of the Buddhist monastic education system, where recitation, manuscript animation, and illustrations coactive, in a supportive, respectful, and multimodal pedagogy long before the term multimodal was coined.

The development of new forms of cultural expression in digital contexts has been made possible by the Khmer script's digitization, which was completed because of the Unicode standardization and the national ICT policies construction. Chheang and Huot (2025) state that this can be described as a reassertion of linguistic sovereignty as it gives Khmer speakers the ability to create and share digital content in the Khmer language. Furthermore, the sociolinguistics studies of Hornberger and Skilton-Sylvester (2000) demonstrate Cambodia's unique multilingualism because of the country's English, French, Chinese, and regional language contacts. This can be observed in classrooms and social media and in informal contexts where teachers and students use a variety of linguistic codes along with visual and digital elements to construct meaning. The narratives and symbolic traditions of Cambodia must intertwine with multimodal literacies.

For centuries, classical art forms such as dance, theatre, shadow puppetry, and mural storytelling, have exemplified multimodal communication with gesture, costume, sound, and movement. Cambodia's performative literacies create an indigenous foundation towards developing digital multimodal literacies. As Ziguras (2001) says, Cultural Continuity in Education is the preservation of traditional expressions and the reinterpretation of those art forms using new digital technologies. In Cambodia, educators use local cultural motifs to teach digital and visual literacy, such as using Buddhist stories or Reamker (Cambodian Ramayana) narratives for digital storytelling and moral education (Huot, 2025b).

One example of multimodal literacy that is culturally responsive is in Khmer classrooms, where teachers combine contemporary digital storytelling and other new media with traditional oral narratives. Buckingham (2015) mentioned that digital literacy to be effective, it must be relevant to learners lived experiences. In this sense, Cambodian learners digitally storyboard and retell episodes of the Reamker, incorporating Khmer texts, audio, and images of temples. As Jewitt (2009) explains, such practices are examples of semiotic orchestration, in which participants draw upon multiple modes to construct meaning. In this regard, Huot and Chheang (2025) also recognize the multimodality of Cambodian literacy in the dual practices of monastic recitation and illustration, which also demonstrates the point that digital innovation, especially in education, is at its most effective when it is rooted in local cultural practices (Ziguras, 2001).

The identity and inclusivity aspects of the cultural dimension of multimodality are intertwined. As Buckingham (2015) states, for digital literacy to be meaningful and impactful, it must connect with the lived experiences, cultures, and languages of the learners. This has been the case in Cambodia, where the use of Khmer and English multimodal resources in bilingual education has helped learners articulate their local identity and constructed global citizenship.

These new hybrid pedagogies are in accordance with UNESCO (2021) culturally responsive digital education, which advocates the use of Indigenous technologies and systems.

Lastly, the intersection of Cambodia's multimodal literacy, linguistics, and culture evokes issues of equity. Cambodian educational policy, therefore, must embrace the complexity of constructing multimodal literacies that incorporate global frameworks while remaining locally relevant, particularly in relation to strategies that drive the preservation of culture, the technology of language, and the education of teachers.

Practical Illustrations

The integration of multimodal literacy principles in Cambodia's educational landscape is becoming more evident across schools, universities, and community projects. There is a conscious attempt at primary and secondary levels, to examine the use of multimodal, (visual, auditory). and (kinesthetic) approaches. In the MoEYS (2024), pilot project in Kampong Cham province, learners created digital Khmer illustrated storybooks and voice-recorded and text-captioned environmental folktales. Teachers noted that these activities increased learners' involvement, understanding, and confidence in expression, particularly among those who had difficulties with traditional text-based teaching methods. In the same way, several private and NGO-supported schools in Phnom Penh have begun blended learning initiatives in which students use mobile applications to record speeches, create video diaries, and design infographics that summarize scientific ideas. In these practices, however, Jewitt (2009) describes meaning orchestration, the use of diverse semiotic resources to collaboratively build understanding.

Cambodian universities experiment with multimodal integration in teaching and learning. For example, students in a digital communications course at Royal University of Phnom Penh (RUPP) use AI translation and visualization tools to analyze texts in different languages and create multimodal research portfolios (RUPP, 2023). At University of Puthisastra, students use AI writing assistants and presentation design tools that guide them in creating integrated text and visuals, as well as data narratives. Students at the National Institute of Education's Pre-Service Education Program practice design-based pedagogy, where rubrics for multi-modal assessment are created with emphasis on students' creativity and the responsible, constructive, and equitable use of digital tools. As noted by Lim and Querol-Julián (2024), these efforts are significant in the context of Southeast Asia after the pandemic, when the shift to fully online and hybrid forms of education has made digital and visual communication primary.

Within the community and NGO context, multimodal literacy practices can be seen as empowering and inclusive. Open Learning Cambodia and Women in Tech Cambodia have started using AI training modules tailored to the needs of marginalized learners, incorporating local storytelling with digital scoping (Huot, 2025a). Community training workshops, for instance, empower women and youth to use mobile artificial intelligence (AI) editing tools to create podcasts and micro-documentaries. Such initiatives are what Mills (2015) refers to as critical multimodal literacy, which combines constructive, active citizenship, and advocacy for social justice. In remote regions, some NGOs have used AI to design appropriate, offline, multi-language educational resources for learners with little or no internet.

The potential of Transformative Pedagogies Innovation framed within the Cambodian sociocultural context also reveals the lack of teacher training on the integration of different modes of teaching, the inadequate teaching and learning support, and the need for localized digital resources. However, as Kress (2009) suggests, the aspiration of multimodal education is not to achieve the same end, but rather to achieve design diversity, the ability of learners to draw on the semiotic resources available to them to construct meaning in ways that are relevant to their immediate context and accessible to wider audiences. This is certainly the case for Cambodia and its emerging practices in the use of multimodal resources. It is testimony to the country's rich effort to balance the old and the new for purposeful, equitable, and sustainable education, as illustrated in Figure 1.

Figure 1.

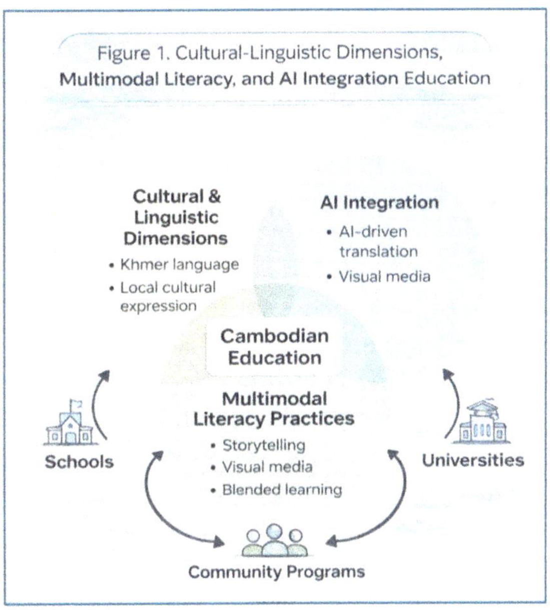

AI INTEGRATION AND EDUCATIONAL REFORM

The way educators teach and assess learners is being transformed in Cambodia due to the integration of AI in educational technologies. AI is being utilized in support of adaptive learning, writing, translation, and formative assessments in formal education. Smart EduTech Cambodia and Sabaicode AI are companies that have built AI-based tools which evaluate and provide feedback on students' writing and adapt teaching materials to different levels of students. These tools are examples of what Luckin's (2018) refers to as intelligent tutoring systems, which educational technology systems that provide personalized learning and data analysis and, therefore, mimic some aspects of human teaching.

AI-integrated programs are fostering effective and inclusive means of communication in the teaching of writing and language. Grammarly, ChatGPT, and Microsoft Copilot are supporting writing instruction in grammar, structure, and constituent elements of an argument in English language instruction in higher education and international schools (Huot & Tep, 2025). According to Kafa (2025), these resources help develop linguistic and meta-cognitive skills, as students learn to analyse and assess the value of the recommendations made by the AI. In the teaching of the Khmer language, locally developed academic and tech partnerships, such as AI4Khmer and Khmer NLP, are improving Khmer digital resources by transforming text recognition, spell checking, and machine translation.

AI's implementation in Cambodia's education systems show promises in visual learning, specifically tools that aid both comprehension and creativity such as Canva, DALL·E, and Piktochart Edu. With such tools, students visualize their learning through graphics, infographics, and videos, and present their learning using various modes (text, image, and data). Such activities help students build on their understanding of complex ideas and their multimodal literacy. Holmes et al. (2019) explain that in education, AI's potential is not only in automating the delivery of the content but rather in amplifying human creativity and reflective learning through the different modes of presentation. AI tools such as Kagan EduAI and ClassPoint Smart Analytics serve as analytics for educators that collect data on student learning gaps and adjust pacing of instruction. This way, classrooms become agile ecosystems.

The authors, Huot and Loch (2025b) describe how inequality exists in the application of AI in education in Cambodia. Rural educational institutions such as schools and universities lack the proper AI infrastructure, training, and tools, as opposed to their urban counterparts, which possess such resources. The aim, therefore, is to use AI to address the inequities in the educational system, and not to further the gaps. The objective, then, is to integrate AI to close, rather than widen, the gap in education inequities. The rapid expansion of digital learning environments and AI-enabled applications has begun to transform Cambodian classrooms. Digital Learning Cambodia and E-School Cambodia, at the primary and secondary levels, use AI to support differentiated learning through adaptive quizzes, voice learning, and multimedia assessments. Teachers use AI to generate content and customize learning materials, as well as to translate lesson plans into different languages and adapt them to different visual formats for students at different literacy levels. Such innovations demonstrate a departure from mass instruction toward mass customization (Cope & Kalantzis, 2020). In this educational system, attributes of flexibility, learner centeredness, and multiple modalities apply to educational design.

The Royal University of Phnom Penh (RUPP) and the Institute of Technology of Cambodia (ITC) are two of the largest higher education institutions in Cambodia, and they are pioneering the use of AI-assisted research tools, such as AI for Literature Reviews, Plagiarism Detection, and Data Mapping. Cambodian universities' use of Natural Language Processing (NLP) has resulted in the rapid editing of large quantities of texts and enhancements in the translation of academic texts from English to Khmer. This, in turn, has enhanced the availability of academic content to a wider audience. For example, AI-powered translation tools have been utilized to eliminate the educational content access barriers that have previously existed in remote and rural areas of Cambodia. The use of AI in education in Cambodia is a case of what UNESCO (2025) describes as technological leapfrogging and the use of digital tools to address the persistent challenges posed by poorly developed infrastructure and limited resources.

The use of AI powered multimodal tools in cross cultural and cross linguistic is commendable also in other areas. Google Lens Translate, VoiceThread, and Kaizen AI Classroom merge the visual, auditory, and text modalities. These tools enable more equitable participation of students with learning disabilities and students with language barriers. For example, captioning devices are standard assistive technology used for students with hearing impairments. Text-to-speech technology has been used to create Khmer education materials for students who are visually impaired. Fostering equitable participation and meaning-making through multimodal technologies and inclusive pedagogy will help in bridging the digital divide, albeit with the digital innovations always carrying some ethical and pedagogical issues, as Lim and Querol-Julián (2024) support this position. Students may lose the ability to think critically and write because they rely too much on the tools to generate materials (Knox, 2020). Cambodian educators must use the benefits of AI while also teaching students digital discernment, the ability to understand and explain how to interact with ai, critique ai, and create along with ai. The balance of efficiency and integrity of teaching is the primary concern with the digital transformation of the country.

The Cambodian government has invested considerable time and effort into policies that facilitate the integration of artificial intelligence (AI) into the Cambodian education sector. MoEYS (2024), Education strategic plan 2024-2028, positions innovation as the primary focus of educational policy reform and its integration into education. It also emphasizes equity, innovativeness, and the preservation of culture. Its goals include establishing an ecosystem where AI facilitates teaching and learning, supports teachers in their professional development, and advances curriculum reform. As a result, it also intends to assist teachers and students in underprivileged regions to attain equitable learning. Using inclusive pedagogy based on culturally responsive digital technologies, coupled with appropriate digitally inclusive practices, MoEYS (2024) reinforces the significance of AI in the Cambodian education system in evolving the youth of Cambodia to be a global knowledge economy contributor, while preserving the culture.

The Digital Economy and Society Policy Framework 2021-2035 RGC (2021b) along with the Cambodia 4.0 Strategy both aim to position Cambodia as a regional leader in the technological innovation and creative industries. They also span over the Cambodia government's primary policies regarding the use of AI in education and the development of human capital. Together with their global partners through educational development assistance programs (i.e. UNICEF, Asian Development Bank, and UNESCO), the Cambodia Government has developed educational policies that address the use of AI, digital citizenship, and teacher training. Cambodia's use of AI in education is cited by UNESCO (2025) in the AI Readiness Assessment Reports. However, Cambodia's limited connectivity, infrastructure, and the absence of comprehensive, sustainable policies for educational AI are considerable obstacles. Alongside the Government of Cambodia, universities and teacher training colleges are updating curricula to align with the newly established national AI education priorities.

Based on the RGC (2021a, 2021b) Cambodia digital economy and society policy framework (2021–2035) and Cambodia digital government policy 2021–2035, the primary focus on Artificial Intelligence will be taught alongside Digital Ethics and Multimodal Education, which will be regarded as cross-cutting competencies. On the other hand, the Smart Axiata Digital Education Program and other collaborations between the public sector and private tech companies are facilitating Artificial Intelligence (AI)-driven research, hackathons, and co-creation of curricula. These collaborations exemplify the triple-helix model of innovation articulated by Holmes et al. (2019), meaning the integrated and co-evolved roles of academia, public sector, and private sector, to develop a dynamic and sustainable ecosystem for education.

As Huot and Such (2025) observe, a successful policy outcome is contingent upon the range of systemic inequities and localized barriers that need to be addressed. They highlight the insufficient teacher training, patchy and inconsistent monitoring, and the overall greater risk of widening the digital divide between urban and rural educational institutions. Even more so, the cultural adaptation of AI to the Khmer language and the ethical and epistemological frameworks of the Khmer people is a critical area of reform that is still insufficiently addressed (Huot & Hok, 2025). Without such needed improvements, Cambodia's adoption of AI in the educational sector will be a case of advanced technology without balances in cultural and contextual considerations.

Still, there are rural–urban disparities regarding the adoption of AI in Cambodia. While urban institutions have better infrastructure, partnerships, and resources to experiment, rural provinces are limited by poor connectivity, inadequate teacher training, and few resources related to AI (Huot & Loch, 2025b). Selwyn (2021) argues that such inequalities are driven by the technology itself, which creates a dual-speed education system where some students progress faster than others.

Because of this, the first focus of investments should be rural areas, inclusive of Khmer language materials, plus equitable and inclusive AI resource training, so that AI promotes equity and prevents digital divides (UNESCO, 2025). With Cambodia's educational AI systems, the incorporation of AI will go beyond mere technological advancement. Incorporating AI requires changes in pedagogy, communication, and policies. Systems such as adaptive learning, automated translation, and other AI tools will impact and transform levels of knowledge. Concurrently, innovative, flexible, and culturally responsive educational frameworks are being prioritized in national policies and institutional reforms.

However, the challenge remains. Cambodia still needs to ensure that AI is a bridge, and not a barrier; an access point to learning that is also respectful of users' language and culture (Huot & Loch, 2025b). When used responsibly, AI can help transform Cambodia's classrooms into places of creativity, inclusiveness innovation, and the fusion of technology and traditions to create the future of learning, as depicted in Table 1.

Table 1.

Dimension	Description	Key Examples
AI in Teaching and Learning	AI is being applied in adaptive learning, writing assistance, translation, and visualization tools. It supports personalized learning, automated assessment, and interactive feedback in classrooms.	Sabaicode AI, Smart EduTech Cambodia, Grammarly, ChatGPT, KhmerNLP, AI4Khmer, Canva AI, DALL·E, Piktochart Edu.
Digital Innovations in Classrooms	AI-driven platforms and educational software are enabling multimodal learning, real-time analytics, and translation-based inclusivity. These tools are transforming pedagogy and bridging linguistic barriers.	Digital Learning Cambodia, E-School Cambodia, RUPP AI Research Tools, ITC NLP Systems, VoiceThread, Kaizen AI Classroom, Google Lens Translate.
Policy Context and Institutional Reform	National policies and institutional strategies promote AI integration in education through capacity-building, ethical guidelines, and partnerships with international organizations. Focuses on inclusive, culturally grounded AI deployment.	MoEYS Policy on Digital Education (2023–2030), Digital Economy and Society Policy (2021–2035), Cambodia 4.0 Strategy, UNESCO AI Readiness Report (2025), Smart Axiata Digital Education Program.

PATHWAYS OF POSITIVE DEVELOPMENTAL PROGRESS

The intersection of multimodal literacy and the development of human capital in Cambodia illustrates the country's effort to move away from a labour-based economy and towards a knowledge-based economy. As stated in the Royal Government of Cambodia's (RGC, 2021a) Digital Economy and Society Policy Framework (2021–2035), the ideal workforce of the future will be skilled and will possess digital, critical, and communicative competencies, which are the components of multimodal literacy. Multimodal literacy, as defined by Cope and Kalantzis (2020), entails being able to decipher and construct meaning in and from various forms of communication. It allows learners to move beyond traditional education-based economies and to participate in knowledge-based economies, particularly those that value creativity, interpretation, and collaboration.

The AI-related skills in education and the AI-related skills in industry in Cambodia are developing. Cambodia is embedding AI in its curriculum. Education providers are ITC and RUPP. They are teaching data analytics, digital storytelling, and algorithmic thinking. Chheang and Huot (2025) state that these activities help improve students' semiotic agility in a variety of professional contexts. This practice resonates with UNESCO (2023) advocacy for AI education that is human-centred, where technological skills and moral reasoning, cross-cultural empathy, and civic social responsibility are integrated.

In addition, AI multimodal education reinforces and strengthens Cambodia's ability to provide lifelong learning, as it is an indispensable component of the national human capital plans. Mobile learning apps, virtual simulations, and translation tools enable undisturbed and flexible learning for students in distant locations. This creates an equitable framework of skills development that eliminates the urban-rural gap. In this regard, the literacy of the education system and the development of the individual, through the empowerment of the individual, are linked to the global competitiveness of the nation. Strengthening AI-assisted literacy being applied to multiple modes also promotes the development of democracy, social cohesion, and cultural creativity. Jenkins and Ito (2016) explain that multimodal literacy fosters a participatory culture, where people feel they can speak, collaborate, and interact.

In Cambodia, where people have traditionally been less socially active due to a lack of information, digitally enabled and multimodal literacies are a means for increased social participation. Speech-to-text and AI translation technologies facilitate seamless communication between government and citizens, improving access and transparency to government information. Young Cambodians are culturally defining themselves using TikTok, Facebook Reels, YouTube Shorts, and other forms of digital communication. The platforms, paired with AI-assisted editing and captioning tools, allow them to combine global, transnational visual cultures with

Khmer cultural aesthetic forms in the making of their own visual culture. As Lim and Querol-Julián (2024) describe it, this kind of digital hybridity promotes self- cultural confidence and the global culture. Furthermore, the AI enhanced applications for creative expression through storytelling, digital art, and editing, such as Runway ML and Canva AI Art Generator, empower Cambodians, including youth, to digitally recreate apsara iconography, Buddhist symbols, and other traditional motifs. This blend of the old with the new exemplifies the unique ability of multi-modal literacy to fuse the past and the present through the preservation of cultural heritage.

The renewed application of AI-based EdTech to civic education is yet another example. The use of AI-powered tools for translation and visualization to create infographics on climate change, public health, and human rights advocacy are the works of the Cambodia Open Development NGO and the Cambodian Center for Independent Media. These works have gained the ability to facilitate the analysis of the target audience, and particularly the youth, on complex social problems. The combination of culturally adaptive AI and digital tools to create infographics enables the audience to evaluate their level of social awareness and engagement, improving the quality of citizenship in Cambodia and the country's inclusive and sustainable development. The heart of Cambodia's multimodal literacy movement lies in community-based initiatives from NGOs, local educationalists, and social enterprises in rural and marginalised settings. For example, grassroots initiatives combining AI and culturally responsive pedagogy are praiseworthy. The Women in Tech Cambodia initiative and SHE Investments, for instance, conduct AI augmented digital storytelling workshops where participants are trained to communicate business ideas using video narratives, visual data, and multilingual online marketing. These workshops combine digital economic participation with multimodal literacy, thus empowering women economically.

The Open Learning Cambodia Project also employed AI in the translation and text-to-speech services to extend literacy to adults with no schooling and members of ethnic minority groups. The educational resources that these initiatives have developed in spoken Khmer and indigenous dialects mitigate the challenges of limited literacy and translation. For Syed and Özbilgin (2009) such initiatives exemplify the intersectional equity frameworks of practice where the incorporation of technology is intentionally designed to achieve gender, language, and social equity together with the provision of ICT for economic empowerment.

My Library Cambodia and other grassroots digital libraries have begun using AI systems for search and recommendation functions to personalize reading resources for individual learners. In these community contexts, learners practice multimodal literacy by digitally recording and narrating oral histories, documenting local crafts, and translating folk songs into digital formats. As Nash et al. (2026) note, these community-based methods help demonstrate how, when integrated locally, technology repositions marginalized learners from being only consumers of information to being active producers of culturally valuable information. These projects also cultivate community resilience. The ability to assess and create multimodal resources provides tools for civic engagement and increased activism. Developed locally, AI solutions, such as predictive analytics for crop monitoring and mapping for disaster response, showcase the potential of localized AI. Cambodia's digital transformation AI-based problem-solving tools empower communities and facilitate the digital integration of all communities. Among other ASEAN countries, Cambodia's advancements in AI and multimodal literacy corresponds with the region's increasing digital integration. The ASEAN Declaration on Digital Literacy, ASEAN Secretariat (2022) underscores the region's efforts towards an inclusive, innovative, and digitally literate Southeast Asia. In this regard, Cambodia's initiatives hold significant importance at both national and regional levels.

In collaboration with other ASEAN countries, Cambodian educators can participate in partnerships for AI in education hosted by the Southeast Asian Ministers of Education Organization (SEAMEO) and ASEAN University Network (AUN). Such partnerships foster the regional exchange of AI ethics, digital pedagogy, and multimodal learning design. For example, Cambodian and Thai universities conducted collaborative workshops on using AI in language translation for understanding regional research. Simultaneous to this, Cambodia's role in ASEAN's educational integration underscored the positive role in fostering the appreciation of cultural and linguistic diversity (ASEAN, 2020). Cambodia's Khmer language AI tools in the regional databases are examples of the ASEA efforts to include local knowledge systems in the overall digital ecosystem of ASEAN. Pascua-Valenzuela (2025) suggested that ASEAN's digital literacy frameworks should advocate the intersection of technological standardization not devoid of cultural pluralism.

Cambodia's strategy for integrating AI with culture, inclusiveness, ethics, and heritage exhibits exemplary practice within ASEAN for harmonizing innovation and identity. The ascendance of AI-enhanced multimodal literacy as a fundamental driver of progress in Cambodia crosses all boundaries of education, economic and social development, and regional diplomacy. It builds and diversifies human capital, fosters social inclusion via community participation, reinvigorates civic engagement through the expression of arts, and positions Cambodia in the digital ecosystem of ASEAN. The new reality, however, is that sustainability of Cambodia's development will be determined by the innovation and equity, modernity and tradition, automation and agency dichotomies. When guided by culturally responsive and inclusive principles, AI and multimodal literacy can become the foundation for Cambodia's transformation into a dynamic, creative, and knowledge-based society, as seen in the Table 2.

Table 2.

Dimension	Description	Key Examples
Human Capital Development	AI-enhanced multimodal literacy supports national workforce readiness and skill diversification. Learners develop digital, creative, and communicative competencies essential for Cambodia's transition toward a knowledge-based economy.	Integration of AI tools in higher education (RUPP, ITC); use of mobile learning apps; MoEYS Digital Education Policy 2023–2030.
Societal Benefits	Multimodal literacy fosters civic participation, intercultural communication, and creative expression. It enhances inclusivity and democratizes information through AI translation and visual storytelling.	Digital storytelling using Canva AI and Runway ML; multimedia civic campaigns by Open Development Cambodia; AI-assisted public engagement tools.
Community Initiatives	Grassroots organizations and NGOs leverage AI for literacy promotion, entrepreneurship training, and social inclusion. Projects emphasize gender equity and accessibility for marginalized groups.	Women in Tech Cambodia, SHE Investments, Open Learning Cambodia, MyLibrary Cambodia – use of AI for storytelling, translation, and capacity-building.
ASEAN Dimension	Cambodia contributes to regional digital literacy integration through ASEAN collaborations focused on AI ethics, cultural preservation, and innovation.	ASEAN Digital Masterplan 2025; SEAMEO and AUN collaborations; joint AI-assisted education programs between Cambodia and Thailand.

CHALLENGES AND ETHICAL CONSIDERATIONS

Rural Cambodia has limited and unequal digital education infrastructure. While, (RGC, 2021b), the Digital Economy and Society Policy Framework (2021–2035), and (RGC, 2022), the Digital Education Policy (2022–2035) seek to change this, inequities prevail across geography and rural teacher digital readiness. (World Bank, 2023) data shows that rural internet access lags well behind urban access; only fifty-two percent of rural households have reliable internet compared to eighty-eight percent of urban households. The constraints surrounding rural engagement in new opportunities for AI learning are evident. Rural participation in emerging AI learning opportunities is effectively limited.

The educational field in Cambodia suffers from digital access inequity, resulting in inequitable access to digital literacy, and in some cases, digital illiteracy. In rural areas, gaps in training on digital pedagogy and the use of AI tools for teaching, contribute to the inequitable use of digital pedagogy and AI tools in the education field. Huot and Tep (2025) point out that, AI inclusion, without infrastructural equity, runs the risk of deepening the digital divide rather than closing it. Furthermore, the lack of digital devices and affordable education resources further cements the socioeconomic divides in rural areas. Educational equity is further shattered as economically disadvantaged students lack the internet or digital devices needed to participate in higher-order learning activities. It is crucial to stress that, in a full sense, the digital divide also entails an ethical, social, and infrastructural problem. Broadband accessibility, digital educator training, and public and private collaborations, especially with telecom companies, must deal with the constructive synthesis of AI and education: the potential deepening of the education divide. Infrastructure with intent describes the pattern of digital resource provisioning in less privileged contexts. It refers to equity, local relevance, and sustainable, adaptive resource capacity building (UNESCO, 2025).

Lack of cultural and linguistic sensitivity in the rapidly digitized teaching and learning environments, especially in the AI-embedded environments, is a challenge. The rich, multi-faceted, and multi-layered Cambodian culture located in the Khmer language, Buddhism, and traditional arts is in danger of being lost with the hegemonic and dominating global AI-driven education systems. "Technological modernization must coexist with cultural continuity; otherwise, development becomes dislocated from identity," as Fahruddiana (2025) points out. The Cambodian classroom, especially the Khmer language classrooms, is dominated and even in the Western influenced and designed AI systems, the resources are designed to be English dominant in the linguistics and the underlying world views. There is often no place for Khmer expressions, visual arts, or traditional Cambodian cultures.

The Khmer language has yet to be fully digitized, despite the advancements with Khmer-NLP and Unicode Khmer. Khmer translation systems driven by AI have not accurately captured or translated the complexities of Khmer sentence structure, idioms, and culturally based metaphors, often resulting in absurd translations and culturally inappropriate outputs. This leads to concerns of epistemic injustice as the world's algorithms seem to dismiss the value of the local language and its accompanying cultural knowledge (Fricker, 2007).

Also, the cultural aspect goes further than the language and includes worldviews. In Cambodian classrooms, Buddhist ethics teach mindfulness, and ethics such as compassion and collective responsibility. Such values may differ from the logic of AI algorithms focused on productivity and efficiency. Thus, cultural sensitivity must inform the design of AI and the integration of AI into the curriculum. Using Khmer stories, and traditional paintings, and integrating traditional Cambodian arts with digital educational materials can be a way of making sure that the educational technology of the digital age is not a means of cultural erasure, but a means of cultural preservation. As Huot et al. (2025) write, Cambodia's educational future depends on technologies that speak the language of its people, literally and metaphorically.

The Cambodian educational system's adoption of AI carries ethical implications on top of the technical aspects that pertain to surveillance, control, and bias. The most pressing of these issues is of data privacy. As educational institutions continue to adopt online learning management systems, student data, including but not limited to, their academic records, behaviour records, and even biometric data, are collected and stored by foreign tech companies. Given the absence of adequate data protection laws, the data is unprotected and is prone to misuse, breach, and commercial exploitation. Another potential problem is known as algorithmic bias. Several AIs receive training based on a data set that fails to include the Southeast Asian region, resulting in a failure of representation and a lack of discrimination. For example, bias in AI translation tools may favor some urban dialects, ignore some languages altogether, and thus worsen the inequitable distribution of linguistic resources. Likewise, local contexts can reveal the sexism and racism embedded in image recognition systems (Buolamwini & Gebru, 2018). If unaddressed, this bias will further entrench systemic inequalities in Cambodia's digital learning environments.

The more we use AI to create content, the more complicated the ethics of education. Using AI tools like ChatGPT raises concerns of students substituting an authentic understanding of the world for an understanding of how to get the algorithms to work. This lack of understanding creates an erosion of critical thought, creativity, and problem solving, the very goals of critical multimodal literacies. AI, as Knox (2020) rightly states, may automate not only tasks, but thought itself, leading to epistemic complacency. This is why education in Cambodia must include an understanding of the ethics of AI, which includes understanding algorithms, and interacting with them in responsible and critical ways. The Ethical governance frameworks, like the UNESCO Recommendation on the Ethics of Artificial Intelligence (2021), provides Cambodia with a starting point. These governance guidelines display the beginnings of a relationship of trust between governance and the use of Artificial Intelligence in education. Perhaps the greatest ethical challenge of Cambodia's AI-driven educational reform is addressing digital inequity and ensuring that women, people in rural areas, language minorities, and people with disabilities can all equally reap the benefits of digital transformation (Huot & Hok, 2025). While the use of AI and the development of multimodal literacies help in democratizing the education sector, the prevailing social and historical hierarchies that exist in any community will continue to create barriers to equitable participation in education. This is why we must ensure that measures aimed at promoting inclusivity take centre stage in the design of any AI-driven educational reforms.

The gap in access to technology and tech-related education continues to persist. According to the International Labor Organization ILO (2021), only thirty-two percent of rural Cambodian women report feeling confident using digital tools while sixty percent of rural Cambodian men report feeling confident using digital tools. This gap signifies economic challenges and sociocultural attitudes that minimize women's participation in technology. Initiatives such as Women in Tech Cambodia and Digital Her Future are attempting to address these challenges through AI-based learning and mentorship. These programs are an example of what Eubanks (2018) calls data justice from below, where tech tools are used to empower rather than disempower marginalized communities.

Inaccessible AI tools, like voice and screen readers and other assistive technologies, hold potential but are not consistently used. The absence of Khmer as an interface and help language is a barrier to many digital services and tools. Indigenous people and ethnic minorities are often excluded from the digital educational tools that focus on English and standardized Khmer. Providing policies include design that are safe and constructive which digital world can be closed from these groups. Providing infrastructure, appropriate education that includes gender-sensitive curriculum, plain language (or appropriate language), and social dialogue are all part of the first steps in closing the gap. Huot and Such (2025) go as far as to suggest that the primary condition for true inclusivity in AI education is the redistribution of voice and agency rather than the mere distribution of devices. Camouflage and the AI and multimodal literacy in Cambodia are two sides of the same coin, progress on one side, and responsibility on the other. The limited social infrastructure, the risks of cultural homogenization, the lack of adequately responsive education, the risks of data exposure and social exclusion are all real and present dangers that will thwart the transformative potential of AI within education.

There is a need for Cambodia's ethical challenges to be firmed into policies. Digital inequity means rural inclusive infrastructure and teacher training; muddying of the linguistic streams means Khmer-centered AI and responsive curricula (Huot & Hok, 2025). UNESCO (2021) notes that the balancing of risks, such as the right to be forgotten, the right to know, and the absence of bias, with the use of local data, and the accountability of the designer is a necessary, but insufficient, measure to protect these rights. Cambodia runs the risk of treating AI purely as a tool and a means to improve technology rather than improve the literacy shift that Cambodia needs to embrace socially. The challenges do not mean that the potential of technology needs to be abandoned, especially with a focus on the central goals of equity, culture, and human dignity, which can provide a basis for innovation and justice. The challenge for Cambodia, on the other hand, is not just to embrace AI, but to determine its character. Everything, including algorithms, policies, and digital systems, should reflect the aspirations, values, and goals of the collective as per the illustration and summary in Table 3.

Table 3.

Dimension	Description	Examples
Infrastructure and Inequality	Persistent disparities in connectivity, device access, and digital literacy hinder equitable AI adoption. Rural schools often lack stable internet and trained teachers, creating an uneven digital learning environment.	Limited rural internet coverage; high cost of digital devices; lack of teacher training; urban-rural divide in AI implementation.
Cultural Sensitivity	Balancing technological modernization with the preservation of Khmer cultural identity and linguistic diversity. Global AI tools often lack cultural and linguistic adaptation to Khmer values.	KhmerNLP, AI4Khmer projects; inclusion of Buddhist ethics and local narratives in AI curricula; risk of cultural homogenization from English-centric AI tools.
Ethical Issues	Concerns about data privacy, algorithmic bias, and over-reliance on AI-generated content. AI must be governed through transparent and accountable frameworks to prevent misuse.	Student data vulnerability in cloud systems; bias in translation and recognition tools; UNESCO AI ethics guidelines as frameworks for responsible AI in education.
Inclusivity	Ensuring equitable access to AI-enhanced education for marginalized groups, including women, rural learners, and persons with disabilities. Emphasizes gender-responsive and accessible technology design.	Women in Tech Cambodia, SHE Investments, Open Learning Cambodia initiatives; text-to-speech and captioning tools for accessibility; localized Khmer AI learning applications.

CONCLUSION

There is a growing sense of hope for the future of digital literacy in Cambodia, as the ongoing expansion of AI-based multimodal literacy education signifies further advancement within the country's developing education system. However, the rapid change that new technologies bring to the Cambodia's educational landscape means that the country must be particularly careful in attempting to find a balanced approach to the impacts of innovation and the associated value of inclusivity, ethics, and preservation of culture. The promise of AI in literacy education is twofold: providing the means to transform learning through the democratization of education and interactive multimode that promotes creative self-expression; and, through the expansion of learning literacy resources, education accessibility, and educator creativity, the creation of transformative risks associated with inequity, sociocultural dissolution, and ungoverned fragmentation. The greatest challenge is to influence change to ensure that technology is used for the benefit of all.

The ongoing changes to education in Cambodia will require the incorporation of multimodal literacies across all levels of learning, formal and informal. There is a need for schools to teach multimodal (i.e. visual, textual, auditory and digital) literacies by embedding these in the national curricula, such that all learners will master the skills necessary for success in a technology-infused workforce. Furthermore, curricula should be designed in a manner that fosters critical thinking and creative problem solving, as well as ethical digital citizenship, to ensure that learners become responsible creators and collaborators rather than mere consumers of technology. Additionally, universities as a part of higher education need to become innovation hubs by implementing AI-driven pedagogy, fostering interdisciplinary collaboration, and supporting the co-creation of tools that incorporate local languages, cultures, and other contextual needs.

Building and sustaining these changes will require a robust approach to teacher professional development. Teachers' proficiency and adaptability with the tools will be essential for the successful implementation of AI-enhanced literacy initiatives. The provision of professional development for trainers and teacher advocacy, the establishment of digital skills mentorship programs, and the establishment of cooperative mentorship programs that pair experienced teachers with novices all contribute to increased educator competence and confidence.

Moreover, investment in Khmer language digital resources and culturally pertinent materials will ensure that technological advancement is aligned with the local culture. Systematic progress requires continued collaboration. Innovations in social justice and culture need to be rooted in coordinated efforts by policymakers, educators, and tech developers within a streamlined ecosystem. Responsible AI in education can be advanced through multi-stakeholder partnerships that include government ministries, universities, private tech companies, and civil society. Such partnerships have the potential to minimize the digital divide by developing inclusive and accessible infrastructures, ethically designed AI, and safe digital environments.

Culturally situated and inclusive policy making is necessary to protect Cambodia's cultural and educational sovereignty in the digital age. Policies need to state, advocate, and support the equal representation of all genders, linguistic variations, and community voice in AI education. Policies should establish ethical boundaries for data, biases from algorithms, and transparency on the use of AI in the classrooms. A policy environment that is culturally attuned, inclusive, and protective of the learners, will also enable learners to engage digital environments in safe and ethically responsible ways.

Going forward, in addition to national reform, Cambodia should integrate regional and global engagement. Within ASEAN, Cambodia can be a regional collaborator and advocate for an inclusive, creative, and interculturally appreciative digital literacy agenda. Cambodia can position itself as a regional advocate and lead in digital transformation in Southeast Asia by collaborating with other ASEAN countries. The Cambodian model, as a manifestation of cultural sensitivity, ethical governance, and social inclusion, can be an emerging exemplar of cultural and responsible innovation for developing countries.

Therefore, Cambodia's journey toward AI-driven multimodal literacy must seek a paradoxical balance between progress and preservation, and between technology and the human spirit. By bringing multilayered education into the classroom, building teacher capacity, and creating cross-sector partnerships and inclusive frameworks, Cambodia aspires to a future in which technology enhances rather than replaces human potential. Cambodia does not seek the simple adoption of AI; rather, the vision for the use of AI is to sustain cultural identity, provide equitable access to cultural identity, and promote active and meaningful participation in the digital world.

REFERENCES

ASEAN. (2020). *Joint statement from the Conference on the digital transformation of education systems throughout ASEAN*. Association of Southeast Asian Nations. https://cil.nus.edu.sg/wp-content/uploads/2020/11/2020-JS-Digital-Transformation-of-Education-Systems.pdf

Buckingham, D. (2015). Defining digital literacy — What do young people need to know about digital media? *Nordic Journal of Digital Literacy*, *10*(Jubileumsnummer), 21–35. DOI: 10.18261/ISSN1891-943X-2015-Jubileumsnummer-03

Buolamwini, J., & Gebru, T. (2018). Gender shades: Intersectional accuracy disparities in commercial gender classification. *Conference on fairness, accountability and transparency, 81*, 1–15. http://proceedings.mlr.press/v81/buolamwini18a.html

Chheang, S., & Huot, S. (2025). A narrative review of teacher engagement in career guidance across Cambodian high schools. *Journal of Social and Educational Research*, *4*(2), 189–198. DOI: 10.5281/zenodo.17868433

Cope, B., & Kalantzis, M. (2020). *Making sense: Reference, agency, and structure in a grammar of multimodal meaning*. Cambridge University Press. DOI: 10.1017/9781316459645

Eubanks, V. (2018). *Automating inequality: How high-tech tools profile, police, and punish the poor*. St. Martin's Press.

Fahruddiana, Y. (2025). Education at the cultural crossroads: Navigating identity and globalization in Southeast Asia. *International Education Trend Issues*, *3*(1), 33–38. DOI: 10.56442/ieti.v3i1.1055

Fricker, M. (2007). *Epistemic injustice: Power and the ethics of knowing*. Oxford University Press. DOI: 10.1093/acprof:oso/9780198237907.001.0001

Gee, J. P. (2003). What video games have to teach us about learning and literacy. [CIE]. *Computers in Entertainment*, *1*(1), 1–4. DOI: 10.1145/950566.950595

Holmes, W., Bialik, M., & Fadel, C. (2019). *Artificial intelligence in education: Promises and implications for teaching and learning*. Center for Curriculum Redesign.

Hornberger, N. H., & Skilton-Sylvester, E. (2000). Revisiting the continua of biliteracy: International and critical perspectives. *Language and Education*, *14*(2), 96–122. DOI: 10.1080/09500780008666781

Huot, S. (2025a). Digital tutors in the kingdom: Exploring ChatGPT's influence on Cambodian students' academic and cognitive growth. In Pandya, J. D., & Patel, K. C. (Eds.), *Interdisciplinary insights: Exploring multiple perspectives* (Vol. 2, pp. 36–54). Meadow Publication.

Huot, S. (2025b). Temples to policy plans: Tracing the political trajectory of education and governance in Cambodia, from antiquity to contemporary reforms. *Journal of Political Science and International Relations*, *8*(3), 122–132. DOI: 10.11648/j.jpsir.20250803.12

Huot, S., & Chheang, S. (2025). Unwriting empire: Decolonizing Khmer language, literature, and cultural memory. *The Context: Journal of English Studies*, *12*(6), 280–293. DOI: 10.5281/zenodo.17061523

Huot, S., & Hok, C. (2025). Enhancing English language teaching for multilingual learners: Leveraging heritage languages in the classroom. *Journal of Social and Educational Research*, *4*(1), 87–95. DOI: 10.5281/zenodo.15698964

Huot, S., & Loch, S. (2025a). Digital practices in Cambodian EFL classrooms: Teacher narratives from remote learning. In K. Khette & Tayade (Eds.), *Proceeding of one day national conference on English language, literature, cultural studies and media studies* (Vol. 2, pp. 19–31). Centre for Learning, Research and Development, Savda, Maharashtra. DOI: 10.5281/zenodo.16921807

Huot, S., & Loch, S. (2025b). Educating in the age of AI: Preparing Cambodian teachers and students for an AI-augmented learning future. *Journal of Educational Technology and E-Learning Innovations*, *1*(2), 31–38. DOI: 10.54536/jeteli.v1i2.5170

Huot, S., Loch, S., Nget, R., & Em, S. (2025). Exploring multiliteracies in the digital era: A framework for 21st-century learning. [CJESS]. *Cambodian Journal of Educational and Social Sciences*, *2*(1), 7–27. DOI: 10.69496/cjess.v2i1.50

Huot, S., & Such, C. (2025). Leveraging social media for language learning: Opportunities and challenges. [JEILT]. *Journal of Education Innovation and Language Teaching*, *1*(2), 10–29. DOI: 10.63381/jeilt.v1i2.56

Huot, S., & Tep, P. (2025). Advancing ChatGPT for pedagogical innovation in Cambodia: Insight from global evidence and local implications. *The Context: Journal of English Studies*, *12*(4), 115–135. DOI: 10.5281/zenodo.15806972

ILO. (2021). *The gender divide in digital skills is another – sadly unsurprising – divide*. International Labour Organization. https://www.ilo.org/media/378741/download

Jenkins, H., & Ito, M. (2016). *Participatory culture in a networked era: A conversation on youth, learning, commerce, and politics*. John Wiley & Sons.

Jewitt, C. (2005). Multimodality,“reading”, and “writing” for the 21st century. *Discourse (Abingdon), 26*(3), 315–331. DOI: 10.1080/01596300500200011

Jewitt, C. (2009). *The Routledge handbook of multimodal analysis*. Routledge London.

Kafa, A. (2025). Exploring integration aspects of school leadership in the context of digitalization and artificial intelligence. *International Journal of Educational Management, 39*(8), 98–115. DOI: 10.1108/IJEM-11-2024-0703

Knox, J. (2020). Artificial intelligence and education in China. *Learning, Media and Technology*, *45*(3), 298–311. DOI: 10.1080/17439884.2020.1754236

Kress, G. (2009). *Multimodality: A social semiotic approach to contemporary communication*. Routledge. DOI: 10.4324/9780203970034

Lim, F. V., & Querol-Julián, M. (2024). *Designing learning with digital technologies*. Routledge. DOI: 10.4324/9781003359272

Long, D., & Magerko, B. (2020). What is AI literacy? Competencies and design considerations. In R. Bernhaupt & F. F. Mueller (Eds.), *Proceedings of the 2020 CHI conference on human factors in computing systems* (pp. 1–16). Association for Computing MachineryNew YorkNYUnited States. DOI: 10.1145/3313831.3376727

Luckin, R. (2018). *Enhancing learning and teaching with technology: What the research says*. ERIC.

Luckin, R., & Holmes, W. (2016). *Intelligence unleashed: An argument for AI in education*. Pearson. https://www.pearson.com/content/dam/corporate/glob

Mills, K. A. (2015). *Literacy theories for the digital age: Social, critical, multimodal, spatial, material and sensory lenses* (Vol. 45). Multilingual Matters.

MoEYS. (2024). *Education strategic plan 2024-2028*. Phnom Penh, Cambodia: Ministry of Education, Youth and Sport. https://moeys.gov.kh/storage/uploads/documents//67316f9d3a57f.pdf

Nash, B. L., Sweinhart, A., & Batchelor, K. (2026). Building the foundations of critical literacy: Collaborative engagement with interactive, multimodal narratives. *Journal of Adolescent & Adult Literacy*, *69*(5), 1–11. DOI: 10.1002/jaal.70040

Ng, D. T. K., Leung, J. K. L., Chu, S. K. W., & Qiao, M. S. (2021). Conceptualizing AI literacy: An exploratory review. *Computers and Education: Artificial Intelligence*, *2*, 1–10. DOI: 10.1016/j.caeai.2021.100041

OECD. (2023). *OECD digital education outlook 2023: Towards an effective digital education ecosystem*. OECD Publishing., DOI: 10.1787/c74f03de-

Pascua-Valenzuela, E. A. (2025). *Digital literacy and transformation in ASEAN: A call for education policy reforms*. ASEAN. https://asean.org/wp-content/uploads/2025/05/ASCC-RD_Policy-Brief_FoE-19_2025_Digital-Literacy-and-Transformation.pdf

RGC. (2021a). *Cambodia digital economy and society policy framework (2021–2035)*. Royal Government of Cambodia, Phnom Penh: Supreme National Economic Council. https://asset.cambodia.gov.kh/mptc/media/EN-Policy-Framework-of-Digital-Economy-and-Society.pdf

RGC. (2021b). *Cambodia digital government policy 2021–2035*. Royal Government of Cambodia, Phnom Penh: Ministry of Post and Telecommunications. https://asset.cambodia.gov.kh/mptc/media/Cambodia_Digital_Government_Policy_2022_2035_English.pdf

RGC. (2022). *Cambodia digital government policy 2022–2035*. Royal Government of Cambodia. https://asset.cambodia.gov.kh/mptc/media/Cambodia_Digital_Government_Policy_2022_2035_English.pdf

RUPP. (2023). *Institutional repository project report, 2020–2023*. Phnom Penh, Cambodia: Royal University of Phnom Penh Library. https://rupp.edu.kh/center/library

Secretariat, A. S. E. A. N. (2022). *Digital policy action areas for a connected ASEAN: ASEAN best practice benchmarking and an action plan for regional harmonization*. ITU Publications Asia-Pacific Region. https://asean.org/wp-content/uploads/2024/03/Digital-Policy-Action-Areas-for-a-Connected-ASEAN.pdf

Selwyn, N. (2021). *Education and technology: Key issues and debates*. Bloomsbury Publishing.

Swisscontact. (2020). *Recognition of prior learning in Cambodia: Implementation guideline*. Skill Development Programme. https://www.swisscontact.org/_Resources/Persistent/6/6/5/c/665c4d57f8eb7ee257d1bef3190e4016794e7a6e/SDP-Recognition%20of%20Prior%20Learning%20%28RPL%29%20Implementation%20Handbook.pdf

Syed, J., & Özbilgin, M. (2009). A relational framework for international transfer of diversity management practices. *International Journal of Human Resource Management, 20*(12), 2435–2453. DOI: 10.1080/09585190903363755

UNESCO. (2021). *Reimagining our futures together: A new social contract for education*. Paris: UNESCO. https://unevoc.unesco.org/pub/futures_of_education_report_eng.pdf

UNESCO. (2023). *Guidance for generative artificial intelligence (GenAI) in education and research: A human-centered approach.* United Nations Educational Scientific and Cultural Organization. https://policycommons.net/artifacts/6942367/guidance-for-generative-ai-in-education-and-research/7852269

UNESCO. (2025). *Cambodia artificial intelligence readiness assessment report.* United Nations Educational Scientific and Cultural Organization. https://unesdoc.unesco.org/ark:/48223/pf0000394553

World Bank. (2023). *Individuals using the Internet (% of population) – Cambodia.* FRED, Federal Reserve Bank of St. Louis, https://fred.stlouisfed.org/series/ITNETUSERP2KHM

Yang, Y., Zhang, Y., Sun, D., He, W., & Wei, Y. (2025). Navigating the landscape of AI literacy education: Insights from a decade of research (2014–2024). *Humanities & Social Sciences Communications*, *12*(1), 1–12. DOI: 10.1057/s41599-025-04583-8

Ziguras, C. (2001). Educational technology in transnational higher education in South East Asia: The cultural politics of flexible learning. *Journal of Educational Technology & Society*, *4*(4), 8–18. https://www.jstor.org/stable/jeductechsoci.4.4.8

KEY TERMS AND DEFINITIONS

Artificial Intelligence (AI): Artificial Intelligence (AI) refers to the phenomenon where human intelligence is replicated in machines through reasoning, learning, language processing, and problem solving. In the field of education, AI enhances teaching and learning through adaptive learning, automated assessment, translation, and data-driven decision making.

Cambodia: The Southeastern Asian country experiencing rapid educational reform and digital transformation, where AI and multimodal literacy are integrated into schools, universities, and community education for national development.

Cultural Sensitivity: The respectful use of innovative educational content and technologies that incorporate and preserve the identity of culture and the locality using traditional and modern cultural practices, values, and languages.

Digital Education: The use of digital technologies to design, deliver and assess the learning process. Digital education includes online learning platforms, interactive tools, AI-assisted learning tools, and student-centred methodologies.

Educational Reform: The improvement of educational systems through policies, pedagogy, and technology. In the case of Cambodia, this means integrating AI and multimodal literacy to improve the quality, relevance, and equity of learning.

Inclusivity: The removal of barriers through equitable design and policy to ensure that everyone, regardless of gender, socioeconomic status, disability, and location, has equal access to learning opportunities.

Multimodal Literacy: The ability to understand and construct meaning through textual, visual, oral, and digital forms. The 21st century requires the ability to engage with information in different forms, and this fosters creative and critical thinking and collaboration in learning environments.

Chapter 12
Toward an Effectual Stance of Reading

Jason D. DeHart
http://orcid.org/0009-0005-5210-4738
The University of Tennessee, USA

ABSTRACT

This chapter revisits Rosenblatt's theories on the stances that readers can adopt and sums up both the efferent and aesthetic stances, while further exploring possibilities in the changing world of text and literacy. In particular, the author advances the possibility of an effectual stance of rewriting and social justice orientation, which positions the reader as an active agent in evaluating texts and applying them to real-world circumstances. Implications from this work are focused on the role of readers or possibilities for instruction.

INTRODUCTION

As texts evolve and change from print to digital formats, and as text generation is transformed over time by the affordances of tools, how does the role of the reader change? Moreover, as readers develop knowledge, practice critical literacy and engage in digital citizenship, does the role of the reader change? Societal shifts, transformative and courageous conversations, and increased focuses on access and equity continue to shape educational discourse. This article is intended to advance these ideas and questions, and offer possible, tentative, and theoretical solutions for further inquiry and development particularly when considering the reading process.

To that end, this work is intended to add to the conversation around Rosenblatt's formulation of transactions in reading/readers and responding. This theory has been seminal for many decades now, and continues to inform policy, practice, and academic

DOI: 10.4018/979-8-3373-6986-0.ch012

work. Representative works for the transaction reading theory can be traced to a 1986 article, "The Aesthetic Transaction," in which the author noted foundational thinking of aesthetic education and transactional theory, linking the relationship of reader and text/author in response. Rosenblatt has posited that readers approach texts from a particular stance and delineated these stances as the aesthetic and efferent. In the aesthetic stance, readers are engaging with a text because of some sense of satisfaction or joy that is part of the experience; that is, they read because it is an activity that makes them enjoyment and appreciation at some level. Readers, in this view, are linked with nature, following from work of Dewey in connecting actors in relationship, rather than expressing a Cartesian duality between humanity and the world outside of self (Rosenblatt, 1986). In the efferent stance, readers engage with a text primarily for information-seeking purposes and seek to learn and grow, or gather particular data to inform a specific thought process.

These stances, from Rosenblatt's (1981) view are dynamic in nature, and do not exist as completely separate dualities; they flow and interweave as needed by the reader, and do not necessarily follow a replicable path. Knowledge of the affordances of these stances can also shape policy, as many institutional and systemic approaches value the efferent stance over the aesthetic stance. Rosenblatt questioned this hierarchical view, expressed in the New Criticism paradigm, and drew attention to the need for aesthetic stance. The notion of a response, according to Rosenblatt (1982), entails an object. The reader is not completely separate or merely cognitively considering this object, but is bringing a set of experiences and ideas to the text. Thus, the reader is not separating themselves into a purely knowledge-based pursuit.

In the case of reading, this object to which response is assigned/involved is the text itself. Rosenblatt's work continued to have impacts on the ways that scholars view texts and readers in relationship, even as definitions of text and further examples emerge socially and culturally. The legacy of this work includes close analysis of a variety of texts, from poetry to video game storytelling (Guanio-Uluru, 2022; Wilson, 2022). Moreover, the aesthetic stance of the reader has continued to inform interactions and engagements with literacy practices in digital spaces (Storm, 2024). Conversations continue to circle around this theory and build upon Rosenblatt's work.

In the spirit of continued work in advancing ideas, I suggest that there might be additional stances that readers can adopt, and that these stances, in particular, can relate to concepts of advocacy and social justice. To continue building on what it means to be a reader, I posit a third stance or lens for reading – the effectual stance, in which the reader engages with text to create a sense of change either/both in themselves and in their outer locus of control. There is a social justice aspect that is endemic to this approach as readers engage with a self → community → global perspective dynamic. This is not a completely separate stance, in any regard, from the efferent and aesthetic views, but rather a dimension that acts as a compliment and theoretically exists in the dynamic.

THE ORIGINS OF THE EFFECTUAL

An effectual stance, at the time of this writing, exists in business and economic research as a conceptualization of a means of influence (Read et al., 2009). This notion includes both adaptability and a sense of expertise that arrives from action and choice rather than preexisting ontology; the effect arises from deliberate and intentional agency rather than an intrinsic, already extant quality. The term effectual stance has also been used in social sciences research to denote a set of motivational mechanisms that enable individuals to act in spite of perceived or concrete disadvantages (Bohas et al., 2024). In this case, both psychological reactance and theories of self-enhancement serve as foundational aspects of the theory, and is linked to effectual thinking. Bohas et al. (2024) included the idea of drivers in their work, a term which I will borrow and conceptualize as it related to the theoretical concept I am describing.

In the case of reading instruction, I posit a reader stance that not only seeks to learn but to enact through reading. I further trace and define this stance as a *reading to represent* orientation as well as *reading to transform* orientation. These two categorizations are not meant to be all-inclusive for this theoretical stance, but are rather intended to a starting point for a more comprehensive theoretical development and refinement. Yet, there is more work to be done with social justice literacy beyond what exists on a page or within a text; this is socially active work and literacy applies to this sense of community, as well (Cho, 2017). This is not to imply, from Read et al.'s (2009) work that a direction of intrinsic social justice orientation does not also emerge from outward environment; discretely, that the types of reading engagements I am describing are not focused on those who have yet to attain a sense of social justice and do so through the active reading of text, but that this sense of social justice is already extant in the reader, just as prior knowledge and experiences would be in any transaction, and that the social justice orientation within a reader acts as a driver based on what is encountered in the text.

A case of the previous description, in which a reader was equipped with a developed or more developed social justice orientation through reading, would likely be considered efferent in nature. The origin of the orientation itself, for a reader who operates in the effectual stance, is not at stake in this description; I posit it is the result of both external and internal interactions from self, family, and wider community, and might be the result of encountering particular instances of social injustice or being in relationship with those who possess and have developed this orientation.

Molla (2024) has explored the impact of AI on creative expression, including both the potential for augmentation and further evolution of creative practices and the potential pratfalls and inequities present with the application of technology.

To this end, Zhou and Sterna (2024) presented the notion of beginning with an AI-generated product and then engaging in a process of rewriting and augmentation to explore creativity possibilities. In this way, the use of AI can be partnered with instead of substituted for human creativity, acting in conversation with the human voice. The process could be rendered in reverse order, as well; that is, a creative expression that is expressed and then reworked with AI tools. In effect, this would be a concert rather than solo creative endeavor and notions of technology assistance have further potential for increasing access and equity for individuals with diverse abilities.

Bohas et al. (2024) shared the caveat that the presence of an effectual stance does not act as a rationale for exonerating actors who engage in lived experience in unjust ways or whose actions, in the case of Bohas et al's study, continue to foster disadvantage. Nor is this approach to reading intended to conflate instances of social injustice with any perceived or concrete disadvantage. In this case, I would be more inclined to define these terms as attempted disenfranchisement or inaccurate/incomplete representation within the composition and/or communication of a text. When encountered, the social justice orientation of the reader is a driver to transact with the text from the effectual stance.

As part of their work on the active view of reading, Burns et al. (2023) noted the importance of reading as a component of social justice; indeed, the weight that educators feel for ensuring that all readers succeed, and the advocacy that is part of noticing and naming the rich literacy practices that are already part of a child's repertoire are all part of the what thoughtful reading instruction entails. Reading has also been considered a tool for social justice work (Dewan, 2016), and a crucial feature of progressive instructional practices (Shannon, 2017). In considering the change agents of reading and its effect on social justice practices, Simpson and Cremin (2022) noted the critical role of the teacher. For some time, social justice-oriented teaching has been linked with developing the types of skills that are valued in close and critical reading practices (Dover, 2015).

This line of thought in literacy is founded upon, in many ways, the work of Freire in articulating the relationships of literacy and liberation. This work points to the agency of readers and the ways in which pedagogical approaches can foster freedom and empowerment for students. Additionally, Gramsci explored the social and political relationships of those who are oppressed and those who oppress them. Gramsci suggested a dynamic of cyclical oppression, while I advance a more hopeful position of social improvement, including increased equity and access.

A Further Note on the Nature of Text

A number of scholars have documented the changing nature of texts and what text means, particularly in light of digital creation and democratized access to digital tools. Bezemer and Kress (2008) noted both the social dimensions of texts as constructions and co-constructions of reality, as well as the continued semiotic affordances of texts which communicate meaning through multiple modes, or spaces/sites, for messaging. These multimodal texts thus appeal to a sense of design and contain particular affordances – said another way, particular types of texts can perform tasks or construct meaning in ways that others cannot (Voss, 2011). This access to a variety of means of communication and text production can include profound implications for students who benefit from messaging in diverse ways, and shapes what literacy and communication, as well as writing and composing, mean at social and cultural levels.

Additionally, the growth of access to artificial intelligence (AI) tools has potential implications for literacy in ways that scholars are working to document in the field (Mills et al., 2024; Sperling et al., 2024). This exploration can be traced from conceptualization to the ways in which educators, institutions, and even students are actively exploring the possibilities of reading, writing, and composing with AI tools (Almatrafi et al., 2024).

TOWARD AN EFFECTUAL STANCE IN READING

The possibility of an effectual stance does not preclude aesthetic or efferent lenses for reading texts, but rather is posited as an additional step and intentionality in the reading experience. Rosenblatt (1982) expanded on the role of reader and text, noting that any multitude of transactions can occur based on the prior knowledge and experiences of the reader. Where does this theoretical knowledge not take us as we explore and enact our role as citizens embracing literacy in traditional, digital, and deictic ways?

Luke (2008) emphasized the essential criticality of literacy, as well as the social dimensions of what it means to be literate, considering communication in both lived and digital lived experiences. From a critical viewpoint, we might ask: Is engaging with a text from a critical framework the same as an efferent or aesthetic lens? To that, I suggest the possibility of both *yes* and *more.* A reader might be engaging with a text from a critical viewpoint from the stance of learning information/discovering something new, and/or a sense of pleasure in the experience; however, they are often reading with the intention of utilizing their knowledge in some social justice orientation.

The reading experience itself acts as a precursor to any subsequent effect, but can have a direct influence on that effect, either in creating or shaping the effect. In this view, the reading stance is informed by the subsequent action and, transactionally, informs the ways that action can take place. For a working definition, Luke (2008) included the utilization of both coding and messaging in conveying the notion of what literacy is. These dimensions do have impacts of approaches to schooling and the ways in which text is taken up, defined, and explored by individuals and institutions. Williamson (2017) offered that this work of social justice engagement requires exposure to shared stories, and access to these stories and truths subsequently shapes curriculum.

Through the threads of literacy's impact, there is a sense of power that is one aspect of what it means to be both justice-focused and literate – a person who navigates codes, messages, communications, and spaces with the intention of supportive work and positive transformation (Blackledge, 2000). Alongside and operating in juxtaposition to notions of power, there is perhaps an aspect of social justice literacy that is moral in nature (Janks, 2017). While morality might be a complicated concept to delineate, the values and ideas that are communicated by a group of people within a particular culture, as well as those ideas and values shared across multiple cultural boundaries, might be thought of either as moral or ethical in nature.

Reading to Represent

In some cases, readers seek a representation of a particular identity/intersection of identities, including noting the absence of representation. While literacy practices themselves are depicted culturally (Williams & Zenger, 2007), this notion of reading to represent – one prong of what effectual reading stance might entail – is more reader-centered, in keeping with the agency that is part of this sense of stance. In this formulation, a reader is encountering a text either to see themselves in some way reflected through characters or some other element of the story; sometimes, this effectuality is possible because of the absence of such characters, while at other times, the presence of a representation that is authentic might inspire, or an inauthentic representation might ignite action.

Breunig (2019) noted the importance of literacy as students (indeed, readers, in general) take stock of where they are and as they move/transform/become a more ideal self. This is the internalized and personalized work of literacy, particularly through a social justice orientation, which considers the importance of identity and representation. In some ways, the linking to becoming is informed by the efferent stance, but at times this dynamic can encompass both the already and the in process aspects of an individual's intersections of identity. The entropic nature of AI as a tool for gathering the sum of what has been shared carries the potential for further obfuscating the nuances of representation; this means that advances in tools should always be considered in light of what we have learned as a society about inclusivity and expression, as well as the central role of the individual voice as a source of advocacy.

Basu et al. (2008) linked notions of literacy with identity; from this, we can glean that a component of the reading process includes a sense of who we are, as represented. Thus, the reading experience might be poised on a heuristic of self, not in terms of transformation, but in terms of ensuring a space is occupied in textual worlds. In this type of stance, the reader is actively looking for themselves not simply to learn from the text but in some cases to underscore or disrupt it. The reader acts as commentator, drawing on their experiences and knowledge not as an end in itself, but as a means of enacting and practicing critique of representation. Given the nature of text, representations can occur as written examples, images, or a combination of both. They can also be intrinsically related to other elements of design, particularly in multimodal texts.

So, the reader perhaps encounters some dimension of the aesthetic – the enjoyment derived from seeing a representation that links with their experiences. This is the reading seeing the reader within another person's construct. At other points, even within the same text, there might be a dynamic of learning about how one is seen or can be seen, linking to the efferent. However, these dimensions do not fully satisfy how a reader might transact with a text; that is, they are experiencing the text with intention for action that is either reified or reshaped by their emotional and intellectual transactions with the text in question. As with literacy more broadly conceived, notions of representation include questions of power and politic (Gainer, 2010). This again circles back to notions of reading to disrupt, which might center on racial and ethnic representations (Oto et al., 2023), or more broadly in terms of disrupting any number of problematic ideas or underdeveloped perspectives (Ebarvia et al., 2021). Thus, the reader is not learning so much as they are reading for opportunities to reify or revoke. As readers who are also authoring their experiences, they can stand with or in opposition to authors based on particular forms of representation.

This model of reading, like the stance I describe in the next section, is one which acknowledges and even builds upon the authority of the reader as a voice in their own right who engages with the written word as both reader and, in some conceptualizations of the term, author or (re)author. Some might suggest that encountering a representation or reflection of one's self in a text is essential aesthetic; I contend that this experience is far more vital than reduction to appreciation or pleasure. It is life-giving textual experience, and can reaffirm or profoundly harm a reader. This concept of reader harm is again a place to advance the position that readers can then take on the reciprocal role of reauthoring or authorizing a particular account – especially when this account is rendered from an etic/outsider perspective, or when one experience is lifted as a monolith while other considerations should be part of discourse.

Reading to Transform

Part of social justice work is noticing the need for change, and appreciating what transformation might affect in the world around us. This is fundamentally Freirean in epistemology, as literacy results in liberation and this sense of empowerment thus results in the continued work of troubling definitions, representations, and ideas that are limited or altogether uninformed.

As a second, though not secondary, prong of effectual reading stance, I posit the existence of a transformational sense of transaction, either with the individual reader in mind or by means of considering how to transform, or actually taking steps to transform, the world around the reader. In this way, the action subsequent to reading as antecedent is not only a precursor but a crucial aspect of the reading process *in media res*. From a wider vantage, one might consider the use of social media as a means of influencing – text creation or consumption with the idea of social and cultural influence in mind (Rachmad, 2025). This influence results in a kind of behavioral or economic transformation. In some ways, for reading, this work of enacting transformation as part of reading is a movement from consuming and considering text to reauthoring/engaging as a rewriter of what has been improperly or inadequately offered.

The idea of action does not end with the individual in all cases. Pahl and Rowsell (2020) linked their ideas about literacy and the ways in which people navigate and communicate now with wider concerns of the world, including concepts of ecology and human rights. Central to this concept of transformation is both participation (e.g., the presence of individuals/ideas/voices), as well as emancipation – the active process of liberating practices that can be part of literacy (e.g., voicing support and/or dissent) (Valladares, 2021). In this dimension of reader stance, the action of critique and informed commentary further undergird agency and decision-making, from asking questions to further demonstrating advocacy.

The central agent, again, is the reader. Unlike paradigms for disrupting/transforming notions of literacy due to changes in technology (Ciampa et al., 2023), this transformative lens of effectual reading, as described here, is focused on the agential choices of the reader based on their use of text and communication. This is not an external group of authorities or setting or authorized ideas that are then applied to a text; this is the reader themselves, recognizing who they are, noticing moments of inequity, and making intentional choices to move and act in this context. The difference is in the fundamental direction of the sense of agency. The dynamic of efferent and aesthetic might be present, as well as the dynamic or the representational lens. When a positive or more complete representation is present, the reader engages with an effectual sense of witness. When the representation is incomplete, the approach is more critical and can be drawn upon to refine an incomplete perspective or redirect an inaccurate representation entirely.

Is the reader, then, a rewriter or (re)author I posited earlier?

In this type of engagement, is the reader seeking to learn? They are the primary voice of the experience that has been represented in some way, or an already-established voice in their own right or troubling or disrupting a less-developed set of principles and practices. Thus, their agency does not come from the text but is a fundamental aspect of their response based on their background, knowledge, and insight. In some cases, the reader might approach a text to learn; in other cases, they know all too well what they will likely encounter, or at least hope that they encounter something more developed. In some ways, approaches to reading position the author as expert who is sharing knowledge; it is perhaps that case in the paradigmatic shift I am suggesting that the reader takes the role of member checking or realignment for the author, thus engaging in a transaction that offers questioning and redefining/reframing as a primary action. Their voice, in this way, *authorizes* a text or advances with textual tools and space for ways that a text can be made true(r).

When a text is appropriately framed, the agency and advocacy that is part of the transformative lens reifies or further disseminates the text. In some ways, this might be seen as liking and tagging on social media, or populating a digital page with the statements and ideas of other posts which align with an ideology or set of values. Just as users of social media curate their space, the transformational reader seeks to curate or distill what is most accurate and informative – not so that they can be informed, but so that their role as reader can serve as a means of educating others. It is work of acknowledgement and transmission.

In keeping with the world that might be based on reading and engaging with literacy practices, there is a speculative aspect of this approach, as well as an authorial dimension. Dewey (1934) offered, "Words furnish a record of what has happened and give direction by request and command to a particular future action" (p. 359). In the same way that narrative inquiry from the spaces of qualitative literature offers an account of an experience, both with its antecedents and careful documentation of its sequence (Labov, 2004), the work of the reader operating from the transformative lens is both to hold historical accuracy to account, as well as support or facilitate the envisioning of a next chapter. In some cases, the reader can point to an extant example of what is intended in their vision as a textual and social agent of literacy.

CONCLUSIONS AND IMPLICATIONS

As with all theoretical work, this exploration is tentative and is intended as a conversation starter and continuation of voice from prior research and leading, hopefully, to subsequent thinking. This is not intended as a closed loop of analysis, but as a step in developing further inquiry. The context in which this thinking occurs is one that seems poised on both the old and the new, aspects of which include both the problematic and promising.

I acknowledge the need for further pruning, refining, and tailoring; indeed, Rosenblatt was not without criticism. Indeed, like the best of thinkers, Rosenblatt (1993) continued to add to and explore her thinking, refining positions and pushing back on dualisms (Rosenblatt, 1981). The author, in this case, is in reader response with themselves, always pushing and striving, both authorizing and reauthoring aspects of a text as they come to know and become experts in their cultural and social spheres. This is not to suggest something postmodern or inherently palimpsest about the nature of theory, but it is to suggest the rewriting nature of theoretical development as more details are studied, reflected on, and known, and other cases come to be noticed, named, and explored.

What we might note as a means of concluding is that readers now exist at the vortex of a variety of textual engagements. With continued thinking sources, validity, and accuracy, including an age of AI in which texts can be generated from culling multiple sources, leaving the reader to sift through for final conclusions, the role of reader has been and will be vital. Given this multitextual space, readers can engage with texts to enjoy them, learn from them, and critique them. This critical dimension also means that there are times a reader might engage with a text in order to effect a subsequent personal or social change. In the case of the personal, this might involve an individual's efferent search for truth; in the case of the social, the reader might already possess knowledge but is engaged in literacy to refine that knowledge or test the text itself.

This work holds potential implications for research, teaching, and policy including:

- Continued inquiry into social justice orientations in their development and impact on literacy.
- Continued inquiry into the stances that a reader adopts, adapts, and flows between/among in addition to those posited here and in Rosenblatt's work.
- Continued inquiry into the implications for Rosenblatt's work and extensions as texts continue to evolve and transform.
- Exploration of ethnographic, autoethnographic, and case study examples of how posited reading stances work in transaction.

- Increased attention to strategies which support critical reading stances, including moments at which readers note a shift in their thinking when engaged in literacy practice.
- Increased attention to the role of readers as witnesses, authorizers, and reauthors.
- Reconsideration of policies which would seek to advance texts and ideologies that disenfranchise.
- A cyclical and reified commitment to the representation of less represented voices and experiences in the influx of information and content that is generated through a variety of means of production.
- A commitment among educational communities and policymakers to reflect the individual and community, including the role of creative voice and expression, in balance with the means of digital production.

REFERENCES

Almatrafi, O., Johri, A., & Lee, H. (2024). A systematic review of AI literacy conceptualization, constructs, and implementation and assessment efforts (2019–2023). *Computers and Education Open*, *6*, 100173. DOI: 10.1016/j.caeo.2024.100173

Basu, K., Maddox, B., & Robinson-Pant, A. (2008). Literacies, identities and social change: Interdisciplinary approaches to literacy and development. *The Journal of Development Studies*, *44*(6), 769–778. DOI: 10.1080/00220380802057695

Bezemer, J., & Kress, G. (2008). Writing in multimodal texts: A social semiotic account of designs for learning. *Written Communication*, *25*(2), 166–195. DOI: 10.1177/0741088307313177

Blackledge, A. (2000). *Literacy, power and social justice*. Trentham Books.

Bohas, A., Grolleau, G., & Mzoughi, N. (2024). The advantages of being disadvantaged. *Kyklos*, *77*(3), 759–775. DOI: 10.1111/kykl.12388

Breunig, M. (2019). Beings who are becoming: Enhancing social justice literacy. *Journal of Experiential Education*, *42*(1), 7–21. DOI: 10.1177/1053825918820694

Burns, M. K., Duke, N. K., & Cartwright, K. B. (2023). Evaluating components of the active view of reading as intervention targets: Implications for social justice. *School Psychology*, *38*(1), 30–41. DOI: 10.1037/spq0000519 PMID: 36745101

Cho, H. (2017). Navigating the meanings of social justice, teaching for social justice, and multicultural education. *International Journal of Multicultural Education*, *19*(2), 1–19. DOI: 10.18251/ijme.v19i2.1307

Ciampa, K., Wolfe, Z. M., & Bronstein, B. (2023). ChatGPT in education: Transforming digital literacy practices. *Journal of Adolescent & Adult Literacy*, *67*(3), 186–195. DOI: 10.1002/jaal.1310

Dewan, P. (2016). Economic well-being and social justice through pleasure reading. *New Library World*, *117*(9/10), 557–567. DOI: 10.1108/NLW-03-2016-0019

Dewey, J. (1934). The supreme intellectual obligation. *Science*, *79*(2046), 240–243. DOI: 10.1126/science.79.2046.240 PMID: 17731609

Dover, A. G. (2016). Teaching for social justice and the Common Core: Justice-oriented curriculum for language arts and literacy. *Journal of Adolescent & Adult Literacy*, *59*(5), 517–527. DOI: 10.1002/jaal.488

Ebarvia, T., Germán, L., Parker, K. N., & Torres, J. (2021). "literacy Is liberation": A Conversation with# disruptTexts leaders. *English Journal, 111*(1), 25–31. DOI: 10.58680/ej202131388

Freire, P. (2021). *Pedagogy of hope.* Bloomsbury Academic. DOI: 10.5040/9781350190238

Gainer, J. S. (2010). Critical media literacy in middle school: Exploring the politics of representation. *Journal of Adolescent & Adult Literacy, 53*(5), 364–373. DOI: 10.1598/JAAL.53.5.2

Gramsci, A. (2000). *The Gramsci reader: selected writings, 1916-1935.* NYU Press.

Guanio-Uluru, L. (2022). The Reader as Player: Exploring the Notion of Aesthetic and Efferent Gaming. *International Research in Children's Literature, 15*(3), 338–352. DOI: 10.3366/ircl.2022.0471

Janks, H. (2017). Critical literacy and the social justice project of education. *English Teaching, 16*(2), 132–144. DOI: 10.1108/ETPC-09-2016-0111

Labov, W. (2004). Ordinary events. In Fought, C. (Ed.), *Sociolinguistic Variation: Critical Reflections* (pp. 31–43). Oxford University Press. DOI: 10.1093/oso/9780195170399.003.0003

Luke, A. (2018). *Critical literacy, schooling, and social justice.* Routledge. DOI: 10.4324/9781315100951

Mills, K., Ruiz, P., Lee, K. W., Coenraad, M., Fusco, J., Roschelle, J., & Weisgrau, J. (2024). *AI Literacy: A Framework to Understand, Evaluate, and Use Emerging Technology*. Digital Promise.

Molla, M. (2024). AI in creative arts: Advancements and innovations in artificial intelligence. *International Journal of Advanced Research in Science Communication and Technology, 4*(1), 513–517. DOI: 10.48175/IJARSCT-19163

Oto, R., Rombalski, A., & Grinage, J. (2023). The role of racial literacy in US K-12 education research: A review of the literature. *Race, Ethnicity and Education, 26*(1), 94–111. DOI: 10.1080/13613324.2022.2047635

Pahl, K., & Rowsell, J. (2020). *Living literacies: Literacy for social change.* MiT Press. DOI: 10.7551/mitpress/11375.001.0001

Rachmad, Y. E. (2025). *The Power of the Influencer: How Viral and Gimmick Marketing Transform Behavior.* United Nations Economic and Social Council.

Read, S., Dew, N., Sarasvathy, S. D., Song, M., & Wiltbank, R. (2009). Marketing under uncertainty: The logic of an effectual approach. *Journal of Marketing*, *73*(3), 1–18. DOI: 10.1509/jmkg.73.3.001

Rosenblatt, L. M. (1981). On the aesthetic as the basic model of the reading process. *Bucknell Review*, *26*(1), 17.

Rosenblatt, L. M. (1982). The literary transaction: Evocation and response. *Theory into Practice*, *21*(4), 268–277. DOI: 10.1080/00405848209543018

Rosenblatt, L. M. (1986). The aesthetic transaction. *Journal of Aesthetic Education*, *20*(4), 122–128. DOI: 10.2307/3332615

Rosenblatt, L. M. (1993). The transactional theory: Against dualisms. *College English*, *55*(4), 377–386. DOI: 10.58680/ce19939301

Shannon, P. (2017). *Progressive reading education in America: Teaching toward social justice*. Routledge. DOI: 10.4324/9781315182391

Simpson, A., & Cremin, T. M. (2022). Responsible reading: Children's literature and social justice. *Education Sciences*, *12*(4), 264. DOI: 10.3390/educsci12040264

Sperling, K., Stenberg, C. J., McGrath, C., Åkerfeldt, A., Heintz, F., & Stenliden, L. (2024). In search of artificial intelligence (AI) literacy in teacher education: A scoping review. *Computers and Education Open*, *6*, 100169. DOI: 10.1016/j.caeo.2024.100169

Storm, S. (2024). Aesthetic literacies in digital learning ecologies: Tracing aesthetic tools and functions in a youth literary salon. *Literacy Research: Theory, Method, and Practice*, *73*(1), 85–104. DOI: 10.1177/23813377241285818

Valladares, L. (2021). Scientific literacy and social transformation: Critical perspectives about science participation and emancipation. *Science & Education*, *30*(3), 557–587. DOI: 10.1007/s11191-021-00205-2 PMID: 33867683

Voss, S. M. (2011). *The affordances of multimodal texts and their impact on the reading process*. University of Minnesota.

Williams, B., & Zenger, A. (2007). *Popular culture and representations of literacy*. Routledge. DOI: 10.4324/9780203008492

Williamson, T. (2017). Listening to many voices: Enacting social justice literacy curriculum. *Teaching and Teacher Education*, *61*, 104–114. DOI: 10.1016/j.tate.2016.10.002

Wilson, A. (2022). The reader, the text, the poem: The influence and challenge of Louise Rosenblatt. *International Journal of Primary, Elementary, and Early Years Education*, *49*(1), 79–95.

Zhou, D., & Sterman, S. (2024, June). Ai. llude: Investigating Rewriting AI-Generated Text to Support Creative Expression. In *Proceedings of the 16th Conference on Creativity & Cognition* (pp. 241-254). DOI: 10.1145/3635636.3656187

KEY TERMS AND DEFINITIONS

Aesthetic Stance: The transaction or engagement with text for the purposes of finding a sense of joy or pleasure, from Rosenblatt's work. A reader who is transacting with a text and who encounters a representation of their lived experiences likely does so from a dimension of this stance, as well as the effectual stance.

Agency: The means of engagement that the reader draws upon, not as a passive recipient of pleasure or knowledge, but as a critic or witness with a text.

Driver: Adapted from social sciences work broadly, this term is used to denote the motivational influences that exist in a text and serve as a catalyst or textual space for effectual reading.

Effectual Stance: The proposed additional stance in which the reader is engaging with a text/transacting primarily as an authorizer or reauthor, in this case from a social justice orientation.

Efferent Stance: The transaction or engagement with text for the purposes of learning/gathering information, from Rosenblatt's work. A reader who is transacting with a text to further develop or understand a sense of social justice would likely be operating in this stance.

Reauthor: The agency-related task of a reader engaged in or subsequent to engaging in the effectual stance of reading in which an inaccurate or incomplete account is revised textually and in discourses of critique.

Representation: A textual image, imagining, or depiction of an individual, community, or experience which either aligns with or incompletely renders a reader's lived experiences.

Transaction: The relationship of reader and text, from Rosenblatt's work.

Compilation of References

Aarthi, S., Ravikumar, R. N., Khudayberganov, S., Ismailov, A., & Khujaniyozova, O. (2025). Using Intelligent Tutoring Systems to enhance student engagement. In *Advances in Computational Intelligence and Robotics* (pp. 155–188). IGI Global. DOI: 10.4018/979-8-3373-1827-1.ch008

Abas, S. (2023). Critical multimodal literacy practices in student-created comics. *Literacy*, *57*(2), 161–170. DOI: 10.1111/lit.12324

Adiguzel, T., Kaya, M. H., & Cansu, F. K. (2023). Revolutionizing education with AI: Exploring the transformative potential of ChatGPT. *Contemporary Educational Technology*, *15*(3), ep429. DOI: 10.30935/cedtech/13152

Afifah, L., Indriwardhani, S. P., Retnantiti, S., & Usman, R. (2023). Digitalization: Improving the literacy of foreign language learners through multimodal texts. [Journal of Linguistics and Literature]. *Lire Journal*, *7*(1), 177–192. DOI: 10.33019/lire.v7i1.171

Ahmed, R. (2024). Reading the Visual: An Introduction to Teaching Multimodal Literacy:(Book Review). *Journal of English Studies in Arabia Felix*, *3*(1), 24–27. DOI: 10.56540/jesaf.v3i1.92

Akgun, S., & Greenhow, C. (2022). Artificial intelligence in education: Addressing ethical challenges in. *AI and Ethics*, *2*(3), 431–440. DOI: 10.1007/s43681-021-00096-7 PMID: 34790956

Al Farabi, M. R. F., & Rohmah, Z. (2023). Teaching Multimodal Literacy Through Integrated Learning of Advertisement Texts. *Journal of English Teaching* [JETALL]. *Applied Linguistics and Literatures*, *6*(1), 73–88.

Alam, A. (2023a). Media multitasking with M-learning technology in real-time classroom learning: Analysing the dynamics in formal educational settings for the future of E-learning in India. In *2023 2nd International Conference on Smart Technologies and Systems for Next Generation Computing (ICSTSN)* (pp. 1-6). IEEE.

Alam, A. (2023b). The secret sauce of student success: Cracking the code by navigating the path to personalized learning with educational data mining. In *2023 2nd International Conference on Smart Technologies and Systems for Next Generation Computing (ICSTSN)* (pp. 1-8). IEEE.

Alam, A., & Mohanty, A. (2022, December). Facial analytics or virtual avatars: competencies and design considerations for student-teacher interaction in AI-powered online education for effective classroom engagement. In *International Conference on Communication, Networks and Computing* (pp. 252-265). Cham: Springer Nature Switzerland.

Alam, A., & Mohanty, A. (2023, January). Learning on the move: a pedagogical framework for state-of-the-art mobile learning. In *International Conference on Data Management, Analytics & Innovation* (pp. 735-748). Singapore: Springer Nature Singapore. DOI: 10.1007/978-981-99-1414-2_52

Alam, A. (2022). Impact of university's human resources practices on professors' occupational performance: empirical evidence from India's higher education sector. In *Inclusive businesses in developing economies: Converging people, profit, and corporate citizenship* (pp. 107–131). Springer International Publishing. DOI: 10.1007/978-3-031-12217-0_6

Alam, A. (2023c). Intelligence unleashed: An argument for AI-enabled learning ecologies with real world examples of today and a peek into the future. In *International Conference on Innovations in Computer Science, Electronics & Electrical Engineering*-2022 (Vol. 2717, No. 1, p. 030001). AIP Publishing LLC. DOI: 10.1063/5.0129803

Alam, A., & Mohanty, A. (2024). Integrated constructive robotics in education (ICRE) model: A paradigmatic framework for transformative learning in educational ecosystem. *Cogent Education*, *11*(1), 2324487. DOI: 10.1080/2331186X.2024.2324487

Albadarin, Y., Saqr, M., Pope, N., & Tukiainen, M. (2024). A systematic literature review of empirical research on ChatGPT in education. *Discover Education*, *3*(1), 60. DOI: 10.1007/s44217-024-00138-2

Alduais, A., Qadhi, S., Chaaban, Y., & Khraisheh, M. (2025). The ETHICAL protocol for responsible use of generative AI for research purposes in higher education. *AI Magazine*, *46*(4), e70047. Advance online publication. DOI: 10.1002/aaai.70047

Alford, J., & Yousef, A. (2023). Unveiling the power of critical multimodal literacy: Exploring cultural difference in children's literature through 'The Proudest Blue—a Story of Hijab and Family'. *Australian Journal of Language and Literacy*, *46*(3), 301–316. DOI: 10.1007/s44020-023-00049-z

Ali, S. I., ... (2023). Causal convolution employing Almeida–Pineda recurrent backpropagation for mobile network design. *ICTACT Journals, 2023(0460).* https://ictactjournals.in/paper/IJCT_Vol_14_Iss_4_Paper_10_3091_3096.pdf

Ali, S. I. (2025). Reinforcement learning for autonomous optimization in intelligent engineering. In Babulak, E. (Ed.), *AI-driven approaches for fully automated smart engineering* (pp. 313–344). IGI Global Scientific Publishing., DOI: 10.4018/979-8-3373-4839-1.ch011

Ali, S. I., Ravuri, H. K., Lakshmi, V. T., Ramya, A., Lavanya, K., & Bahade, S. (2024). The role of nanomaterials in the development of high-performance batteries. *Nanotechnology Perceptions*, *20*(S11). Advance online publication. DOI: 10.62441/nano-ntp.v20iS11.2098

Alm, A. (2025). Reconceptualising literacy as co-literacy in language education with AI. In *Insights into AI and Language Teaching and Learning* (pp. 53–76). Castledown., DOI: 10.29140/9781763711600-04

Almatrafi, O., Johri, A., & Lee, H. (2024). A systematic review of AI literacy conceptualization, constructs, and implementation and assessment efforts (2019–2023). *Computers and Education Open*, *6*, 100173. DOI: 10.1016/j.caeo.2024.100173

Almeida, L. D. S. G., Sabota, B., & Rodrigues, O. S. (2023). Multimodal literacy in the learning of the chronicle genre: a possibility of pedagogical mediation. *Revista e-Curriculum, 21.*

Alotaibi, N. S., & Alshehri, A. H. (2023). Prospers and obstacles in using artificial intelligence in Saudi Arabia Higher Education institutions—The potential of AI-based learning outcomes. *Sustainability (Basel)*, *15*(13), 10723. DOI: 10.3390/su151310723

Amer, L. (2025). Writing Matters: Let's Spread Queer Joy through Multimodal Literacy Practices! *Language Arts*, *102*(5), 274–278. DOI: 10.58680/la20251025274

Amin, F. M. (2023). Exploring Students' Reading Interest Through Tiktok Multimodal Literacy. [JETL]. *Journal Of Education And Teaching Learning*, *5*(2), 157–164.

Amiri, S. M. H., Islam, M. M., & Akter, N. (2025). Educating the future: AI's role in shaping next-generation pedagogies. *International Journal of Science and Research Archive*, *15*(1), 621–636. DOI: 10.30574/ijsra.2025.15.1.1036

Analido, B., & Pratiwi, M. A. (2025). Multimodal Literacy: The Use of Web Blog As Media of Teaching Writing At English Department of STKIP PGRI West Sumatera. *Ethical Lingua. Journal of Language Teaching and Literature*, *12*(1). Advance online publication. DOI: 10.30605/25409190.229

Apata, S. B., Owojori, O. M., Shogbesan, Y. O., & Ugom, M. K. (2025). Artificial intelligence and multiliteracies: Preparing learners for a technologically evolving world. *International Journal of Nursing Education, 15*(15). Advance online publication. DOI: 10.24310/ijne.15.2025.21332

Aragón, M. J. (2025). "They're like slash": Multimodality and embodied agency in digital literacy practices. *Reading Research Quarterly*. Advance online publication. DOI: 10.1002/rrq.585

Arellano, R. (2024). Promoting multilingual and multimodal literacy discourses: From silence to advocacy in Chilean EFL teacher education. *Reimagining Literacies Pedagogy in the Twenty-first Century: Theorizing and Enacting Multiple Literacies for English Language Learners*, 97.

Aridasarie, Z., & Rohmah, Z. (2024). Enhancing multimodal literacy: Puppetry for English-speaking skills development. *Cogent Education, 11*(1), 2370754. DOI: 10.1080/2331186X.2024.2370754

Asad, M. M., Shahzad, S., Shah, S. H. A., Sherwani, F., & Almusharraf, N. M. (2024). ChatGPT as artificial intelligence-based generative multimedia for English writing pedagogy: Challenges and opportunities from an educator's perspective. *International Journal of Information and Learning Technology, 41*(5), 490–506. DOI: 10.1108/IJILT-02-2024-0021

ASEAN. (2020). *Joint statement from the Conference on the digital transformation of education systems throughout ASEAN*. Association of Southeast Asian Nations. https://cil.nus.edu.sg/wp-content/uploads/2020/11/2020-JS-Digital-Transformation-of-Education-Systems.pdf

Atari. (1972). *Pong* [Video game]. Atari.

Atlus. (2016). *Persona 5* [Video game]. Atlus.

Avila, K. E., Dinc, Y., Hortmann, C., & Revenga, N. (2025). On opportunities and challenges of large multimodal foundation models in education. npj Science of Learning, 10(1), 13. DOI: 10.1038/s41539-025-00301-w

Bacalja, A. (2018). What critical literacy has to offer the study of video games. *Australian Journal of Language and Literacy, 41*(2), 111–122. DOI: 10.1007/BF03652016

Bacon, C. K. (2017). Multilanguage, multipurpose: A literature review, synthesis, and framework for critical literacies in English language teaching. *Journal of Literacy Research, 49*(3), 424–453. DOI: 10.1177/1086296X17718324

Bahroun, Z., Anane, C., Ahmed, V., & Zacca, A. (2023). Transforming education: A comprehensive review of generative artificial intelligence in educational settings through bibliometric and content analysis. *Sustainability (Basel), 15*(17), 12983. DOI: 10.3390/su151712983

Barthes, R. (1972). *Mythologies* (Lavers, A., Trans.). Hill and Wang. (Original work published 1957)

Basu, K., Maddox, B., & Robinson-Pant, A. (2008). Literacies, identities and social change: Interdisciplinary approaches to literacy and development. *The Journal of Development Studies, 44*(6), 769–778. DOI: 10.1080/00220380802057695

Bekturova, M., Gaipov, D., Dyankova, G. H., & Tulepova, S. (2025). Examining Multimodal Literacy Skills Among EMI Teachers in Kazakhstan. *International Journal of Cognitive Research in Science. Engineering and Education, 13*(1), 217–222.

Beltrán-Palanques, V. (2023). Multimodal Literacy in ESP/EAP. *The Future of Teacher Education: Innovations across Pedagogies. Technology in Society, 7*, 101.

Beltrán-Palanques, V. (2024). Assessing video game narratives: Implications for the assessment of multimodal literacy in ESP. *Assessing Writing, 60*, 100809. DOI: 10.1016/j.asw.2024.100809

Beltrán-Palanques, V. (2024). Teaching elevator pitch presentations through a multimodal lens: Insights from ESP students' experiences. *TESOL Journal, 15*(1), e769. DOI: 10.1002/tesj.769

Beltrán-Palanques, V., & Querol-Julián, M. (2024). The genre of PechaKucha presentations: Analysis and implications for enhancing multimodal literacy at university. *English for Specific Purposes, 75*, 102–118. DOI: 10.1016/j.esp.2024.05.002

Bender, E. M., Gebru, T., McMillan-Major, A., & Shmitchell, S. (2021). On the Dangers of Stochastic Parrots. *Proceedings of FAccT*, 610–623. DOI: 10.1145/3442188.3445922

Bethesda Game Studios. (1997–2018). *Fallout series* [Video game series]. Bethesda Softworks.

Bewersdorff, A., Hartmann, C., Hornberger, M., Seßler, K., Bannert, M., Kasneci, E., Kasneci, G., Zhai, X., & Nerdel, C. (2025). Taking the next step with generative artificial intelligence: The transformative role of multimodal large language models in science education. *Learning and Individual Differences, 118*, 102601. DOI: 10.1016/j.lindif.2024.102601

Bezemer, J., & Cowan, K. (2021). Exploring reading in social semiotics: Theory and methods. *Social Semiotics, 31*(3), 331–348. DOI: 10.1080/10350330.2020.1810553

Bezemer, J., & Kress, G. (2008). Writing in multimodal texts: A social semiotic account of designs for learning. *Written Communication, 25*(2), 166–195. DOI: 10.1177/0741088307313177

Bezemer, J., & Kress, G. (2015). *Multimodality, learning and communication.* Routledge., DOI: 10.4324/9781315687537

Biagini, G. (2024). Assessing the assessments: Toward a multidimensional approach to AI literacy. *Medical Education, 15*(1), 91–101. DOI: 10.36253/me-15831 PMID: 38279173

Bjork, O. (2025). Towards a multimodal dialogic understanding of early writing development in school. *Language and Education.* Advance online publication. DOI: 10.1080/09500782.2025.2471506

Blackledge, A. (2000). *Literacy, power and social justice.* Trentham Books.

Black, N. B., George, S., Eguchi, A., Dempsey, J. C., Langran, E., Fraga, L., Brunvand, S., & Howard, N. (2024a). A framework for approaching AI education in Educator Preparation Programs. *Proceedings of the AAAI Conference on Artificial Intelligence, 38*(21), 23069–23077. DOI: 10.1609/aaai.v38i21.30351

Blizzard Entertainment. (2004). *World of Warcraft* [Video game]. Blizzard Entertainment.

Boden, M. A. (1998). Creativity and artificial intelligence. *Artificial Intelligence, 103*(1–2), 347–356. DOI: 10.1016/S0004-3702(98)00055-1

Bogost, I. (2011). *How to do things with videogames.* University of Minnesota Press. DOI: 10.5749/minnesota/9780816676460.001.0001

Bohas, A., Grolleau, G., & Mzoughi, N. (2024). The advantages of being disadvantaged. *Kyklos, 77*(3), 759–775. DOI: 10.1111/kykl.12388

Bolívar, V. P. (2023). Rethinking Multimodal Literacy in Theory and Practice. *RaeL: Revista Electrónica de Lingüística Aplicada, 22*(1).

Bretaño, J. A. (2025). Towards multimodal literacy in translation studies. *Estudios de traducción*, (15), 25-32.

Breunig, M. (2019). Beings who are becoming: Enhancing social justice literacy. *Journal of Experiential Education, 42*(1), 7–21. DOI: 10.1177/1053825918820694

Brouwer, C. L., Dinkla, A. M., Vandewinckele, L., Crijns, W., Claessens, M., Verellen, D., & van Elmpt, W. (2020). Machine learning applications in radiation oncology: Current use and needs to support clinical implementation. *Physics and Imaging in Radiation Oncology, 16*, 144–148. DOI: 10.1016/j.phro.2020.11.002 PMID: 33458358

Brown, S., Hao, L., & Zhang, R. (2023). Assessing the multimodal literacy practices of young emergent bilinguals. In *Handbook of multilingual TESOL in practice* (pp. 373–401). Springer Nature Singapore. DOI: 10.1007/978-981-19-9350-3_25

Buckingham, D. (2015). Defining digital literacy — What do young people need to know about digital media? *Nordic Journal of Digital Literacy, 10*(Jubileumsnummer), 21–35. DOI: 10.18261/ISSN1891-943X-2015-Jubileumsnummer-03

Buckingham, D. (2019). *The media education manifesto*. Polity Press.

Buolamwini, J., & Gebru, T. (2018). Gender shades: Intersectional accuracy disparities in commercial gender classification. *Conference on fairness, accountability and transparency, 81*, 1–15. http://proceedings.mlr.press/v81/buolamwini18a.html

Burnett, C., & Merchant, G. (2020). Returning to text: Affect, meaning making, and literacies. *Reading Research Quarterly, 56*(2), 355–367. DOI: 10.1002/rrq.303

Burns, M. K., Duke, N. K., & Cartwright, K. B. (2023). Evaluating components of the active view of reading as intervention targets: Implications for social justice. *School Psychology, 38*(1), 30–41. DOI: 10.1037/spq0000519 PMID: 36745101

Campbell, C., & Olteanu, A. (2024). The challenge of postdigital literacy: Extending multimodality and social semiotics for a new age. *Postdigital Science and Education, 6*(2), 572–594. DOI: 10.1007/s42438-023-00414-8

Cappello, M., & Ojeda, A. G. (2023). Teaching Multimodal and Digital Literacies. In *Handbook of Research on Teaching the English Language Arts* (pp. 96–115). Routledge. DOI: 10.4324/9781003334392-6

Cappello, M., Wiseman, A. M., & Turner, J. D. (2019). Framing equitable classroom practices: Potentials of critical multimodal literacy research. *Literacy Research: Theory, Method, and Practice, 68*(1), 205–225. DOI: 10.1177/2381336919870274

Carcamo, B. (2024). Within the'Educational Chasm': The Chilean ELT Textbook and the Development of Multimodal Literacy. *Language Teaching Research Quarterly, 40*, 161–174. DOI: 10.32038/ltrq.2024.40.10

Carcamo, B. (2025). Exploring the impact of multimodal artifact creation in Canva on the understanding of multimodal texts in EFL Learners. *Technology in Language Teaching & Learning*, *7*(4), 103022–103022. DOI: 10.29140/tltl.v7n4.103022

Carcamo, B., & Carmona, C. (2025). Improving EFL students' multimodal literacy through infographics. *ELT Journal*, *79*(2), 205–215. DOI: 10.1093/elt/ccae049

Carcamo, B., & Pino, B. (2025). Developing EFL students' multimodal literacy with the use of infographics. *Asian-Pacific Journal of Second and Foreign Language Education*, *10*(1), 16. DOI: 10.1186/s40862-025-00322-3

Casal-Otero, L., Catala, A., Fernández-Morante, C., Taboada, M., Cebreiro, B., & Barro, S. (2023). AI literacy in K-12: A systematic literature review. *International Journal of STEM Education*, *10*(1), 29. Advance online publication. DOI: 10.1186/s40594-023-00418-7

Chantajinda, V. (2024). Research into practice: Digital multimodal composition in second language writing. *Language Teaching*, *57*(4), 546–560. DOI: 10.1017/S0261444824000235

Cheng, L. M. Y., Powell, S. J., & Davis, B. (2025). Critical Multimodal Literacy: An Analysis of Young Children's Picture Books About Refugees: L. Cheng et al. *International Journal of Early Childhood*, 1-27.

Chen, L., Chen, P., & Lin, Z. (2020). Artificial intelligence in education: A review. *IEEE Access : Practical Innovations, Open Solutions*, *8*, 75264–75278. DOI: 10.1109/ACCESS.2020.2988510

Chen, Y. (2024). Perceptions of AI-facilitated creativity in language education: A study on digital storytelling. *The JALT CALL Journal*, *20*(3), 1–27. DOI: 10.29140/jaltcall.v20n3.2089

Chesney, R., & Citron, D. K. (2019). Deep fakes: A looming challenge for privacy, democracy, and national security. SSRN *Electronic Journal, 107*, 1–68. DOI: 10.2139/ssrn.3213954

Chess, S. (2017). Playing with Identity. In Ready Player Two: Women Gamers and Designed Identity (pp. 31–58). University of Minnesota Press. DOI: 10.5749/j.ctt1pwt7z7.5

Cheung, K. K. C., Erduran, S., & Oancea, A. (2025). Affordances and Challenges of Multimodal Literacy-Infused Science Pedagogy: A Case of Hong Kong EMI Science Classroom. *Designing Learning with Multimodality in English Medium of Education (EME) Classrooms Across Asia*, 47.

Cheung, K. K. C., Pun, J., Kenneth-Li, W., & Mai, J. (2024). Exploring students' multimodal representations of ideas about epistemic reading of scientific texts in generative AI tools. *Journal of Science Education and Technology*. Advance online publication. DOI: 10.1007/s10956-024-10182-0

Chheang, S., & Huot, S. (2025). A narrative review of teacher engagement in career guidance across Cambodian high schools. *Journal of Social and Educational Research*, *4*(2), 189–198. DOI: 10.5281/zenodo.17868433

Chiu, T. K. F. (2024). Future research recommendations for transforming higher education with generative AI. *Computers and Education: Artificial Intelligence*, *6*, 100197. DOI: 10.1016/j.caeai.2023.100197

Chiu, T. K. F., Ahmad, Z., Ismailov, M., & Sanusi, I. T. (2024). What are artificial intelligence literacy and competency? A comprehensive framework to support them. *Computers and Education Open*, *6*, 100171. DOI: 10.1016/j.caeo.2024.100171

Chiu, T. K. F., Xia, Q., Zhou, X., Chai, C. S., & Cheng, M. (2023). Systematic literature review on opportunities, challenges, and future research recommendations of artificial intelligence in education. *Computers & Education: Artificial Intelligence*, *4*, 100118. DOI: 10.1016/j.caeai.2022.100118

Cho, H. (2017). Navigating the meanings of social justice, teaching for social justice, and multicultural education. *International Journal of Multicultural Education*, *19*(2), 1–19. DOI: 10.18251/ijme.v19i2.1307

Christ-Brendemühl, S. (2025). Leveraging generative AI in higher education: An analysis of opportunities and challenges addressed in university guidelines. *European Journal of Education*, *60*(1), e12891. Advance online publication. DOI: 10.1111/ejed.12891

Christian, I. S., Rohmah, Z., & Jalaluddin, I. (2024). Exploring Studies on Multimodal Literacy in English Learning: A Bibliometric Analysis. [Journal of English Education and Linguistics Studies]. *JEELS*, *11*(2), 821–848. DOI: 10.30762/jeels.v11i2.3681

Ciampa, K., Wolfe, Z. M., & Bronstein, B. (2023). ChatGPT in education: Transforming digital literacy practices. *Journal of Adolescent & Adult Literacy: A Journal From the International Reading Association*, *67*(3), 186–195. DOI: 10.1002/jaal.1310

Claman, D., & Sezgin, E. (2024). Artificial intelligence in Dental Education: Opportunities and Challenges of large language models and Multimodal foundation Models (Preprint). *JMIR Medical Education*, *10*, e52346. DOI: 10.2196/52346 PMID: 39331527

Cohn, C., Snyder, C., & Fonteles, J. H., Ashwin, Montenegro, J., & Biswas, G. (. (2025). A multimodal approach to support teacher, researcher and AI collaboration in STEM +C learning environments. *British Journal of Educational Technology: Journal of the Council for Educational Technology*, *56*(2), 595–620. DOI: 10.1111/bjet.13518

Cope, B., & Kalantzis, M. (2009). "Multiliteracies": New literacies, new learning. *Pedagogies*, *4*(3), 164–195. DOI: 10.1080/15544800903076044

Cope, B., & Kalantzis, M. (2015). *A pedagogy of multiliteracies: Learning by design*. Palgrave. DOI: 10.1057/9781137539724

Cope, B., & Kalantzis, M. (2020). *Making sense: Reference, agency, and structure in a grammar of multimodal meaning*. Cambridge University Press. DOI: 10.1017/9781316459645

Cope, B., & Kalantzis, M. (2024). Literacy in the time of artificial intelligence [Preprint]. *EdArXiv*. https://doi.org/DOI: 10.35542/osf.io/es5kb

Cope, B., & Kalantzis, M. (Eds.). (2000). *Multiliteracies: Literacy learning and the design of social futures*. Routledge.

Cornfield, O., Rodriquez Vazquez, B., & Holtaway, K. (2025). Fostering creative confidence and multimodal literacy in practice at the Children's Creativity Museum. *Journal of Early Childhood Literacy*, *25*(4), 14687984251382045. DOI: 10.1177/14687984251382045

Crawford Camiciottoli, B., & Campoy-Cubillo, M. C. (2018). Introduction: The nexus of multimodality, multimodal literacy, and English language teaching in research and practice in higher education settings. *System*, *77*, 1–9. DOI: 10.1016/j.system.2018.03.005

Crescenzi-Lanna, L. (2020). Multimodal learning analytics research with young children: A systematic review. *British Journal of Educational Technology*, *51*(5), 1485–1504. DOI: 10.1111/bjet.12959

Crompton, H., & Burke, D. (2020). Mobile learning and pedagogical opportunities: A configurative systematic review of PreK-12 research using the SAMR framework. *Computers & Education*, *156*, 103945. DOI: 10.1016/j.compedu.2020.103945

Cross, R., Condon, L., & McNamara, M. (2022). Dialogic theories, literacy practices and initial teacher education. *Australian Journal of Language and Literacy*, *45*(3), 362–376. DOI: 10.1007/s44020-022-00025-z

Cruz, F. R. (2022). *Jogando palavras: Tecnologia e gamificação no ensino de língua portuguesa*. InterSaberes.

Cruz, F. R. (2024). "Papers, Please": transposições entre o real e o imaginário de comunidades de refugiados. *RE@D - Revista de Educação a Distância e E-learning, 7*(2), e202416. DOI: 10.34627/redvol7iss2e202416

Cummings, R. E., Monroe, S. M., & Watkins, M. (2024). Generative AI in first-year writing: An early analysis of affordances, limitations, and a framework for the future. *Computers and Composition, 71*, 102827. DOI: 10.1016/j.compcom.2024.102827

Cun, A. (2025). Creating more opportunities through multimodal literacy and positioning in online and in-person Chinese heritage language classrooms. *Language and Education, 39*(2), 357–379. DOI: 10.1080/09500782.2024.2352428

Dada, C. (2025). Integrating Technology for Multimodal Literacy in English Studies. *NIU Journal of Humanities, 10*(1), 237–245.

Dada, C., & Akande, R. M. (2025). Assessing Multimodal Literacy in Higher Education: Impact on Student Learning Outcomes in Selected Universities in Edo State, Nigeria. *NIU Journal of Educational Research, 11*(1), 51–59.

Dahlquist, M. (2023). Toward a framework for information creativity. *College & Research Libraries, 84*(3). Advance online publication. DOI: 10.5860/crl.84.3.441

Damayanti, I. L., & Febrianti, Y. (2020). Multimodal literacy: Unfolding reading path in children's picture book and its potential for EFL classrooms. *Indonesian Journal of Applied Linguistics, 9*(3), 616–627. DOI: 10.17509/ijal.v9i3.23212

Daniele, S., Murcia, K., & Chappell, J. (2025). Beyond museum walls: A transmedia approach to fostering multimodal literacy and STEM engagement in science discovery children's museums. *Journal of Early Childhood Literacy, 25*(4), 14687984251379603. DOI: 10.1177/14687984251379603

Danielsson, K., & Selander, S. (2016). Reading multimodal texts for learning – a model for cultivating multimodal literacy. *Designs for Learning, 8*(1), 25–36. DOI: 10.16993/dfl.72

Daulay, E., & Dewi, U. (2025). Reading comprehension through multimodal literacy approach for English education. [English Teaching Journal]. *ETERNAL, 16*(2), 397–404. DOI: 10.26877/eternal.v16i2.1910

Davis, G. A., & Woodward, J. (2020). *Creativity is forever*. Hunt Publishing.

De Oliveira, J. M. (2024, November). Enhancing multimodal literacy through community service learning in higher education. [). Frontiers Media SA.]. *Frontiers in Education*, *9*, 1448805. DOI: 10.3389/feduc.2024.1448805

de Saussure, F. (2011). *Course in General Linguistics* (P. Meisel & H. Saussy, Eds.; W. Baskin, Trans.). Columbia University Press. (Original work published 1916)

Derunova, E. N., & Sagyntaeva, Z. K. (2025). Creolized texts as a tool for developing multimodal literacy of schoolchildren learning Russian in Kazakhstan. *Russian Language Studies*, *23*(1), 132–152. DOI: 10.22363/2618-8163-2025-23-1-132-152

Detrick, R., & Li, N. (2025). Students-generative AI interaction patterns and its impact on academic writing. *Journal of Computing in Higher Education*. Advance online publication. DOI: 10.1007/s12528-025-09444-6

Dewan, P. (2016). Economic well-being and social justice through pleasure reading. *New Library World*, *117*(9/10), 557–567. DOI: 10.1108/NLW-03-2016-0019

Dewanthi, F., Marsakawati, N. P. E., & Sari, R. A. (2024). Text-based language teaching flipbook for guest relation officer to enhance students multimodal literacy. [TATEFL]. *The Art of Teaching English as a Foreign Language*, *5*(2), 124–136. DOI: 10.36663/tatefl.v5i2.759

Dewey, J. (1934). The supreme intellectual obligation. *Science*, *79*(2046), 240–243. DOI: 10.1126/science.79.2046.240 PMID: 17731609

Domínguez Figaredo, D., & Stoyanovich, J. (2023). Responsible AI literacy: A stakeholder-first approach. *Big Data & Society*, *10*(2), 20539517231219958. Advance online publication. DOI: 10.1177/20539517231219958

Domínguez Romero, E., Bobkina, J., Stefanova Radoulska, S., & Herrero, C. (2023). *Rethinking multimodal literacy in theory and practice*. Peter Lang. DOI: 10.3726/b20792

Dover, A. G. (2016). Teaching for social justice and the Common Core: Justice-oriented curriculum for language arts and literacy. *Journal of Adolescent & Adult Literacy*, *59*(5), 517–527. DOI: 10.1002/jaal.488

Duraisamy, S. (2025). Exploring the impact of multimodal learning on literacy and social-emotional development in early childhood. *Journal of Language and Culture in Education*, *2*(2b), 88–108.

Ebarvia, T., Germán, L., Parker, K. N., & Torres, J. (2021). "literacy Is liberation": A Conversation with# disruptTexts leaders. *English Journal*, *111*(1), 25–31. DOI: 10.58680/ej202131388

Eubanks, V. (2018). *Automating inequality: How high-tech tools profile, police, and punish the poor.* St. Martin's Press.

Fahruddiana, Y. (2025). Education at the cultural crossroads: Navigating identity and globalization in Southeast Asia. *International Education Trend Issues, 3*(1), 33–38. DOI: 10.56442/ieti.v3i1.1055

Farias-Gaytan, S., Aguaded, I., & Ramirez-Montoya, M. S. (2023). Digital transformation and digital literacy in the context of complexity within higher education institutions: A systematic literature review. *Humanities & Social Sciences Communications, 10*(1), 386. DOI: 10.1057/s41599-023-01875-9

Floridi, L., & Chiriatti, M. (2020). GPT-3: Its nature, scope, limits, and consequences. *Minds and Machines, 30*(4), 681–694. DOI: 10.1007/s11023-020-09548-1

Floridi, L., Cowls, J., Beltrametti, M., Chatila, R., Chazerand, P., Dignum, V., Luetge, C., Madelin, R., Pagallo, U., Rossi, F., Schafer, B., Valcke, P., & Vayena, E. (2018). AI4People—An Ethical Framework for a Good AI Society: Opportunities, risks, principles, and recommendations. *Minds and Machines, 28*(4), 689–707. DOI: 10.1007/s11023-018-9482-5 PMID: 30930541

Fortanet-Gómez, I., & Querol-Julián, M. (2025). Multimodal literacy at the university: The ins and outs of educating in English as an additional language. In *Multimodal Literacy in English as an Additional Language in Higher Education* (pp. 3–19). Routledge. DOI: 10.4324/9781003429876-2

Forte, M. (2025). Exploring multiverses: Generative AI and neuroaesthetic perspectives. *Heritage, 8*(3), 102. DOI: 10.3390/heritage8030102

Fountoulakis, M. S. (2024). Evaluating the impact of AI tools on language proficiency and intercultural communication in second language education. *International Journal of Second and Foreign Language Education, 3*(1), 12–26. DOI: 10.33422/ijsfle.v3i1.768

Fradana, A. N., Suwarta, N., & Sotlikova, R. (2025). Strengthening multimodal literacy through digital literary text learning: Enhancing students' achievement in the age of disruption. *Journal of Language and Literature Studies, 5*(1), 216–225. DOI: 10.36312/jolls.v5i1.2635

Freire, P. (1985). Reading the world and reading the word: An interview with Paulo Freire. *Language Arts, 62*(1), 15–21. DOI: 10.58680/la198525786

Freire, P. (1987). *Reading the word and the world.* Bergin & Garvey.

Freire, P. (2021). *Pedagogy of hope*. Bloomsbury Academic. DOI: 10.5040/9781350190238

Fricker, M. (2007). *Epistemic injustice: Power and the ethics of knowing*. Oxford University Press. DOI: 10.1093/acprof:oso/9780198237907.001.0001

Fu, S., Lee, A. J., Wang, A., Momennejad, I., Bihl, T., Lu, H., & Webb, T. W. (2025, March 29). *Evaluating compositional scene understanding in multimodal generative models*. arXiv.org. https://arxiv.org/abs/2503.23125?utm_source=chatgpt.com

Gainer, J. S. (2010). Critical media literacy in middle school: Exploring the politics of representation. *Journal of Adolescent & Adult Literacy*, *53*(5), 364–373. DOI: 10.1598/JAAL.53.5.2

Galactic Cafe. (2013). *The Stanley Parable* [Video game]. Galactic Cafe.

García, C. G. (2024). YOUTUBE videos to develop multimodal literacy. *ELIA: Estudios de Lingüística Inglesa Aplicada*, (24), 209–244. DOI: 10.12795/elia.2024.i24.7

Gass, A. B. (2022). *The body in play: Embodiment in and through videogames* (Doctoral dissertation). University of Chicago.

Gavaler, C., & Goldberg, N. (2019). *Superhero thought experiments: Comic book philosophy*. University of Iowa Press. DOI: 10.2307/j.ctvn5twvb

Gearbox Software. (2009–2025). *Borderlands series* [Video game series]. 2K Games.

Gee, J. P. (2003). What video games have to teach us about learning and literacy. [CIE]. *Computers in Entertainment*, *1*(1), 1–4. DOI: 10.1145/950566.950595

Gee, J. P. (2007). *What video games have to teach us about learning and literacy* (2nd ed.). Palgrave Macmillan.

Gee, J. P. (2008). Video games and embodiment. *Games and Culture*, *3*(3-4), 253–263. DOI: 10.1177/1555412008317309

Giant Sparrow. (2017). *What remains of Edith Finch* [Video game]. Annapurna Interactive.

Gideon, L.A. (2025). The role of Ai in English education: Opportunities, challenges, and future directions. *International Journal of Law, Politics and Humanities Research*. DOI: 10.70382/caijlphr.v9i6.057

González, N., Moll, L. C., & Amanti, C. (Eds.). (2005). *Funds of knowledge: Theorizing practices in households, communities, and classrooms*. Lawrence Erlbaum Associates.

Gordon, F. (2019). Virginia Eubanks (2018) automating inequality: How high-tech tools profile, police, and punish the poor. New york: Picador, st martin's press. *Law. Technology and Humans*, *1*(1), 162–164. DOI: 10.5204/lthj.v1i0.1386

Gramsci, A. (2000). *The Gramsci reader: selected writings, 1916-1935*. NYU Press.

Group, N. N. L.The New London Group. (1996). A Pedagogy of Multiliteracies: Designing Social Futures. *Harvard Educational Review*, *66*(1), 60–93. DOI: 10.17763/haer.66.1.17370n67v22j160u

Guanio-Uluru, L. (2022). The Reader as Player: Exploring the Notion of Aesthetic and Efferent Gaming. *International Research in Children's Literature*, *15*(3), 338–352. DOI: 10.3366/ircl.2022.0471

Guerrero-Sosa, J. D. T., Romero, F. P., Menéndez-Domínguez, V. H., Serrano-Guerrero, J., Montoro-Montarroso, A., & Olivas, J. A. (2025). A Comprehensive review of multimodal analysis in Education. *Applied Sciences (Basel, Switzerland)*, *15*(11), 5896. DOI: 10.3390/app15115896

Güneş, A., & Kaban, A. L. (2025). A Delphi study on ethical challenges and ensuring academic integrity regarding AI research in higher education. *Higher Education Quarterly*, *79*(4), e70057. Advance online publication. DOI: 10.1111/hequ.70057

Guo, M., & Wang, J. (2024). Robotic Badges for Girl Scouts: Coding Exploration Integrated with Multimodal Literacy. *Journal of Technology-Integrated Lessons and Teaching*, *3*(2), 30–40. DOI: 10.13001/jtilt.v3i2.8763

Guo, X., Chen, S., & Guo, Y. (2024). Advancing multimodal teaching: A bibliometric and content analysis of trends, influences, and future directions. *Humanities & Social Sciences Communications*, *11*(1), 1527. DOI: 10.1057/s41599-024-04254-0

Guo, Y.-X., & Zhang, X. (2025). The impact mechanism of algorithmic transparency on user trust in intelligent recommendation systems of internet platforms. *Journal of Computers*, •••, 335–348. DOI: 10.63367/199115992025063603022

Gu, X., & Ericson, B. J. (2024). AI literacy in K-12 and higher education in the wake of generative AI: An integrative review. In *Proceedings of the 2025 ACM Conference on International Computing Education Research* V.1 (pp. 367-381). DOI: 10.1145/3702652.3744217

Hadjiconstantinou, S. (2023). Developing multimodal literacy through critical practices: an examalpe from an english for the media university program. In *5th International Conference Literacy and Contemporary Society: Creativity, Equity, Social Action*.

Hafner, C. A. (2014). Embedding digital literacies in English language teaching: Students' digital video projects as multimodal ensembles. *TESOL Quarterly*, *48*(4), 655–685. DOI: 10.1002/tesq.138

Hambally Yacouba, Y., Diabagate, A., Diaby, M., Coulibaly, A., & Azmani, A. (2025). AI in african schools: Obstacles, perspectives and pedagogical strategies. *International Journal of Advanced Research*, *13*(9), 764–784. DOI: 10.21474/IJAR01/21760

Haoming, W., Chengliang, W., Zhan, C., Fa, L., Chunjia, B., & Xianlong, X. (2025). Impact of AI-agent-supported collaborative learning on the learning outcomes of university programming courses. *Education and Information Technologies*, *30*(12), 1–34. DOI: 10.1007/s10639-025-13487-8

Hardukiewicz, J. (2024). Multimodal Literacy in Teaching Foreign Languages: The Example of Power Point Presentations. *XLINGUAE*, *17*(4), 251–261. DOI: 10.18355/XL.2024.17.04.15

Harrington, L., & Cox, K. (2024). On These Haunted Streets: A Photopoetic Process of Transmedia Storytelling as Critical Multimodal Literacy. In *Transmedia Applications in Literacy Fields* (pp. 238-261). IGI Global. DOI: 10.4018/979-8-3693-3302-0.ch011

Harry, A., & Sayudin, S. (2023). Role of AI in education. [INJURITY]. *Interdiciplinary Journal and Hummanity*, *2*(3), 260–268. DOI: 10.58631/injurity.v2i3.52

Hartmann, E. C. (2025). Multimodal literacy learning in The big word factory: Exploring a trilingual picturebook app with bilingual student teachers. In *Multimodal Mediation Through Picturebooks and Graphic Narratives* (pp. 167–186). Routledge. DOI: 10.4324/9781003378136-11

Hashim, H. U., Saragih, E., & Gapur, A. (2024). Enhancing Augmented Reality (AR) Technology to Improve Medical English Literacy. *International Journal Linguistics of Sumatra and Malay, 2*(2), 49â-55.

Hawreliak, J. (2019). *Multimodal semiotics and rhetoric in videogames*. Routledge.

Heilala, V., & Araya, R. (2025). Beyond text-to-text: An overview of multimodal and generative artificial intelligence for education using topic modeling. *Proceedings of the 40th ACM/SIGAPP Symposium on Applied Computing*, 1594–1603. DOI: 10.1145/3672608.3707764

Henderson, R. (2023). Between worlds: Extending students' multimodal literacy practices with augmented reality. *Literacy Learning: The Middle Years*, *31*(1), 66–68.

Hendricks-Sturrup, R., Simmons, M., Anders, S., Aneni, K., Wright Clayton, E., Coco, J., Collins, B., Heitman, E., Hussain, S., Joshi, K., Lemieux, J., Lovett Novak, L., Rubin, D. J., Shanker, A., Washington, T., Waters, G., Webb Harris, J., Yin, R., Wagner, T., & Malin, B. (2023). Developing ethics and equity principles, terms, and engagement tools to Advance Health Equity and Researcher Diversity in AI and machine learning: Modified Delphi approach. *JMIR AI*, *2*, e52888. DOI: 10.2196/52888 PMID: 38875540

Hesti, D. A., Ozora, G., Silalahi, V. M., Hanoselina, Y., & Helmi, R. F. (2025). Pemberdayaan Siswa dan Siswi dalam Pemanfaatan Kecerdasan Buatan (AI) Secara Etis dan Produktif di Lingkungan Sekolah. *Sosial Simbiosis : Jurnal Integrasi Ilmu Sosial Dan Politik*, *2*(2), 163–178. DOI: 10.62383/sosial.v2i2.1588

Higgins, L., Long, E., & Flower, L. (2006). Community literacy: A rhetorical model for personal and public inquiry. *Community Literacy Journal*, *1*(1), 9–43. DOI: 10.25148/CLJ.1.1.009529

Holmes, W., Bialik, M., & Fadel, C. (2019). *Artificial intelligence in education: Promises and implications for teaching and learning*. Center for Curriculum Redesign.

Holmes, W., Porayska-Pomsta, K., Holstein, K., Sutherland, E., Baker, T., Shum, S. B., Santos, O. C., Rodrigo, M. T., Cukurova, M., Bittencourt, I. I., & Koedinger, K. R. (2022). Ethics of AI in education: Towards a community-wide framework. *International Journal of Artificial Intelligence in Education*, *32*(3), 504–526. DOI: 10.1007/s40593-021-00239-1

Holmes, W., & Tuomi, I. (2022). State of the art and practice in AI in education. *European Journal of Education*, *57*(4), 542–570. DOI: 10.1111/ejed.12533

hooks, b. (2014). *Teaching to transgress*. Routledge.

Hornberger, N. H., & Skilton-Sylvester, E. (2000). Revisiting the continua of biliteracy: International and critical perspectives. *Language and Education*, *14*(2), 96–122. DOI: 10.1080/09500780008666781

Hradilová, A. (2025). Generative AI in teaching academic writing: Guiding students to make informed and ethical choices. *Language Learning in Higher Education*, *15*(2), 447–461. DOI: 10.1515/cercles-2024-0103

Hryciw, B. N., Seely, A. J. E., & Kyeremanteng, K. (2023). Guiding principles and proposed classification system for the responsible adoption of artificial intelligence in scientific writing in medicine. *Frontiers in Artificial Intelligence*, *6*, 1283353. DOI: 10.3389/frai.2023.1283353 PMID: 38035200

Huang, L. T., & Huang, T. (2025). Generative bias: Widespread, unexpected, and uninterpretable biases in generative models and their implications. *AI & Society*. Advance online publication. DOI: 10.1007/s00146-025-02533-1

Hull, G. A., & Nelson, M. E. (2005). Locating the semiotic power of multimodality. *Written Communication*, *22*(2), 224–261. DOI: 10.1177/0741088304274170

Hulston, S. J. (2019). Embodied meaning making: A case study investigating the use of gesture in the responses of year 1 children to a wordless picturebook. *Cambridge Open-Review Educational Research e-Journal, 6*, 13–33.

Huot, S., & Loch, S. (2025a). Digital practices in Cambodian EFL classrooms: Teacher narratives from remote learning. In K. Khette & Tayade (Eds.), *Proceeding of one day national conference on English language, literature, cultural studies and media studies* (Vol. 2, pp. 19–31). Centre for Learning, Research and Development, Savda, Maharashtra. DOI: 10.5281/zenodo.16921807

Huot, S. (2025a). Digital tutors in the kingdom: Exploring ChatGPT's influence on Cambodian students' academic and cognitive growth. In Pandya, J. D., & Patel, K. C. (Eds.), *Interdisciplinary insights: Exploring multiple perspectives* (Vol. 2, pp. 36–54). Meadow Publication.

Huot, S. (2025b). Temples to policy plans: Tracing the political trajectory of education and governance in Cambodia, from antiquity to contemporary reforms. *Journal of Political Science and International Relations*, *8*(3), 122–132. DOI: 10.11648/j.jpsir.20250803.12

Huot, S., & Chheang, S. (2025). Unwriting empire: Decolonizing Khmer language, literature, and cultural memory. *The Context: Journal of English Studies*, *12*(6), 280–293. DOI: 10.5281/zenodo.17061523

Huot, S., & Hok, C. (2025). Enhancing English language teaching for multilingual learners: Leveraging heritage languages in the classroom. *Journal of Social and Educational Research*, *4*(1), 87–95. DOI: 10.5281/zenodo.15698964

Huot, S., & Loch, S. (2025b). Educating in the age of AI: Preparing Cambodian teachers and students for an AI-augmented learning future. *Journal of Educational Technology and E-Learning Innovations*, *1*(2), 31–38. DOI: 10.54536/jeteli.v1i2.5170

Huot, S., Loch, S., Nget, R., & Em, S. (2025). Exploring multiliteracies in the digital era: A framework for 21st-century learning. [CJESS]. *Cambodian Journal of Educational and Social Sciences*, *2*(1), 7–27. DOI: 10.69496/cjess.v2i1.50

Huot, S., & Such, C. (2025). Leveraging social media for language learning: Opportunities and challenges. [JEILT]. *Journal of Education Innovation and Language Teaching*, *1*(2), 10–29. DOI: 10.63381/jeilt.v1i2.56

Huot, S., & Tep, P. (2025). Advancing ChatGPT for pedagogical innovation in Cambodia: Insight from global evidence and local implications. *The Context: Journal of English Studies*, *12*(4), 115–135. DOI: 10.5281/zenodo.15806972

Hutchison, A., & Woodward, L. (2014). A planning cycle for integrating digital technology into literacy instruction. *The Reading Teacher*, *67*(6), 455–464. DOI: 10.1002/trtr.1225

Hwang, Y., & Wu, Y. (2025). Graphic design education in the era of text-to-image generation: Transitioning to contents creator. *International Journal of Art & Design Education*, *44*(1), 239–253. DOI: 10.1111/jade.12558

Hysaj, A., & Freeman, M. (2025). Exploring the purposes and uses of generative artificial intelligence tools in academic writing for multicultural students. *Higher Education Research & Development*, *44*(7), 1686–1700. Advance online publication. DOI: 10.1080/07294360.2025.2488862

Ibrahim, A. B. (2024). Assessing the knowledge and perception of artificial intelligence for teaching and research among lecturers in the faculties of arts in Nigeria. *Journal of Global Research in Education and Social Science*, *18*(2), 25–33. DOI: 10.56557/jogress/2024/v18i28671

Ibrahim, R. A., & Lianingsih, N. (2025). Digital rhetoric and algorithmic ethics: A literature review of digital communication. *International Journal of Linguistics. Communication & Broadcasting*, *3*(2), 45–49. DOI: 10.46336/ijlcb.v3i2.224

Igbokwe, I. C. (2024). Artificial intelligence in educational leadership: Risks and responsibilities. *European Journal of Arts. Humanities and Social Sciences*, *1*(6), 3–10. DOI: 10.59324/ejahss.2024.1(6).01

ILO. (2021). *The gender divide in digital skills is another – sadly unsurprising – divide*. International Labour Organization. https://www.ilo.org/media/378741/download

Ilomäki, L., Paavola, S., Lakkala, M., & Kantosalo, A. (2023). Critical digital literacies at school level: A systematic review. *Review of Education*, *11*(3), e3425. DOI: 10.1002/rev3.3425

Indhra, F. M., Anshori, M., & Solihin, M. (2025). Adapting Palabe folk tales into multimodal literacy for early childhood education. [IJED]. *Indonesian Journal of Educational Development*, *6*(3), 874–892. DOI: 10.59672/ijed.v6i3.5365

Insani, N. H., Suwarna, S., & Triyono, S. (2024). Effect of Multimodal Literacy on Reading Ability of Indonesian Javanese Learners. *Issues in Language Studies, 13*(2), 17–33. DOI: 10.33736/ils.6472.2024

Isbister, K. (2017). *How games move us: emotion by design.* The MIT Press.

Jandrić, P., Knox, J., Besley, T., Ryberg, T., Suoranta, J., & Hayes, S. (2018). Post-digital science and education. *Educational Philosophy and Theory, 50*(10), 893–899. DOI: 10.1080/00131857.2018.1454000

Janks, H. (2017). Critical literacy and the social justice project of education. *English Teaching, 16*(2), 132–144. DOI: 10.1108/ETPC-09-2016-0111

Jayanti, E. D., & Damayanti, I. L. (2023). Exploring teachers' perceptions of integrating multimodal literacy into English classrooms in Indonesian primary education. *Child Education Journal, 5*(2), 98–109. DOI: 10.33086/cej.v5i2.5240

Jenkins, H. (2012). *Textual poachers: Television fans and participatory culture.* Routledge. DOI: 10.4324/9780203114339

Jenkins, H., Clinton, K., Purushotma, R., Robison, A. J., & Weigel, M. (2006). *Confronting the challenges of participatory culture: Media education for the 21st century.* The John D. and Catherine T. MacArthur Foundation.

Jenkins, H., & Ito, M. (2016). *Participatory culture in a networked era: A conversation on youth, learning, commerce, and politics.* John Wiley & Sons.

Jewitt, C. (2005). Multimodality,"reading", and "writing" for the 21st century. *Discourse (Abingdon), 26*(3), 315–331. DOI: 10.1080/01596300500200011

Jewitt, C. (Ed.). (2009). *The Routledge handbook of multimodal analysis.* Routledge.

Jewitt, C., Bezemer, J., & O'Halloran, K. (2016). *Introducing multimodality.* Routledge., DOI: 10.4324/9781315638027

Jiang, J. (2024). When generative artificial intelligence meets multimodal composition: Rethinking the composition process through an AI-assisted design project. *Computers & Composition. Computers and Composition, 74,* 102883. DOI: 10.1016/j.compcom.2024.102883

Jin, Y., Echeverria, V., Yan, L., Zhao, L., Alfredo, R., Tsai, Y., Gašević, D., & Martinez-Maldonado, R. (2024). FATE in MMLA: A Student-Centred Exploration of Fairness, Accountability, Transparency, and Ethics in Multimodal Learning Analytics. *arXiv (Cornell University).* https://doi.org//arxiv.2402.19071DOI: 10.48550

Jobin, A., Ienca, M., & Vayena, E. (2019). The global landscape of AI ethics guidelines. *Nature Machine Intelligence*, *1*(9), 389–399. DOI: 10.1038/s42256-019-0088-2

Jordão, C., & Fogaça, F. (2007). Ensino de inglês, letramento crítico e cidadania: um triângulo amoroso bem-sucedido [English teaching, critical literacy and citizenship: A harmonious intersection. *Línguas & Letras*, *8*(14), 79–105. DOI: 10.5935/rl&l.v8i14.906

Kafa, A. (2025). Exploring integration aspects of school leadership in the context of digitalization and artificial intelligence. *International Journal of Educational Management*, *39*(8), 98–115. DOI: 10.1108/IJEM-11-2024-0703

Kajiwara, Y., & Kawabata, K. (2024). AI literacy for ethical use of chatbot: Will students accept AI ethics? *Computers and Education Artificial Intelligence*, *6*, 100251. DOI: 10.1016/j.caeai.2024.100251

Kalan, A. (2024). Metatextual Dimensions of Multimodal Literacy Engagement. *Handbook of Research in Online Learning: Insights and Advances*, 196.

Kalantzis, M., Cope, B., & Zapata, G. C. (2024). Literacy in a time of multimodal generative AI. *Reading Research Quarterly*, *59*(4), 534–556. DOI: 10.1002/rrq.591

Kang, J., & Kim, H. G. (2024). Multimodality in English Language Teaching: A Review of L2 Multimodal Composition. *Multimedia-Assisted Language Learning*, *27*(4).

Kang, J., & Yi, Y. (2023). Beyond ChatGPT: Multimodal generative AI for L2 writers. *Journal of Second Language Writing*, *62*, 101070. DOI: 10.1016/j.jslw.2023.101070

Kankainen, V. (2024). Curating the Self-Identity: Tabletop Game Hobbyist Online Practices as an Extended Leisure Experience. *Leisure Sciences*, •••, 1–20. DOI: 10.1080/01490400.2024.2305666

Kargin, T. (2023). Exploring Critical Multimodal Literacy in Reconstructing Fairy Tales. *Educational Policy Analysis and Strategic Research*, *18*(3), 158–175. DOI: 10.29329/epasr.2023.600.8

Kasneci, E., Sessler, K., Küchemann, S., Bannert, M., Dementieva, D., Fischer, F., Gasser, U., Groh, G., Günnemann, S., Hüllermeier, E., Krusche, S., Kutyniok, G., Michaeli, T., Nerdel, C., Pfeffer, J., Poquet, O., Sailer, M., Schmidt, A., Seidel, T., & Kasneci, G. (2023). ChatGPT for good? On opportunities and challenges of large language models for education. *Learning and Individual Differences*, *103*, 1–13. DOI: 10.1016/j.lindif.2023.102274

Kayumova, A., & Sadykova, G. (2019). Implementing a multimodal online program for very young learners of Russian: Educators' perspective. *Indonesian Journal of Applied Linguistics*, *9*(1). Advance online publication. DOI: 10.17509/ijal.v9i1.13323

Keane, K. (2023). *Reading in the Digital Age: Teacher and Students' Experiences with Multimodal Literacy and Varied Text Types*. Stanford University.

Kellner, D., & Share, J. (2019). *The critical media literacy guide engaging media & transforming education*. Brill., DOI: 10.1163/9789004404533

Khosronejad, M., Weber, L., & Ryan, M. (2023). Teacher learning as a polyphonic endeavor: A context sensitive model of teacher professional development. *Teachers and Teaching*, *129*(7-8), 104154. DOI: 10.1080/13540602.2023.2215709

Knox, J. (2020). Artificial intelligence and education in China. *Learning, Media and Technology*, *45*(3), 298–311. DOI: 10.1080/17439884.2020.1754236

Komninos, N. (2023). Tracking Multimodal Literacy in Schools: A Case Study. *REVIJA ZA ELEMENTARNO IZOBRAŽEVANJE*, *16*(Special Issue), 157–171. DOI: 10.18690/rei.16.Spec.Iss.2990

Kooli, C. (2023). Chatbots in education and research: A critical examination of ethical implications and solutions. *Sustainability (Basel)*, *15*(7), 5614. DOI: 10.3390/su15075614

Kostopolus, E. (2024). Student use of generative AI as a composing process supplement: Concerns for intellectual property and academic honesty. *Computers & Composition. Computers and Composition*, *75*, 102894. DOI: 10.1016/j.compcom.2024.102894

Kress, G. R. (2003). *Literacy in the new media age*. http://eprints.ioe.ac.uk/14914/

Kress, G. (2003). *Literacy in the new media age*. Routledge., DOI: 10.4324/9780203299234

Kress, G. (2010). *Multimodality: A social semiotic approach to contemporary communication*. Routledge.

Kress, G., & van Leeuwen, T. (2001). *Multimodal discourse: The modes and media of contemporary communication*. Arnold.

Kress, G., & van Leeuwen, T. (2021). *Reading images: The grammar of visual design* (3rd ed.). Routledge., DOI: 10.4324/9781003099857

Krompák, E., & Hartmann, E. (2023). Multimodal literacy and linguistic landscape: A digital tandem project in European Teacher Education. *Alsic. Apprentissage des Langues et Systèmes d'Information et de Communication, 26*(1).

Kumar, J. T., Babu, H., & Srinivasan, N. (2024, February). Comic Generation Using AI–A Review. In *International Conference on Computational Intelligence in Data Science* (pp. 156-166). Cham: Springer Nature Switzerland.

Kustini, S. (2023). A project-based multiliteracies instruction to improve students' multimodal literacy. In *Advances in Social Science, Education and Humanities Research* (pp. 632–647). Atlantis Press SARL. DOI: 10.2991/978-2-38476-054-1_54

Kustini, S. (2023, May). A project-based multiliteracies instruction to improve students' multimodal literacy. In *20th AsiaTEFL-68th TEFLIN-5th iNELTAL Conference (ASIATEFL 2022)* (pp. 632-647). Atlantis Press.

Labov, W. (2004). Ordinary events. In Fought, C. (Ed.), *Sociolinguistic Variation: Critical Reflections* (pp. 31–43). Oxford University Press. DOI: 10.1093/oso/9780195170399.003.0003

Lam, K. Y., & Putri, E. W. (2024). A study on the affordances of digital fairy-tale rewriting: A critical literacy approach to digital multimodal composing. *System, 127*, 103536. DOI: 10.1016/j.system.2024.103536

Lankshear, C., & Knobel, M. (2003). *New literacies* (1st ed.). Open University Press.

Leander, K. M., & Burriss, S. K. (2020). Critical literacy for a posthuman world: When people read, and become, with machines. *British Journal of Educational Technology, 51*(4), 1262–1276. DOI: 10.1111/bjet.12924

Ledy, N. M. (2023). Multimodal Literacy in Learning English at Senior High School: Students' Perspective. *ICOTEL Proceeding MPBING, 4*(1), 33-41.

Lemke, J. (2006). *Everywhere now: Three dialogues on kids, games and learning.*

Lérias, E., Guerra, C., & Ferreira, P. (2024). Literacy in artificial intelligence as a challenge for teaching in higher education: A case study at Portalegre Polytechnic University. *Information (Basel), 15*(4), 205. DOI: 10.3390/info15040205

Liao, C.-H., & Wu, J.-Y. (2022). Deploying multimodal learning analytics models to explore the impact of digital distraction and peer learning on student performance. *Computers & Education, 190*, 104599. DOI: 10.1016/j.compedu.2022.104599

Li, J., & Huang, Q. (2025). Navigating ethical dilemmas in AI-enhanced education. *International Journal of Knowledge Management, 21*(1), 1–21. DOI: 10.4018/IJKM.382384

Lim, F. V. (2024). The future of TESOL with multimodality. *International Journal of TESOL Studies, 241213*.

Lim, F. V. (2021). Investigating intersemiosis: A systemic functional multimodal discourse analysis of the relationship between language and gesture in classroom discourse. *Visual Communication, 20*(1), 34–58. DOI: 10.1177/1470357218820695

Lim, F. V., & Nguyen, T. T. H. (2024). A pedagogical approach towards designing for multimodal literacy learning with picture books. In *Developing Future-ready Learners for a Global Age* (pp. 195–210). Routledge. DOI: 10.4324/9781003455721-18

Lim, F. V., Nguyen, T. T. H., & Kubler, M. (2022). Multimodality in the English language classroom: A systematic review of literature. *Linguistics and Education, 69*, 101048. DOI: 10.1016/j.linged.2022.101048

Lim, F. V., & Querol-Julián, M. (2024). *Designing learning with digital technologies*. Routledge. DOI: 10.4324/9781003359272

Lim, F. V., & Tan-Chia, L. (2023). Multimodal literacy learning with digital texts. In Lim, F. V., & Tan-Chia, L. (Eds.), *Designing learning for multimodal literacy* (pp. 1–18). Routledge., DOI: 10.4324/9781003198741

Lim, F. V., & Unsworth, L. (2023). Multimodal composing in the English classroom: Recontextualising the curriculum to learning. *English in Education, 57*(2), 102–119. DOI: 10.1080/04250494.2023.2187696

Li, N., & Wu, D. (2025). The auxiliary function and realization mechanism of artificial intelligence in cross-cultural traditional music education. *Journal of Cases on Information Technology, 27*(1), 1–18. DOI: 10.4018/JCIT.388947

Lin, A. M. Y., & Siu, P. (2026). 'Fractalizing' the Multimodalities-Entextualization Cycle: Towards a theoretical model for integrating multimodal literacy in bilingual teacher education. *International Journal of Bilingual Education and Bilingualism, 29*(3), 376–401. Advance online publication. DOI: 10.1080/13670050.2025.2610367

Lin, C.-S. (2026). Co-creating with AI: How communication students learn, think, and rely on intelligent systems. *Journal of Educational Computing Research, 64*(1), 155–179. DOI: 10.1177/07356331251385944

Lin, C., Zhou, K., Li, L., & Sun, L. (2024). Integrating generative AI into digital multimodal composition: A study of multicultural second-language classrooms. *Computers & Composition. Computers and Composition, 75*, 102895. DOI: 10.1016/j.compcom.2024.102895

Linder, R., & Falk-Ross, F. (2024). Multimodal resources and approaches for teaching young adolescents: A review of the literature. *Education Sciences, 14*(9), 1010. DOI: 10.3390/educsci14091010

Lin, H.-C. K. (2025). Writing is Coding. *International Journal of Online Pedagogy and Course Design, 15*(1), 1–23. DOI: 10.4018/IJOPCD.385016

Lin, Z., Dai, Y., & Ng, O.-L. (2025). Constructionism in K-12 AI literacy education: A systematic review of pedagogical designs, student outcomes, and learning mechanisms. *Journal of Educational Computing Research, 63*(7–8), 1748–1781. DOI: 10.1177/07356331251360442

Li, S. (2025). Generative AI and second language writing. *Digital Studies in Language and Literature, 2*(1), 122–152. DOI: 10.1515/dsll-2025-0007

Liu, H., Liu, L., & Li, H. (2024). Multimodal discourse studies in the international academic community (1997–2023): A bibliometric analysis. *SAGE Open, 14*(4), 21582440241305454. Advance online publication. DOI: 10.1177/21582440241305454

Liu, J. E., & Lim, F. V. (2024). Educational Context and Teacher Beliefs Matter: Multimodal Literacy in the Greater Bay Area of China. *RELC Journal, •••*, 00336882241304136. DOI: 10.1177/00336882241304136

Liu, J. E., & Lo, Y. Y. (2025). Multimodality in CLIL assessment: Implications for teacher assessment literacy. *Journal of Multilingual and Multicultural Development, 46*(5), 1459–1477. DOI: 10.1080/01434632.2024.2357140

Liu, M., Zhang, L., & Biebricher, C. (2024). Investigating students' cognitive processes in generative AI-assisted digital multimodal composing and traditional writing. *Computers & Education, 211*, 104977. DOI: 10.1016/j.compedu.2023.104977

Liu, X., Wang, J., & Luo, Y. (2025). Acceptance and use of technology on digital learning resource utilization and digital literacy among Chinese engineering students: A longitudinal study based on the UTAUT2 model. *Behavioral Sciences (Basel, Switzerland), 15*(6), 728. DOI: 10.3390/bs15060728 PMID: 40564510

Löfgren, M. (2025). Literacy and multimodality for all. Swedish educational policy for reading and writing in the age of global assessments. *Scandinavian Journal of Educational Research, •••*, 1–19.

Lomelí, K. (2023). The work of growing young people con Cariño: A reconstructive lens on one white teacher's anti-racist approach to teaching immigrant-origin Latinx students. *English Teaching, 22*(1), 45–60. DOI: 10.1108/ETPC-03-2022-0040

Long, D., & Magerko, B. (2020). What is AI literacy? Competencies and design considerations. *Proceedings of the 2020 CHI Conference on Human Factors in Computing Systems*, 1–16. DOI: 10.1145/3313831.3376727

López-Pérez, M. V., & Bobadilla-Pérez, M. (2023). Multimodal literacy and pluriliteracy in the Primary School classroom through a transmedia narrative El niño, el topo, el zorro y el caballo, by Charlie Mackesy. *Texto Livre*, *16*, e41879. DOI: 10.1590/1983-3652.2023.41879

Lubis, B. N. A. (2025). Multimodal-Based Approaches in Teaching Ecological Literacy: Enhancing Environmental Awareness through Textual, Visual, and Auditory Integration. *STAIRS: English Language Education Journal*, *6*(1), 53–68. DOI: 10.21009/stairs.6.1.6

Luckin, R., & Holmes, W. (2016). *Intelligence unleashed: An argument for AI in education*. Pearson. https://www.pearson.com/content/dam/corporate/glob

Luckin, R. (2018). *Enhancing learning and teaching with technology: What the research says*. ERIC.

Luckin, R. (2018). *Machine learning and human intelligence: The future of education for the 21st century*. UCL Institute of Education Press.

Luke, A. (2012). Critical literacy: Foundational notes. *Theory into Practice*, *51*(1), 4–11. DOI: 10.1080/00405841.2012.636324

Luke, A. (2018). *Critical literacy, schooling, and social justice*. Routledge. DOI: 10.4324/9781315100951

Luo, H. (2023). Editorial: Advances in multimodal learning: Pedagogies, technologies, and analytics. *Frontiers in Psychology*, *14*, 1286092. DOI: 10.3389/fpsyg.2023.1286092 PMID: 38022937

Ly, C. N., & Forzani, E. E. (2023). Let's Learn from Them: Using the Integrative Multimodal Literacy Assessment Tool to Support Instruction for Young Children. *The Reading Teacher*, *77*(3), 407–413. DOI: 10.1002/trtr.2243

Lysne, M. S. (2023). Aesthetic engagement with Mouse Bird Snake Wolf–Literary multimodal literacy in English language education. *Children's Literature in English Language Education*, *11*(2), 54–79.

Maamuujav, U. (2025). Multimodal Writing in Multilingual Space. *Education Sciences*, *15*(11), 1446. DOI: 10.3390/educsci15111446

Makinde, S. O., Sakariyahu, S., Abdullahi, A., & Ibrahim, A. (2025). Multimodal Literacy and Sociocultural Dynamics in Online Communication: An Interdisciplinary View. In *Sociocultural and Multicultural Meanings in Online Communication* (pp. 409-436). IGI Global Scientific Publishing.

Ma, N., & Zhong, Z. (2025). A meta-analysis of the impact of generative artificial intelligence on learning outcomes. *Journal of Computer Assisted Learning*, *41*(1), 70117. DOI: 10.1111/jcal.70117

Maxis. (2014). *The Sims 4* [Video game]. Electronic Arts.

Mc Evander, M. F. (2024). Exploring Multimodal Literacy Instruction on Reading Comprehension and Abilities in Critical Thinking of College Students. *Research Journal of Humanities and Social Sciences*, *15*(3), 175–179.

McGonigal, J. (2011). *Reality is broken: Why games make us better and how they can change the world.* Penguin Books.

Meylani, R. (2024). Artificial Intelligence in the education of teachers: A qualitative synthesis of the cutting-edge research literature. *Journal of Computer and Education Research (ISSN 2148-2896), 12*(24), 600–637. DOI: 10.18009/jcer.1477709

Midgette, E., Stewart, O., & González, J. (2023). Teaching with multimodal texts through a critical literacy lens within an English as a foreign language classroom context. *Anglistics and Americanistics*, (20), 72–77. DOI: 10.15421/382313

Miller, S. M. (2013). A research metasynthesis on digital video composing in classrooms. *Journal of Literacy Research*, *45*(4), 386–430. DOI: 10.1177/1086296X13504867

Mills, K. A., Brown, A., & Gutierrez, A. (2025). Virtual Reality Street Art with L2 Learners as Multimodal Literacy. In *Multiliteracies, Multimodality, and Learning by Design in Second Language Learning and Teacher Education* (pp. 86-102). Routledge. DOI: 10.4324/9781032620497-8

Mills, K. A. (2010). A review of the "digital turn" in the new literacy studies. *Review of Educational Research*, *80*(2), 246–271. DOI: 10.3102/0034654310364401

Mills, K. A. (2015). *Literacy theories for the digital age: Social, critical, multimodal, spatial, material and sensory lenses* (Vol. 45). Multilingual Matters.

Mills, K. A., Heck, E., Brown, A., & Funnell, P. (2023). *Senses Together: Multimodal Literacy Learning in Primary Education.* Australian Catholic University. DOI: 10.24268/acu.8zy8y

Mills, K. A., Scholes, L., & Brown, A. (2022). Virtual Reality and Embodiment in Multimodal Meaning Making. *Written Communication, 39*(3), 335–369. DOI: 10.1177/07410883221083517

Mills, K., Ruiz, P., Lee, K. W., Coenraad, M., Fusco, J., Roschelle, J., & Weisgrau, J. (2024). *AI Literacy: A Framework to Understand, Evaluate, and Use Emerging Technology*. Digital Promise.

Moalla, D. (2023). The dynamics of multimodal literacy development: The Tunisian EAP context as a case study. *Journal of Linguistics and Communication Studies, 2*(1), 47–65. DOI: 10.56397/JLCS.2023.03.07

MoEYS. (2024). *Education strategic plan 2024-2028*. Phnom Penh, Cambodia: Ministry of Education, Youth and Sport. https://moeys.gov.kh/storage/uploads/documents//67316f9d3a57f.pdf

Molla, M. (2024). AI in creative arts: Advancements and innovations in artificial intelligence. *International Journal of Advanced Research in Science Communication and Technology*, *4*(1), 513–517. DOI: 10.48175/IJARSCT-19163

Moll, L. C., Amanti, C., Neff, D., & González, N. (1992). Funds of knowledge for teaching: Using a qualitative approach to connect homes and classrooms. *Theory into Practice*, *31*(2), 132–141. DOI: 10.1080/00405849209543534

Mulcahy, C., & Shaw, L. (2024). Centering Critical Engagement, Multimodal Learning, and Compassion through Language and Literacy. *The Intersections of Critical Pedagogy, Critical Literacy, and Social Justice: Toward Empowerment, Equity, and Education for Liberation*, 15.

Mu, S., Cui, M., & Huang, X. (2020). Multimodal data fusion in learning analytics: A systematic review. *Sensors (Basel)*, *20*(23), 6856. DOI: 10.3390/s20236856 PMID: 33266131

Nagapushpa, Kanchana, & Monish. (2024). Revolutionizing art and design through AI: Balancing innovation, Ethics, and future preparedness. *INTERANTIONAL JOURNAL OF SCIENTIFIC RESEARCH IN ENGINEERING AND MANAGEMENT, 08*(11), 1–7. DOI: 10.55041/IJSREM38443

Nash, B. L., Dunham, H., Murdter-Atkinson, J., & Mosley Wetzel, M. (2024). A culturally sustaining approach to multimodal literacies: Building from students' funds of knowledge in field-based teacher education. *Literacy Research and Instruction*, *63*(2), 151–175. DOI: 10.1080/19388071.2022.2153766

Nash, B. L., Sweinhart, A., & Batchelor, K. (2026). Building the foundations of critical literacy: Collaborative engagement with interactive, multimodal narratives. *Journal of Adolescent & Adult Literacy*, *69*(5), 1–11. DOI: 10.1002/jaal.70040

Ng'ambi, D., Brown, C., Bozalek, V., Gachago, D., & Wood, D. (2016). Technology enhanced teaching and learning in South African higher education – A rearview of a 20 year journey. *British Journal of Educational Technology*, *47*(5), 843–858. DOI: 10.1111/bjet.12485

Ng, D. T. K., Leung, J. K. L., Chu, K. W. S., & Qiao, M. S. (2021). AI literacy: Definition, teaching, evaluation and ethical issues. *Proceedings of the Association for Information Science and Technology*, *58*(1), 504–509. DOI: 10.1002/pra2.487

Ng, D. T. K., Leung, J. K. L., Chu, S. K. W., & Qiao, M. S. (2021). Conceptualizing AI literacy: An exploratory review. *Computers and Education: Artificial Intelligence*, *2*, 100041. DOI: 10.1016/j.caeai.2021.100041

Noble, S. U. (2018). *Algorithms of oppression: How search engines reinforce racism*. New York University Press., DOI: 10.18574/nyu/9781479833641.001.0001

Norvig, P. (1992). *ELIZA: Paradigms of artificial intelligence programming*. Morgan Kaufmann Publishers.

Nouri, J. (2019). Students multimodal literacy and design of learning during self-studies in higher education. *Technology Knowledge and Learning*, *24*(4), 683–698. DOI: 10.1007/s10758-018-9360-5

Nurjamin, A. S. E. P., Nurjamin, L. R., Fajriah, Y. N., Nurjamin, A. K., & Nugraha, I. R. S. Y. A. D. (2025). Developing and evaluating an augmented reality (AR) digital storytelling video to foster multimodal literacy and narrative comprehension. *Journal of Engineering Science and Technology*, *20*(4), 919–956.

O'Halloran, K. L., Bateman, J. A., & Schmidt, K. H. (2017). *Multimodality: Foundations, research and analysis – A problem-oriented introduction*. de Gruyter Mouton. DOI: 10.1515/9783110479898

O'Halloran, K. L. (2023). Matter, meaning and semiotics: Exploring multimodal processes. *Visual Communication*, *33*(2), 123–140. DOI: 10.1177/14703572221128881

OECD. (2023). *OECD digital education outlook 2023: Towards an effective digital education ecosystem*. OECD Publishing., DOI: 10.1787/c74f03de-

Oermann, M. H., Owens, J. K., Carter-Templeton, H., Peterson, G., & Bailey, H. E. (2025). Using artificial intelligence for scholarly writing. *The American Journal of Nursing*, *125*(11), 52–55. DOI: 10.1097/AJN.0000000000000179 PMID: 41128585

Ojeda-Ramirez, S., Ritchie, D., & Warschauer, M. (2024). AI literacy for multilingual learners: Storytelling, role-playing, and programming. *The CATESOL Journal, 35*(1). Advance online publication. DOI: 10.5070/B5.35861

Olvah, M., Alfan, M., Nusantara, T., Suyitno, I., & Anggraini, A. E. (2024). Pemanfaatan Berbagai Media dalam Pembelajaran untuk Meningkatkan Literasi Siswa dalam Perspektif Multimodal Literacy. *JIIP-Jurnal Ilmiah Ilmu Pendidikan, 7*(7), 6391–6398. DOI: 10.54371/jiip.v7i7.4689

Online dialog posted to http://community.macfound.org/openforum

Ostertag, M. K. (2017). *The witch boy*. Graphix.

Oto, R., Rombalski, A., & Grinage, J. (2023). The role of racial literacy in US K-12 education research: A review of the literature. *Race, Ethnicity and Education, 26*(1), 94–111. DOI: 10.1080/13613324.2022.2047635

Ouhaichi, N., Hammami, S., & Souissi, N. (2024). *A systematic review of multimodal learning analytics systems design frameworks*. IATED Digital Library., DOI: 10.21125/edulearn.2024.1299

Pahl, K., & Rowsell, J. (2020). *Living literacies: Literacy for social change*. MiT Press. DOI: 10.7551/mitpress/11375.001.0001

Parker, M. (2024). Multimodal literacy: Supporting children as effective communicators. *Rattler (Sydney)*, (146), 15–18.

Park, H., Zong, J., Polat, N., & Schallert, D. L. (2024). Bilingual/ESL preservice teachers' heritage language and language identity: Evidence from multimodal literacy autobiographies. *Teaching and Teacher Education, 152*, 104775. DOI: 10.1016/j.tate.2024.104775

Partington, A. (2010). Game literacy, gaming cultures and media education. *English Teaching, 9*(1), 73–86.

Pascua-Valenzuela, E. A. (2025). *Digital literacy and transformation in ASEAN: A call for education policy reforms*. ASEAN. https://asean.org/wp-content/uploads/2025/05/ASCC-RD_Policy-Brief_FoE-19_2025_Digital-Literacy-and-Transformation.pdf

Pattanaik, B., Kumari, S. S., Kumar, C. K., Pattnaik, M., Ali, S. I., & Kumarasamy, M. (2023). An innovation of algebraic mathematical-based statistical analysis model for complex number theory. In *Proceedings of the 2023 International Conference on Disruptive Technologies (ICDT)* (pp. 94–99). IEEE. DOI: 10.1109/ICDT57929.2023.10151169

Peng, P., Xu, L., Ng, D. T. K., Lee, C. S. Y., & Chu, S. K. W. (2025). Exploring the impact of AI -generated image, story and song creations on AI literacy and well-being among older adults: A mixed-methods study. *Proceedings of the Association for Information Science and Technology*, *62*(1), 1045–1050. DOI: 10.1002/pra2.1337

Pereira, Í. S. P., Gil, M., & Sylla, C. M. (2023). Meeting the challenges of designing multimodal texts to promote multiliteracies pedagogy. *Comunicação e sociedade*, (43), e023008.

Peristeris, K. (2017). Culturally sustaining pedagogies: Teaching and learning for justice in a changing world. *Journal of Teaching and Learning*, *11*(1), 35–37. DOI: 10.22329/jtl.v11i1.4987

Pernaa, J., Ikävalko, T., Takala, A., Vuorio, E., Pesonen, R., & Haatainen, O. (2024). Artificial intelligence chatbots in chemical information seeking: Narrative educational insights via a SWOT analysis. *Informatics (MDPI)*, *11*(2), 20. DOI: 10.3390/informatics11020020

Pool, S., Rowsell, J., & Sun, Y. (2023). Towards literacies of immanence: Getting closer to sensory multimodal perspectives on research. *Multimodality & Society*, *3*(2), 130–149. DOI: 10.1177/26349795231158741

Pope, L. (2013). [Video game]. *Papers, Please*, *3909*, LLC.

Prensky, M. (2007). *Digital Game-Based Learning*. Paragon House.

Prinsloo, M., & Rowsell, J. (2012). Digital literacies as placed resources in the globalised periphery. *Language and Education*, *26*(4), 271–277. DOI: 10.1080/09500782.2012.691511

Prinsloo, P., Slade, S., & Khalil, M. (2023). Multimodal learning analytics—In-between student privacy and encroachment: A systematic review. *British Journal of Educational Technology*, *54*(6), 1566–1586. DOI: 10.1111/bjet.13373

Proctor, W. (2017). Schrödinger's cape: The quantum seriality of the Marvel multiverse. Retrieved from http://eprints.bournemouth.ac.uk/29352/7/Quantum_Seriality.pdf

Purdy, S. B. (1999). Is there a multiverse in "Finnegan's wake", and does that make it a religious book? *James Joyce Quarterly*, *36*(3), 586–602.

Pym, A. (2009). *Exploring translation theories*. Routledge., DOI: 10.4324/9780203869291

Qiu, G. (2025). On the relationship between students' perceived support, students' self-efficacy, and affect-emotions in AI -enhanced learning environments. *European Journal of Education, 60*(3), e70180. Advance online publication. DOI: 10.1111/ejed.70180

Qi, W. (2023). Developing multimodal literacy in the Business English reading class: A case study of students' presentation PowerPoint slides. *Journal of Language Teaching and Research, 14*(3), 820–827. DOI: 10.17507/jltr.1403.30

Quan, Y. (2025). The influence of teachers' clarity and credibility on Chinese EFL students' willingness to attend AI -powered classrooms: A qualitative inquiry. *European Journal of Education, 60*(4), e70295. Advance online publication. DOI: 10.1111/ejed.70295

Querol-Julián, M., & Fortanet-Gómez, I. (Eds.). (2025). *Multimodal literacy in English as an additional language in higher education*. Taylor & Francis. DOI: 10.4324/9781003429876

Querol-Julián, M., & Lo, Y. Y. (2025). Multimodal literacy in the professional development of bilingual educators. *International Journal of Bilingual Education and Bilingualism*, •••, 1–11.

Rachmad, Y. E. (2025). *The Power of the Influencer: How Viral and Gimmick Marketing Transform Behavior*. United Nations Economic and Social Council.

Rafique, G. M., Mughari, S., & Khan, H. A. (2025). Unlocking potential: The role of AI literacy and creativity in medical librarians' task performance in Pakistan. *Information Development, 41*(3), 559–575. DOI: 10.1177/02666669251325444

Rana, P., Bhardwaj, P., & Singh, J. (2018). Artificial Intelligence (AI) in Video Games. *International Journal of Computer Applications, 181*(19), 1–3. DOI: 10.5120/ijca2018917818

Ranes, B. (2025). AI integration in facilitating learning: Its benefits, challenges and strategies for enhancement. *Divine Word International Journal of Management and Humanities (DWIJMH) (ISSN: 2980-4817), 4*(3), 2095–2109. DOI: 10.62025/dwijmh.v4i3.181

Rasul, S., Razia, A., & Mumtaz, S. (2023). Literacy as a Social Practice: Mapping out Multimodal Literacy Practices in Middle-Class Beauty Salons. *Human Nature Journal of Social Sciences, 4*(2), 734–749. DOI: 10.71016/hnjss/r9d6vr56

Ravikumar, R. N., Aarthi, S., Rai, P. K., & Mamadiyarov, Z. (2025). Intelligent code analysis and feedback generation. In *Advances in Computational Intelligence and Robotics* (pp. 137–170). IGI Global Scientific Publishing. DOI: 10.4018/979-8-3373-0598-1.ch006

Ravikumar, R. N., Aarthi, S., Ruzimova, F., & Mamadiyarov, Z. (2025). Training and development in AI-driven education scaling solutions. In *Advances in Computational Intelligence and Robotics* (pp. 267–298). IGI Global Scientific Publishing. DOI: 10.4018/979-8-3373-2185-1.ch010

Ravikumar, R. N., Aarthi, S., Sapaeva, B., Jumaniyozov, Y., Manoj Praveen, V., & Siddheswaran, V. (2025). Revolutionizing education with NLP and ML. In *Advances in Computational Intelligence and Robotics* (pp. 293–324). IGI Global Scientific Publishing. DOI: 10.4018/979-8-3373-6791-0.ch011

Ravikumar, R. N., & Aarthi, S. (2025). Federated Learning and privacy-preserving search. In *Role of Library Resources for Higher Education in the Digital Era* (pp. 71–108). IGI Global Scientific Publishing., DOI: 10.4018/979-8-3373-3005-1.ch004

Ray, S., & Ray, D. P. (2024). Artificial Intelligence in education: Navigating the nexus of innovation and ethics for future learning landscapes. *International Journal of Research -GRANTHAALAYAH, 11*(12). DOI: 10.29121/granthaalayah.v11.i12.2023.5464

Read, S., Dew, N., Sarasvathy, S. D., Song, M., & Wiltbank, R. (2009). Marketing under uncertainty: The logic of an effectual approach. *Journal of Marketing*, *73*(3), 1–18. DOI: 10.1509/jmkg.73.3.001

RGC. (2021a). *Cambodia digital economy and society policy framework (2021–2035)*. Royal Government of Cambodia, Phnom Penh: Supreme National Economic Council. https://asset.cambodia.gov.kh/mptc/media/EN-Policy-Framework-of-Digital-Economy-and-Society.pdf

RGC. (2021b). *Cambodia digital government policy 2021–2035*. Royal Government of Cambodia, Phnom Penh: Ministry of Post and Telecommunications. https://asset.cambodia.gov.kh/mptc/media/Cambodia_Digital_Government_Policy_2022_2035_English.pdf

RGC. (2022). *Cambodia digital government policy 2022–2035*. Royal Government of Cambodia. https://asset.cambodia.gov.kh/mptc/media/Cambodia_Digital_Government_Policy_2022_2035_English.pdf

Rocamora, M. S., & Baguio, J. B. (2025). Multimodal Literacy and Creative Teaching Practices of Public Elementary School Teachers. *Archives of Current Research International*, *25*(7), 199–212. DOI: 10.9734/acri/2025/v25i71325

Rod, P., & Jamie, M. (2021). Critical literacy and semiotic juxtaposition: The possibilities of multimodal pedagogy in Korea. *STEM Journal*, *22*(2), 73–92. DOI: 10.16875/stem.2021.22.2.73

Rosenblatt, L. M. (1981). On the aesthetic as the basic model of the reading process. *Bucknell Review*, *26*(1), 17.

Rosenblatt, L. M. (1982). The literary transaction: Evocation and response. *Theory into Practice*, *21*(4), 268–277. DOI: 10.1080/00405848209543018

Rosenblatt, L. M. (1986). The aesthetic transaction. *Journal of Aesthetic Education*, *20*(4), 122–128. DOI: 10.2307/3332615

Rosenblatt, L. M. (1993). The transactional theory: Against dualisms. *College English*, *55*(4), 377–386. DOI: 10.58680/ce19939301

Rowsell, J., & Walsh, M. (2011). Rethinking literacy education in new times: Multimodality, multiliteracies, & new literacies. *Brock Education Journal*, *21*(1). Advance online publication. DOI: 10.26522/brocked.v21i1.236

RUPP. (2023). *Institutional repository project report, 2020–2023*. Phnom Penh, Cambodia: Royal University of Phnom Penh Library. https://rupp.edu.kh/center/library

Ryu, H., & Kim, D. (2024). Multimodal Literacy in the Singaporean English Language Syllabus: Implications for Korea's 2022 Revised English Curriculum. *The SNU Journal of Education Research*, *33*(4), 79–107. DOI: 10.54346/sjer.2024.33.4.79

Sabatini, J., Graesser, A. C., Hollander, J., & O'Reilly, T. (2023). A framework of literacy development and how AI can transform theory and practice. *British Journal of Educational Technology*, *54*(5), 1174–1203. DOI: 10.1111/bjet.13342

Salen, K. (2007). Gaming literacies: A game design study in action. *Journal of Educational Multimedia and Hypermedia*, *16*(3), 301–322.

Salen, K., & Zimmerman, E. (2004). *Rules of play: Game design fundamentals*. MIT Press.

Samo, A., & Highhouse, S. (2025). Artificial intelligence and art: Identifying the aesthetic judgment factors that distinguish human- and machine-generated artwork. *Psychology of Aesthetics, Creativity, and the Arts*, *19*(5), 1084–1098. DOI: 10.1037/aca0000570

Saputra, D. T., Rahmawati, L. E., & Markhamah, M. M. (2024). The Fostering of Multimodal Text Literacy in Elementary School Learning. *Lensa: Kajian Kebahasaan, Kesusastraan, dan Budaya, 14*(1), 187-210.

Saputra, D. T., Rahmawati, L. E., & Markhamah, M. (2025). Implementation strategy of multimodal literacy text as a means to optimize literacy in Indonesian language lessons for elementary school students. *BAHASTRA, 45*(1), 155–164. DOI: 10.26555/bs.v45i1.1260

Sari, A. P. (2025). Representation or Misrepresentation of Autistic Agency? Multimodal Literacy Analysis of Makayla's Voice. *Jurnal Ilmiah Bina Bahasa, 18*(1), 91–101. DOI: 10.33557/hyw3hy31

Satar, M., Hauck, M., & Bilki, Z. (2023). Multimodal representation in virtual exchange: A social semiotic approach to critical digital literacy. *Language Learning & Technology, 27*(2), 72–96. DOI: 10.64152/10125/73504

Secretariat, A. S. E. A. N. (2022). *Digital policy action areas for a connected ASEAN: ASEAN best practice benchmarking and an action plan for regional harmonization.* ITU Publications Asia-Pacific Region. https://asean.org/wp-content/uploads/2024/03/Digital-Policy-Action-Areas-for-a-Connected-ASEAN.pdf

Selwyn, N. (2019). *Should robots replace teachers?: AI and the future of education.* Polity Press.

Selwyn, N. (2021). *Education and technology: Key issues and debates.* Bloomsbury Publishing.

Selwyn, N. (2022). The future of AI and education: Some cautionary notes. *European Journal of Education, 57*(4), 620–631. DOI: 10.1111/ejed.12532

Seneechai, W., & Ampon, R. K. (2025). Designing Learning for Multimodal Literacy: Teaching Viewing and Representing. *Reflections: The SoL Journal, 32*(1). Advance online publication. DOI: 10.61508/refl.v32i1.277805

Serafini, F. (2015). Multimodal Literacy: From Theories to Practices. *Language Arts, 92*(6), 412–423. https://www.jstor.org/stable/24577533. DOI: 10.58680/la201527389

Serafini, F. (2023). Implications of multimodal theories for literacy research and pedagogy. In *Rethinking Multimodal Literacy in Theory and Practice* (pp. 17–35). Peter Lang AG.

Shah, P. (2023). *AI and the future of education: Teaching in the age of artificial intelligence.* Jossey-Bass.

Shannon, P. (2017). *Progressive reading education in America: Teaching toward social justice*. Routledge. DOI: 10.4324/9781315182391

Shen, Y. A. N. A. N., Ab Jalil, H., & Jamaluddin, R. (2024). A 10-year systematic review on the incorporation of digital games for multimodal literacy education. *WSEAS Transactions on Computer Research, 12*, 463–474. DOI: 10.37394/232018.2024.12.46

Shen, Y., & Ab Jalil, H. (2023). Using digital game-based learning to foster multimodal literacy in left-behind children of migrant workers: Possibilities and challenges. *Migration Letters : An International Journal of Migration Studies, 20*(5), 469–486. DOI: 10.59670/ml.v20i5.3993

Shen, Y., Jalil, H. A., & Jamaluddin, R. (2025). Exploring adolescents' multimodal literacy as critical and creative prosumers in digital game-based multimodal composition. *Journal of Educational Technology & Society, 28*(1), 1–17.

Shiri, A. (2024). Artificial intelligence literacy: A proposed faceted taxonomy. *Digital Library Perspectives, 40*(4), 681–699. Advance online publication. DOI: 10.1108/DLP-04-2024-0067

Simpson, A., & Cremin, T. M. (2022). Responsible reading: Children's literature and social justice. *Education Sciences, 12*(4), 264. DOI: 10.3390/educsci12040264

Sinar, T. S., Budiman, M. A., Ganie, R., & Rosa, R. N. (2023). Students' perceptions of using Roblox in multimodal literacy practices in teaching and learning English. *World Journal of English Language, 13*(7), 146. DOI: 10.5430/wjel.v13n7p146

Smith, M. P. (2022). Dialogic authorial academic language learning: An alternative to genre pedagogy. *Dialogic Pedagogy: A Journal for Studies of Dialogic Education, 10*, DP34–DP66. DOI: 10.5195/dpj.2022.495

Smith, B. E., Pacheco, M. B., & Warrington, A. (2025). Multimodal composing with generative AI: Examining opportunities and challenges for literacy education. *Computers and Composition, 68*, 102785. DOI: 10.1016/j.compcom.2024.102785

Smith, B. E., Shimizu, A. Y., Burriss, S. K., Hundley, M., & Pendergrass, E. (2024). Multimodal composing with generative AI: Examining preservice teachers' processes and perspectives. *Computers & Composition. Computers and Composition, 75*, 102896. DOI: 10.1016/j.compcom.2024.102896

Sodiq, S., Indarti, T., Resdianto, P. R., & Wijaya, T. (2023, December). Implementation of Multimodal Literacy Principles in Scientific Journal Article Writing Course: Enhancing Learning Experience in Indonesian Language Education. In *International Joint Conference on Arts and Humanities 2023 (IJCAH 2023)* (pp. 893-899). Atlantis Press. DOI: 10.2991/978-2-38476-152-4_86

Sofkova Hashemi, S. (2025). Fostering AI literacy in higher education: students' multimodal prompting. In *ARLE SIG TALE 3rd Symposium: Digital technologies, literacy and schooling-Responding to 'newness'? 10–13 June 2025, Larnaca, Cyprus*.

Solanke Shweta A, P., & Assistant Professor PR Pote Patil College of Engineering and Management Amravati Maharashtra India Southern Asia, C. S. E. D. (2024). The prospects of generative AI in higher education. *INTERANTIONAL JOURNAL OF SCIENTIFIC RESEARCH IN ENGINEERING AND MANAGEMENT, 08*(05), 1–5. DOI: 10.55041/IJSREM32533

Sperling, K., Stenberg, C. J., McGrath, C., Åkerfeldt, A., Heintz, F., & Stenliden, L. (2024). In search of artificial intelligence (AI) literacy in teacher education: A scoping review. *Computers and Education Open*, *6*, 100169. DOI: 10.1016/j.caeo.2024.100169

Srinivasan, M., Venugopal, A., Venkatesan, L., & Kumar, R. (2024). Navigating the pedagogical landscape: Exploring the implications of AI and chatbots in nursing education. *JMIR Nursing*, *7*, e52105. DOI: 10.2196/52105 PMID: 38870516

Srivastava, S. S., Ali, S. I., Srivastava, A. K., & Goswami, C. (2024). *Improving 5G network performance with MIMO technology using beamforming algorithm*. ICTACT Journal on Communication Technology., DOI: 10.21917/ijct.2024.0472

Srivastava, S. T. C., Sharmiladevi, D., Sugumar, D., Ali, S. I., Jones Mary, T. A., & Kumar, S. (2023). Using a smart wearable device monitoring the social distance in smart cities. In *2023 International Conference on Research Methodologies in Knowledge Management, Artificial Intelligence and Telecommunication Engineering (RMKMATE)* (pp. 1–5). IEEE. DOI: 10.1109/RMKMATE59243.2023.10369118

Stahl, G., Koschmann, D., & SuthersDan, S. (2006). Computer-supported collaborative learning: An historical perspective. In R. K. Sawyer (Ed.), (pp. 1–20). Cambridge University Press. DOI: 10.1017/CBO9781139519526.029

Stahl, G. (2017). Group practices: A new way of viewing CSCL. *International Journal of Computer-Supported Collaborative Learning*, *12*(1), 113–126. DOI: 10.1007/s11412-017-9251-0

Steinkuehler, C. (2006). Massively multiplayer online video gaming as participation in a discourse. *Mind, Culture, and Activity*, *13*(1), 38–52. DOI: 10.1207/s15327884mca1301_4

Steinkuehler, C. (2008). Cognition and literacy in massively multiplayer online games. In Coiro, J., Knobel, M., Lankshear, C., & Leu, D. J. (Eds.), *Handbook of research on new literacies* (pp. 611–634). Erlbaum.

Steinkuehler, C. (2010). Video games and digital literacies. *Journal of Adolescent & Adult Literacy*, *54*(1), 61–63. DOI: 10.1598/JAAL.54.1.7

Storm, S. (2024). Aesthetic literacies in digital learning ecologies: Tracing aesthetic tools and functions in a youth literary salon. *Literacy Research: Theory, Method, and Practice*, *73*(1), 85–104. DOI: 10.1177/23813377241285818

Strat, T. T. S., Henriksen, E. K., & Jegstad, K. M. (2024). Inquiry-based science education in science teacher education: A systematic review. *Studies in Science Education*, *60*(2), 191–249. DOI: 10.1080/03057267.2023.2207148

Street, B. V. (1984). *Literacy in theory and practice*. Cambridge University Press.

Subiyantoro, H., Hartono, R., Fitriati, S. W., & Faridi, A. (2024). Recovering multilingual children's literacy loss through multimodal literacy practices in a pull-out program. *Indonesian Journal of Applied Linguistics*, *13*(3), 513–523. DOI: 10.17509/ijal.v13i3.66937

Sudarwati, E., Lestari, I. P., & Daniswara, R. A. (2025). Digital Multimodal Literacy Model of English Language Education in Indonesian Higher Education. [Journal of English Education and Linguistics Studies]. *JEELS*, *12*(2), 615–640. DOI: 10.30762/jeels.v12i2.2612

Suhaimi, I., & Permatasari, F. (2024). Integrating Literature in English Learning to Improve Multimodal Literacy through a Sociocognitive Approach. *Essence. Journal of English Language Teaching, Linguistics, and Literature*, *1*(2), 37–49.

Su, J., Ng, D. T. K., & Chu, S. K. W. (2023). Artificial intelligence (AI) literacy in early childhood education: The challenges and opportunities. *Computers and Education: Artificial Intelligence*, *4*, 100124. DOI: 10.1016/j.caeai.2023.100124

Sultan, H. (2023). Measurement of Multimodal Literacy of EFL Iraqi Students. *Journal of Namibian Studies, 34*.

Sun, L., & Zhou, L. (2024). Does generative artificial intelligence improve the academic achievement of college students? A meta-analysis. *Journal of Educational Computing Research*, *62*(8), 2161–2191. DOI: 10.1177/07356331241277937

Suthar, B., & Ali, S. I. (2025). A survey on hand gesture sign language recognition with Arduino Leonardo. In *2025 International Conference on Computational, Communication and Information Technology (ICCCIT)* (pp. 111–115). IEEE. DOI: 10.1109/ICCCIT62592.2025.10927994

Sutrisno, D. B. (2024, February). Multimodal literacy and multimodal assignments in Indonesian EFL classrooms. In *7th International Conference on Language, Literature, Culture, and Education (ICOLLITE 2023)* (pp. 139-145). Atlantis Press. DOI: 10.2991/978-94-6463-376-4_19

Sutrisno, D., Abidin, N. A. Z., Pambudi, N., Aydawati, E., & Sallu, S. (2024). Exploring the benefits of multimodal literacy in English teaching: Engaging students through visual, auditory, and digital modes. *Global Synthesis in Education Journal*, *1*(2), 1–14. DOI: 10.61667/xh184f41

Swisscontact. (2020). *Recognition of prior learning in Cambodia: Implementation guideline*. Skill Development Programme. https://www.swisscontact.org/_Resources/Persistent/6/6/5/c/665c4d57f8eb7ee257d1bef3190e4016794e7a6e/SDP-Recognition%20of%20Prior%20Learning%20%28RPL%29%20Implementation%20Handbook.pdf

Syafei, M., & Nuraeningsih, N. (2025). Leveraging artificial intelligence in writing: ELT students' perspectives and experiences. *International Journal of Learning. Teaching and Educational Research*, *24*(5), 416–430. DOI: 10.26803/ijlter.24.5.22

Syed, J., & Özbilgin, M. (2009). A relational framework for international transfer of diversity management practices. *International Journal of Human Resource Management*, *20*(12), 2435–2453. DOI: 10.1080/09585190903363755

Tadimalla, S. Y., & Maher, M. (2025). AI literacy as a core component of AI education. *AI Magazine*, *46*(2), e70007. Advance online publication. DOI: 10.1002/aaai.70007

Tan, L., & Guo, L. (2009). From print to critical multimedia literacy: One teacher's foray into new literacies practices. *Journal of Adolescent & Adult Literacy: A Journal From the International Reading Association, 53*(4), 315–324. DOI: 10.1598/JAAL.53.4.5

Tan, S. A. C. Y., Jill, L. S. S., Tan, S., & AkhaviZadegan, R. (2023). Exploring the Inclusivity of Assessment ePortfolio for Multimodal Literacy During the Pandemic: A Case Study in Malaysian Higher Education. In *Improving Inclusivity in Higher Education: Addressing the Digital Divide in the COVID Pandemic* (pp. 139-161). Singapore: Springer Nature Singapore.

Tan, X., Xu, W., & Wang, C. (2024, March 28). *Purposeful remixing with generative AI: Constructing designer voice in multimodal composing*. arXiv.org. https://arxiv.org/abs/2403.19095?utm_source=chatgpt.com

Tan, T., Yan, Y., Yuan, X., & Gao, Z. (2025). Shaping Sustainable Futures on T ik T ok? Media Literacy, Youth Education and the SDG s. *European Journal of Education, 60*(4), e70270. Advance online publication. DOI: 10.1111/ejed.70270

Tavinor, G. (2009). *The art of videogames.* Wiley-Blackwell. DOI: 10.1002/9781444310177

Tchetgen, P. V. N. (2025). Designing a Culturally Grounded Ecology for Mediating Multimodal Literacy Experiences through Parent-Child Technology Interactions. In *Proceedings of the 19th International Conference of the Learning Sciences-ICLS 2025, pp.* 2572-2574. International Society of the Learning Sciences. DOI: 10.22318/icls2025.203690

The Stanley Parable. (n.d.). https://www.stanleyparable.com/

Thomas, R., Pugh, S., & Mulvihill, P. (2002). *The island of Dr. Moreau (JLA).* DC Comics.

Thomson, T. J., Pfurtscheller, D., Lobinger, K., Laba, N., & Christ, K. (2025). Visual literacies in transition: Multimodal co-production with generative AI. *Journal of Visual Literacy, 44*(4), 305–329. DOI: 10.1080/1051144X.2025.2566592

Tinmaz, H., Lee, Y. T., Fanea-Ivanovici, M., & Baber, H. (2022). A systematic review on digital literacy. *Smart Learning Environments, 9*(1), 21. DOI: 10.1186/s40561-022-00204-y PMID: 40478098

Tlili, A., Saqer, K., Salha, S., & Huang, R. (2025). Investigating the effect of artificial intelligence in education (AIEd) on learning achievement: A meta-analysis and research synthesis. *Information Development, 33*(3), 825–842. Advance online publication. DOI: 10.1177/02666669241304407

Topalidou Laskaridou, A., Papadopoulos, N., & Koutsogiannis, D. (2022). Contemplating post-digital narrativity: Co-active, multimodal meaning-making on Instagram and its implications on learning. *Punctum International Journal of Semiotics, 08*(02), 119–142. DOI: 10.18680/hss.2022.0019

Trisanti, N., Sukyadi, D., & Hermawan, B. (2024). University EFL teachers' stance and engagement in digital multimodal composing as multimodal literacy practices. *International Journal of Education, 17*(1), 61–70. DOI: 10.17509/ije.v17i1.56188

Ulu Bilim, H., & Erdem, C. (2025). The mediating role of critical thinking disposition in the relationship between multimodal literacy and media analysis skill: Evidence from pre-service teachers. *Education and Information Technologies, 30*(17), 1–22. DOI: 10.1007/s10639-025-13697-0

UNESCO. (2021). *Reimagining our futures together: A new social contract for education.* Paris: UNESCO. https://unevoc.unesco.org/pub/futures_of_education_report_eng.pdf

UNESCO. (2023). *Guidance for generative artificial intelligence (GenAI) in education and research: A human-centered approach.* United Nations Educational Scientific and Cultural Organization. https://policycommons.net/artifacts/6942367/guidance-for-generative-ai-in-education-and-research/7852269

UNESCO. (2025). *Cambodia artificial intelligence readiness assessment report.* United Nations Educational Scientific and Cultural Organization. https://unesdoc.unesco.org/ark:/48223/pf0000394553

Unsworth, L. (2024). Multimodal Literacy in a New Era of Educational Technology: Comparing Points of View in Animations of Children's and Adult Literature. *ECNU Review of Education, 7*(2), 384–405. DOI: 10.1177/20965311231179738

Valladares, L. (2021). Scientific literacy and social transformation: Critical perspectives about science participation and emancipation. *Science & Education, 30*(3), 557–587. DOI: 10.1007/s11191-021-00205-2 PMID: 33867683

Van Brummelen, J., Heng, T., & Tabunshchyk, V. (2021). Teaching tech to talk: K-12 conversational artificial intelligence literacy curriculum and development tools. *Proceedings of the AAAI Conference on Artificial Intelligence, 35*(17), 15655–15663. DOI: 10.1609/aaai.v35i17.17844

van Leeuwen, T. (2004). *Introducing social semiotics.* Routledge. DOI: 10.4324/9780203647028

van Leeuwen, T. (2015). Multimodality in education: Some directions and some questions. *TESOL Quarterly, 49*(3), 582–589. DOI: 10.1002/tesq.242

Vartiainen, H., Kahila, J., Tedre, M., López-Pernas, S., & Pope, N. (2024). Enhancing children's understanding of algorithmic biases in and with text-to-image generative AI. *New Media & Society.* Advance online publication. DOI: 10.1177/14614448241252820

Vartiainen, H., & Tedre, M. (2024). How text-to-image generative AI is transforming mediated action. *IEEE Computer Graphics and Applications, 44*(2), 12–22. DOI: 10.1109/MCG.2024.3355808 PMID: 38285567

Vélez-Ibáñez, C. G., & Greenberg, J. B.Carlos G. Vélez-Ibáñez ProfessorJames B. Greenberg Associate Research Professor. (1992). Formation and transformation of funds of knowledge among U.S. Mexican households. *Anthropology & Education Quarterly, 23*(4), 313–335. DOI: 10.1525/aeq.1992.23.4.05x1582v

Venuti, L. (2000). *The translation studies reader*. Routledge. DOI: 10.4324/9780203446621

Verma, V., & Varghese, J. (2025). Mapping multi-modal learning analytics in techno-driven learning environments: A bibliometric analysis. *Discover Education, 3*(1), 242. DOI: 10.1007/s44217-025-00789-9

Voss, S. M. (2011). *The affordances of multimodal texts and their impact on the reading process*. University of Minnesota.

Wang, C. (2025). Exploring students' generative AI-assisted writing processes: Perceptions and experiences from native and nonnative English speakers. *Technology Knowledge and Learning, 30*(3), 1825–1846. DOI: 10.1007/s10758-024-09744-3

Wang, H., Wu, Y., Chen, L., & Zhao, Y. (2023). Key factors predicting problem-based learning in online environments: Evidence from multimodal learning analytics. *Frontiers in Psychology, 14*, 1080294. DOI: 10.3389/fpsyg.2023.1080294 PMID: 36814653

Wang, J. (2024). Bridging the Self's worlds: Young girls' creative TikTok expressions of multimodal literacy during Covid-19. *Journal of Early Childhood Literacy*, •••, 14687984241270820.

Wang, L., & Ren, B. (2024). Enhancing academic writing in a linguistics course with generative AI: An empirical study in a higher education institution in Hong Kong. *Education Sciences, 14*(12), 1329. DOI: 10.3390/educsci14121329

Wang, X., Wu, Z., Huang, W., Wei, Y., Huang, Z., Xu, M., & Chen, W. (2023). VIS+AI: Integrating visualization with artificial intelligence for efficient data analysis. *Frontiers of Computer Science, 17*(6), 1–12. DOI: 10.1007/s11704-023-2691-y

Wang, Y., & Hao, L. (2025). "I'll play the role of you": a case study of multimodal literacy practice with an international family. In *Handbook of Literacy in Families and Communities* (pp. 378–397). Edward Elgar Publishing. DOI: 10.4337/9781035326983.00028

Wareham, J. (2019). "Murdered, hanged and lynched: 331 trans people killed this year." Retrieved from https://www.forbes.com/sites/jamiewareham/2019/11/18/murdered-hanged-and-lynched-331-trans-people-killed-this-year/#4ca3092a2d48

Warriner, D. S. (2023). Literacy. In *The routledge handbook of applied linguistics* (pp. 245–257). Routledge. DOI: 10.4324/9781003082644-21

Warschauer, M. (2011). *Learning in the cloud: How (and why) to transform schools with digital media*. Teachers College Press.

Wertsch, J. V., del Río, P., & Alvarez, A. (Eds.). (2021). *Sociocultural studies of mind*. Cambridge University Press., DOI: 10.1017/CBO9781139174299

Williams, B., & Zenger, A. (2007). *Popular culture and representations of literacy*. Routledge. DOI: 10.4324/9780203008492

Williamson, B. (2015). Digital education governance: Data visualization, predictive analytics, and 'real-time' policy instruments. *Journal of Education Policy*, *31*(2), 123–141. DOI: 10.1080/02680939.2015.1035758

Williamson, B., & Eynon, R. (2020). Historical threads, missing links, and future directions in AI in education. *Learning, Media and Technology*, *45*(3), 223–235. DOI: 10.1080/17439884.2020.1798995

Williamson, T. (2017). Listening to many voices: Enacting social justice literacy curriculum. *Teaching and Teacher Education*, *61*, 104–114. DOI: 10.1016/j.tate.2016.10.002

Wilson, A. (2022). The reader, the text, the poem: The influence and challenge of Louise Rosenblatt. *International Journal of Primary, Elementary, and Early Years Education*, *49*(1), 79–95.

Wong, N. (2025). Transmodal Pedagogy in Action: Multilingual Experiences of Disciplinary Literacy in an Elementary Art Classroom. *Literacy Research and Instruction*, •••, 1–23.

World Bank. (2023). *Individuals using the Internet (% of population) – Cambodia*. FRED, Federal Reserve Bank of St. Louis, https://fred.stlouisfed.org/series/ITNETUSERP2KHM

Wu, Q., Li, B. J., & Zhang, H. (2025). Observers, seekers, and professionals in AI adoption: An investigation of AI divide through social cognitive perspective. *Proceedings of the Association for Information Science and Technology*, *62*(1), 1121–1125. DOI: 10.1002/pra2.1350

Xu, Y., Zhu, J., Wang, M., Qian, F., Yang, Y., & Zhang, J. (2024). The impact of a digital game-based ai chatbot on students' academic performance, higher-order thinking, and behavioral patterns in an information technology curriculum. *Applied Sciences (Basel, Switzerland)*, *14*(15), 6418. DOI: 10.3390/app14156418

Yakubu, F. M., & Obafemi, K. E. (2023). Systematic review of multiliteracies skills, multimodal tools to facilitate learning in early childhood classroom. *J Inov Teknol Pendidik*, *10*(4), 431–440. DOI: 10.21831/jitp.v10i4.66343

Yang, W. (2022). Artificial intelligence education for young children: Why, what, and how in curriculum design and implementation. *Computers and Education: Artificial Intelligence*, *3*, 100061. DOI: 10.1016/j.caeai.2022.100061

Yang, Y., Zhang, Y., Sun, D., He, W., & Wei, Y. (2025). Navigating the landscape of AI literacy education: Insights from a decade of research (2014–2024). *Humanities & Social Sciences Communications*, *12*(1), 1–12. DOI: 10.1057/s41599-025-04583-8

Yan, Y., Liu, H., & Chau, T. (2025). A systematic review of AI ethics in education. *Journal of Global Information Management*, *33*(1), 1–50. DOI: 10.4018/JGIM.386381

Yaşar, M. S., & Arı, G. (2023). Turkish Language Teacher Candidates' Multimodal Literacy Levels and Their Attitudes Towards Information and Communication Technologies. *Sakarya University Journal of Education, 13*(5-Special Issue-World Language Turkish), 916-932.

Yim, I. H. Y., & Su, J. (2024). Artificial intelligence (AI) learning tools in K-12 education: A scoping review. *Journal of Computers in Education*. Advance online publication. DOI: 10.1007/s40692-023-00304-9

Yim, I. H. Y., & Wegerif, R. (2024). *Teachers' perceptions, attitudes, and acceptance of artificial intelligence (AI) educational learning tools: An exploratory study on AI literacy for young students*. Future in Educational Research., DOI: 10.1002/fer3.65

Yi, Z., & Siquan, X. (2025). The impact of pre-service language teachers' basic psychological needs on behavioural intentions to utilise artificial intelligence (AI) in teaching: AI literacy and self-efficacy as mediators. *European Journal of Education*, *60*(3), e70160. Advance online publication. DOI: 10.1111/ejed.70160

Yue, M., Jong, M. S.-Y., & Dai, Y. (2022). Pedagogical design of K-12 artificial intelligence education: A systematic review. *Sustainability (Basel)*, *14*(23), 15620. DOI: 10.3390/su142315620

Zaidi, R., & Sah, P. K. (2024). Affordances of multilingual and multimodal literacy engagements of immigrant high school students: A scoping review. *SAGE Open*, *14*(1), 21582440241228122. DOI: 10.1177/21582440241228122

Zawacki-Richter, O., Marín, V. I., Bond, M., & Gouverneur, F. (2019). Systematic review of research on artificial intelligence applications in higher education – where are the educators? *International Journal of Educational Technology in Higher Education*, *16*(1), 39. Advance online publication. DOI: 10.1186/s41239-019-0171-0

Zhai, C., Wibowo, S., & Li, L. D. (2024). The effects of over-reliance on AI dialogue systems on students' cognitive abilities: A systematic review. *Smart Learning Environments*, *11*(1), 1–37. DOI: 10.1186/s40561-024-00316-7

Zhang, D., Li, D., & Guo, K. (2026). From passive consumers to critical creators: Enhancing university students' new media literacy through AI-enhanced digital multimodal composing. *Interactive Learning Environments*, 1–25. Advance online publication. DOI: 10.1080/10494820.2026.2617985

Zhang, H., Lee, I., Ali, S., DiPaola, D., Cheng, Y., & Breazeal, C. (2022). Integrating ethics and career futures with technical learning to promote AI literacy for middle school students: An exploratory study. *International Journal of Artificial Intelligence in Education*, *33*(2), 1–35. DOI: 10.1007/s40593-022-00293-3 PMID: 35573722

Zhang, S., Ganapathy Prasad, P., & Schroeder, N. L. (2025). Learning about AI: A systematic review of reviews on AI literacy. *Journal of Educational Computing Research*, *63*(5), 1292–1322. DOI: 10.1177/07356331251342081

Zhao, L., Wu, X., & Luo, H. (2022). Developing AI literacy for primary and middle school teachers in China: Based on a structural equation modeling analysis. *Sustainability (Basel)*, *14*(21), 14549. DOI: 10.3390/su142114549

Zhao, Z., An, Q., & Liu, J. (2025). Exploring AI tool adoption in higher education: Evidence from a PLS-SEM model integrating multimodal literacy, self-efficacy, and university support. *Frontiers in Psychology*, *16*(1619391), 1619391. DOI: 10.3389/fpsyg.2025.1619391 PMID: 40989284

Zheng, B., Lin, C.-H., & Kwon, J. B. (2020). The impact of learner-, instructor-, and course-level factors on online learning. *Computers & Education*, *150*, 103851. DOI: 10.1016/j.compedu.2020.103851

Zhou, D., & Sterman, S. (2024, June). Ai. llude: Investigating Rewriting AI-Generated Text to Support Creative Expression. In *Proceedings of the 16th Conference on Creativity & Cognition* (pp. 241-254). DOI: 10.1145/3635636.3656187

Ziguras, C. (2001). Educational technology in transnational higher education in South East Asia: The cultural politics of flexible learning. *Journal of Educational Technology & Society*, *4*(4), 8–18. https://www.jstor.org/stable/jeductechsoci.4.4.8

Zimmerman, E. (2008). Gaming literacy: Game design as a model for literacy in the twenty-first century. In Perron, B., & Wolf, M. J. P. (Eds.), *The video game theory reader 2* (pp. 23–31). Routledge.

About the Contributors

Jason D. DeHart is a passionate educator, actively engaged in finding what works for connecting readers with literacy practices. DeHart earned his PhD from The University of Tennessee, Knoxville in 2019. He served as a middle grades English teacher for eight years, has worked at the university level at Lee University in Cleveland, Tennessee, as well as at The University of Tennessee, Knoxville and Appalachian State University, and currently works with high school students in Wilkesboro, North Carolina. DeHart's publications include Building Critical Literacy and Empathy with Graphic Novels (NCTE), as well as a number of edited volumes for Routledge and IGI Global. He has written articles and posts for The ALAN Review, English Journal, The Journal of Adolescent & Adult Literacy, Edutopia, Steve Bickmore's YA Wednesday, and Middleweb.

***

Ashraf Alam is currently serving as an Assistant Professor in the Department of Education at NIT Calicut, Kerala, India. He has been recognised among the *World's Top 2% Scientists* by Stanford University and Elsevier. His academic contributions include more than 75 Scopus-indexed publications and over 100 conference presentations delivered at national and international academic forums. His work has appeared in reputed research publication platforms including Elsevier, Springer, Taylor & Francis, CRC Press, Routledge, Atlantis Press, Springer Nature, Palgrave Macmillan, and IEEE. He earned his Ph.D. from IIT Kharagpur, where his research engaged with foundational concerns in educational policy, curriculum design, educational technology, philosophy of education, innovation in education, educational administration, governance, and pedagogical transformation. His work is grounded in a transdisciplinary orientation that draws from educational sciences, digital pedagogy, curriculum theory, learning analytics, sustainability education, instructional design, artificial intelligence, ethics of technology, and socio-technical studies. Dr. Ashraf's scholarship strives to interrogate and expand the boundaries of educational thought by examining the epistemological, ethical, and social dimensions of digital and post-digital pedagogies. His work critically engages with the changing nature of knowledge production, learner agency, pedagogical mediation, and institutional transformation in technologically saturated educational environments. He is particularly invested in advancing inclusive digital learning, gamified instructional strategies, AI-mediated educational ecosystems, and ethically governed technology integration in education. His research agenda is animated by the pursuit of design-oriented, ethically attuned, and contextually responsive frameworks that can support meaningful educational reform. Through his work, he seeks to contribute to the development of pedagogical models that are not only technologically innovative but also socially just, epistemically inclusive, developmentally sensitive, and aligned with the broader goals of sustainable and human-centred education.

Syed Ibad Ali holds a distinguished academic background with a Bachelor of Engineering in Electronics and Communication Engineering (ECE), a Master of Technology in VLSI Design, and a Ph.D. in Electronics and Communication Engineering. With over 13 years of rich academic and research experience, Dr. Ali has been at the forefront of interdisciplinary innovation, merging traditional ECE principles with cutting-edge advancements in artificial intelligence and data science. Currently serving as an associate professor in the Department of Artificial Intelligence and Data Science at Parul Institute of Engineering and Technology, Parul University, Gujarat, he is recognized for his commitment to fostering analytical thinking and research-led pedagogy. His work often bridges theory with impactful applications, inspiring the next generation of engineers and AI specialists. Dr. Ali's passion lies in advancing transparent and ethical AI systems, a vision that is deeply embedded in the themes of this book.

Sovannaroth Chheang earned her bachelor's degree in English from Build Bright University, Phnom Penh, in 2016, where she built a solid foundation in language studies, communication, and pedagogy. She began her teaching career in 2013 as a Tutor at the Kindergarten Association, conducting both part-time and full-time English programs. Since 2018, she has served as a Teacher of English and General Assistant at Sovanna Elton Foreign Language School. Through these roles, she has developed broad expertise in classroom management, language instruction, curriculum design, and student engagement, supporting the school's mission of advancing foreign language learning. Ms. Chheang's academic interests center on pursuing a master's degree in English education or related fields within the humanities and social sciences. Passionate about integrating global research methodologies into her practice, she aims to enhance pedagogy, foster classroom innovation, and promote effective, research-informed teaching. Her commitment lies in bridging academic research with real-world practice to advance English education in Cambodia and beyond.

Deepak Gupta is a distinguished academician with over 20 years of teaching experience and expertise in Computer Science and Engineering. He holds a Ph.D. in Computer Engineering and has an extensive research portfolio, including many international journal papers, multiple conference proceedings, and several books. His research interests span machine learning, artificial intelligence, and data mining. Currently, Dr. Gupta serves as an Associate Professor and Head of Department of CSE (Emerging Branches) at ITM Gwalior, MP, India. He has also contributed significantly to the field through patents and copyrights and actively engages as a reviewer, conference chair and editor.

Hok Chheangkhy is a lecturer at the Department of Khmer Literature, University of Heng Samrin Thbongkhmum. With a strong dedication to the study and preservation of Khmer language, literature, and culture, he has contributed to advancing literary education and research in Cambodia. His academic interests include classical and modern Khmer literature, linguistic analysis, and cultural studies. Mr. Chheangkhy is passionate about inspiring students to explore Cambodia's rich literary heritage and promoting the value of Khmer identity through education. In addition to teaching, he actively engages in academic writing and community cultural initiatives, aiming to strengthen the role of literature in contemporary Cambodian society.

Sovanna Huot is a PhD candidate in Political Science at the University of Delhi, New Delhi, India. He is a vice principal at a Government Public High School of Cambodia and is responsible for the school academic and institutional leadership. He is a very proficient academic across many disciplines. He has completed a two-year teacher training program from 2010-2012 and has obtained bachelor's degrees in English and in Educational Administration. He also has two master's degrees in law and in TEFL obtained through a very competitive scholarship, and a Master of Education, specialized in School Leadership, Upper Secondary School Principalship, from the National Institute of Education (NIE), Phnom Penh, 2021. He specializes in educational reform and in the practice-policy nexus of digit pedagogy and in glonacal (global–national–local) education systems. He has formal academic training in political science and education and has published scholarly work in both disciplines, including articles indexed in Scopus (Author ID: 59316244400).

Amit Kumar Jain is a distinguished academic and researcher in Electronics and Communication Engineering with a PhD from Poornima University (2025), an M.Tech in VLSI, and a B.Tech in ECE. With over 14 years of teaching experience, he currently serves as an Associate Professor at Poornima University, Jaipur. He has taught a range of subjects including Microwave Engineering, Analog Electronics, and Microprocessors, and has significantly contributed to engineering education through textbooks and numerous research publications in reputed SCOPUS and ABDC-indexed journals. Dr. Jain's research interests include wireless networks, machine learning, and sensor networks. He has presented his work at both national and international conferences. In addition to academics, he plays a pivotal role in institutional operations, managing CRM systems and admission analytics, and leading large administrative teams. His dedication to teaching, research, and university development continues to make a lasting impact in the field of technical education.

Sovanna Loch is a prominent figure at the Cambodian Monastery Rajgir, serving as a deputy in charge. He is also a PhD research scholar and ICCR Fellow in the Dept. of English at Nava Nalanda Mahavihara (Deemed University), an institution under the Ministry of Culture, Govt. of India. His academic background includes a bachelor's degree in Pāli and a master's in English, both obtained from NNM. His research primarily focuses on Cambodian classical and Buddhist English literature.

Khajoboeva Nodira is affiliated with the Department of Uzbek and Eastern Languages at Mamun University, Khiva, Uzbekistan. Her academic interests focus on Uzbek language studies, Eastern languages, linguistics, and literature. She is actively involved in teaching and academic activities that promote the development of language proficiency, cultural understanding, and literary appreciation among students. Her work emphasizes the preservation and advancement of linguistic heritage, effective language teaching methodologies, and the integration of cultural studies in language education. Khajoboeva Nodira also contributes to academic discussions related to comparative linguistics, translation studies, and the study of classical and modern literature of Eastern cultures. Through her teaching and scholarly engagement, she aims to strengthen language education and support the development of students' communication, analytical, and intercultural skills.

Kishin Khajiboyev is affiliated with the Department of Uzbek and Eastern Languages at Mamun University, Khiva, Uzbekistan. His academic interests focus on Uzbek language studies, Eastern languages, linguistics, and literature. He is actively engaged in teaching and academic activities that promote language proficiency, cultural understanding, and the study of literary traditions of the region. His work emphasizes effective language teaching methodologies, linguistic analysis, and the preservation and promotion of cultural and linguistic heritage. Kishin Khajiboyev also contributes to academic discussions related to comparative linguistics, translation studies, and the development of modern approaches to language education. Through his teaching and scholarly engagement, he aims to strengthen language education and support the development of students' communication skills, critical thinking, and intercultural competence.

Ravikumar R. Natarajan is an experienced academician with over 12+ years of teaching and research expertise across institutions in India, the UAE, and the Maldives. He currently serves as an Assistant Professor at Marwadi University, Rajkot, specializing in Machine Learning, Recommender Systems, and AI-driven applications in healthcare and security. He holds a Ph.D. in Machine Learning and Recommender Systems from Amity University, Jaipur, a Master of Engineering in CSE from VMRF University, Salem, and a Bachelor of Engineering in CSE from Anna University. He also has a MiniMBA from the Swiss eLearning Institute. Dr. Ravikumar has authored more than 8+ multiple SCIE/Scopus-indexed journal articles, 25+ IEEE/Springer conference papers, and co-authored a book on Artificial Intelligence. He has also published 9 patents and contributed 95+ book chapters in emerging domains such as Federated Learning, Blockchain, and Digital Twins for IGI Global, Wiley and Springer publisher. He actively mentors students through initiatives like the Research Activities Club (RAC) and Student Research Internship Training (SRIT), promoting innovation and research culture.

Fabielle Rocha Cruz is a PhD student at the university of Calgary, and a Brazilian scholar, teacher, and gamer who believes in critical and gaming literacies as a tool for fairer education. With experience in education and research across Brazil, the United States, and Canada, her practice is shaped by plurilingualism, migration, and a deep engagement with culturally sustaining pedagogies.

Aarthi S is a dedicated Assistant Professor in Computer Science with over six years of teaching experience. She is currently pursuing her Ph.D. at Marwadi University, Gujarat, and holds an M.Phil. and MCA from Bharathiar University, Tamil Nadu. Throughout her academic career, Aarthi has specialized in programming languages such as C++, Java, and C, and contributed to research in recommender systems and AI-related data privacy. She has published journal articles, contributed to book chapters, and actively participated in technical workshops. Known for her student mentorship and engagement in academic events, Aarthi remains committed to fostering innovation and excellence in computer science education.

Turdiev Abdullo Sagdullaevich is an Associate Professor in the Department of Finance at Alfraganus University, Tashkent, Uzbekistan. His academic and research interests focus on financial management, banking systems, investment analysis, and modern financial practices. He is actively involved in teaching and scholarly activities aimed at strengthening finance education and developing analytical and decision-making skills among students. His work emphasizes the application of contemporary financial tools, financial policy analysis, and effective financial management strategies within both academic and professional contexts. Turdiev Abdullo Sagdullaevich also contributes to academic discussions related to corporate finance, economic development, and financial system modernization. Through his teaching, research, and academic engagement, he aims to promote high-quality finance education and support the preparation of professionals capable of addressing modern financial and economic challenges.

|Phearun Tep - Contributing Author|Phearun Tep is a committed researcher with academic interests in South Asian literature, Translation Studies, Indian Literary Theory & Criticism, literature, fiction, cultural and post-conflict studies, and identity representation. His research examines how historical trauma, cultural memory, and narrative imagination inform human experience, with the broader aim of contributing to literary scholarship and interdisciplinary studies.

Dilmurod Turaev is affiliated with the Department of Information Technology and Exact Sciences at Termez University of Economics and Service, Termez, Uzbekistan. His academic interests focus on information technology, computer science, and the application of computational methods in scientific and educational environments. He is actively involved in teaching and academic activities that aim to strengthen students' knowledge in programming, data analysis, and modern computing technologies. His work emphasizes the integration of digital technologies, problem-solving skills, and analytical approaches to address real-world technological challenges. Dilmurod Turaev also contributes to academic discussions related to emerging technologies, information systems, and the advancement of IT education. Through his teaching and scholarly engagement, he seeks to promote innovation in technology education and support the development of skilled professionals capable of contributing to modern digital and scientific advancements.

Index

A

C

D

E

F

G

H

I

L

M

P

R

S

T

V

www.ingramcontent.com/pod-product-compliance
Lightning Source LLC
LaVergne TN
LVHW062325300926
849161LV00007B/1575